The Economics and Politics of East-West Trade

JOZEF WILCZYNSKI

Andrew S. Thomas Memorial Library
MORRIS HARVEY COLLEGE, CHARLESTON, W. VA.

FREDERICK A. PRAEGER, *Publishers*
New York · Washington

BOOKS THAT MATTER

Published in the United States of America in 1969
by Frederick A. Praeger, Inc., Publishers
111 Fourth Avenue, New York, N.Y. 10003

© 1969, in London, England, by Jozef Wilczynski

All rights reserved
Library of Congress Catalog Card Number: 72-93449

Printed in Great Britain

Contents

List of Tables and Diagrams	9
Foreword by Professor Harry G. Johnson	11
Preface	15

I. *EAST-WEST TRADE IN PERSPECTIVE*

1	East-West Trade	19
	A. Distinctive Features of East-West Trade	21
	B. East-West Trade in the International Scene	24
2	Structure	34
	A. Western Exports to the Socialist Bloc	34
	B. The Bloc's Exports to the West	37
	C. Some General Observations	41
3	Changing Patterns of Direction	44
	A. Tendencies in Western Foreign Trade	44
	B. Tendencies in Socialist Foreign Trade	47
	C. Trends in East-West Trade	52

II. *PRINCIPLES, POLICIES, PRACTICES*

4	Ideological and Theoretical Background	59
	A. The Essence of Foreign Trade under Each System	59
	B. Foreign-Trade Theory	63
	C. The Theory of Comparative Costs	69
5	Organization	75
	A. General Organizational Framework	75

	B. Foreign-Trade Corporations	78
	C. The Relation of Trading to Producing and Using Enterprises	82
	D. Foreign-Trade Promotion and Services	86

6 Prices, Exchange Rates and Tariffs ... 90
   A. Prices ... 90
   B. Exchange Rates ... 96
   C. Tariffs ... 100

7 Weapons of Trade Policy ... 103
   A. General Foundations ... 103
   B. Directive and Motivational Means ... 105
   C. A General Appraisal of the Weapons ... 116

III. *MAJOR ISSUES IN EAST-WEST TRADE*

8 Equality of Trading Opportunity ... 121
   A. The MFN Reciprocity ... 121
   B. Possibilities of Evasion of Equal Trading Opportunity ... 123
   C. The Question of Safeguards ... 130

9 Dumping ... 138
   A. Do Western Countries Pursue Dumping in the Socialist Bloc? ... 140
   B. Western Charges of Socialist Dumping ... 146
   C. Price Discrimination Practised by Socialist Countries ... 162
   D. Protection against Dumping Originating from a Different Economic System ... 171
   E. Gains from Dumping ... 176
   F. Weaknesses in the Anti-dumping Arrangements in East-West Trade ... 187

10 Payments and Finance ... 191
   A. Trade and Payment Flows ... 191
   B. The Bloc's Reserves and International Liquidity ... 194
   C. Bilateralism ... 203

CONTENTS 7

    D. Multilateralization of Trade and Payments   207
    E. Credits   226
    F. Payment Record   232

11 Politics in Partnership with Trade   236
    A. The Cold War and East-West Trade   236
    B. Denial of Trade   241
    C. Politics in Aid of Trade   246
    D. Competition for Support in Developing Countries   252
    E. Oil, Wheat and Technology   259
    F. Conclusions   267

12 Strategic Embargo   271
    A. Development of Western Strategic Export Controls   271
    B. Rationale of the Embargo   274
    C. The Bloc's Vulnerability   278
    D. The Effect of the Embargo on the Bloc   283
    E. Effects on the West   289

13 Trade Disputes   294
    A. Settlement of Foreign-Trade Disputes   294
    B. Sources of Conflict   299
    C. A General Appraisal   304

14 Gains and Waste   308
    A. Gains from Trade under Free Enterprise and under Central Planning   308
    B. Foreign-Trade-Efficiency Calculations in the Socialist Bloc   311
    C. Recent Reforms in Eastern Europe and Gains from Trade   330
    D. Which Side Gains more from East-West Trade?   334
    E. Forms of Waste   342

15 East-West Trade as an Avenue of Convergence   348
    A. Broad Patterns of Convergence   348
    B. 'Pecunia Non Olet'   357
    C. Institutional Convergence   361

    D. Joint East-West Ventures   377
    E. Solving East-West Trade Problems   384
    F. Barriers to Convergence   389

A Selected Bibliography   396

Index of Names   406

Subject Index   410

Tables and Diagrams

I. Participation in World Trade, 1967 — 24
II. The Degree of Dependence of Western Countries on Trade with the Socialist Bloc — 29
III. The Degree of Dependence of Socialist Countries on Trade with the West — 32
IV. Percentage Composition of Western Exports to the Socialist Bloc — 35
V. Percentage Share of Manufactures in Western Exports to the West, the Socialist Bloc and the Developing World — 37
VI. Percentage Composition of Socialist Exports to the West — 38
VII. Percentage Share of Manufactures in Socialist Exports to the Socialist Bloc, the West and the Developing World — 40
VIII. Manufactures in East-West Trade, 1955–1966 — 42
IX. Western and Socialist Participation in World Trade, 1938, 1948, 1953–1967 — 45
X. Intra-Western and Intra-Socialist Foreign Trade, 1938, 1948, 1953–1967 — 46
XI. The Development of East-West Trade, 1938, 1948, 1953–1967 — 52
XII. The Role of East-West Trade in Western and Socialist Foreign Trade, 1938, 1948, 1953–1967 — 54
XIII. Western and Socialist Annual Rates of Growth in Foreign Trade, 1953–1967 — 55
XIV. The Role of the Main Weapons of Trade Policy in East-West Trade — 106
XV. East-West Bilateral Trade Agreements, 1957 and 1968 — 108
XVI. Normal Values, and Prices Obtained from the Socialist Countries for Australian Wheat, 1960/61–1967/68 — 142
XVII. Subsidization of the Australian Wheat Exports to the Socialist Bloc, 1960/61–1967/68 — 143

XVIII.	Examples of Western Accusations of Socialist Dumping	149
XIX.	Australian Dumping Complaints against the Socialist Bloc by Commodity Groups, 1961–1967	156
XX.	Established Cases of Socialist Dumping in Australia, 1961–1967	157
XXI.	Prices Obtained by the USSR for Diesel Fuel Exported to Different Countries, 1965	165
XXII.	Prices Obtained by Poland for Black Coal Exported to Different Countries, 1965	166
XXIII.	Prices Obtained by the USSR for Selected Products Exported to Different Countries, 1965	167
XXIV.	Prices Obtained by Poland for Selected Products Exported to Different Countries, 1965	168
XXV.	United Kingdom's Balance of Trade with the Socialist Bloc, 1938, 1948, 1953–1967	194
XXVI.	The Degree of Multilateral Balancing in East-West Trade, 1938, 1948, 1957 and 1960–1967	209
XXVII.	East-West Diplomatic Relations, 1968	247
XXVIII.	Western and Socialist Trade with the Third World, 1938, 1948, 1953–1967	257
XXIX.	The Third World's Trade with the West and with the Socialist Bloc, 1938, 1948, 1953–1967	258
XXX.	A Recent Strategic Embargo List	279
XXXI.	Exports to the Socialist Bloc in Selected Years	290
XXXII.	Western and Socialist Membership of International Organizations Relevant to East-West Trade, 1954 and 1966.	368
XXXIII.	Recent Examples of Joint East-West Undertakings	379
Diag. A.	East-West Trade in the World Scene	27
Diag. B.	Flow of Trade between the Socialist Bloc and Major Areas of the World	192
Diag. C.	Flow of Trade between the United Kingdom, the Socialist Bloc and the Oversea Sterling Area	193

Foreword

It is a great pleasure to me to have the opportunity to write the Foreword to this book. My own work has been largely on the pure theory of international trade, with excursions into the trade and monetary policy problems of the advanced Western industrial countries and the revisions of trade policy required to promote the development of the poor nations of the world. But the growth of East-West trade, and the trend towards market socialism in the Socialist countries, had made me increasingly aware of the existence of both a range of problems with which I should become more familiar, and a growing number of fellow scholars of international trade theory in the Socialist countries working on fundamental problems of common interest.

Under the rules of London University, a doctoral candidate prepares his thesis more or less on his own, and it then has to be examined by an 'internal' and an 'external' examiner. I was asked to be internal examiner for Dr Wilczynski, the external being Professor Alec Nove; and I took on the assignment because I saw it as a convenient opportunity to take a crash course in the economics of East-West trade.

It was a far better course than I could possibly have expected. Dr Wilczynski has assembled a mass of evidence and argument on all relevant aspects of the economics and politics of East-West trade; and he has presented it admirably clearly and readably. The work was not a PhD thesis in the common sense, with more references per page in the footnotes than ideas per chapter in the text, but a first-class work of mature scholarship and judgment, which will be of service to scholars and policy-makers for many years ahead.

Reading the book, and thinking about the current situation with respect to East-West trade, prompts me to make some observations which I hope will be found helpful by other readers.

The first is that both Western experience of trade liberalization and the experience of East-West trade tend to confirm the basic general proposition of the English classical tradition from which both Western and Eastern contemporary economic theory started, that international trade is beneficial or at least potentially beneficial to the various nations whatever the nature of their political systems. An important relevant point in this connection is that attempts to restrict trade for political reasons, on either side, do far more damage to the country imposing the restrictions than to the intended victims of the restrictions, and especially so – for well-known theoretical reasons – when the restriction-imposing countries are small and would normally be heavily engaged in trade. Large countries imposing trade restrictions for political reasons suffer relatively little economic damage therefrom; but they also derive relatively little political gain, at least in the longer run, because it is always possible to substitute for imports though at an economic cost. This point, or so I hope, is gradually being recognized on both sides of the East-West division, and should lead to mutual agreement to lower barriers to East-West trade.

My second observation is that, while the gains from freer trade on classical lines can easily be demonstrated in pure theory, the application of that analysis to the practical world is not as easy as it might seem. The real world constantly throws up problems which can only be solved by a combination of high theoretical ability and detailed institutional understanding. There are two sorts of problem here.

On the one hand, in any actual trading situation, the personnel actually involved in trading relationships will be led by the situation to conceive of the problem in a way which may deflect attention from the economics of the problem to its political, commercial, or administrative aspects. This problem is exemplified by the question of 'dumping', discussed at length by our author, where economic calculation is usually conspicuous by its absence. More generally, the defects of the present international monetary system promote a concern on the part of Western policy-makers with the balance-of-payments aspects of commercial policy which differs in its implications from the concern of Eastern trade officials with various kinds of real balances.

On the other hand, in the modern world it is increasingly difficult for the trade theorist to bridge the gap between the pure abstract theory of comparative advantage, which applies to any economic system because it is no more than the basic principles of intelligent choice, and its application to concrete economies in specific trading situations. A potent red herring here is the contention that comparative advantage theory is 'static' and that somehow 'dynamic' considerations overrule it; this contention is a useless diversion to the conscientious economist, because any 'dynamic' consideration with scientific content can be specified and brought into quantification as an aspect of investment choice. The real difficulty is that comparative advantage can only be applied if policy determination can penetrate through the veil of distorted money prices and costs to the underlying social alternative opportunity costs. In this connection, Eastern scholars (so far as my observations can claim validity) have wasted much effort in rediscovering principles that were present in traditional Western theory but not easily recognizable because of their expression in the language of a competitive market economy. Western scholars, on the other hand, have been too easily inclined to point to the irrationality of the price structure in Socialist economies, without recognizing the manifold irrationalities in pricing in their own economies produced by such typical phenomena as agricultural price support policies, fixing of wages by collective bargaining and minimum-wage laws, tariffs and other restraints on international trade, and complex subsidies to particular industries provided by defence contracts, foreign-aid tying, and governmental support of scientific research in particular fields. In my view, scholars from both East and West could help each other a great deal both to understand the possibilities and limitations of gaining from international trade between the two groups of countries, and to assist in the specification of optimal international trading policies, if they had more opportunity – by either personal or literary contact – for scholarly interchanges aimed at sorting out fundamental principles from the semantic and institutional contexts in which such principles are usually buried when they come to the attention of economists working in a particular economic and political environment.

My third and final observation is that Western and Eastern international economists alike face a major analytical challenge, which traditional comparative advantage theory has so far not recognized but which is increasingly important in the modern world. This challenge may be termed the problem of analysing, positively and normatively, the use of knowledge as a factor of production. Trade theory has typically treated knowledge as a datum: in the Ricardian tradition, differences in knowledge appear as unexplained differences in labour cost ratios between countries; in the Heckscher–Ohlin–Samuelson theory, knowledge is assumed to be a free good equally available everywhere. In fact, knowledge is a form of capital, created by investment in learning and in research, which yields a return so long as it retains a scarcity value, maintained by the patent system, or by 'industrial leadership', but which eventually becomes a free good.

The problem posed by knowledge as a factor of production is that it is an essential feature of modern industrial production, whether that production is organized on 'Capitalist' or on 'Socialist' lines. In the former system it is responsible for most of the problems raised, or thought to be raised, by the modern corporation; in the latter system it is responsible for many of the problems both of educational and scientific policy and of decentralization *versus* centralization in the structuring of the economy. It is, in an important sense, fundamental to the problem of 'American domination' in the developed countries, and of 'colonialism' and 'imperialism' in the newly-independent developing countries.

Yet neither orthodox nor Marxian theory provided an easy and self-evident way of coming to grips with the problem, because in both systems of thought the concept of property and its rights and powers cannot easily be extended from the ownership of material capital, which is appropriable and alienable, to knowledge, which is appropriable and alienable by institutional convention but not by the inherent necessity of the laws of scarcity.

The relaxation of existing barriers to East-West trade, and the development of freer trade – and investment – between the market and the Socialist economies, which I expect in the future, is very likely to raise in an increasingly acute form the problem of knowledge as a factor of industrial production, and the related problems of the equity and efficiency of rival Western and Eastern systems for generating and applying it. These problems are the next item on the agenda of research in the pure theory of international trade, if it is to remain both relevant to the practical world of commercial relations among countries and the practical problems of commercial policy formation.

HARRY G. JOHNSON

The London School of Economics
   and Political Science
November 1968

Preface

THIS is a study of trade between two antagonistic economic and political systems in a rapidly changing world. The accent is on 'economics' and on the 'East'. Trade is after all an essentially economic process, and the East is less familiar and (considering recent reforms) more enigmatic than the well-established Western order. Political considerations entering into East-West trade are brought out where warranted and their extent, relative importance and effects are critically evaluated. The usual pattern followed is to bring out briefly the salient characteristics of Western trade and against this background to discuss the Socialist side in detail. The aim is to highlight differences and striking similarities.

Neither the East nor the West is homogeneous. However, the task undertaken in this enquiry is not to dwell exhaustively on the details of the foreign trade of the twenty-five Western and the twelve Socialist countries, but rather to bring out essential characteristics peculiar to each system. One of the difficulties experienced in a comparative study of this nature is to formulate significant generalizations in the face of exceptions obscuring broad patterns.

The book consists of fifteen chapters divided into three parts. Part I, 'East-West Trade in Perspective', provides a concise factual background. The position, size and composition of East-West trade are considered in the world scene, and these are further examined in a historical perspective. In Part II, 'Principles, Policies, Practices', the Western and Socialist foreign trade systems are confronted with each other. The discussion is concentrated on the peculiarities of thinking, the institutional framework and the accepted procedures conditioning East-West trade on each side.

The main body of the study is contained in Part III, 'Major Issues in East-West Trade', in which controversial problems are examined from both sides. Issues of economic as well as of non-economic content are analysed, special attention being given to the evolutionary changes taking place in the West and the reforms being implemented in Eastern Europe. In the concluding chapter, a proposition is examined as to what extent East-West trade is a factor in promoting the convergence of the two systems.

Hardly any other field of international relations since World War II has been more bestrewn with hastily formed views or plain distortions than East-West trade. These have been prevalent on both sides of the Iron, or Gold, Curtain. The attitude which the author has striven to maintain is that of a detached observer and critic rather than that of an enthusiastic protagonist or an unflinching antagonist of one system or the other. The author is aware of the fact that his critical evaluations will please neither Western nor Socialist readers who have their own views on each system. Should the results of this investigation contribute to greater moderation in East-West relations and to sensible solutions of the many outstanding issues, its purpose would be achieved and the author would consider it as his greatest reward.

This study was carried out as a doctorate thesis for the University of London. It is based on both Western and Socialist sources. Of the former, mostly American, Australian, British, West German, Italian and Japanese publications have been employed, whilst of the latter mainly Bulgarian, Chinese, Czechoslovak, East German, Hungarian, Polish and Soviet material has been utilized. In addition, sources published by the United Nations and those in Hong Kong have been used.

Some of the propositions advanced in this book were first tested in American, Australian, British, Italian and Norwegian journals. The author wishes in particular to thank the editors of *Economia Internazionale*, the *Economic Journal*, the *Economic Record*, *Economics of Planning*, the *Journal of Political Economy* and *Soviet Studies* for permission to use parts of his articles.

J. WILCZYNSKI

Royal Military College of Australia, Duntroon,
  and University of London

PART ONE

East-West Trade in Perspective

1 East-West Trade

IT is customary nowadays to distinguish three major divisions of the world – the Developed Countries, or vaguely the 'West', the Centrally Planned Economies, or the 'East', and the Developing Countries, or the 'Third World'.[1] The task undertaken in this study is to enquire into the trade between the first two economic and political systems confronting each other today. Trade with the Third World is considered only where it helps to place East-West trade in a proper perspective and throws additional light on it.

The West is interpreted broadly as embracing the 25 Developed countries of North America, Western Europe, Japan, Australia, New Zealand and South Africa (the so-called 'Economic Class I' in United Nations sources).[2] The East is taken as comprising the 12 centrally planned economies – 8 European (Albania, Bulgaria, Czechoslovakia, East Germany,[3] Hungary, Poland, Rumania, the USSR) and 4 Asian countries (Mainland China,[3] Mongolia, North Korea[3] and North Vietnam[3]). The 12 countries are referred to as the 'Socialist Bloc', or individually as 'Socialist' or 'Bloc' countries.[4]

---

[1] 'Developed' and 'Developing' countries combined are referred to in this study as the 'Capitalist World'. The description 'Free World' is not used in this study; it is not generally realized that one in five of the Capitalist countries is under military or semi-military rule (23 out of 105 in 1967).

[2] Several minor European States (such as Liechtenstein, Malta, Monaco) are also included in this division.

[3] Throughout this study, the well-established descriptive names 'East Germany', 'North Korea', 'North Vietnam' and 'Mainland China' are used rather than the formalistic but officially correct designations 'German Democratic Republic', 'Democratic People's Republic of Korea', 'Democratic Republic of Vietnam' and 'People's Republic of China'. Similarly, for the sake of consistency, the descriptions 'West Germany', 'South Korea', 'South Vietnam' and 'Taiwan' will be used rather than 'Federal Republic of Germany', 'Republic of Korea', 'Republic of Vietnam' and 'Republic of China'.

[4] The description 'Socialist' Bloc or countries is used in this study instead of 'Communist' Bloc or countries. All the 12 countries are still in the first stage of Communism

Although Yugoslavia and Cuba are regarded by the Socialist countries as belonging to the Socialist family of nations (and included in their statistics as such since 1962), there are several reasons for not treating them as part of the 'Bloc' which is taken here as a continuous group of countries characterized by a high degree of centralized economic planning and administration. In the overall treatment, we shall follow the usual United Nations classification, and thus include Yugoslavia as part of the West and Cuba as belonging to the Developing World. However, as these two countries represent obvious and interesting exceptions in several respects, occasional references will be made to them.

Neither the West nor the Socialist Bloc are homogeneous entities nor are capable of acting as unified groups of countries. No two countries in each division are alike economically or politically, and the divergent national interests and polycentric tendencies obstinately reasserting themselves both in the West and in the East are well known. In particular, the use of the term 'Bloc' to describe the twelve Socialist countries, may be considered outdated.

Nevertheless, each of these two groups has enough common characteristics to make it a distinct world division. To generalize, these include free enterprise, political democracy, highly developed economies and high standards of living on the Western side, and allegiance to the Marxist-Leninist philosophy, economic democracy, central economic planning and – above all – a distinctive manner of conducting foreign trade on the Eastern side. As to the term 'Bloc', owing to its use for two decades now, its brevity and the lack of another simple designation, it will be frequently used in this study.

Originally, i.e. in the early post-war years, the phrase East-West trade was used to denote trade between Eastern and Western European countries, and in its narrow meaning the expression is still used in that sense. However, as the trade of the remaining Western and Socialist countries respectively conforms to the same principles, bears a similar

---

called by Marx 'lower phase' or 'Socialism' (during which some elements of Capitalism are still retained) and all these countries refer to themselves as 'Socialist', not 'Communist' countries. The USSR, the most advanced 'Socialist' country at present, is scheduled to start entering the 'higher phase', or 'Communism' not earlier than 1980, and other Bloc countries much later (vaguely after the year 2000). See V. I. Lenin, *The State and Revolution*, ch. I; *The Road to Communism.* Documents of the 22nd Congress of the CPSU, FLPH, Moscow 1961, pp. 196–246, 509–12.

CH. I EAST-WEST TRADE

character and faces the same type of problems, the meaning has soon been extended to cover trade between the Developed countries and the Socialist Bloc. It is in this broad sense that East-West trade is approached in this study.

By this token, East Germany, Poland, Czechoslovakia and Hungary, whose people have been proud to identify themselves with Western civilization for a thousand years, must be treated as Eastern partners in East-West trade. At the same time, such countries as Turkey and Japan are taken as part of the West.[1]

Sometimes, 'East-West trade' is vaguely meant to describe trade between the Socialist Bloc and the Capitalist World (i.e. the Developed and the Developing non-Socialist countries lumped together). However, it is considered that its use in this sense is not justified and it will not be applied in this meaning in the present enquiry.

So much for the clarification of the scope of this study. We shall now consider the general peculiarities of East-West trade and then its place in the world scene.

A. DISTINCTIVE FEATURES OF EAST-WEST TRADE

East-West trade has several characteristics deriving from the differences in the economic and political systems which, naturally, condition trade in different ways on each side. What may be described as 'normal practice' in intra-Western or in intra-Bloc trade breaks down when it comes to East-West trade. The distinctive features of trade are the subject of analysis in the remaining chapters, so that only an overall view is presented in this section.

The West has no clearly defined ideological attitude to trade with Socialist countries. It is generally accepted that trade should be entrusted to the market mechanism and be conducted in pursuance of private interest. Government intervention, although greater than in

[1] A Dutch lawyer (Pieter Sanders) was obviously still thinking in terms of the old colonial days preceding World War II, when he recently wrote an article entitled 'Trade Arbitration between East and West' (*International and Contemporary Law Quarterly*, London, July 1966). He identified East-West trade as that between the countries belonging to the Oriental (Japan included) and Western (including Eastern European countries) civilizations.

trade with other Capitalist countries, is only of a supplementary nature. In Socialist countries, trade is viewed as a macro-social activity in which non-commercial considerations necessarily play a legitimate role. Whilst in the West the mainsprings of trade are the profit motive and the consumer's sovereignty, in Socialist countries developmental needs reflected in the general economic plan essentially determine the flow of trade.

The second feature is that the processes involved in pricing articles entering East-West trade differ on each side. In the West, where market economies prevail, prices are basically determined by the interplay of supply and demand; all factor costs are normally reflected in prices although the latter may be modified to some extent by government intervention in the form of indirect taxes and subsidies. In each Socialist country the domestic price structure is, as a rule, centrally planned and, owing to the ideological acceptance of the labour theory of value, the costs of natural and man-made resources are not fully, or otherwise arbitrarily, reflected. Prices do not necessarily perform an allocative function and they are almost entirely insulated from world market forces.

Third, on the Western side, trade is carried on predominantly by privately owned and operated firms, some large but otherwise mostly of medium size. This in effect means a considerable degree of decentralization of decision-making. In Socialist countries, trade is centrally determined by the state planning commission on the advice of the ministry of foreign trade. On the operational side, there is a relatively small number of specialized state instrumentalities each, in general, with a monopoly of foreign trade in certain classes of articles; even where the right to engage in foreign trade has been delegated to other entities, as in some Eastern European countries recently, their number is small and their size is large.

In Western countries, competition is regarded as highly desirable, as it promotes efficiency and is conducive to the consumers' welfare and traders, generally speaking, operate under competitive conditions. In Socialist countries, on the other hand, competition has a very limited scope and it is largely incompatible with central planning and the existing institutional set-up.

As a corollary of the conditions outlined above, there is a difference in emphasis in the weapons of trade policy employed by governments in

East-West trade. In free enterprise countries, the authorities endeavour to attain their policy objectives mainly through influencing the operation of the market mechanism, while direct controls are of secondary importance. On the other hand, Socialist governments rely chiefly on directive measures whilst material incentives play a subsidiary role. However, it may be observed that Western countries resort to direct controls more extensively in trade with Socialist countries than with other Capitalist nations. Similarly, the role of material incentives employed by Socialist authorities is much greater in application to trade with Western countries than in intra-Bloc trade.

As East-West trade is conditioned in different ways on each side, such problems as access to the market, MFN reciprocity, the manipulation of exchange rates, dumping and trade disputes have different implications under each system. These problems are thorny enough if they arise in trade between economies of the same type, but when different economic and political systems are involved the issues are likely to degenerate, as they often have, into intolerant diatribes leading to no solution.

By whose standards are the issues to be judged? The story is told of a Western and a Socialist economist, both cross-eyed, who attended a United Nations conference on trade. Walking from opposite directions in an empty, straight corridor they bumped into each other. 'You idiot', said one, 'why don't you look where you are going?' To which the other retorted, 'You pervert, why don't you go where you are looking?' There is no lack of extremists on either side who believe that the strained atmosphere in which East-West trade is conducted can never be removed, and that normal trading relations between countries with opposing social systems are in fact not possible.

Other characteristics of a general nature for which East-West trade is noted may be briefly stated. The influence of politics in obstructing, and occasionally promoting, commercial relations between the two camps has been obvious ever since World War II (and even earlier if we study Soviet trade). To a large extent, trade between the two camps can be viewed as a barometer reflecting ups and downs in the East-West political scene. To the list of the distinctive features discussed, we must add the wide fluctuations in the size, structure and direction of trade, its uncertainty, the persistence of the strategic embargo and a virtual absence of capital movements. These features explain another characteristic of East-West trade, viz. its relatively small size. We shall examine this question in some detail in the next section.

B. EAST-WEST TRADE IN THE INTERNATIONAL SCENE

The participation in world trade by the West and by the Socialist Bloc in relation to their area, population and industrial output is indicated in Table I. For the sake of comparison, data for the Developing World are also given.

TABLE I   PARTICIPATION IN WORLD TRADE, 1967

WORLD DIVISION	% SHARE IN THE WORLD'S:			FOREIGN-TRADE TURNOVER		
	Area	Population	Industrial Output[4]	Total £ Million[5]	% Share[5]	Per Head (£)
The West[1]	26·4	21·5	55 (63)	107,490	69·3	142
The Socialist Bloc[2]	25·6	35·5	38 (23)	17,520	11·3	14
The Third World[3]	48·0	43·0	7 (14)	29,580	19·1	20
THE WORLD	100·0	100·0	100 (100)	155,170	100·0	43

[1] Canada, USA, all Europe except the 8 Socialist countries, Japan, South Africa, Australia and New Zealand.
[2] Albania, Bulgaria, Czechoslovakia, East Germany, Hungary, Poland, Rumania, the USSR, Mainland China, Mongolia, North Korea and North Vietnam.
[3] Countries other than under [1] and [2].
[4] In the world's national income in brackets.
[5] The world total includes £580 m. for trade of unknown destination.
Sources. Based mainly on: United Nations, *Monthly Bulletin of Statistics*, June 1968; *Voprosy ekonomiki*, Moscow, 9/1967, p. 124.

If we average each division's share in the world's area, population and industrial output, we find that according to this rough test each division represents one-third of the world. The relatively high degree of participation in world trade by the West (69%) and the low share claimed by the Bloc (only 11%) patently stand out.

The reasons for this contrast are numerous and complex, partly economic, partly political, and well rooted in geography and history. First of all, there are more than twice as many countries in the West as in the Socialist Bloc, which means that the average size of a Socialist country is twice as large. Besides, two Bloc countries are disproportionately large – the USSR is larger in area and industrial output, and China in population, than the remaining Socialist countries combined. Thus, some of the trade (intra-Western) appearing as 'foreign' in the West naturally falls under 'domestic' in the Bloc, because it is merely between one part of the same large country and another, instead of between two small countries.

A rough indication of the role of foreign trade in a country's economy can be provided by the proportion represented by the foreign-trade turnover in its National Income. Taking the West as a whole, foreign trade works out at about a quarter, and in the Bloc it constitutes roughly one-tenth. The percentage shares for selected Western countries in 1966 were: USA: 10%, Turkey: 14%, Japan: 25%, France: 30%, Australia: 33%, Italy: 34%, U.K.: 38%, W. Germany: 42%, Canada: 49%, Switzerland: 58% and the highest share attained was in the case of the Netherlands: 87%.[1] For the most important Socialist countries the approximate proportions were in the same year: China: 4%, USSR: 8%, and for the other European CMEA countries the percentages ranged from 25% to 70%, the highest proportions having been attained in the case of Bulgaria (60%) and Hungary (70%).[2]

As is well known, participation in foreign trade is as a rule positively correlated with *per capita* income.[3] Although one can have doubts as to

[1] Based on: IMF and IBRD, *Direction of Trade*, Annual 1961–66; United Nations, *Monthly Bulletin of Statistics*, 7/1968.

[2] The proportion for China is the author's estimate based on the assumption that her foreign-trade turnover was US $4,300 m. and her National Income $100,000 m. The figures for the remaining Socialist countries are based on various Socialist sources (rough adjustments were made to bring the Socialist national income figures to the Western basis).

[3] The foreign-trade turnover per head of the population attained by selected Western countries in 1967 was (in US dollars): Turkey 37, Yugoslavia 148, Japan 210, USA 302, France 477, UK 583, Australia 624, West Germany 680, Canada 1,070, Sweden 1,168, Netherlands 1,240, Switzerland 1,253 and Belgium–Luxemburg 1,435. The estimated figures for the most important Socialist countries in the same year were (also in US dollars): China 6, USSR 80, Rumania 160, Poland 165, Czechoslovakia 415, Hungary 415 and the highest was attained in the case of Bulgaria 445. In the foreign-trade turnover figures, all imports were brought to a c.i.f. basis. For the average weighted Western and Bloc averages, see Table I.

the precise figures, it is fairly certain that the National Income per head in the Bloc is only half of that in the West.[1] Historically speaking, trade has undoubtedly been promoted by such factors as the possession of dependencies (as sources of raw materials and markets for finished products) and the export of capital. The trade links so established do not easily fade away, even if trade patterns undergo transformation, following the political emancipation of colonies. Compared with most Western nations, the present Socialist countries' role in these two fields has been nil or negligible.

Another obvious reason is the difference in the authorities' attitude to foreign trade. Owing to the high significance attached to the consumers' welfare, employment-creation and private profit-making, foreign trade has been traditionally viewed with favour in Western countries. On the other hand, the fascination with autarky ('balanced development') in each Socialist country – even though less pronounced now than in the Stalinist era – is still strong.[2]

The place of East-West trade in the world scene is shown in Diag. A on p. 27. The size of the squares is in proportion to each division's share in world trade (exports + imports); the unshaded areas in the squares represent intra-foreign trade whilst the shaded portions indicate trade with the respective world divisions. It will be noted that the value of East-West trade in recent years has averaged £4,000 m. annually, constituting only 2·8% of the world foreign trade turnover. Considering that this inter-trade is contributed by two-thirds of the world, its small

[1] Several Western economists have endeavoured to demonstrate the degree of the Socialist countries 'under-trading'. Two different approaches deserve to be mentioned here. Pryor based his estimates of 'trade potential' on *per capita* trade turnover and *per capita* industrial production. Cornelisse made estimates of potential exports (which he called 'calculated exports') using the GNP of the exporting country, the GNP of the importing country and the distance between them. Accepting the degree of trade intensity of the 8 leading Western nations as a yardstick, Pryor demonstrated that in 1955 not one CMEA country realized even 50% of its 'potential' trade *per capita*. Cornelisse showed that the exports of the 7 leading Western nations and of the 5 leading European Socialist countries (including Yugoslavia) to each other in 1957 and in 1961 were less than 25% of what they should have been by the intra-Western trading intensity standards. See F. L. Pryor, *The Communist Foreign Trade System*, Allen & Unwin, London 1963, pp. 27, 277–80; P. A. Cornelisse, 'The Volume of East-West Trade', *Co-existence*, Nov. 1964, pp. 99–106.

[2] However, the role of autarkic policies pursued by Socialist countries can easily be exaggerated (as indeed they have been by Western observers in the past). Even before the war, the share of these countries in world trade was small – in fact smaller then (8%) than now (11%). See Table IX, p. 45.

Diag. A. East-West Trade in the World Scene
*Annual Averages, 1966–1967**

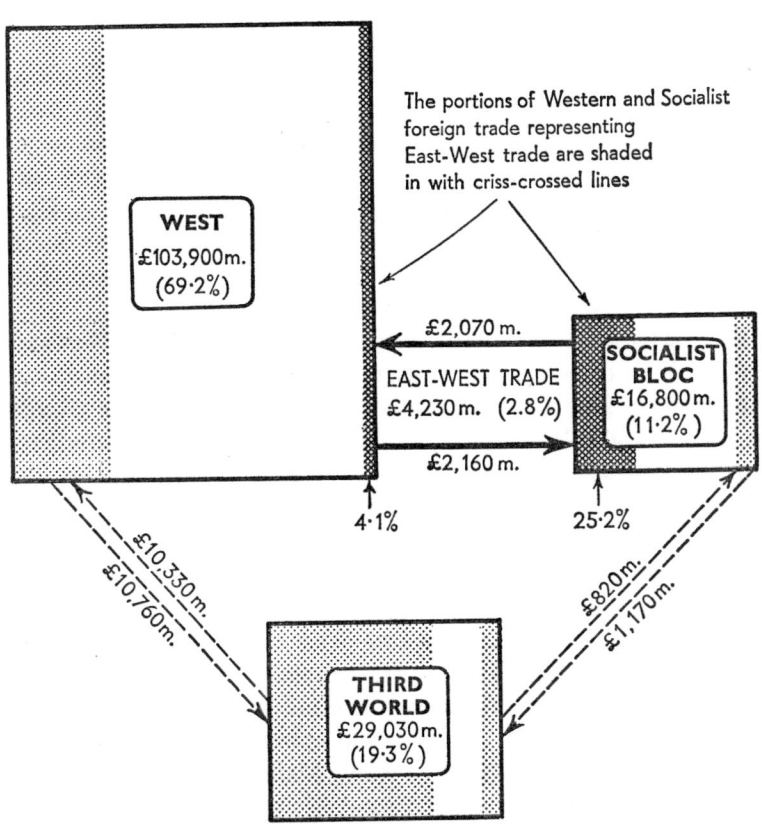

* Both exports and imports are valued f.o.b. The percentage figures, indicating each division's share in the world foreign trade turnover, do not add up to 100·0% because the world total includes trade of unknown destination, worth £370 m. (or 0·3%).

Source. Based on, United Nations, *Monthly Bulletin of Statistics*, June 1968, p. xii.

size is most conspicuous. Its value is considerably less than the total foreign trade of the Netherlands, and only one-third of the British and only one-half of the Soviet foreign trade. This can be compared with the trade between the West and the Less Developed world (the two divisions which roughly also constitute two-thirds of the world) the value of which has recently reached £20,000 m., representing over 14% of world trade.

The explanation for the relatively small size of East-West trade consists partly in the Bloc countries' small participation in foreign trade in general, already discussed. Otherwise, political intervention on each side must largely bear the blame – the desire to become independent of the other camp, especially for strategic imports (see Ch. 11 A, B), the strategic embargo administered by the West (Ch. 12) and the Socialist drive to expand trade with the Third World (see Ch. 11 D, esp. Tables XXVIII and XXIX, pp. 257 and 258).

What is the relative importance of East-West trade to the West and to the Bloc? As demonstrated in Diag. A, Western dependence on the trade with the Bloc is comparatively small – it represents only 4% of the Western countries' foreign trade turnover. On the other hand, trade with the West consititutes as much as 25% of the Socialist countries' foreign trade. Thus to sum up, East-West trade represents:

3% of world foreign trade turnover;
4% of the Western countries' foreign trade;
25% of the Bloc countries' foreign trade.

The degree of dependence on East-West trade naturally differs from one country to another. This is demonstrated in Tables II and III. Of the Western countries, Yugoslavia, Finland and Iceland are the most active, and South Africa, New Zealand and the United States the least active traders with the Socialist Bloc. Mainland China, Poland and Rumania are the most dependent, and Mongolia, North Vietnam and North Korea the least dependent Socialist countries on the West for trade.[1]

In spite of the small value of East-West trade, its role in international relations since World War II has been extraordinary. East-West trade has been intimately interwoven with foreign policy and with many crucial

[1] The share of the West and of the Socialist Bloc in Cuba's trade over the 2 years 1966–67 was 13% and 68% respectively.

issues of our time, forcing Western and Socialist countries into intricate patterns of relationships. It has received more publicity than other trade, and it has been a frequent subject of international conferences, parliamentary debates, ministerial enquiries, special reports, etc., far beyond the nominal value of the trade involved. The importance of trade in East-West relations, as seen by an American writer, is reflected in the following recollection: '... Khrushchev's beginning point was almost always the problem of trade and the U.S. restrictive policy. He harangued about it, pleaded against it, joked about it, stormed at it, and openly puzzled over it'.[1]

[1] Mose L. Harvey, *East-West Trade and United States Policy*, National Association of Manufacturers, New York 1966, p. 30.

TABLE II THE DEGREE OF DEPENDENCE OF WESTERN COUNTRIES ON TRADE WITH THE SOCIALIST BLOC

Annual Averages, 1966–1967[1]

COUNTRY	Annual Value of Trade with the Bloc	Trade with the Bloc as a Percentage of the Country's Total Trade	The 4 Main Socialist Trade Partners
	£m.	%	
1. Yugoslavia	340	32·8	USSR, E. Germany, Czechoslovakia, Poland
2. Finland	210	18·0	USSR, Poland, E. Germany, Czechoslovakia
3. Turkey	60	14·0	USSR, Hungary, E. Germany, Czechoslovakia
4. Austria	185	12·6	USSR, Hungary, Czechoslovakia, Poland
5. Greece	70	11·5	USSR, Bulgaria, Czechoslovakia, Hungary

TABLE II—*Continued*

COUNTRY	Annual Value of Trade with the Bloc	Trade with the Bloc as a Percentage of the Country's Total Trade	The 4 Main Socialist Trade Partners
	£m.	%	
6. Iceland	13	7·5	USSR, Poland, Czechoslovakia, E. Germany
7. Italy	415	6·6	USSR, Rumania, Poland, China
8. Japan	480	6·5	China, USSR, Rumania, Bulgaria
9. Sweden	150	4·6	USSR, Poland, E. Germany, China
10. W. Germany[2]	620	4·4	USSR, Rumania, China, Poland
11. United Kingdom	490	4·3	USSR, Poland, China, Czechoslovakia
AVERAGE (weighted)	—	4·1	
12. France	335	4·0	USSR, China, Rumania, Poland
13. Australia	90	3·6	China, USSR, Poland, Czechoslovakia
14. Denmark	85	3·5	Poland, USSR, E. Germany, Czechoslovakia
15. Switzerland	90	3·4	Czechoslovakia, USSR, China, Hungary
16. Norway	50	3·2	USSR, Poland, Czechoslovakia, E. Germany
17. Canada	195	2·6	USSR, China, Poland, Czechoslovakia
18. Spain	45	2·5	Poland, USSR, Rumania, E. Germany

TABLE II—*Continued*

COUNTRY	Annual Value of Trade with the Bloc	Trade with the Bloc as a Percentage of the Country's Total Trade	The 4 Main Socialist Trade Partners
	£m.	%	
19. Netherlands	130	2·4	USSR, E. Germany, Czechoslovakia, China
20. Belgium–Lux.	110	2·2	USSR, E. Germany, Poland, China
21. Ireland	9	1·4	Poland, USSR, E. Germany, Czechoslovakia
22. Portugal	7	1·2	Poland, Czechoslovakia, Rumania, Bulgaria
23. New Zealand	8	1·1	USSR, China, Poland, Czechoslovakia
24. United States	140	0·7	Poland, USSR, Czechoslovakia, E. Germany
25. South Africa	3	0·2	Poland, Czechoslovakia, Hungary, E. Germany

[1] The values and percentages shown are minimal figures, as in the trade totals of each country trade with undisclosed partners is included.

[2] West Germany's trade with East Germany is recorded in statistics as intra-German (domestic) trade. If it is treated as foreign, its average value in 1966–67 was £250 m., West Germany's trade with the Bloc amounted to £870 m. representing 6·2% of the country's total foreign trade, and East Germany ranked ahead of the USSR as a trading partner.

Sources. Based on: IMF and IBRD, *Direction of Trade*; United Nations, *Monthly Bulletin of Statistics*.

TABLE III THE DEGREE OF DEPENDENCE OF SOCIALIST COUNTRIES ON TRADE WITH THE WEST

Annual Averages, 1966–1967[1]

COUNTRY	Annual Value of Trade with the West £m.	Trade with the West as a Percentage of the Country's Total Trade %	The 4 Main Western Trade Partners
1. Mainland China	680	45	Japan, W. Germany, U.K., Australia
2. Rumania	340	35	W. Germany, Italy, France, U.K.
3. Poland	600	30	U.K., W. Germany, Italy, USA
4. Hungary	300	25	W. Germany, Italy, Austria, Yugoslavia
AVERAGE (weighted)	—	25	
5. USSR	1,350	24	U.K., Finland, Japan, Yugoslavia
6. East Germany[2]	480	21	Yugoslavia, France, U.K., Sweden
7. Czechoslovakia	420	20	W. Germany, Yugoslavia, U.K., Italy
8. Bulgaria	230	20	W. Germany, Italy, France, Yugoslavia
9. Albania	10	12	Italy, Canada, Yugoslavia, W. Germany
10. North Korea	20	10	Japan, France, Greece, Australia
11. North Vietnam	10	6	Japan, France, Belgium, U.K.

TABLE III—*Continued*

COUNTRY	Annual Value of Trade with the West	Trade with the West as a Percentage of the Country's Total Trade	The 4 Main Western Trade Partners
	£m.	%	
12. Mongolia	4	4	USA, Belgium, Japan, U.K.

[1] See footnote [1] to Table II.
[2] Trade with West Germany and West Berlin is normally regarded as intra-German (domestic) trade. If treated as foreign, the value of this trade averaged £250 m. in 1966–67, East Germany's trade with the West amounted to £730 m., representing 30% of the country's total trade, and West Germany ranked ahead of Yugoslavia as a trading partner.

Sources. Based on: IMF and IBRD, *Direction of Trade.* Supplementary adjustments were made from the official statistical yearbooks of Albania, Bulgaria, Czechoslovakia, East Germany, Hungary, North Korea, Poland, Rumania, USSR, and from: Far Eastern Economic Review, *China Trade Report.*

2 Structure

EAST-WEST trade, involving as it does two-thirds of the world, is as varied as world trade in general. Apart from items of strategic significance, it would be difficult to find articles normally entering world trade absent in East-West trade. However, the purpose of this chapter is not to dwell on details but rather to bring out meaningful patterns.[1] Attention is focused on the role of primary products and manufactures, and tendencies that can be discerned in the last decade. The plan adopted is first to examine Western exports to the Socialist Bloc, then the Bloc's exports to the West. This factual discussion is followed by some general observations on the composition of East-West trade.

A. WESTERN EXPORTS TO THE SOCIALIST BLOC

The structure of Western exports to the Bloc is shown in a simplified form in Table IV. The commodities are divided into broad classes and expressed in value percentages covering selected years in the last decade.

It is evident from the Table that roughly one-third of the exports to the Bloc consists of foodstuffs and raw materials. The main commodities include grains (mainly from Australia, Canada, USA, France, West Germany, Sweden), wool (Australia, Britain, New Zealand),[2] hides and skins (Australia, USA, Canada), synthetic rubber and fibres (USA, France, West Germany, Britain) and copper (West Germany, Britain, Australia). Of these the largest single item by value is wheat, averaging

---

[1] Apart from national statistical publications, details can be found in the voluminous annual issues of the United Nations *Commodity Trade Statistics* where articles of trade are brought to common classification and value bases.

[2] Britain has traditionally been a re-exporting centre for Australian, South African and New Zealand wool to the Bloc countries, although her role has declined in recent years. Beginning in 1964 (the USSR in 1960), the Bloc has virtually ceased importing wool from South Africa.

TABLE IV PERCENTAGE COMPOSITION OF WESTERN EXPORTS TO THE SOCIALIST BLOC

CLASS OF EXPORT*	1957–59		1962–64		1965		1966	
	Annual Averages							
Food, beverages, tobacco	12·8		25·1		22·2		20·1	
Crude materials (except fuels)	18·2	31·2	13·2	38·6	12·0	34·5	10·2	30·5
Mineral fuels	0·2		0·3		0·3		0·2	
Chemicals	10·7		9·6		12·7		12·5	
Machinery and transport equipment	22·0	68·4	27·5	60·7	27·0	65·0	30·1	69·1
Other manufactures	35·7		23·6		25·3		26·5	
Unclassified	0·4		0·7		0·5		0·4	
TOTAL	100·0		100·0		100·0		100·0	
	(£810 m.)		(£1,390 m.)		(£1,780 m.)		(£2,060 m.)	

* Based on the uniform *SITC* (Standard International Commodity Classification) *Revised*, applying to the whole period.

Source. Based on United Nations, *Monthly Bulletin of Statistics.*

£300 m. in recent years, constituting about one-sixth of Western exports to the Bloc (for further details, see Ch. 11 E(b), pp. 262–64).

Manufactures, comprising some two-thirds of the total, include a wide variety of articles ranging from semi-finished simple chemicals to complete industrial plants. This group of exports is clearly dominated by machinery and other forms of capital equipment such as (in descending order of value) electrical machinery and equipment, ships, locomotives and other vehicles, heating and cooling equipment, metalworking machinery, paper-processing machinery, pumps and filtering equipment, textile machinery and scientific apparatus and computers.

This class of exports also includes complete plants and factories for chemical, glass-making, oil refining, textile, pulp and paper, iron and steel, food processing and other industries. Some recent examples of such deliveries may be mentioned: fertilizer plants (from Britain to Czechoslovakia, Hungary, Poland, and the USSR, from West Germany to Rumania, from the Netherlands and Japan to China), oil refineries (Britain, West Germany and Italy to China, the USA to Rumania), a polyvinyl plant (Japan to the USSR), a vinylon plant (Japan to China) and metallurgical plants (a West German, French and Belgian consortium to China, Italy to Czechoslovakia, West Germany to Rumania). Amongst the largest of such deals in recent years we may mention a complex of passenger car plants (worth £300 m.) from Italy (FIAT) and France to the USSR, of chemical plants (£40 m.) from the Italian Montecatini to the USSR, and of dacron plants (£40 m.) from Britain to the USSR.

The remaining manufactured exports comprise a variety of iron and steel products, fertilizers, pharmaceuticals, plastics, metal-working tools, ball-bearings, man-made fibres, cables and industrial fittings. In contrast to the situation before the Communist regimes took over in the present Bloc countries, a relatively small proportion is represented by 'non-essential' consumer goods. The proportion of highly sophisticated manufactured exports to the Bloc containing highly advanced technology might be higher were it not for the strategic embargo administered by the leading Western countries (see Ch. 12 A, B, pp. 271–78).

If we examine the course of Western exports to the Bloc over the last decade, we can observe a sharp increase in the export of food over the period 1962–65 which was noted for widespread agricultural failures in Eastern Europe and continued food shortages in China. It is interesting to note a corresponding decline of manufactured exports, machinery and transportation equipment excepted, which suggests that the Socialist countries' liquid reserves (with the possible exception of the USSR) are pretty limited (see Ch. 10 B). The decline was particularly sharp in the case of China, to whom Western exports of manufactures slumped to a third of what they had been before. The decline was not so noticeable in the case of the Soviet Union who, being a substantial gold producer, financed part of the imports by substantial gold sales in the West, as well as generous long-term credits (see Ch. 10 B, E).

The proportion of manufactures in Western exports to the Socialist Bloc is not much different from that obtaining in Western exports to Capitalist countries – Western or Developing, see Table V, p. 37.

TABLE V PERCENTAGE SHARE OF MANUFACTURES IN WESTERN EXPORTS TO THE WEST, THE SOCIALIST BLOC AND THE DEVELOPING WORLD

(*Figures in brackets represent non-manufactured exports*)

DESTINATION OF WESTERN EXPORTS	1957–59	1962–64	1965	1966
	Annual Averages			
To the West	60 (40)	66 (34)	68 (32)	70 (30)
To the Socialist Bloc	68 (32)	61 (39)	65 (35)	69 (31)
To the Developing World	78 (22)	77 (23)	77 (23)	77 (23)

Source. Derived from Table IV and its sources.

B. THE BLOC'S EXPORTS TO THE WEST

If we divide the Bloc's exports to the West into primary products and manufactures, we find that the former constitute as much as two-thirds whilst the latter is only one-third of the total. Thus, as compared with Socialist imports from the West, the proportions are reversed. The relative importance of the different types of exports is brought out in Table VI.

The Socialist Bloc is still an important exporter of food to the West, even though in recent years (on account of the large purchases of grains) it has turned into a net importer. The ten leading foodstuffs exported to the West are the following (in order of value):

cereals and preparations (chiefly by the USSR, China, Rumania, East Germany);

sugar (USSR, Czechoslovakia, Poland, China, Hungary, East Germany);

meats (Poland, Hungary, East Germany, Rumania, China);

fruits and vegetables (Hungary, Poland, China, Bulgaria, Czechoslovakia);

eggs (Poland, China, Bulgaria, Czechoslovakia);

fish and preparations (USSR, China, Poland);

dairy products (Poland, Hungary);

soybeans and kernels (China, Rumania);

TABLE VI PERCENTAGE COMPOSITION OF SOCIALIST EXPORTS TO THE WEST

CLASS OF EXPORT*	1957–59		1962–64		1965		1966	
	Annual Averages							
Food, beverages, tobacco	23·8		21·0		19·6		20·3	
Crude materials (excl. fuels)	23·4	64·3	23·0	62·6	24·4	59·2	25·1	59·6
Mineral fuels	17·7		18·6		15·2		14·2	
Chemicals	6·8		5·8		5·9		5·4	
Machinery and transport equipment	7·9	33·0	7·5	36·8	7·3	39·9	7·6	38·9
Other manufactures	18·8		23·5		26·7		25·9	
Unclassified	2·7		0·6		0·9		1·5	
TOTAL	100·0		100·0		100·0		100·0	
	(£800 m.)		(£1,280 m.)		(£1,660 m.)		(£1,990 m.)	

* Based on the uniform *SITC Revised*, applying to the whole period.
Source. Based on: United Nations, *Monthly Bulletin of Statistics*.

tea (China);
beverages (Hungary, China).
Crude materials include a large variety of animal, plant and mineral products. We shall list only the ten most important items (also in order of value):
timber (mainly from the USSR, Rumania, Poland, Czechoslovakia);
furs (USSR, China, Poland);
animal hair and feathers (China, USSR);
cotton (USSR);
pulp and waste paper (USSR, Czechoslovakia, Poland);
industrial animal and vegetable oils (USSR, Rumania, China);
silk (China, USSR);
manganese (USSR);
chromium (USSR);
asbestos (USSR).

CH. 2 §B STRUCTURE 39

The Socialist Bloc is amply endowed with mineral fuels and, owing to its relatively small requirements, the Bloc is an important exporter to the West. Oil and products, exported from the USSR and Rumania (oil products also from East Germany, Czechoslovakia, Poland and Hungary) now consititute one-tenth of the Bloc's exports to the West [for details, see Ch. 11 E(a)]. Nearly as important by value are exports of coal, coke and briquettes, almost exclusively from the USSR, Poland, East Germany, Czechoslovakia and North Vietnam.

So far as manufactured exports are concerned, they are mostly unsophisticated consumer goods and semi-finished materials which need further processing in the West; in fact some of them are re-imported, as is the case with Chinese pig iron re-imported as steel from Japan. The most important groups by value may be briefly listed: iron and steel semi-manufactures (especially from the USSR, Poland, Czechoslovakia, China, Hungary, East Germany, Rumania), textiles (China, Czechoslovakia, East Germany, Poland, USSR, Hungary, Bulgaria, Rumania), fertilizers (East Germany, USSR, Poland), a variety of organic and inorganic chemicals (East Germany, USSR, Poland, Czechoslovakia, China), wood manufactures (USSR, Poland, East Germany, Hungary, China), non-ferrous metallic – aluminium, zinc, tin and lead – semi-manufactures (USSR, China, Poland, Hungary), glass and pottery (Czechoslovakia, East Germany, Poland, China) and some others.

The Bloc's export of machinery to the West, about £130 m. annually, is only one-tenth of what Britain alone exports to the West.[1] There is virtually no machinery exported to the West from the Asian Socialist countries and Albania. The machinery exported by the remaining Socialist countries, in descending order of value, includes the following types: machine tools (Czechoslovakia, East Germany, USSR, Poland, Hungary), vehicles – locomotives, trucks, cars, motor-cycles (Czechoslovakia, USSR, Hungary, East Germany, Poland), electric machinery and appliances (East Germany, Czechoslovakia, USSR, Hungary, Poland), construction and mining machinery (USSR, Czechoslovakia, East Germany, Rumania), office machines (East Germany, Czechoslovakia) and printing and book-binding equipment.

If we turn to Table VII, it can be seen that in their exports to other Socialist countries and to the Developing World, manufactures con-

[1] United Nations *Monthly Bulletin of Statistics*, 3/1968, p. xxviii.

TABLE VII PERCENTAGE SHARE OF MANUFACTURES IN SOCIALIST EXPORTS TO THE SOCIALIST BLOC, THE WEST AND THE DEVELOPING WORLD

(Figures in brackets represent non-manufactured exports)

DESTINATION OF SOCIALIST EXPORTS	1957–59 Annual	1962–64 Averages	1965	1966
To the Socialist Bloc	57 (43)	67 (33)	68 (32)	68 (32)
To the West	33 (67)	37 (73)	40 (60)	39 (61)
To the Developing World	60 (40)	68 (32)	68 (32)	68 (32)

Source. Derived from Table VI and its sources.

stitute two-thirds of the total in each case. In addition, these manufactures include a large proportion of machinery and complete industrial plants, such as agricultural machinery, power plants, textile machinery, steel mills, sugar refineries, oil refineries, ocean-going vessels, telecommunication apparatus, military equipment, etc. Some of the above items, especially agricultural machinery, textile plants and military equipment, are exported in sizeable quantities even by China. After all, manufacturing is responsible for one-half of the Gross National Product (of the European Socialist countries at least[1]) and the Socialist Bloc as a whole claims some two-fifths of the world's industrial output (see Table I, p. 24).

The relatively small proportion of manufactures in Socialist exports to the West can be explained by several contributing causes. First of all, Socialist countries – particularly those within CMEA – give preference to satisfying member countries' requirements for carrying out their planned development schemes.[2] On the other hand, many Socialist manufactures do not easily meet the standards demanded in the highly competitive buyers' markets in the West. Central planning and collective ownership of the means of production are not conducive to immediate

[1] V. Rutgaizer, *Voprosy ekonomiki*, 8/1964, p. 69.
[2] Of the total value of Socialist manufactured exports £4,930 m. in 1966, 68% was channelled to other Socialist countries; the Developing World and the West each absorbed only 16%. Based on United Nations *Monthly Bulletin of Statistics*, 3/1968, pp. xviii–xxxi.

adaptation, or anticipation, of models to rapidly changing technological possibilities and tastes. Western opposition to importing a higher proportion of manufactures is deplored in Socialist countries, and it is interpreted as politically motivated. It is thought that, with the Cold War still lingering on, the West would like the Socialist countries to serve as a source of raw materials and a market for its finished products, as they did before the Communist regimes took over.[1]

C. SOME GENERAL OBSERVATIONS

From the preceding discussion of Western and Socialist exports to each other, it can be concluded that East-West trade is still largely vertical, i.e. in the main the Bloc's primary products are exchanged for Western manufactures. Thus in its trade with the West, the Socialist Bloc can be looked upon as an underdeveloped part of the world. This contrasts with the Bloc's trade with the Developing World, to which Socialist countries mostly export manufactures but import foodstuffs and other raw materials in exchange – trade which also bears vertical characteristics.

Considering that the Socialist Bloc supplies mainly primary products to the West, its exports are greatly exposed to the fluctuations typical of such products in the highly competitive world markets. Moreover, these exports have to encounter several forms of discrimination in the West on account of agricultural protectionism, economic integration and political considerations (see Ch. 8 B, and Ch. 11 B, E). Besides, being mainly importers of manufactures from the West, the Bloc in common with the Developing World has been suffering from long-run deterioration in its terms of trade (also see Ch. 14 D, pp. 334–41).

Although the Bloc in trade with the West still largely exchanges primary products for manufactures, this structure is gradually undergoing a transformation, bearing (imperfect) witness to the rapidly proceeding industrialization in Socialist countries. The proportion of manufactured goods has been steadily rising, not only in the Bloc's total exports to the world but also to the West (see Table VIII). Their

[1] See, e.g., T. Földi (ed.), *Studies in International Economics*, Akademiai Kiado, Budapest 1966, pp. 79–89, 103–33; S. Toczek, *Handel zagraniczny* (Foreign Trade), Warsaw, 3/1967, pp. 107–12.

Table VIII MANUFACTURES IN EAST-WEST TRADE, 1955–1966*

YEAR	WESTERN EXPORTS OF MANUFACTURES TO THE SOCIALIST BLOC		THE BLOC'S EXPORTS OF MANUFACTURES TO THE WEST	
	In £ Million at Current Prices (Machinery and Vehicles in brackets)	% of Total Exports to the Bloc	% of Total Exports to the Bloc	In £ Million at Current Prices (Machinery and Vehicles in brackets)
1955	270 (95)	57	28	170 (40)
1956	390 (125)	63	31	210 (50)
1957	460 (155)	63	32	250 (65)
1958	570 (165)	70	35	270 (65)
1959	620 (210)	72	33	290 (65)
1960	770 (270)	72	33	330 (75)
1961	750 (310)	65	35	380 (75)
1962	790 (375)	68	38	410 (90)
1963	810 (365)	61	35	450 (90)
1964	900 (410)	55	38	560 (120)
1965	1,160 (480)	65	40	670 (120)
1966	1,420 (620)	69	39	780 (150)

* Based on the United Nations *SITC Revised;* manufactures are taken as Classes 5–8, i.e. chemicals are included.
Sources. Calculated from: United Nations, *Monthly Bulletin of Statistics* and *Commodity Trade Statistics.*

proportion in the Bloc's exports to the West rose from less than 30% in the mid-1950s to 40% in the mid-1960s.

However, in these developments one notable trend can be detected, concerning the Bloc's imports of machinery and complete industrial plants. In the mid-1950s Socialist countries as a whole imported twice as much machinery from the West as they exported to it, but now they import four times as much (see Table VIII). This indicates the important role the West is playing in Socialist industrialization even today.

Although in general the Bloc's ability to influence Western markets is small, owing to its small overall share in Western trade (see Ch. 1, pp. 24-28), its impact can be considerable in the case of certain commodities and countries. Thus Sweden, France and Italy substantially rely on Polish and Soviet coal; Britain, France and the Netherlands on Soviet and Rumanian timber; West Germany on East German lignite and briquettes; Italy, Austria, Finland and Iceland on Soviet oil; Japan on Chinese iron and oil seeds; and Australia on Chinese tung oil (used as a drying agent in paint manufacture) and bristles.

On the Western export side, practically all Socialist countries provide a valuable market, in particular for such products as Australian and Canadian wheat, barley and oats, and for Australian and New Zealand wool.[1] Western European countries and Japan have come to rely on the steadily growing exports of machinery, fertilizers and other manufactures to the Bloc. In contrast to the USA, these countries have rather limited domestic markets and sales to Socialist countries provide a welcome opportunity to utilize idle capacity.[2]

[1] In recent years the Bloc has absorbed one-half of Australian and Canadian wheat exports, and in odd years a quarter of Australian and Canadian barley, and normally nearly a tenth of Australian and New Zealand wool exports. Occasionally, large proportions of Australian oats and of Icelandic fish were also purchased by the Bloc. The proportion of Western exports as a whole absorbed by the Bloc is 4%.

[2] In 1966, of their manufactured exports to the world, the highest proportions directed to the Bloc were recorded in the case of the following Western countries: Yugoslavia: 35%, Austria: 25%, Finland: 25%, Italy: 6%, Japan: 6%, Denmark: 5%, Sweden: 4%, West Germany: 4%. The proportion for the United Kingdom was 3% and for the USA less than 0·2%. Based on United Nations *Commodity Trade Statistics 1966*.

3 Changing Patterns of Direction

IN the introductory chapter we presented a static picture of the Western and Socialist countries' trade in an international setting as it is today. In this chapter we shall examine the direction of their trade historically, going back to pre-war times to assess any significant trends. To provide a background, we shall first consider the tendencies in Western trade followed by a similar analysis of Socialist trade. We shall then draw an overall picture (motion, if you like) of trends in East-West trade.

A. TENDENCIES IN WESTERN FOREIGN TRADE

Since the war, the world as a whole has experienced an impressive expansion in foreign trade.[1] In this remarkable development the West and the Socialist Bloc have both exhibited a higher rate of growth than the world as a whole. This is indicated by the rising proportions of world trade claimed by the two divisions, as demonstrated in Table IX, p. 45.

If we consider the relatively normal period since the Korean War, the percentage of world trade contributed by Western nations rose from 63% in 1953 to 69% in 1967, and the share claimed by Socialist countries from 9% to 11% in the same period. (This means that the share of the Developing countries in world trade declined from 28% to 20%.)

However, in the expansion of the trade in the West, intra-Western trade has been increasing at a slightly faster rate than that with the rest of the world taken as a whole. Thus up to the mid-1950s, less than two-thirds of Western countries' trade was with one another, but the proportion has gradually increased to three-quarters since that time. This is shown in Table X, p. 46.

[1] 10 times in nominal (US dollar) values or about 4 times in real terms. See various issues of United Nations *Yearbook of International Trade Statistics* and *Monthly Bulletin of Statistics*, June 1968, p. xvi.

CH. 3 §A CHANGING PATTERNS OF DIRECTION

TABLE IX WESTERN AND SOCIALIST PARTICIPATION IN WORLD TRADE, 1938, 1948, 1953–1967[1]

YEAR	WESTERN COUNTRIES' FOREIGN TRADE TURNOVER[2]		SOCIALIST COUNTRIES' FOREIGN TRADE TURNOVER[3]	
	In £ Million at Current Prices	% of World Trade	% of World Trade	In £ Million at Current Prices
1938	6,460	67·3	8·6	830
1948	18,150	63·6	6·3	1,800
1953	36,990	62·9	9·3	5,470
1954	38,500	62·9	9·9	6,040
1955	42,750	64·2	9·7	6,490
1956	48,040	65·0	9·5	6,990
1957	51,670	64·9	9·9	7,920
1958	49,030	63·8	11·2	8,570
1959	52,720	64·1	12·2	10,040
1960	59,520	70·9	12·8	10,730
1961	62,730	65·9	11·6	11,090
1962	66,390	66·1	12·3	12,370
1963	72,960	66·5	11·9	13.030
1964	82,740	67·4	11·6	14,270
1965	90,670	68·1	11·5	15,270
1966	100,090	69·0	11·1	16,110
1967	107,490	69·3	11·3	17,520

[1] All exports and imports are valued f.o.b. The world total includes shipments to unknown destinations, usually constituting less than 2% of world trade. No data are available on inter-trade among the four Asian Socialist countries (M. China, Mongolia, N. Korea and N. Vietnam), and thus to this extent the Bloc's as well as the world's totals are understated, but the amount involved is believed to be less than 1% of world trade. The values were converted from US dollars at the rate current at the time.
[2] Canada, USA, all Europe except the eight Socialist countries, Japan, South Africa, Australia and New Zealand.
[3] Albania, Bulgaria, Czechoslovakia, East Germany, Hungary, Poland, Rumania, USSR, Mainland China, Mongolia, North Korea and North Vietnam.

Sources: Based on: United Nations, *Yearbook of International Trade Statistics* and *Monthly Bulletin of Statistics.*

This tendency can be attributed to several causes. The disintegration of the colonial empires of some of the leading Western traders (the Netherlands, Britain, France, Belgium), has naturally led to some re-orientation of the former dependencies' trade away from the imperial powers. At the same time, owing to a rapidly increasing productivity and standard of living, Western countries are well-placed to produce and purchase manufactures. In this they have found that, in general, their best customers and sources of supply for such goods are other Western

TABLE X INTRA-WESTERN AND INTRA-SOCIALIST FOREIGN TRADE, 1938, 1948, 1953–67*

	INTRA-WESTERN FOREIGN TRADE TURNOVER		INTRA-SOCIALIST FOREIGN TRADE TURNOVER	
YEAR	In £ Million at Current Prices	% of Trade with the World	% of Trade with the World	In £ Million at Current Prices
1938	4,260	65·9	12·8	110
1948	11,890	64·4	44·4	800
1953	24,110	65·2	79·6	4,350
1954	25,400	66·0	76·9	4,640
1955	29,060	68·0	73·6	4,770
1956	32,780	68·2	70·6	4,940
1957	35,430	68·6	71·7	5,570
1958	33,180	67·7	71·5	6,130
1959	36,640	69·5	74·7	7,500
1960	42,090	70·7	72·1	7,740
1961	44,950	71·7	69·1	7,660
1962	48,140	72·5	66·9	8,270
1963	53,340	73·1	67·9	8,850
1964	61,060	73·8	66·1	9,430
1965	67,830	74·8	64·6	9,860
1966	75,860	75·8	61·5	9,910
1967	80,160	75·7	62·1	10,730

* For explanations and sources, see Table IX, p. 45.

countries. Membership of such organizations as the Consultative Group (on strategic exports, see Ch. 12 A, p. 271), NATO and the OECD (and its predecessor the OEEC), to which most Western countries belong, has also favoured the expansion of mutual trade.

As a factor in the diversion of trade in certain parts of the West, we must also mention the development of regional groupings, namely the European Economic Community (since 1957), the European Free Trade Association (since 1958) and (of minor consequence) the Australia and New Zealand Free Trade Area (since 1965). Much of the diversion of trade into intra-grouping channels has been (in relative, not absolute, terms) at the expense of other Western countries, but other parts of the world have also been adversely affected. Thus the share of the non-Western world in the EEC's foreign trade declined from 26% in 1957 to 21% in 1967, and in EFTA's from 29% to 22%.[1]

Regional integration in the West, especially the EEC, has been viewed by Socialist countries as scheming directed economically and politically against the non-Western world. In the well-publicized 'Theses', proclaimed by the Institute of World Economics and International Relations, under the auspices of the Soviet Academy of Sciences, the Common Market was described as 'a kind of holy alliance of reactionary powers directed against Socialism, workers, national liberation and general democratic movements, and designed to strengthen the economic base of the aggressive North Atlantic Bloc in Europe.'[2]

Although intra-Western trade has been growing faster than Western trade with the rest of the world, Socialist countries have little justification for complaint on this score. The 'losers' in the lagging growth of extra-Western trade have been not the Socialist countries but the Third World (see Table XIII, p. 55, and Ch. 11 D, pp. 257–58).

B. TENDENCIES IN SOCIALIST FOREIGN TRADE

We can identify three distinct stages in the development of Socialist foreign trade since World War II:

[1] Based on United Nations *Yearbook of International Trade Statistics 1963*, pp. 20–29, and *Monthly Bulletin of Statistics*, June 1968, pp. xii–xiii.
[2] *Pravda*, 26/8/1962.

(i) Restrained commercial co-operation with the Capitalist world during the early post-war reconstruction period 1945–48.
(ii) Drive towards intra-Bloc trade, 1948–53.
(iii) Expansion of extra-Bloc trade since 1953.

These stages can be distinguished by examining the tendencies in intra-Bloc trade in Table X, p. 46.

It will also be noted that the proportion of the present Socialist countries' trade with one another was only 13% before the war; this contrasts with the high degree of intra-Western trade concentration already at that time. Intra-Bloc trade reached the highest proportion in the later stages of the Korean War when it reached four-fifths of the Bloc's total trade. However, since 1953 trade with the Capitalist World has been rising faster than with other Socialist countries, so that intra-Bloc trade now represents less than two-thirds of the total. We shall now discuss these tendencies in some detail.

Up to Stalin's death (1953), the Socialist countries' trade policies were dominated by national autarkic ambitions. Their extreme dependence on the West under pre-Communist regimes was still fresh in their memories. 'Balanced development' and particularly rapid industrialization appealed to them because they thought that not only could these lead to economic independence but they also promoted social processes favourable to Communist ideology. It was assumed that the Soviet model of near-self-sufficiency was an ideal to strive for. With these attitudes prevailing, trade was basically regarded not as an avenue for economizing resources but chiefly as a means to rapid industrialization and a practical way for overcoming bottlenecks. Although since the mid-1950s the ideal of national autarky has been abandoned, even by the USSR, nostalgia for national self-sufficiency and their 'own path to Socialism' still lingers on.

Reorientation of trade in favour of intra-Bloc channels had already begun with the resumption of trade after World War II. But the most determined effort was staged during the period 1948–53, when the proportion of intra-Socialist foreign trade rose from 44% (£800 m.) to 80% (£4,350 m.); see Table X.[1] Shortly before he died, Stalin was able

---

[1] Proportions are a better guide than absolute figures, owing to the devaluation of the pound sterling (in 1949), a slight fall in world prices between the two dates and doubts as to the valuation of Socialist trade from year to year. Expressed in US dollars,

to take pride in the fact that the single world market 'disintegrated' into 'two parallel world markets.'[1]

Several factors have favoured the growth of intra-Bloc trade. Quite apart from geographical proximity, the changeover to Communist regimes roughly coincided with changes in boundaries involving all the twelve Socialist countries, which naturally tended to increase their mutual dependence. The identity, or at least similarity, of ideological, political and economic interests have also, in general, helped promote trade among Bloc members, whilst rapidly growing industrialization has been broadening the sources of supply. At the same time, there have been prodding forces operating from outside the Bloc, such as the difficulty of access to Capitalist markets, Western strategic embargo, shortage of convertible exchange and the Cold War in general.

The growth of trade amongst the European Socialist countries has been fostered on a systematic basis by the Council for Mutual Economic Assistance (COMECON, CMEA, CEMA or CEA).[2] Up to the mid-1950s this co-operation was achieved mostly through reciprocal planning of trade and commitment to agreed import and export targets. A new stage was entered upon in 1956, since when the member countries have embarked upon far-reaching economic integration through the co-ordination of long-term production plans. A long-lasting basis for mutual growth of trade is laid down by planned national specialization in agreed branches of industry. It is pointed out that CMEA countries have established a new model of international specialization – not the typically Capitalist vertical form between the producers of raw materials and those of manufactures but a horizontal one involving all stages of production. It was stressed in a Socialist study on international economics that

---

intra-Bloc trade increased from $3,230 m. in 1948 to $12,290 m. in 1953, whilst trade with the Capitalist World declined from $3,950 m. to $3,220 m. The level of world market prices was roughly 4% lower in 1953 as compared with 1948. Based on: United Nations *Yearbook of International Trade Statistics 1961*, pp. 20–31.

[1] J. V. Stalin, *Economic Problems of Socialism in the USSR*, Foreign Languages Publishing House, Moscow, 1952, pp. 34–35.

[2] Albania ceased participating in the work of the Council in 1961, whilst Mongolia was admitted to full membership in 1962. Yugoslavia was accepted as an 'associate' member in 1964. Mainland China, North Korea, North Vietnam and Cuba have an 'observer' status. China's interest in CMEA's work began declining after 1962, and beginning in 1966 she has ceased attending CMEA sessions.

Expanding trade among themselves, Socialist countries are creating a new type of the international division of labour. A distinguishing feature of this division is that it is not one-sided. In contrast to the international division of labour which has developed in the Capitalist world, this specialization is not between manufacturing countries on the one hand and agricultural and raw material producing countries on the other. It has all-sided characteristics in that each country specializes in all branches of industry and agriculture.[1]

Particular importance is attached to specialization and trade in key industrial raw materials, iron and steel, non-ferrous metals, machinery, chemicals and certain consumer goods.[2]

To promote trade among member countries along the desired lines CMEA established Permanent Commissions for 'Foreign Trade' (1956), for 'Transport' (1958), and for 'Currency and Finance' (1962). In 1963 it was resolved to take new measures to transform the member countries' trade from a bilateral to a multilateral basis, and in the following year the International Bank for Economic Co-operation started operations towards this goal (see Ch. 10 D, pp. 218–22).[3]

However, in spite of the efforts under CMEA, the proportion of intra-Bloc trade has been steadily declining since the Korean War (see Table X, p. 46). As can be observed from the Table, this decline contrasts with the tendency in intra-Western trade. There are many reasons for the weakening predisposition on the part of Socialist countries to trade with one another.

There are too many divergent forces reasserting themselves in the Bloc, some of which are economic, whilst others are ideological and political in nature. Most member countries refuse to acknowledge the competence of CMEA over national interests and, in contrast to EEC

---

[1] Z. Kamecki, J. Sołdaczuk and W. Sierpiński, *Miedzynarodowe stosunki ekonomiczne* (International Economic Relations), PWE, Warsaw 1964, p. 79.

[2] For further details see United Nations, *Economic Integration and Industrial Specialization Among the Member Countries of the Council for Mutual Economic Assistance*, New York 1966.

[3] A thorough account of the integration in CMEA covering the period 1949–75 can be found in: L. Ciamaga, *Od współpracy do integracji*. Zarys organizacji i działalności RWPG w latach 1949–64 (From Co-operation to Integration. An Outline of the Organization and Activity of CMEA over the Period 1949–64), KiW, Warsaw 1965 (with a summary in English); A. Bodnar, *Gospodarka europejskich krajów socjalistycznych*. Zarys rozwoju w latach 1950–75 (The Economies of the European Socialist Countries. An Outline of the Development in the Years 1950–75), KiW, Warsaw 1962.

there is still no supranational authority to override the opposition of individual member countries, such as Rumania and Bulgaria in particular. The Sino-Soviet dispute has also been reflected in China's diversion of trade away from the USSR and also other CMEA members. Thus between 1958 and 1968 CMEA's share in China's trade dwindled from two-thirds to less than one-quarter. In spite of several efforts directed towards multilateralism, intra-Bloc trade is still bedevilled by bilateral trade and payments.

But the fundamental obstacle to the further growth of intra-Bloc trade derives from the inability of the present Socialist economic system to evaluate the relative efficiency of such specialization and trade to the satisfaction of all countries concerned, as was stated bluntly in a Socialist source:

> the lack of objective criteria for the calculation of production costs and the effectiveness of international specialization present the ultimate stumbling block in the development of the international Socialist division of labour.... The fundamental difficulty lies in the impossibility of a direct comparison of real costs of production in individual countries, while the existing system of prices does not as yet afford a sound basis for the rational calculation of economic costs, not only on an international scale but even in individual countries.[1]

At the same time, Socialist countries have found it expedient to expand trade with Capitalist nations. Guided partly by economic and partly by political motives, the Bloc has embarked on a trade drive with the Developing countries, with some spectacular results. The share of the Developing World in the Bloc's trade soared from 5% (£260 m.) in 1953 to 12% (£2,000 m.) in 1967 (for further details see Ch. 11 D, pp. 252–58, esp. Tables XXVIII, p. 257 and XXIX, p. 258). There has also been a remarkable expansion of trade with the West since 1953.[2] We shall consider these developments in our overall discussion of the trends in East-West trade in the following section.

---

[1] Z. Kamecki, J. Sołdaczuk and W. Sierpiński, *op. cit.*, p. 85. However, see Ch. 14 B, C, pp. 311–34.
[2] The first move towards the expansion of trade with Capitalist countries can be traced back to the International Economic Conference in Moscow, April 1952.

C. TRENDS IN EAST-WEST TRADE

The course of East-West trade over the last three decades is shown in Table XI, The small size of this trade is conspicuous throughout the period. It will be noted that even before the war, when all the present Socialist countries except the USSR and Mongolia were under Capital-

TABLE XI THE DEVELOPMENT OF EAST-WEST TRADE, 1938, 1948, 1953–67*

YEAR	In £ Million at Current Prices	As a Percentage of World Trade
1938	610	6·4
1948	750	2·6
1953	770	1·3
1954	880	1·4
1955	1,090	1·6
1956	1,320	1·8
1957	1,500	1·9
1958	1,590	2·1
1959	1,730	2·1
1960	2,060	2·5
1961	2,200	2·3
1962	2,330	2·3
1963	2,590	2·4
1964	3,100	2·5
1965	3,410	2·6
1966	4,000	2·8
1967	4,410	2·8

* For explanations and sources, see Table IX, p. 45.

ism, trade between what we now call the East and West represented only 6% of world trade.

The changeover to Communist regimes after World War II was followed by a gradual reorientation of Western and Socialist trade, which was dictated by economic as well as political calculations. This tendency was further hastened by the outbreak of the 'Cold War' in 1948 (see Ch. 11 A, pp. 236–41) and the Korean War (1950–53). The trough in East-West trade was reached in 1953 when its value was no greater than the trade between the United Kingdom and North America.

An interesting trend can, however, be observed since the Korean War. The share of East-West trade in total world trade has doubled. This unmistakable tendency clearly contradicts the prognostications of Stalin about the disintegration of the world market, and his postulation that a gradual reduction of East-West trade would lead to Western economic ruin.[1] Stalin believed, no doubt on the basis of his understanding of the writings of Marx and Lenin, that barring the Bloc market to Western countries would lead to idle capacity, bankruptcies, widespread unemployment and social unrest, which would pave the way for the collapse of Capitalism. It is rather ironical that during the 1958 recession the Western countries' trade with other Capitalist countries declined by 5% whilst with the Socialist Bloc it rose by more than 6%.[2]

The relatively fast expansion of East-West trade derives chiefly from the high rates of economic growth, both in the Bloc and in the West, and especially from the composition of that growth – faster growth of industrial output than of other forms of production. As industrialization has been entering more sophisticated stages in Socialist countries, the need for Western instruments, machinery, complete plants and other manufactures, and even for certain industrial raw materials and components, appears to be increasing rather than declining. The relaxation of Western strategic export controls since 1954 (see Ch. 12 A, pp. 272–74), the extension of currency transferability since 1958 (see Ch. 10 D, pp. 211–12) and the liberalization of import quotas especially since 1963 (see Ch. 7 B(b), pp. 110–11) in favour of Socialist countries have afforded improving access to Western markets. The development of trade has, no doubt, been also facilitated by a gradual improvement (although marked with occasional setbacks) in the political climate in East-West relations.

As the size of East-West trade has been changing, so has its role to the

[1] Stalin, *op. cit.*, p. 36.
[2] Based on: United Nations *Yearbook of International Trade Statistics 1961*, pp. 20–29.

West and to the Bloc. Before the war one-tenth of Western trade was with the present Socialist countries, the proportion slumped to 2% during the Korean War and it has since recovered to 4% (see Table XII,). Because of the Socialist countries' smaller absolute participation in world trade, trade with the West has traditionally represented a fairly high proportion to the Bloc – nearly three-quarters before the war, and even today it is one-quarter. Although the Western share in

TABLE XII THE ROLE OF EAST-WEST TRADE IN WESTERN AND SOCIALIST FOREIGN TRADE, 1938, 1948, 1953–67*

YEAR	Trade with the S. Bloc as a % of Total Western Countries' Trade with the World	VALUE OF EAST-WEST TRADE In £ Million at Current Prices	Trade with the West as a % of Total Socialist Countries' Trade with the World
1938	9·5	610	73·8
1948	4·1	750	41·6
1953	2·1	770	14·0
1954	2·3	880	14·5
1955	2·5	1,090	16·7
1956	2·7	1,320	18·6
1957	2·9	1,500	19·0
1958	3·2	1,590	18·5
1959	3·3	1,730	17·2
1960	3·5	2,060	19·2
1961	3·1	2,200	17·9
1962	3·7	2,330	18·8
1963	3·6	2,590	19·1
1964	3·8	3,100	21·7
1965	3·8	3,410	22·4
1966	4·0	4,000	24·8
1967	4·1	4,410	25·2

* For explanations and sources, see Table IX, p. 45.

the trade of the Socialist countries was drastically reduced during the Korean War, it can be seen from Table XII that the Bloc's dependence on the West has been steadily increasing since that time.

To place the development of East-West trade in its proper perspective,

TABLE XIII   WESTERN AND SOCIALIST ANNUAL RATES OF GROWTH IN FOREIGN TRADE, 1953–67*

WORLD DIVISION	1953–62	1963–65	1966	1967
	Annual averages†			
WESTERN TRADE				
Total	6·8	11·0	10·4	5·6
Intra-Western	8·2	12·1	11·8	6·2
With the S. Bloc	13·3	13·7	17·0	7·1
With the Third World	3·9	8·0	8·6	3·0
SOCIALIST TRADE				
Total	9·6	7·3	5·5	7·3
Intra-Bloc	5·8	6·1	0·5	8·5
With the West	13·3	13·7	17·0	7·1
With the Third World	19·8	13·0	7·0	0·0
WORLD TRADE	6·2	9·8	9·1	2·7

* For general explanations and sources, see Table IX, p. 45.

† Calculated as a percentage increase (or decrease) over the preceding year, the percentages added and the total averaged.

we shall conclude with a comparison of the rates of growth in Western and Socialist trade. The relevant figures are presented in Table XIII. As world market prices were, in spite of fluctuations from year to year, practically the same in 1967 as in 1953, these rates may be taken as also roughly indicating growth in the volume of trade.[1]

Socialist countries have often been accused in the West of autarkic policies. Whilst this criticism was certainly justified before Stalin's

[1] See United Nations *Yearbook of International Trade Statistics 1965*, pp. 32–34, and *Monthly Bulletin of Statistics*, June 1968, p. xvi.

death, there is little foundation in it so far as the growth of trade is concerned since that time. If we take the period 1953–67 as a whole, the average annual rate of growth in the Socialist countries' trade is 8·6. This compares with the Western rate of 7·9 and the world average of only 7·0.

But the most interesting observation that can be made from the Table is that on the growth of East-West trade. Over the period covering fifteen years, trade between the West and the Bloc was growing at an average annual rate of 13·3. Thus East-West trade over the entire period was growing much faster than either intra-Western (6·2) or intra-Socialist foreign trade (5·6), and nearly twice as fast as world trade as a whole (7·0).

PART II
Principles, Policies, Practices

4 Ideological and Theoretical Background

THE course of East-West trade has often been bedevilled by mutual mistrust and suspicion. The interchange of accusations freely dispensed in academic polemics, at international conferences and in trade negotiations, can be partly traced to the implicit assumptions that the same principles apply to both systems, that the same rule (e.g. under GATT) can be given the same meaning and that its application should be the same. To provide a basic explanation for Western and for Socialist foreign trade behaviour, we shall bring out the distinguishing general features of foreign trade, highlight the evolution of the foreign-trade theory and conclude with an examination of the significance of the theory of comparative costs under each system.

A. THE ESSENCE OF FOREIGN TRADE UNDER EACH SYSTEM

Fundamentally, under each system foreign trade is (naturally) regarded as a means towards the maximum improvement of welfare. But the concept of welfare, value judgments, and consequently the extent to which foreign trade is to be employed and within what institutional framework, differ markedly in each case. These differences are essentially a logical consequence of the political and social philosophy subscribed to.

In a developed market economy, where ideologically the main emphasis is on individualism and political democracy, foreign trade is basically a generalization of the exchange conditions applying to individual persons. On the other hand, in a centrally planned economy of the collectivist type, paramount importance is attached to socio-economic democracy, and external trade is understood as a reflection of the economic relations between societies.

In market economies, the size, composition and course of foreign trade are essentially determined by the market mechanism. Trade decisions are decentralized and are made predominantly by private firms guided by their own profit motive and operating normally under competitive conditions. Even where state agencies directly engage in foreign trade they are, in general, subject to the same market forces and commercial considerations as private traders. In most market economies nowadays governments intervene in the market to modify the prices paid or obtained through tariffs, subsidies and in some cases manipulation of exchange rates. But governments essentially endeavour to achieve their objectives through the ordinary market forces, i.e. influencing supply or demand but without interfering with the market mechanism as a system.

Government intervention may also assume the form of quantitative import (or export) restrictions, or in some cases complete prohibitions. Where such direct controls exist, they are normally regulated by the rules of the GATT and of the IMF, of which most Western countries are members. A special case of direct government intervention is that of controls on exports of strategic significance.

In centrally planned economies of the Socialist type, the market mechanism is fundamentally superseded by planning. The size, structure and direction of foreign trade are subject to long-term (10-20 years), medium-term (5-7 years) and short-term (12 and 3 months) plans.

The foreign-trade plan is worked out by the ministry of foreign trade (see Ch. 5 A) assisted by other interested ministries and by the foreign-trade corporations, industrial branch associations and the relevant producing and using enterprises. This plan is integrated by the central planning authority into the general economic plan within the ramifications of government policy and the general social objectives laid down by the Communist Party. The competence of the latter to make optimum overall value judgments is accepted as axiomatic. Whereas in the developed market economies the emphasis appears to be on exports, in the centrally planned economies it is imports that occupy the focus of attention. Imports are the starting side in the planning process, since they are considered as indispensable to meet developmental targets. Exports are essentially looked upon as a sacrifice to

CH. 4 §A THEORETICAL BACKGROUND 61

secure the required imports. The practice in the less developed Socialist countries (Albania and the four Asian countries) is to treat the foreign-trade plan as a residual supplement of the general economic plan to help attain the quantitative targets laid down and to overcome arising bottlenecks. The recent tendency in the European CMEA countries is for the foreign-trade plan to be worked out in value terms and from the standpoint of the maximum feasible efficiency of exports and, to some extent, of imports, and of the whole economy in general.[1]

As a rule, in market economies the spontaneous operation of the market mechanism and of profit motivation are considered as stimulating healthy competition and efficiency, and thus promoting an international pattern of production and trade which yields maximum returns from the resources employed. On the other hand, in centrally planned economies greater importance is attached to stability and orderly development; free working of the market forces would cause too many disruptions. In recent years considerable attention has been given in most Socialist countries to competition and profit. It is now widely accepted that these are not necessarily incompatible with central planning,[2] and indeed they are being partly incorporated in the recent economic reforms in Eastern Europe (see Ch. 14 C, pp. 330–34).

However, the working of market forces is still clearly circumscribed within the framework of planning, collective ownership of the means of production and the State monopoly of foreign trade. Where it is allowed to operate, its purpose is not to displace planning but rather to strengthen it by helping to achieve the planned import and export targets in more efficient ways. 'It is unquestionable', pointed out a Socialist economist in a recent study on the role of the market, 'that the optimization of allocative decisions in a Socialist economy requires a substantial degree of central planning. The scale of the central planners'

[1] For further details, see Ch. 14 B, C and the following references: H. Kosk, *Gospodarka planowa* (Planned Economy), Warsaw, 6/1966, pp. 23–28; B. Wojciechowski, *Gosp. plan.*, 2/1967, pp. 12–16.

[2] E.g. see G. Gräbig, *Wirtschafts Wissenschaft*, East Berlin, 10/1966, pp. 1,598–1,610; J. Głowacki and W. Trzeciakowski, *Gosp. plan.*, 11/1966, pp. 35–39; L. Leontyev, *Kommunist*, Moscow, 3/1967, pp. 62–73. For a broader treatment see: W. Wilczynski, *Rachunek ekonomiczny a mechanizm rynkowy* (Economic Calculation and Market Mechanism), PWE, Warsaw 1965; E. D. Kaganov, *Sotsialisticheskoe vosproizvodstvo i rynok* (The Role of the Market in Economic Growth under Socialism), Ekonomika, Moscow 1966.

preferences most fully reflects the structure of needs of the national economy, as well as the ways of the most rational utilization of the available resources.'[1]

There are some nonsensical views still held in the West on the role of foreign trade in a Socialist economy, such as that 'The basic aim of foreign trade, communist economists explain, is to eliminate the need for foreign trade.'[2] This opinion is now at least ten years out of date. In the past, the importance of foreign trade in economic development was largely overlooked because of the presence of extensive growth factors. But the slackening rates of growth in the late 1950s and the economic stagnation that followed in the more mature Socialist economies made it clear that the only way to maintain the high rates was to turn to 'intensive growth factors', i.e. by rapidly raising labour productivity. International division of labour and thus a substantial expansion of foreign trade have assumed new and critical importance. A prominent Hungarian economist described the present Socialist view on the subject in the following words:

> Economic growth is a demand of our era that is so unequivocally accepted and corresponds so fully to its needs that it cannot be renounced under any circumstances. The problem must be solved ... by greatly increased activity on the world market. ... We attach great significance to the development of all potentialities of world trade as a means of strengthening peaceful and friendly relations between nations.[3]

In fact, an East German economist went further when he pointed out:

> However, not only is trade in goods *per se* a source of growth for national income but so too are other elements of foreign trade relations. New elements in the system of foreign trade relations such as scientific-technological co-operation, production co-operation, exchange of data from science, research technology and development, exchange of licences, credit relations, tourism, etc., are gaining a continually larger importance.[4]

[1] W. Wilczyński, *op. cit.*, p. 25.
[2] Mose L. Harvey, *East-West Trade and United States Policy*, National Association of Manufacturers, New York 1966, p. 46.
[3] Imre Vajda, *The Role of Foreign Trade in a Socialist Economy*, Corvina Press, Budapest 1965, p. 298.
[4] G. Schermer, 'The Role of Foreign Trade in the GDR', *Der nationale Demokrat*, East Berlin, 1/1967 (translation in: US Dept. of Commerce, Joint Publications Research Service, *Translations on East European Foreign Trade*, 27/2/1967, p. 3).

B. FOREIGN-TRADE THEORY

The theory of foreign trade has traditionally received more than its fair share of attention from Western economists. An exaggerated emphasis was given particularly by mercantilists. However, a systematic body of principles was developed later, mainly by the classical economists – notably D. Hume, H. Thornton, D. Ricardo and J. S. Mill. Their interest centred on the optimum utilization of natural and man-made resources, and consequently on the international division of labour.

The rigorous basis for proving some of their propositions was embodied in the theory of comparative costs which was subsequently supplemented with several refinements and additions. The demand side of trade was also considered, with such techniques as the reciprocal demand and supply analysis developed by A. Marshall and F. Y. Edgeworth. To attain maximum gains from trade, classical as well as neo-classical writers postulated unrestricted competition and free trade. This work was later supplemented with studies by P. T. Ellsworth, Joan Robinson, E. Chamberlin and others on the significance of monopoly elements in international trade.

Classical and particularly later economists have preoccupied themselves with the mechanism of international exchanges and the problem of equilibrium. The most notable contributions have been made in the sphere of the balance of payments, exchange rates, terms of trade, income effects, trade policy and welfare by such writers as V. Pareto, A. Marshall, J. Viner, C. Bresciani-Turroni, G. Haberler, F. Machlup, L. A. Metzler and J. E. Meade. Structural aspects of international trade received some attention, particularly from French writers, namely M. Byé, J. Perroux and J. Weiller.

In general, up to World War II, foreign-trade theory was considered in terms of short-run periods, but since the war increasing attention has been devoted to long-run dynamic analysis. This has been conditioned by such developments as factor-price equalization models and the theory of growth and customs unions, to which notable contributions have been made by E. Heckscher and B. Ohlin, H. G. Johnson, R. F.

Harrod, R. Nurkse, N. Kaldor, A. O. Hirschman, P. Samuelson, J. Viner and many others.[1]

By contrast, Socialist thinkers have never worked out such a systematic body of principles, and even today the theory of foreign trade is still in its infancy as compared with Western attainments. The early Socialist writers, such as K. Marx and F. Engels, did not preoccupy themselves with foreign trade as a separate field of study. But they sketchily analysed such questions as the reasons for international trade, the role of world trade and markets in the development of Capitalist methods of production, the influence of foreign trade on the rate of profit, international values and the nature of foreign-trade policy under Capitalism.[2]

Rosa Luxemburg carried on these discussions further and developed them to finer conclusions. Her interest centred on the significance of the expansion of exports in the development of Capitalism.[3] She also made the famous pronouncement, supported by some Soviet theoreticians later, that a collectivist economy, including its foreign trade, would not be subject to any economic laws, as the overthrow of the Capitalist system constitutes the 'last act of political economy.'[4] At the same time, Lenin dwelt mostly on the uneven economic and social development under Capitalism and its significance in international trade, especially the role of monopolies in the imperialist penetration of underdeveloped dependencies.[5]

After the establishment of the first Socialist State, for many years hardly any interest was shown in the theory of foreign trade under the conditions of Socialism. Soviet thinkers, pragmatically, identified the problem of foreign trade under central planning with that in the USSR. Owing to the possession of large and varied resources and the hostility

---

[1] There are hundreds of excellent sources, but the best concise accounts will be found in: G. Haberler, *A Survey of International Trade Theory*, Princeton University, 1961; W. M. Corden, *Recent Developments in the Theory of International Trade*, Princeton University, 1965. The above sources also include extensive bibliographies.

[2] The best collection of their writings on the subject in one volume can be found in K. Marx and F. Engels on *Colonialism*, Foreign Languages Publishing House, Moscow.

[3] See Rosa Luxemburg, *The Accumulation of Capital*, Routledge & Kegan Paul, London 1951, esp. pp. 419–67.

[4] Rosa Luxemburg, *Einführung in die Nationalökonomie*, East Berlin 1951, vol. 1, p. 491 [quoted from Oskar Lange, *Ekonomia polityczna* (Political Economy), Warsaw 1959, vol. 1, p. 78].

[5] V. I. Lenin, *Selected Works*, Lawrence & Wishart, London, vol. 5, pp. 14–119.

of the Capitalist World, the Soviet Union's development strategy was based overwhelmingly on domestic sources. After World War II, Soviet thinking on the subject was also adopted in other Socialist countries, and up to Stalin's death (1953) there were practically no theoretical writings on foreign trade.

But the attitude to foreign trade began to change in the early 1950s. The period of post-war reconstruction 'at any price' was over. Owing to the exaggerated early autarkic ambitions, bottlenecks soon began to reappear impairing further growth. The gains that could be derived from increased participation in the international division of labour were soon becoming increasingly obvious. The Council for Mutual Economic Assistance, which until Stalin's death had been in a dormant stage, became revitalized and given the mission of forging the member countries into a Socialist 'common market'. Prospects for trade with the West began to brighten with the gradual liberalization of the strategic embargo. For a variety of reasons, closer political and economic links began to be established with the Developing countries, which provided a new opportunity for examining the role of foreign trade.

It is noteworthy that in this rejuvenated Socialist thinking on foreign trade, the USSR has contributed practically nothing of originality, and instead she has largely turned for ideas to her Eastern European associates, and – in contrast to other fields of economic theory – the Soviet writers' role has been virtually limited to eclecticism. The Eastern European countries, as compared with the Soviet Union (and China) have small resources and yet great ambitions for development and improvement of living standards. There is also a more vigorous and sophisticated opinion, where memories of pre-Communist intellectualism are still quite vivid. Their discussions have been most fruitful in three aspects of foreign-trade theory: the role of foreign trade in Socialist development, the efficiency of foreign trade and the significance of international trade in the context of underdevelopment.

In the writings on the role of external trade in Socialist economic development, two major lines of interest have been followed. Firstly, to what extent, quantitatively and qualitatively, foreign trade should be employed to accelerate the rate of development under the conditions of central planning. It is repeated time and again (rather naïvely, as it appears to a Western scholar) that international trade provides a possibility of obtaining required goods at a smaller resource outlay from imports than from domestic production. This saving of resources (i.e. the economy of 'social labour' in the ultimate analysis) enables a higher rate of growth. In particular it is argued that Socialist countries have attained a stage of industrialization when new investment programmes cannot be consummated by reference to national (input and output) markets only, if they are to yield optimal results. In view of the economic stagnation, which was particularly prevalent in the Bloc during 1962–64, it is now realized that foreign trade is about the only major reservoir to tap to sustain high rates of growth. Secondly, a good deal of attention has been devoted to the principles to govern international specialization and trade among Socialist countries, especially those within CMEA.[1]

The studies on foreign-trade efficiency began to arouse the interest of theoreticians in the middle 1950s. Some penetrating studies were pioneered in Hungary, Czechoslavakia, Poland and East Germany. Amongst the leading contributors we may mention A. Marias and J. Kornai (of Hungary), V. Černiansky and J. Nykryn (of Czechoslovakia), A. Rolow and W. Trzeciakowski (of Poland) and H. J. Nitz and L. Rouscik (of East Germany). The essence of these studies has consisted in a search for criteria of foreign-trade efficiency and, further in devising indices and coefficients of foreign-trade effectiveness under the conditions of central planning, given a predominantly collective ownership of the means of production, a distorted domestic price structure and unrealistic official exchange rates. The studies have proceeded along three distinct although, naturally, closely related lines: the efficiency of exports, the efficiency of imports and the foreign-trade efficiency of investments. In the indices and models devised, domestic costs expressed in national currency are related to the receipts (or expenditure) of foreign exchange. The details of the indices and their evaluation are discussed in Ch. 14 B, pp. 311–30.

[1] Literature on this subject is extensive and only a selection of the more important contributions can be given here. R. Brauer, *Probleme der Ermittlung des ökonomischen Nutzens der sotsialistischen internationalen Arbeitsteilung und des Aussenhandels sotsialistischen Staaten*, Die Wirtschaft, East Berlin 1962; Imre Vajda, *The Role of Foreign Trade in a Socialist Economy*, Corvina Press, Budapest 1965; S. Góra and Z. Knyziak, *Współpraca krajów RWPG a rachunek ekonomiczny* (Co-operation amongst CMEA Countries and the Calculation of Economic Efficiency), PWE, Warsaw 1966; B. S. Vaganov, *Vneshnaya torgovlya sotsialisticheskikh stran. Voprosy teorii* (Foreign Trade of Socialist Countries. Problems of Theory), Mezhdunarodnye Otnosheniya, Moscow 1966.

CH. 4 §B THEORETICAL BACKGROUND

The writings on the role of foreign trade in the context of underdevelopment are of relatively recent origin, stimulated as they are by the expanding relations with the Developing World of Asia, Africa and Latin America. The discussions have naturally highlighted the historical causes of backwardness and the ways in which foreign trade has perpetuated dependence on the industrially developed countries of the West. The role of protection and direct controls as well as the relevance of certain elements of central planning have featured prominently in the discussions. In dealing with the strategy for accelerated growth, appropriate basic models have been developed, in which the debt owed to Western economists stands out pretty conspicuously. Attempts have also been made to systematize the distinguishing features characterizing the trade of the Third World with the West and with the Socialist Bloc.[1]

The fields of interest among Capitalist and Socialist theoreticians, naturally, largely overlap. But in general, Western foreign trade theory has been preoccupied with (i) gains from foreign trade, and (ii) the adjustment mechanism of international trade. On the other hand, the Socialist interest has mostly centred on: (i) the socio-economic foundations and consequences of international trade, and (ii) the role and conduct of foreign trade under the conditions of controlled economic development. The unique contribution by the Socialist thinkers, to which special tribute must be paid, is the study of foreign-trade efficiency.

Each approach, naturally, to some extent reflects the basic social and political thinking. This is more obvious in the case of Socialist writers. However, in the last decade it is possible to detect a certain 'convergence' of major interests. Socialist economists have turned to a profound study of the gains from trade, and both Capitalist and Socialist thinkers have branched off to the study of the principles of foreign trade applicable to economic groupings and to Developing economies.

There is little doubt that Western achievements in foreign-trade

[1] E.g. see some of the important recent studies: I. Sachs, *Handel zagraniczny a rozwój gospodarczy* (Foreign Trade in the Context of Economic Development), PWE, Warsaw 1963; J. L. Schmidt, *Die Industrialisierung der Entwicklungsländer und ihre Folgen für die Weltwirtschaft*, VEB deutscher Verlag der Wissenschaften, East Berlin 1964; L. Dvorak, *Mirovaya sistema sotsializma i razvivaiushchiyesya strany* (The World Socialist System and Developing Countries), Mysl, Moscow 1965; M. Falkowski, *Contribution socialiste à l'étude de la croissance économique des pays en voie de dévelopment*, PWN, Warsaw 1966.

theory are far more extensive and varied. This is only natural, at least on historical grounds. By comparison, the Socialist contribution – especially to the pure theory of international trade – has been rather modest. Socialist economists have been mostly preoccupied with the operational problems of foreign trade, and the principles formulated are rather deductive *ex post* generalizations.

To what extent are the Western and Socialist achievements in foreign-trade theory of mutual value? On closer examination, the extent of applicability is in fact rather limited. Thus, the Capitalist theory dealing with the price mechanism, exchange rates, tariffs, balance-of-payments equilibrium, capital movements, income effect and cyclical fluctuations are of limited use for guiding trade among Socialist countries. However, in two respects the study of Western theory can be of value to the Bloc countries. First, if they understand the laws governing the operation of Capitalist markets, they are in a better position to maximize their gains by appropriate planning and execution of their policies in trade with the West. The increasing share of the West in the volume and proportion of the Bloc's trade (see Table XII, p. 54) makes this study a compelling necessity.

Secondly, the reforms in the foreign trade of most CMEA countries, where several elements of the market mechanism are being tested and adopted, place the theory of international trade evolved in the West in a new light. Some of these principles with appropriate adaptations may be applied to perfect the working of the Socialist foreign trade system. The Socialist interest is testified by the increasing output of publications in CMEA countries on Capitalist foreign trade. There is little in the Socialist foreign trade theory that is of applicable value to the highly developed Western countries. But the principles concerned with the role of foreign trade and its social repercussions have found applications in the less developed Capitalist countries embarking on accelerated development under the conditions of economic planning.

The main fields of common interest (not necessarily of common agreement) between Capitalist and Socialist foreign trade theory, according to a notable Socialist economist, are three: elasticity of demand, problems of the terms of trade and the theory of comparative costs.[1] Of these, the last one has proved most controversial. In the next

[1] Imre Vajda, *op. cit.*, p. 245.

CH. 4 §C THEORETICAL BACKGROUND

section we shall examine the Western and Socialist attitude to the theory and its applicability in a market economy and under central planning, as each reflects the nature and role of foreign trade under each system.

C. THE THEORY OF COMPARATIVE COSTS

The theory of comparative costs was first put forward by R. Torrens in 1815, but it is D. Ricardo who is generally regarded as its founder. Other classical, neo-classical and modern economists have elaborated on it, gradually relaxed a number of limiting assumptions and applied tools of linear programming, so that in its modern form it is a highly involved doctrine.[1]

The essence of the theory is that countries should specialize in the articles which they can produce relatively cheaply and import those in which they have a comparative disadvantage. In this rationalization of international specialization and trade, the traditional view emphasized the productive efficiency, whilst the modern approach stresses the relative abundance of factors and the intensity of their use. The theory does not represent a complete explanation of foreign trade and the gains derived from it, even between market economies. It explains only a particular aspect of the supply side. It has commanded varying degrees of acceptance in the Western World, less in Continental Europe than in the English-speaking countries. Nevertheless it has come to occupy a cardinal place in the Capitalist theory of international trade,[2] and it has

---

[1] For details of its development, including bibliographies see: G. Haberler, *The Theory of International Trade*, William Hodge, London 1936, pp. 125–44; G. Haberler, *A Survey of International Trade Theory*, pp. 1–6, 61–70; Corden, *Recent Developments in the Theory of International Trade, op. cit.*, pp. 24–34, 69–78. Also see Bela Balassa, 'An Empirical Demonstration of the Comparative Costs Theory', *Review of Econ. and Stat.*, August 1963, pp. 231–38, and by the same author, 'Trade Liberalisation and "Revealed" Comparative Advantage', *Manchester School of Economic and Social Studies*, May 1965, pp. 99–124; Akihiro Amano, 'Determinants of Comparative Cost: A Theoretical Approach', *Oxford Econ. Papers*, Nov. 1964, pp. 389–400.

[2] It does not necessarily mean that all trade amongst market economies is conducted in accordance with the theory. Quite apart from restrictive practices by private firms and international cartels, governments modify the size, composition and direction of trade through trade agreements, a variety of tariffs, subsidies and bounties, import licensing and quotas, embargoes and various subtle administrative measures. These

attracted bitter criticism from Socialist economists, especially since the late 1950s.

The theory is essentially a product of economic *laissez-faire* and is largely inapplicable to a centrally planned economy of the Collectivist type. First, the theory rests on the assumption of proportionality of prices to real economic costs. But pricing policies and practices in the Socialist Bloc do not allow the free market to operate, whether in the factor or product markets. In each Socialist country price fixing is largely centralized in a price-planning commission. Scarcity is not necessarily reflected in prices, in fact the idea of scarcity as understood in market economies is alien to Marxian economics. Some costs are not reflected in prices or are unduly low, such as certain forms of rent and capital charges. The theory implies that prices of factors are equal to their marginal products and product prices to their marginal costs. But the concept of marginality is again alien to the Socialist economic theory and, in general, prices are not necessarily allowed to respond to changing market conditions. When planners decide to make price re-adjustments the purpose is more often to regulate *distribution* rather than production. In addition, domestic prices are effectively insulated from external influences ('competition stops and starts at the national frontier').

Second, under central planning foreign trade is largely determined in advance to fit into the general economic plan. Imports and exports are not based merely on businessmen's decisions guided by current price differentials. Import needs are, generally, determined first, and exports are then planned accordingly. A forecast of the relative costs of articles (by whatever criteria), especially of those in East-West trade, is always likely to contain elements of error. But fulfilment of the plan once approved is a matter of importance, usually irrespective of subsequent changes in relative costs.

Third, exchange rates operated by Socialist countries do not necessarily relate domestic to foreign prices. All these countries administer the strictest form of exchange control, and by the official exchange rates

---

actions modify cost/benefit to producers and/or consumers. Otherwise, in pursuance of private profit, trade is conducted in accordance with the principle, and (to simplify) the greater the difference in pre-trade comparative costs, the greater the gain from trade to the society.

CH. 4 §C THEORETICAL BACKGROUND

their currencies are overvalued. Some of these countries also operate multiple rates. Thus their exchange rates largely distort domestic-foreign price relationships.

Fourth, even when cost disadvantages are substantial and beyond doubt, they are often disregarded in the name of 'balanced economic development'. In practice this means developing key manufacturing industries at all costs, to the neglect of agriculture and light industries, however efficient the latter may be. This is borne out by the Bloc countries' preoccupation with heavy industries, such as the apparently uneconomic huge steel mills at Kremikovtsi (Bulgaria), Kosice (Czechoslovakia), Dunaujvaros (formerly Sztalinvaros, Hungary), Nowa Huta (Poland), Galati (Rumania) and the backyard furnaces in China during the Great Leap period. It is postulated that the initial cost disadvantage of a particular industry will be overcome in the future within a balanced economic structure.

Quite apart from the above facts, the theory becomes largely irrelevant in the face of certain trading practices which are pursued by Socialist countries for a variety of reasons. A large proportion of the Bloc countries' trade is still carried on on a bilateral basis, and besides non-commercial considerations may be taken into account.

To Socialist economists the theory of comparative costs unmistakably appears as a convenient theoretical justification for the perpetuation of Western economic domination of the less developed countries. Soviet writers appear to be the most caustic in criticism but their attitude is largely shared in other Bloc countries as well.[1] One writer described the theory as 'a pseudo-scientific reactionary doctrine of foreign trade disseminated by bourgeois economists to provide theoretical rationalization for the discriminatory commercial policies pursued by the West against the Socialist Bloc.'[2] It is further pointed out that according to the theory it is economically profitable to preserve the backward and one-sided

---

[1] A. Frumkin, *Voprosy ekonomiki*, 12/1959, pp. 120–28; G. Roginskii and A. Frumkin, *Vneshnaya torgovlya*, 11/1961, pp. 20–31; A. B. Frumkin, *Kritika sovremennykh burzhuaznykh teorii mezhdunarodnykh ekonomicheskikh otnoshenii* (Critique of the Contemporary Bourgeois Theory of International Economic Relations), Vneshnotorgizdat, Moscow 1964, esp. pp. 13–66; Sachs, *op. cit*, pp. 28–33; Z. Kamecki, J. Sołdaczuk and W. Sierpiński, *Miedzynarodowe stosunki ekonomiczne* (International Economic Relations), PWE, Warsaw 1964, pp. 94–126; Imre Vajda, *op. cit.*, pp. 245–64.

[2] Frumkin, *Vop. ek.*, *op. cit.*, p. 120.

structure of the economy when the required goods can be obtained more cheaply from the industrialized nations. A Socialist economist attempted to demonstrate that the most backward countries today are those which specialize in a limited number of staple products in which they have a comparative advantage based on static physical potentialities.[1] It is maintained that international specialization in the name of 'comparative advantages based on the differences in the stage of development tend to perpetuate these differences'.[2]

The ideological basis for the present attitude of the Socialist thinkers to the theory of comparative costs can be traced to Marx's analysis of 'non-equivalent exchange'. When dealing with the intensity of labour and the law of value, Marx made a distinction between their interplay in the domestic and in international markets.

> The average intensity of labour [Marx argued] changes from country to country; here it is greater, there less. These national averages form a scale, whose unit of measure is the average unit of universal labour. The more intense national labour, therefore, as compared with the less intense, produces in the same time more value . . . . But the law of value in its international application is yet more modified by this, that on the world market the more productive national labour reckons also as the more intense, so long as the more productive nation is not compelled by competition to lower the selling price of its commodities to the level of their value. . . . The different quantities of commodities of the same kind, produced in different countries in the same working time, have, therefore unequal international values, which are expressed in different prices. . . .[3]

The point made by Marx is simply that a more developed country has a higher intensity of labour and consequently in trading relations with a less developed one it secures more crystallized labour than it forgoes.[4]

Although Socialist economists have rejected the theory as a rational

[1] Vajda, *op. cit.*, p. 260.　　　　　　[2] *Ibid.*, p. 263.
[3] K. Marx, *Capital*, FLPH, Moscow 1959, vol. I, p. 560.
[4] It is these Marxian deductions that gave ideas to Yugoslavia at first, and later to Rumania and Bulgaria (and China), opposing specialization especially in primary production under CMEA auspices. They have argued that international division of labour can work with fairness only when the less developed member countries have reached a sufficiently advanced stage of industrialization. Only then can the Marxian postulate of equivalent exchange be satisfied.

basis for guiding the foreign trade of the less developed nations, they have not yet evolved a comparable doctrine to take its place. It is conceded in Socialist literature that with regard to the problem of the mechanism of foreign exchanges there is 'a gap' in the Socialist theory of foreign trade.[1]

If the reader is a believer in the 'convergence thesis', he will be gratified by the changing views on the theory both in the West and in the Bloc, suggesting a trend towards a reasonable compromise. In the West, several prominent economists have indicated at different times since the war that the static version of the theory was not sensible in application to underdeveloped countries.[2] Similarly in recent years, the majority of Socialist writers on the subject appear to have made some concessions as to the validity of the theory, even though basically they are still critical of it. It is maintained that the theory in its traditional form can be relevant to Socialist foreign trade only in the short run. In the long run, only a dynamic formulation of the theory, such as that put forward by Chenery, can be accepted where not so much current but *perspective* comparative costs (in 15–20 years) are assumed as valid. Moreover, such anticipated costs must not be viewed on a single Socialist country's scale but in the context of the CMEA grouping as a whole, in which case comparative-advantage considerations find their expression in the co-ordination of investment plans.[3]

Of all Socialist countries, the recognition of the validity of the theory in the sense discussed above is given especially in Czechoslovakia, East Germany, Hungary and Poland. Thus in Poland, at least two profound studies have been recently carried out in which the principle of com-

[1] *Mała encyklopedia ekonomiczna* (Concise Encyclopedia of Economics), PWE, Warsaw 1962, p. 211.
[2] See especially Joan Robinson, 'The Pure Theory of International Trade', *Review of Econ. Studies*, vol. XIV, no. 36, 1946–47, pp. 98–112; T. Balogh, 'Welfare and Freer Trade – a Reply', *Econ. Journal*, March 1951, pp. 72–82 (a reply to: G. Haberler, 'Some Problems in the Pure Theory of International Trade', *Econ. Journal*, June 1950, pp. 223–40); H. Myint, 'The Classical Theory of International Trade and the Underdeveloped Countries', *Econ. Journal*, June 1958, pp. 317–37; H. B. Chenery, 'Comparative Advantage and Development Policy', *Am. Econ. Review*, March 1961, pp. 18–51; B. R. Schiller, 'The Compatibility of the Theory of Comparative Cost with the Development Needs of Today's Economically Less-Developed Countries', *Indian Econ. Journal*, July–Sept. 1965, pp. 1–12.
[3] Z. Kamecki *et al.*, *op. cit.*, pp. 123–26; J. Kotyński, *Ekonomista* (The Economist), Warsaw, 2/1968, pp. 335–56.

parative advantage was thoroughly examined as a criterion of choice for variants under Socialist conditions on the CMEA scale.[1]

It can be expected that as Socialist countries enter higher stages of economic development and become less militant ideologically, they will find the principle of comparative costs, even in its static form, less objectionable on doctrinaire grounds and increasingly acceptable as a guide to international specialization even on a national scale.[2] It is already noticeable that Marxian dicta on international values and their role in economic growth are no longer as uncritically accepted at their face value as they used to be. It is pointed out by some writers on the subject that equivalence of international exchanges is in fact irrelevant to the growth of national income. It is differences in cost and the possibility of saving domestic resources that matter.[3]

[1] S. Góra and Z. Knyziak, *op. cit.*; M. Guzek, *Zasada kosztów komparatywnych a problemy RWPG* (The Principle of Comparative Costs in Relation to the Problems Facing CMEA), PWE, Warsaw 1967.

[2] How the dictates of the principle of comparative costs are obeyed in practice can be illustrated even from the trade of the country which has been the most outspoken critic of it. In the days when the USSR was an important wheat exporter, she found it advantageous to import Canadian wheat to Eastern Siberia whilst exporting her own wheat (grown mostly in the west) through the Black Sea and Baltic ports. More recently, the Soviets have proposed a deal to Canada whereby oil would be exported from the western USSR to eastern Canada and imported from the western Canadian provinces to the Soviet Far East. At the 23rd Congress of the CPSU (in 1966), Kosygin and Brezhnev outlined plans for raising the efficiency of the Soviet economy through a higher proportion of machinery in exports and an increasing share of 'comparative imports'.

[3] See especially Erika Maier, *Wirtschafts Wissenschaft*, 9/1966, pp. 1463–76; M. Guzek, *Gosp. plan.*, 3/1967, pp. 16–22.

5 Organization

A. GENERAL ORGANIZATIONAL FRAMEWORK

IN free enterprise economies the administrative and operational framework within which foreign trade is conducted is highly diversified and, in general, decentralized – a legacy of historical evolution. This is true even at government level. There are practically no countries with just one ministry concerned specifically with foreign trade. Of the twenty-five Western countries, only Italy has a separate Ministry of Foreign Trade.[1]

A ministry of commerce or trade in Capitalist countries is usually concerned with both domestic and foreign trade, as in Sweden and Spain. In some countries trade and industry are combined into one ministry, as is the case of the Irish 'Ministry of Industry and Commerce' and the Japanese 'Ministry of International Trade and Industry'. However, in most Western countries foreign-trade policy is put into effect through several ministries. Thus in the USA, apart from the Department of Commerce, Departments of the State and of the Treasury (some aspects of strategic export controls), Department of Agriculture (marketing of surplus products) and various semi-independent governmental instrumentalities also participate; besides, the power to extend or deny tariff preferences partly rests with the President. In Australia, the ministries concerned with external trade include the Department of Trade and Industry, the Department of Customs and Excise, the Department of Primary Industry (marketing of certain products), the Department of External Affairs (strategic export controls) and the Department of National Development (control of exports of national importance), not to mention several marketing boards.

The operational side of foreign trade is highly diverse and decentral-

[1] Belgium has the Ministry of Foreign Trade and Technical Assistance to Developing Countries.

ized. Trade is carried on by predominantly private interests – by individuals, partnerships, companies and sometimes by large associations. Business firms normally act so as to maximize their own profits. Society relies on the government to supplement private enterprise and influence appropriately the market mechanism to promote a higher level of national welfare. To discharge this responsibility, a government may – apart from its regulatory actions – engage in foreign trade itself, either directly or indirectly.

In the early stages of the Communist regimes, the governmental set-up concerned with foreign trade in Socialist countries was similar to that in Capitalist nations, i.e. there was usually a ministry responsible for both domestic and foreign trade and in addition other ministries were also involved in one way or another. After several changes in the USSR as well as in other Bloc countries, separate ministries were evolved in the late 1940s and early 1950s, so that today (with one exception) there is in all Socialist countries a ministry of foreign trade.[1] The ministry is responsible for drafting foreign-trade plans, administering export and import permits, negotiating trade agreements, protocols and treaties and co-ordinating and supervising other incidental operations to implement government foreign economic policy in general.

Although the forms of conducting and controlling foreign trade have undergone several transformations, the principle of State monopoly has never been abandoned. In the context of central planning of the Socialist type it has several important advantages, and is indeed probably indispensable. First of all, it would be ideologically inconsistent to allow private interests to engage in foreign trade and compete with the State, especially in relation with Capitalist countries. Secondly, it facilitates centralized planning, the regulation and control of foreign trade, as well as dovetailing it into the general economic plan. Thirdly, changes in foreign-trade policy can be put into effect swiftly and in application to any particular country without being undermined by other interests. Fourthly, it affords air-tight protection to domestic industries. Imports

---

[1] Albania, whose foreign trade is very small, has the Ministry of Commerce, responsible for both internal and external trade. In East Germany, the Ministry of Foreign and Internal German Trade (i.e. also responsible for trade with West Germany) was renamed the Ministry of Foreign Trade in 1967. Cuba has a separate Ministry of Foreign Trade, whilst in Yugoslavia the ministry is now called the Federal Secretariat for Foreign Trade.

and exports can be quantitatively controlled in such a way as to safeguard domestic industries and promote their development by suitable imports and by controlling certain exports (for example, of relevant raw materials). Closely related to the above advantage is the insulation of the domestic market from the disruptive effects of fluctuations in market economies, or even in other Socialist countries.

The degree of decentralization in Western, and of centralization in Socialist, countries can, however, be exaggerated. On the one hand, there has been a tendency in the West towards the formation of larger and larger oligopolistic and monopolistic units operating in foreign trade through amalgamations and take-overs and through the creation of national and even international cartels; in some countries, notably in the USA, domestic firms are exempt from anti-monopoly legislation in their operations abroad.

In many Western countries, firms trading with the Bloc often form special councils, associations, *ad hoc* consortia, etc. This is exemplified by the East European Trade Council, the Sino-British Trade Council, and the 'Group of 48' (the latter includes 48 firms trading with China) in Britain; the Eastern Committee of the Federation of Trade and Industry in West Germany; or the China-Japan Exporters' and Importers' Association and the Japan Association for Soviet and East European Trade. Such organizations facilitate dealings and strengthen the position of Western firms, and are usually actively supported by governments. Besides, elements of State trading have been adopted in various countries, particularly in respect of primary products. Some of the leading exports to the Bloc are handled by monopolistic semi-governmental marketing bodies, such as the Australian and the Canadian Wheat Boards.

On the other hand, during the last decade there have been moves in most Socialist countries towards decentralization. In several Eastern European countries the State foreign trade monopoly is no longer concentrated in the ministries of foreign trade but is also partly shared by other ministries, by industrial associations, industrial enterprises and in some cases even by internal trading corporations.[1] Foreign-trade

[1] For examples of the organization of the ministry of foreign trade under the new economic system, see the articles available in English: G. S. Georgiev, 'The Essence and Forms of the Foreign-Trade Monopoly under the New System of Managing the

plans are not as rigidly imposed now from above, and trading and industrial undertakings are being given greater financial independence and, within certain limits, they are encouraged to use their own initiative. Czechoslovakia, East Germany, Hungary and Poland have led the way, recently followed by Bulgaria and Rumania. Bulgaria had never been in the forefront of economic reforms, but a leading administrator recently described the official attitude to the organizational changes in the following statement:

> A new approach, new forms and methods are required to change our views, our attitude toward the problem of our foreign trade relations. This is not the question of a partial solution of the individual problems but of an entire system of forms and methods of economic activities which will help a complete reorganization of the work in the field of foreign trade.[1]

The most far-reaching reorganization of foreign trade away from the old model has taken place so far in Bulgaria and Rumania. For further details concerning institutional trends in the West and in the Bloc, see Ch. 15 C(a), pp. 362–66.

B. FOREIGN-TRADE CORPORATIONS

In each Socialist country the policy of the ministry of foreign trade is put into operation almost entirely through monopolistic foreign trade corporations. Each corporation is monopolistic in the sense that in each country it practically has the exclusive right of importing and/or exporting defined classes of articles or services. As such, it is usually a large buyer or seller in international markets. Thus the average value of trade handled by a Soviet corporation in 1967 amounted to $560 m., which was about one-third of the entire trade of a Western country like

---

National Economy', *Vunshna turgoviya* (Foreign Trade), Sofia, 4/1967, pp. 6–9 (translation in: US Dept of Commerce, Joint Publications Research Service, *Translations on East European Foreign Trade*, 21/6/1967, pp. 12–19); 'A Basic Document on Rumania's Economic Advance', *Rumanian Foreign Trade*, 1/1968, pp. 5–6; J. Biro, 'Directive on the Organization of the Ministry of Foreign Trade', *Külkereskedelmi Ertesito* (Foreign Trade Bulletin), Budapest, 7/2/1968, pp. 51–52 (translation in: *Transl. on E.E.F.T.*, 22/4/1968, pp. 7–10).

[1] K. Sheynov in *Ikonomicheski zhivot* (Economic Life), Sofia, 20/4/1967 (translated in: *Translations on East Europ. For. Tr.*, 26/5/1967, p. 6).

Greece or Portugal, and twice as much as the total trade of Iceland; the figures for China, East Germany, Czechoslovakia and Poland were $300 m., $230 m., $200 m. and $150 m. respectively.[1] Offers of large orders can be, and have often been skilfully used to seduce even critical Western big business circles. As dominant buyers or sellers in particular markets they can behave not unlike international oligopsonies or oligopolies and pursue various forms of discrimination according to the bargaining power of their trading partners (see Chs. 6 A and 9 C).

The corporations are legal entities, formally independent, generally run on the principle of commercial accountability and financial independence, under centralized management headed by a director responsible to the ministry of foreign trade, and in some cases to some other sectoral ministry. Most of them are State-owned, and a few are cooperatives. But some are companies with limited liability, in which shares are owned by State bodies or in some cases by the State, cooperative and even private shareholders. Each corporation has to operate within the limits imposed by the import and export plan, trade agreements and various mandatory directives as to the direction of trade, conditioned by such factors as the hardness of currency, political attitudes, etc. But otherwise it is expected to operate on an ordinary commercial basis as efficiently as possible – to buy in the cheapest market and to sell wherever it is most profitable. The systems of premium and bonuses developed to a varying extent in different Bloc countries are designed to encourage maximum performance, even if not always maximum efficiency.

Disregarding Mongolia, the number of foreign-trade corporations varies in each Bloc country – from 7 in Albania to 37 in Poland. The number is not static as some are occasionally wound up whilst others are being established. But owing to the increasing size and complexity of foreign trade, as well as the propensity towards decentralization, the number of the corporations tends to increase. Thus in the mid-1950s the number in the Bloc was 150. Today the figure stands at 240, and besides in several European Socialist countries a number of economic councils, industrial associations, industrial enterprises and domestic trading corporations have been granted the right of direct dealings in

[1] Based on: United Nations *Monthly Bulletin of Statistics*, July 1968, and a variety of other sources.

foreign markets. In Mongolia there are no specific foreign-trade corporations; their external trade operations are performed by co-operative trading or producing enterprises under the direction of the ministry of foreign trade. In Cuba foreign trade is handled by 18 import and export control boards, whilst in Yugoslavia it is now conducted by several hundred firms.

In the early formative stages, the question naturally arose as to by what criterion the field of operations of each corporation should be circumscribed. This problem first came to the fore in the USSR in the 1920s. For a time the geographical criterion was adopted, i.e. organizations were formed to handle all trade with particular countries or areas. Then the industrial criterion was tested, i.e. entities were set up to take care of all imports needed by a branch of industry and of all output produced by it for export. Each of these approaches had definite disadvantages, and it has been found that the commodity criterion is, on the whole, the most satisfactory approach.

These evolutionary stages were recapitulated in other Socialist countries with a similar result, so that today most corporations are concerned with defined classes of goods or services, irrespective of the geographical or industrial reference.[1] Thus the Soviet *Mezhdunarodnaya Kniga* handles imports and exports of books, periodicals, postcards and gramophone records, and the *China National Tea Export and Import Corporation* trades in tea. The commodity criterion is also taken as a basis for the organization of several divisions of the Ministry of Foreign Trade in each Bloc country.

The system based on the commodity criterion has several advantages:
 (i) This division is clear and easily understood by both the domestic enterprises and trading partners abroad.
 (ii) Specialists are fully utilized and duplication is avoided.
 (iii) The problem of 'apparent competition' (i.e. different corporations of the same country handling the same type of product competing in the same foreign market) can be eliminated.
 (iv) The system is conducive to selling in the most profitable, and buying in the cheapest, markets.

---

[1] There are some exceptions in the USSR. *Vostogintorg* is responsible for all Soviet trade with Mongolia, the Sinkiang district of China, Afghanistan, Iraq and Turkey, *Lenfintorg* with Finland and *Dalintorg* with Japan and certain other countries.

(v) It can be easily adapted to trading conditions in Capitalist countries where traders generally specialize by commodities.[1]

Another problem that arises is whether imports and exports of a particular commodity class should be handled by one or separate corporations. Again the practice varied in the past. At first, exports and imports were handled by the same entities. But then in the late 1940s and in the 1950s there was a drive towards separation of the two functions. However, more recently there has been a tendency to combine exports and imports of the same category of goods in one corporation. Apart from the ordinary economics of scale, it is easier under this system to promote exports in barter or compensation deals where imports can be made conditional upon the trading partner's purchases. Examples of such corporations are the recently established Polish *Metronex* (measurement apparatus, laboratory equipment, computers, nuclear devices), the Hungarian *Agrimpex* (agricultural products) and the North Vietnamese *Fafim* (films). However in many cases the separation is still observed, as illustrated by the Soviet *Machinoeksport* and *Machinoimport*.

Some other features of the corporations may be briefly mentioned. Usually in each Bloc country there is a corporation handling complete factory imports or exports, including surveying work, technical assistance and the training of personnel (e.g. the East German *Unitechna*). In some countries a particular corporation may export just one product (e.g. tobacco by *Bulgartabak*) whilst some corporation may be responsible for handling a variety of articles not handled by other corporations (e.g. *Varimex* of Poland). The USSR recently established a separate corporation (*Zapczasteksport*) to supply all sorts of spare parts for Soviet machinery sold abroad. In most Bloc countries there is a separate corporation to carry out barter or compensation deals (such as the North Vietnamese *Transaf*). There is a Polish corporation (*Impeko*) which has the independent right of buying and retail selling at international fairs, exhibitions, tourist centres, etc. A Czechoslovak corporation (*Tuzex*) handles retail sales of goods in Czechoslovakia for foreign currency (to tourists visiting the country and to local residents who obtain foreign

[1] J. Zieleniewski and S. Szczypiorski, *Zasady organizacji i techniki handlu zagranicznego* (Principles of the Organization and Conduct of Foreign Trade), PWE, Warsaw 1963, esp. pp. 240-44.

exchange from abroad). In East Germany there are nine (out of thirty-three) foreign-trade corporations which also have the right of dealing in the same class of products in the domestic market (e.g. *Glass-Keramik*). Several Bloc countries have recently set up corporations to administer the import and export of patents and licences (e.g. *Litsenzitorg* in the USSR and *Licencia* in Hungary). Forwarding and transport arrangements are generally handled by specialized corporations (such as *Romtrans* of Rumania and *Transshqip* of Albania).[1]

Almost all foreign-trade corporations in each country are under the express control of the ministry of foreign trade. But there are exceptions, e.g. *Soveksportfilm* is directly responsible to the USSR Council of Ministers' State Committee on Cinematography, whilst *Sovfrakht* (international forwarding involving sea transport) is under the USSR Ministry of Merchant Marine. The system of dual control is most developed in East Germany (where one-third of the total number of the corporations is also responsible to a sectoral ministry), and to a lesser extent in Bulgaria, Czechoslovakia, Hungary, Poland, Rumania and China.

C. THE RELATION OF TRADING TO PRODUCING AND USING ENTERPRISES

As a rule the trading function is institutionally separated from production both under Capitalism and more so under Socialism. But historically the relationship has followed varied patterns under each system. The functions were generally separated under pre-capitalist and early Capitalist conditions. Then there was a tendency for commercial and industrial capital to merge so that producing and trading functions were often combined in the larger firms.

This practice is still followed today by many large Western concerns which directly import their key inputs and undertake the export of their

[1] But there are exceptions to this rule in the case of the forwarding and transporting of goods presenting special problems in respect of perishability, packing, loading and unloading. For example, the Polish *Weglokoks* (exporting coal and products) and *Rolimpex* (speciality foods, sugar and products) handle their own forwarding and loading.

key products. This is often done through specially formed subsidiaries, as is the case of Shell, Nestle's, the US Steel, or General Electric. Direct foreign-trade dealings may not only ensure the supply of appropriate raw materials and components, but they can also help in fostering the reputations of the producer; in some cases they are indispensable where installing and servicing can be done most effectively only by the maker. Some large concerns, such as ALCOA, ICI and Volkswagen, combine their export effort with foreign investments by setting up branches abroad.

In the USSR in the 1920s and in other Socialist countries up to the early 1950s, producing and using enterprises were engaging directly in foreign trade. But then the policy was changed to divorcing trade from production and use by evolving independent foreign trade corporations, and this system still, basically, prevails. This approach has received support partly on doctrinaire grounds, because it fits into the Marxian postulate of the separation of distribution from production and because such separation facilitates planning, particularly of the 'command' type.

However, there has been a tendency in most Eastern European countries for many years now to give authority to certain undertakings to handle their own exports or imports. The right is usually extended by the ministry of foreign trade (but in Bulgaria, for example, it is done by the Council of Ministers), and it can be granted to industrial (or economic) associations, defined producing or using enterprises, and internal trading corporations. Besides, *ad hoc* licences to import or export directly may be granted for specific purposes.

This system is most developed in East Germany, where it was already operating in 1953 and it was at its peak in 1955–56; subsequently some restraints were imposed to curb abuses. Such direct export or import dealings are under the supervision of the relevant foreign-trade corporations which participated in working out the foreign-trade plan. At the beginning of 1967 there were fifteen large enterprises producing for export with the right of direct dealings in foreign markets, and the Minister for Foreign Trade announced that the right would be extended to more undertakings in 1968.[1]

After several years of experimentation a similar system has also been partly adopted in Bulgaria, Czechoslovakia, Hungary, Poland and

[1] H. Sölle, *Die Wirtschaft*, East Berlin, 23/2/1967, p. 4.

Rumania. The prevailing trend now is for replacing, where practicable, the previous divided centralized control over foreign trade and production by decentralized co-ordination exercised by industrial associations through their foreign-trade departments. Thus in Bulgaria in 1968 there were 36 foreign-trade corporations, but in addition 13 State economic associations were responsible for production and foreign trade in such products as beer, cars, eggs and sugar. In Hungary, where there are 34 foreign-trade corporations, 31 industrial and domestic trading enterprises have been granted the right to export and import directly.[1] The system is still being further extended. The aim of this reorganization is, as was put by a Hungarian foreign trade expert, to achieve 'economic identity of interest between industry and foreign trade' by making them co-responsible mainly through jointly sharing profits and losses.[2]

If the reader is inclined to believe with Marx that mergers and take-overs are the sole preserve of 'monopoly capitalism', he should study the recent developments in Eastern Europe. Thus in Czechoslovakia, in some cases foreign-trade corporations and industrial enterprises have been linked into joint-stock companies (e.g. *Centrotex*, *Kovo*, *Motokov*), whilst a few corporations have been taken over by large industrial concerns (e.g. *Skoda*, *Jablonex*) and formed into subsidiaries to act as foreign-sales departments. In cases where foreign-trade corporations remain independent entities, whether in Czechoslovakia or elsewhere in the Bloc, industrial producers of the export, or users of the import, in question are now usually allowed to participate in negotiating foreign-trade contracts. Although the economic reforms in the USSR have not been specifically directed at foreign trade, the decision taken in 1965 to replace the territorial system of economic administration with that based on the branch of industry provides a more effective link between production and foreign trade. In 1967 Export Councils were established to co-ordinate the activities of the foreign-trade corporations with those of the enterprises producing for export.

It should be observed that the problem of combining or separating production and trading arises mostly in trade with Capitalist countries. Owing to the mutual co-ordination of economic plans and firm commit-

---

[1] *American Review of East-West Trade*, 2/1968, pp. 85–87; *East Europe*, 6/1968, p. 15.

[2] S. Balazsy, *Gospodarka planowa* (Planned Economy), Warsaw, 2/1967, p. 41.

ments in trade agreements, trade with other Socialist countries, especially those within CMEA, can be satisfactorily handled by foreign-trade corporations. Consequently, the starting point of the issue is to decide to what extent a particular type of goods is to be traded with Capitalist countries. It is worth noting that the right of conducting foreign trade directly by enterprises does not necessarily impair the State monopoly of foreign trade. The right is not automatic; it can be granted or withdrawn as conditions change.

From the point of view of a Socialist country, the possibility of direct dealings in foreign markets obviously has several advantages in specific circumstances. In granting the right to export directly, the authorities are guided by the following considerations:

(i) Planned production targets in the past, in general, tended to emphasize quantity rather than quality. In many cases the quality as normally produced for the domestic market is simply not good enough for export, especially for Western markets. And yet it is Western foreign exchange that the Bloc countries are mostly after. If a producing enterprise conducts its export, it has a greater sense of responsibility in meeting high standards.

(ii) When it comes to complicated engineering, communications or scientific instrument products, a foreign-trade corporation is a faceless nobody. It is often easier to find markets if the export promotion is undertaken by a well-known maker with a long established reputation for quality, reliability and honesty (as is the case, for example, of the Czechoslovak *Skoda*, the East German *Carl Zeiss* and the Polish *Cegielski Engineering Works*).

(iii) In the case of complicated apparatus and equipment, it is highly desirable that the makers themselves undertake installation, technical training and servicing.

(iv) In some lines, a successful export drive depends on quick adaptation to the changing techniques of production and requirements of the market. Such changes can be detected and translated into effect most efficiently by producing enterprises.

(v) Sometimes orders for export involve a large variety of articles, each in small amounts, as in the case of quality foods and handicrafts. Under such conditions an internal trading corporation can effect such orders more economically.

The authority to import directly can be extended when:
(i) The goods involved are highly perishable and usually the enterprise concerned alone has suitable facilities for sorting, storage and further processing.
(ii) The goods are not standardized and yet the choice as to the quality, specifications and timing must be quickly made.
(iii) The imported components are re-exported after further treatment by the enterprise.[1]

When appearing in Capitalist markets, whether through industrial enterprises or foreign-trade corporations, the general policy of the Socialist countries is to deal with the producing and, when practicable, the using enterprises directly. The aim is to by-pass merchants and other intermediaries. 'Direct dealings with foreign exporters and importers in Capitalist countries facilitate continuous contact and a more intimate insight into the current conditions of their markets; this strengthens our independence and enables us to secure greater economic gains.'[2]

D. FOREIGN-TRADE PROMOTION AND SERVICES

In general Capitalist countries do not appear to attach much importance to official and unofficial trade representation in Socialist countries, because its scope in a centrally planned economy is pretty limited. Nevertheless most Western governments maintain official or unofficial permanent representations in roughly half the number of the Socialist countries (see Table XXVII, p. 247). Besides, an increasing number of the leading Western firms are establishing permanent offices in the Bloc or in such convenient centres as Vienna or Hong Kong. Visits by official and unofficial trade missions have become more frequent, especially since 1962.

---

[1] J. Masztalerz, *Wymiana towarowa organizacji handlu wewnętrznego z zagranicą* (Foreign Trade and Internal Trading Corporations), IHW, Warsaw 1964 (roneoed ed.), esp. pp. 7–92; K. Meissner, *Aussenhandel*, East Berlin, 3/1967, pp. 33–35; I. Nikolov, *Vunshna turgoviya*, 2/1967, pp. 8–10; L. Kovacs, *Külkereskedelem* (Foreign Trade), Budapest, 11/1967, 331–32; B. Muszycki, *Handel zagraniczny* (Foreign Trade), Warsaw, 2/1968, pp. 67–70.

[2] Zieleniewski and Szczypiorski, *op. cit.*, p. 216.

Socialist countries attach considerable importance to trade representation in the West. In the more important trading partner countries they maintain permanent 'trade delegations', which include officials of diplomatic status and representatives of relevant foreign trade corporations.[1] Elsewhere, trade attachés, commercial consuls or agents of the foreign-trade corporations may be maintained; for example, Polish foreign trade corporations have agents in more than sixty Capitalist countries.[2]

An important role in Capitalist foreign trade is played by chambers of commerce. In the leading Western trading countries they are very old institutions formed on a voluntary basis (as for example in Belgium, Britain, Sweden, Switzerland and the USA). There are local, regional, and national chambers which are concerned with the promotion of both domestic and foreign trade, and their interest often extends to manufacturing as well. Almost all the important Capitalist trading nations are members of the International Chamber of Commerce (founded in 1919, with its head office in Paris). Socialist countries tend to regard the Western chambers of commerce as 'projecting the interests of the *haute bourgeoisie*', and the International Chamber of Commerce as 'in fact assisting the big international monopolies.'[3]

In a centrally planned economy, the traditional chamber of commerce is largely superfluous. Its functions, especially in domestic trade, are taken over by the State. However, in all Socialist countries chambers of commerce have been retained or established to promote certain aspects of foreign trade, even though their official designation in most of these countries is 'chamber of commerce'.[4] Although the Soviet Chamber of Commerce (*Vsesoiuznaya Torgovaya Palata*) served as a model for

---

[1] E.g., the Soviet Trade Delegation in London has a staff of over 200 (as reported in the *Board of Trade Journal*, 5/7/1968, p. 7). The attitude of the US Government has traditionally been against such permanent delegations in the USA. Soviet trading interests are handled by the Amtorg Trading Corporation (est. in 1924), in which the officials of the Soviet Ministry of Foreign Trade hold all stock. It has no diplomatic immunity and is subject to local laws like any American firm.

[2] *Nowe drogi* (New Paths), Warsaw, 1/1966, p. 21.

[3] Zieleniewski and Szczypiorski, *op. cit.*, p. 301.

[4] There are four exceptions: in Poland and in East Germany its official name is 'Chamber of Foreign Trade', whilst in China and in North Korea it is 'Committee for the Promotion of International Trade'. The set-up in Cuba and in Yugoslavia is similar to that prevailing in the West.

chambers in other Socialist countries, it is an exception to this rule insofar as it is concerned with domestic trade as well.

The chambers have been found necessary to assist in the conduct of foreign trade, particularly with free enterprise countries, as they have a similar set-up. In contrast to the West, the Socialist chambers were established by State legislatures. The chambers are subordinated to their respective ministries of foreign trade, although in most respects they enjoy a good deal of autonomy. Their membership consists of foreign-trade corporations and other bodies concerned with foreign trade (the State bank, State insurance offices, shipping enterprises, harbour authorities, etc.). No Socialist chamber of commerce (or chamber of foreign trade) is a member of the International Chamber of Commerce.

The main functions of the Socialist chambers are the publication of periodicals and monographs on foreign trade,[1] the organization of international trade fairs, exhibitions etc., and the provision of information and miscellaneous services designed to foster commercial relations with other countries. One of the most important of these services is the provision of facilities for the arbitration of disputes arising in foreign trade (see Ch. 13 A). In the case of countries which do not recognize each other diplomatically, the Socialist chamber – acting on behalf of the ministry of foreign trade – may negotiate trade agreements; this is done by the East German Chamber of Foreign Trade. Most European Socialist countries now have joint chambers of commerce with several Western countries. For example, the Soviet Union has entered into such an arrangement with Britain, Finland, France and Italy, and there is a Soviet-Japanese Committee for Business Co-operation. Adoption of the new economic system in the more trade-oriented European Socialist countries is providing the chambers of commerce with a new challenge.

Socialist countries have occasionally been accused of poor delivery performance in respect of quality, specifications, packing, time, etc. (whilst they themselves are most demanding in their contracts with other countries).[2] Such complaints are now treated very seriously in the

---

[1] The most active appears to be the Czechoslovak Chamber, which publishes at least six different important journals on foreign trade in 6 languages (Czech, English, French, German, Russian and Spanish).

[2] For evidence, based on the experience of different countries in the last decade, see: M. L. Hoffman, 'Problems of East-West Trade', *International Conciliation*,

CH. 5 §D ORGANIZATION

Socialist Bloc. In all Bloc countries special State instrumentalities have been established to examine the traded articles for correctness of description and to ensure high standards of quality of both exports and imports. These instrumentalities may be either specialized foreign trade corporations (such as the Czechoslovak *Inspekta*, the East German *Intercontrol*, the Hungarian *Mert* and the Polish *Polcargo*), or, as in Bulgaria, a separate department of the ministry of foreign trade.[1]

Besides, there are standardization control offices, such as the Central Inspectorate of Standardization in Poland. In the case of complex equipment, the certification is occasionally extended to earlier processes of production as well. Designated experts may have to test each stage of construction, and this may apply not only to the articles produced at home for export but also to those contracted for import in the process of manufacturing abroad. For further details of promotional work in East-West trade, see Ch. 15 C, E, pp. 375–77, 387–88.

1/1957, pp. 269–70; European League for Economic Co-operation, *East-West Commercial Relations*, Brussels, 1965, p. 49; J. Wilczyński, 'Trade between Market and Centrally Planned Economies: Australia's Experience with the Communist Bloc', *Economic Record*, Melbourne, Dec. 1965, p. 588; M. I. Goldman and A. Conner, 'Businessmen Appraise East-West Trade', *Harv. Bus. Rev.*, Jan.–Feb. 1966, pp. 24–26; I. M. Drummond, 'Canada and East-West Trade', *East-West Trade*, A Symposium, P. E. Uren (ed.), Canadian Institute of International Affairs, Toronto 1966, p. 164; *Far Eastern Economic Review*, 5/5/1966, p. 241; *American Review of East-West Trade*, 7/1968, p. 68.

[1] For the new system of controls over the activities of the organs of foreign trade on the example of Bulgaria see I. Budinov, 'Regulation on the Organization, Functions, and Activities of the Control Inspectorate Department in the Ministry of Foreign Trade', *Durzhaven vestnik* (State Journal), Sofia, 7/4/1967 (translation in: JPRS, *Translations on East European Foreign Trade*, 26/5/1967, pp. 1–4).

6 Prices, Exchange Rates and Tariffs

IN this chapter we shall consider the general principles, policies and practices underlying prices, exchange rates and tariffs of relevance to East-West trade, and this account will be supplemented in the next chapter on weapons of trade policy. Prices, exchange rates and tariffs, of course, condition the Western and Socialist sides of East-West trade in different ways and, as these elements are of crucial significance in the study of East-West trade problems, they will be analysed further in more specific settings in Part III, especially in Chs. 8, 9, 10 and 14.

A. PRICES

Under free enterprise, basically, both domestic prices and those in foreign trade are defined by the forces of supply and demand, tending to produce price structures reflecting scarcity-preference relations. The prices so formed perform a guidance function to producers and consumers in their continuous quest for the patterns of articles that represent the maximum profit or satisfaction. The operation of the market forces is, of course, modified to some extent by government intervention in the form of tariffs, subsidies, the manipulation of exchange rates and, in isolated cases, direct price fixing. If to this we add various restrictive practices by private and even governmental bodies, and the existence of transport costs, we find that there is a certain degree of insulation of market economies not only from centrally planned but also from other market economies. This insulation is particularly pronounced in respect of agricultural products.[1] Nevertheless, these national distortions apart,

[1] E.g., in 1966/67 the average domestic and export (in that order) prices of wheat in some of the Western countries exporting this product to the Bloc were as follows: Australia: $A1·57 and 1·45 per bushel f.a.q. bulk; France: 49·64 and 32·80 new francs

prices in the principal world markets are formed under reasonably competitive conditions and are fairly uniform.

In centrally planned economies, with minor exceptions, the market mechanism is of course not allowed to operate freely. Price setting is, as a rule, centralized in each country in a State price planning commission which is guided by criteria differing in detail from time to time and from country to country. As, at least on ideological grounds, these countries subscribe to the labour theory of value, certain costs such as rents, interest and depreciation (in spite of some reforms in recent years) are not reflected to the extent they are in free enterprise countries. Similarly, to a far greater extent than in the latter countries, prices are employed under central planning as a deliberate tool of economic policy to attain planned social goals, such as regulating consumption and saving, promoting high rates of growth of socially desirable industries and favouring or penalizing certain social groups.[1]

To facilitate planning, wholesale prices are usually held stable over long periods, even though the costs are known to have changed in the meantime. Retail prices are adjusted more frequently, but the purpose is to regulate consumption rather than production. In general, foreign-trade corporations when acquiring goods from the producing enterprises for exports pay domestic prices, whilst imports are sold in the domestic market at the same prices as domestically produced articles or their close substitutes.

It should be evident from the foregoing that under Socialism the degree of insulation of domestic from foreign prices is much greater than in the case of Capitalist countries. In consequence, the discrepancies in the price levels and structures, both amongst the Bloc countries themselves and between each of them and the rest of the world, are considerable.

With the increasing role being attached to efficiency, intensive

---

per 100 kgs of soft wheat; Italy: 6,545 and 3,974 liras per 100 kgs of soft wheat; Sweden: 59·65 and 33·52 kroner per 100 kgs of winter wheat. See International Wheat Council, *World Wheat Statistics 1968*, London 1968, p. 50; Bureau of Agricultural Economics, *The Wheat Situation*, Canberra, July 1968, p. 11.

[1] An extreme view of pricing was exemplified by Molotov, who in 1938 forbade economists to discuss the principles of price formation because 'prices concerned politics and not economics'. Reported in *Ekonomicheskaya gazeta* (Economic Gazette), Moscow, 13/6/1964.

growth and foreign trade, the need for rational pricing more realistically reflecting costs has become obvious to the more developed Socialist countries. Thus the aim behind the major price reforms in all European Socialist countries since 1963 (still being implemented) has been to reduce the extent of State subsidies on goods sold below costs.[1] There is a growing tendency to account in pricing for not only the use of capital but also of natural resources.

There has also been some decentralization of the price setting process, especially in Bulgaria, Czechoslovakia and Hungary, and to a lesser extent in Poland and the USSR, where price fixing has been partly delegated to industrial associations, producing and marketing enterprises or (as in the USSR) regional price committees. The first three above countries now have the so-called 'flexible price systems' under which most prices are still centrally fixed, but some are free to move within set ranges and some are allowed to fluctuate freely (e.g. in Hungary the proportion of the country's prices to fall within each category was planned to be in 1968 50%, 27% and 23% respectively). Prices of products sold by private farmers, plot holders, fishermen and hunters to private consumers have practically always been determined in all Socialist countries in (relatively) free markets.

There is a growing body of opinion in the more developed European Socialist countries (Czechoslovakia, East Germany, Hungary, Poland) urging that domestic prices of internationally traded goods be brought in line with world market prices, and a start has been made to plan at least a portion of foreign trade in value terms.[2] The recognized need for improved pricing theory and practice is reflected in the large, and growing, output of literature on the law of value.

Although the problem of pricing has been widely debated in China since 1961, it must be pointed out that the new approach advocated and partly adopted in East Europe has been officially rejected in Chinese discussions.[3]

[1] E.g. see O. Tarnovskii, *Voprosy ekonomiki*, 7/1966, pp. 82–93; J. Struminski, *Nowe drogi* (New Paths), Warsaw, 4/1967, pp. 147–50.
[2] See G. Grote, *Aussenhandel*, East Berlin, 1/1964, pp. 1–5, 2/1964, pp. 1–4, 3/1964, pp. 6–7; H. Kosk, *Gospodarka planowa* (Planned Economy), Warsaw, 6/1966, pp. 23–28; F. Hamouz, *Czechoslovak Foreign Trade*, 7/1967, pp. 3–5.
[3] The best recent study of this subject can be found in Nai-Ruenn, 'The Theory of Price Formation in Communist China', *China Quarterly*, July–Sept. 1966, pp. 33–53, esp. p. 36.

Prices in East-West Trade

In general, East-West trade is conducted at the current prices prevailing in the main Capitalist markets.[1] Prices are not usually specified in East-West trade agreements or even in annual protocols, but are subsequently negotiated in the case of each contract and the actual price agreed upon in bargaining sessions may depart from the current world prices. In the following circumstances export prices secured by a Socialist exporter may be lower than those prevailing in world markets:

(i) If a foreign-trade corporation wants to dispose of unwanted surpluses acquired in the first instance as a result of bilateral agreements or straight barter deals. This was the case of the Soviet dumping of Chinese tin in the late 1950s.

(ii) To secure hard currencies, especially if there are urgent needs for unexpected imports.

(iii) To break into a particular market where fierce competition is faced from well-established Western suppliers. Soviet and Rumanian oil in the late 1950s and early 1960s illustrate this case.

(iv) To secure certain non-commercial advantages. For example, in 1948 the USSR shipped low-priced grain to France before elections to strengthen the chances of the Communist Party.

(v) In a recent study by the Political and Economic Planning in Britain the conclusion was reached that Socialist exports are frequently offered in the West at unusually low prices owing to ignorance of the prices and poor marketing techniques.[2]

It is not often that foreign-trade corporations can secure higher than world prices. When it does happen, it is usually a consequence of bilateralism. A Capitalist importer may be compensated for the higher price paid to a Socialist country by a higher price for his export to the

---

[1] In intra-Bloc trade, *average* world market prices over a selected period are taken as a basis and these are 'corrected' by agreement for fluctuations, speculative elements, transport to or from principal world markets and intra-Bloc costs. The periods chosen at different times as an initial basis for intra-CMEA trade include: 1949–50, 1957, 1957–58, 1960–64.

[2] Political and Economic Planning, 'East-West Trade', *Planning*, May 1965, pp. 143, 145.

same country or a third country (in the so-called triangular deals).[1] A Socialist country may also obtain a higher price if it agrees to accept payment in a soft currency. Such cases are more likely to occur in trade with the less-developed countries than in the highly competitive Western markets.

Similarly, the prices paid by Socialist countries for their imports from outside the Bloc may depart from world prices. In the following cases, which occurred frequently enough in the past, the prices paid could be higher:

(i) It occasionally happens that there is an inflation of prices of the commodities for which a large buyer (as a Socialist foreign trade corporation usually is) is known to be in the market. This is well illustrated by Soviet purchases of wool in Australia where bidding at auctions has sometimes been quite reckless, e.g. in order to fill the available shipping space. On one occasion the Soviet behaviour was described in a market report as follows: 'With Russia operating in our markets there were in reality two prices which would quote the market – one quotation for those wools in which Russia was operating and another lower quotation for wools on which Russia was not operating.'[2]

(ii) In dealing with Western suppliers, Socialist countries often insist on counter-purchases, i.e. a foreign-trade corporation agrees to place a particular order provided the Western exporter purchases a quantity of articles which the corporation wants to dispose of. The common practice is for the Western export to carry a mark-up as compensation for the possible loss on the resale of the unwanted purchase.

(iii) A higher price may be paid when the Capitalist exporter is prepared to accept payment through a bilateral clearing account instead of in a convertible currency. This includes the case when a Socialist country treats the commodity in question as a prospective earner of hard currency when subsequently re-exported.

---

[1] E.g. the USSR used to secure higher prices for wheat and sugar exported to Finland, whilst Finland was partly compensated by higher prices for cellulose exported to Poland (thus Poland had to have an export surplus with the USSR to complete the circuit).

[2] Farmers' and Graziers' *Weekly Market Report*, Sydney, 1/5/1955.

CH. 6 §A PRICES, EXCHANGE RATES AND TARIFFS 95

This was illustrated by the Czechoslovak imports of Egyptian cotton in the middle 1950s, later re-exported to Western Europe.

(iv) Prices charged to Socialist countries are sometimes higher than to other customers to compensate Western exporters for the lack of patent safeguards on technology and to circumvent the Socialist disinclination to pay direct high interest charges on credits received.

(v) A higher price may also be paid when the commodity in question is under embargo. Mainland China overpaid Ceylon for rubber in 1952/53 to defeat the Western embargo on this strategic commodity.

(vi) Political or other non-commercial considerations may also induce a Socialist country to offer higher than the current world prices. This was done by the USSR, which overpaid Iceland for herrings in 1958 following the latter's dispute with Britain over fishing grounds.

Although the Socialist foreign trade corporations cannot exercise much monopolistic power, their monopsonistic capacity to depress prices on occasions can be considerable. This happens not only when purchases are made from unorganized small sellers competing for orders, but even from monopolistic semi-governmental marketing boards (see Ch. 9 A, pp. 140–44). Apart from the circumstances considered above, price discrepancies in East-West trade may be a consequence of long-term agreements in which prices may be fixed for considerable periods of time. These periods used to be quite long in the early post-war period but now price revisions are more frequent (say every six months in the case of long-term contracts).

How has Socialist trade affected the movement in world prices? There is no simple answer to this question. For most commodities Socialist sales or purchases represent small proportions of world totals. It also appears that co-operation between the foreign-trade corporations of different Socialist countries to try to manipulate world prices to their advantage is small or non-existent.[1] But there have been cases of market disruption through the unexpected flooding of Western markets and the consequent price slumps of such commodities as coal, tin, aluminium, platinum, cement, cellulose, textiles, chemicals, machine tools, etc. (for

[1] P.E.P., 'East-West Trade', p. 142.

details see Ch. 9 B). On the other hand, the Bloc's purchases have usually exerted stabilizing effects on the prices of rubber, cotton, wool, hides, wheat, barley, rice and sugar.

B. EXCHANGE RATES

In a market economy, exchange rates tend to be determined by the forces of supply and demand operating in the foreign-exchange market, i.e. in effect by a country's balance of payments. Broadly speaking, such exchange rates reflect the relation between the price levels in the economies concerned, i.e. the purchasing power of the currencies, especially in terms of internationally traded goods.

All Western currencies have been linked by institutionally stabilized exchange rates under the general guidance of the International Monetary Fund of which all these countries (except Switzerland) are members. In practically all these countries, the authorities intervene in the market in one way or another in support of the stability of the rates. Changes in the official exchange rates are rare and they are regulated by IMF. Alteration of the rates carries considerable repercussions. For example, depreciation will make imports dearer to the country in question whilst its exports will be made cheaper to other countries. A change in exchange rates, by recasting price differentials, directly affects the very mainspring of Capitalist international trade, i.e. traders' profits. It could, in fact, reverse the flow of trade in particular commodities. It affects prices, the size of imports and exports and patterns of production and consumption not only in the country altering the rate but also in its trading partners, and even further afield.

In contrast to the voluminous literature on the subject in the West, the theory of exchange rates in Socialist countries has been almost completely neglected.[1] The writings on the subject have mostly been, as was pointed out recently by a Socialist economist, 'a mirror of practice',[2] concerned primarily with the operational requirements of the monetary policy in its narrow sense rather than with broader foundations

---

[1] A reasonably good general treatment can be found in M. Orłowski, *Teoria kursów walutowych* (Theory of Exchange Rates), PWG, Warsaw 1961.

[2] A. Zwass, *Finanse* (Finance), Warsaw, 2/1967, p. 36.

reaching into the price and income theory. This is understandable enough, considering that the official exchange rates do not enter into central planners' decisions on the size, composition and direction of foreign trade. Similarly, changes in such rates in the past did not necessarily affect domestic prices.[1] Although most Bloc currencies (of all European members except Albania) are defined in gold, this has no practical significance as no Socialist currency, not even the Soviet rouble, is convertible. East-West trade is conducted in Western currencies, and the Socialist official exchange rates are in fact of no relevance to this trade on either side.

The official commercial exchange rates (applicable to visible trade) are generally fixed at unrealistically low levels whereby the value of the Socialist currency in terms of the convertible Western currencies is grossly overstated. There appear to be two main reasons for this: prestige considerations[2] and a means of providing the State with 'accumulation' (saving in the form of revenue).[3] As was pointed out in the preceding section of this chapter, as a rule foreign-trade corporations when dealing with domestic enterprises do not pay or receive foreign-exchange equivalents in domestic currency, but make settlements at the insulated domestic prices (however, see Ch. 14 C). As at the official commercial rate Socialist currencies are overvalued, the corporations usually have to subsidize exports but they collect levies on imports, both of course in domestic currency. As a rule 'surpluses' on imports exceed 'deficits' on exports and the balance of revenue is absorbed by the State budget.[4]

Although the official commercial exchange rate applicable to a particular foreign currency is nominally uniform, the actual rate in trade in most cases differs according to the amount of the subsidy paid or the levy charged by the foreign-trade corporation. In this sense, Socialist

[1] Thus a change in exchange rates does not necessarily lead to the restructuring of prices (as for example the 'revaluation' of the Soviet rouble in 1961). The reverse is also true – an internal currency conversion need not be followed by a corresponding adjustment in exchange rates (e.g. in the case of the Soviet conversion of 1947).
[2] Frankly stated by Mr A. Korovushkin, chairman of the *Gosbank*; reported in *Pravda*, 15/11/1960.
[3] Orłowski, *op. cit.*, p. 196.
[4] E.g. in Poland in 1959 (when tariffs were practically non-existent, the surplus earned on imports reached 30,000 m. złotys whilst the deficit incurred on exports amounted to 19,000 m. złotys. *Mała encyklopedia ekonomiczna* (Concise Encyclopedia of Economics), PWE, Warsaw 1962, p. 78.

countries, in effect, apply multiple exchange rates even in visible trade. This may also occur in a market economy where bounties and tariffs exist (more so if they are differentiated, as they usually are). However, the mechanism of operation is quite different. In the latter economy such effectively multiple exchange rates enter into decision-making as to each transaction, which is *then* reflected in the modified size, structure and direction of the country's foreign trade. On the other hand, in a centrally planned economy such rates are an *ex post* residual device to reconcile central planners' *ex ante* macro-economic decisions with the operational side of foreign trade in the context of an insulated and distorted domestic price structure and a disequilibrium exchange rate.

Those Socialist countries which carry on advanced foreign-trade-efficiency calculations, in addition to the official commercial exchange rates, also use 'coefficients of the relative value of foreign currencies' and 'marginal exchange rates'. These are fixed by the ministry of foreign trade and/or the ministry of finance and then adjusted periodically according to changing circumstances, and circulated to the foreign-trade corporations and other bodies concerned with foreign trade.

The purpose of the application of these additional rates is to determine the optimum direction and structure of exports and (to a lesser extent) of imports, and to ensure balance-of-payments equilibrium. Coefficients of the relative value of foreign currencies indicate not only 'correct' value relations between foreign currencies from the point of view of the Socialist country, but also, if the marginal exchange rate is applied in addition, their value relation to the domestic currency. These are discussed further in Ch. 14 B(e), pp. 322–24.

At the official commercial rates fixed by Socialist countries, Western currencies are more undervalued in respect of the Socialist domestic prices of retail goods and invisible items than in respect of producers' goods. Consequently, most Socialist countries have found it necessary also to operate non-commercial rates which are more favourable to holders of Western currencies, such as tourists, diplomats, emigrants sending cash remittances, and others. One of the important objectives behind these relatively favourable rates is to maximize foreign-exchange earnings from these sources. The latest list of the official exchange rates of Socialist currencies is given below.[1]

[1] United Nations *Monthly Bulletin of Statistics*, 7/1968, 194.

EXCHANGE RATES OF SOCIALIST CURRENCIES
National Currency per US $1·00
(as of mid-1968)

Country	Unit	Basic Rate	Non-commercial Rate
ALBANIA	Lek	5·00	12·50
BULGARIA	Lev	1·17	2·00
CHINA	Yuan	2·00	—
CZECHOSLOVAKIA	Koruna	7·20	14·36–16·20
GERMANY, EAST	Mark	2·22	4·20
HUNGARY	Forint	11·73	30·00
KOREA, NORTH	Won	1·20	—
MONGOLIA	Tugrik	4·00	—
POLAND	Złoty	4·00	24·00–40·00
RUMANIA	Leu	6·00	12·00–18·00
USSR	Rouble		0·90
VIETNAM, NORTH	Dong	2·94	—

The higher non-commercial rates in the case of Czechoslovakia, Poland and Rumania are allowed to tourists exchanging larger amounts of hard currencies.

Some Socialist countries also operate additional, more favourable non-commercial rates applicable to specified types of transactions. Thus Poland applies a rate of 72 złotys to $1·00 on the so-called PKO cash transfers of hard currencies to Poland. At the same time, the black-market rate has recently fluctuated within the range 90–100 złotys to $1·00. In some studies comparing the Polish National Income with those of Western European countries, the rate used was 30 złotys to $1·00.[1]

Contrary to the opinion sometimes expressed in the West, the exchange-rate policy in Socialist countries is not devoid of rationality. It is certainly more complex and more difficult to pursue than in Capitalist countries. Although the exchange rate cannot play the same role as in a market economy, it does perform useful functions under the

[1] W. Brus, Życie gospodarcze (Economic Life), Warsaw, 13/11/1966, p. 7. Also see J. Wesołowski, Finanse (Finance), Warsaw, 7/1966, pp. 57–64.

peculiar conditions prevailing under central planning of the Socialist type. Its significance to Socialist countries is enhanced by its greater flexibility. It can be varied at short notice in response to changing conditions or to produce specific (however limited) effects.[1] As no Socialist countries are members of IMF, they are not bound by the rules of the game which are applicable to Western countries. For prospects for Socialist currencies becoming convertible, see Ch. 10 D.

C. TARIFFS

As in the case of pricing and exchange rates, the role of tariffs under each system is fundamentally different. Normally, i.e. barring national emergencies (when direct controls are tolerated as legitimate), tariffs are the most important instrument of trade policy at the disposal of the authorities in a market economy. Tariffs directly modify price differentials and thus influence the very mainspring of trade – profits. They are compatible with competition and they distort international prices less than most other instruments. Tariffs cause less opposition in the community than other measures; in fact some well-organized groups (such as manufacturing interests competing with imports) constantly press for their extension.

Under the Socialist economic system, tariffs lose their conventional significance. The virtual insulation of domestic from foreign prices, together with State planning and the monopolization of foreign trade, offer more complete, direct and flexible methods of protecting local industries or collecting revenue.

Taking the Bloc as a whole, the attitude to tariffs passed through three phases. In the early stages of the Communist regimes, there was a tendency to discontinue tariffs to avoid administrative costs, considering that duties in a centrally planned economy are simply paid by one State instrumentality to another. When trade relations with Capitalist countries became normalized, most Socialist countries (the Eastern European ones and China) introduced duties on non-commercial

[1] E.g. in Poland over the two decades following World War II, at least 26 adjustments could be counted in the published exchange rates. See, J. Wesołowski, *Handel zagraniczny* (Foreign Trade), Warsaw, 10/1965, pp. 487-91.

imports (and occasionally on exports). In practice, the import duties were levied on parcels received by private persons, whilst the executors of the foreign-trade plan (i.e. foreign-trade corporations and other importing enterprises) were exempted from such levies.

A revived Socialist interest in tariffs dates from the late 1950s. It has been stimulated by three developments: the economic integration in Western Europe; the growing Socialist tendency towards trade with Capitalist countries; and, more recently, by the economic reforms in East Europe where increasing emphasis is placed on motivational means. Several European Socialist countries have revised their previous tariff schedules or have introduced tariffs as a useful weapon in negotiating commercial treaties and reciprocating minimum duties to countries extending the Most-Favoured-Nation treatment. As of 1968 at least seven Bloc countries (Bulgaria, Czechoslovakia, East Germany, Hungary, Poland, Rumania and the USSR) had two-column tariffs. All these countries, except East Germany but with Albania added, are now members of the International Union for the Publication of Customs Tariffs (see Table XXXII, p. 370). By Western standards their tariff schedules appear very liberal and the level of tariffs is very low. Thus, according to the new Soviet tariff of 1961, the average level of import duties was 2·5% (*ad valorem*), the maximum rates of tariff are on the average 10–15% higher than the minimum (MFN) rates and 60% of Soviet imports were admitted duty-free; since that time (effective January 1965) all duties on imports from Developing Countries (representing 15% of Soviet imports) have been abolished.[1]

Where tariffs are levied in visible trade, their only importance consists in influencing the 'profitability' of the foreign-trade corporations. To maximize their profits, and thus bonuses for their personnel, the corporations are interested in importing those goods and from those countries to which, *ceteris paribus*, the lowest or no tariffs are applicable.[2]

[1] *Vneshnaya torgovlya* (Foreign Trade), Moscow, 10/1961, pp. 5–6 and 9/1966, p. 13; *Izvestiya*, Moscow, 12/1/1965, p. 1.

[2] In general, the corporations resell the imported articles in the domestic market at uniform prices, corresponding to those of the domestically produced articles. However, it appears that some passing on of the tariff is now possible in several European Socialist countries, such as Czechoslovakia, East Germany, Hungary, Poland and the USSR. In the USSR only a minimum tariff can be passed on to Soviet users, whilst the difference between the minimum and maximum duties must be absorbed either by the importing foreign trade corporation or the foreign exporter.

Thus the only effects that tariffs may produce are a modest geographical redistribution of trade and perhaps a slight modification of its commodity structure. Tariffs virtually have no effect on the total level of imports, nor on their structure as far as the fulfilment of the national development plan is concerned.

The different role of tariffs under each system is demonstrated by the different processes of regional economic integration, as illustrated by the European Economic Community and the Council for Mutual Economic Aid. In market economies, the tariff is the principal means by which such integration can be achieved. It is manipulated in such a way as to redirect trade, which in turn leads to restructurization of production within the grouping. Under central planning economic integration is achieved by co-ordination of national economic (especially investment) plans directly, irrespective of tariffs.[1] Trade is rather a consequence, not a forerunner, of such integration.

Of the 75 full members of the General Agreement on Tariffs and Trade, only Czechoslovakia and Poland are full members. As such they are accorded MFN tariff treatment by other member countries.[2] Czechoslovakia is a foundation member; Poland, after ten years of 'observer' and 'special' status, was admitted to full membership in October 1967.[3] Since 1964 these countries have participated in the 'Kennedy Round' of tariff negotiations. Bulgaria, Hungary and Rumania have an 'observer' status in GATT; on several occasions in recent years trade officials of these countries have hinted that their countries may seek full membership. The traditional attitude of Socialist countries to GATT and the problem of MFN reciprocity are considered in Ch. 8, esp. pp. 122, 129 and 135–36.

---

[1] There is no express provision in the CMEA Charter for any preferential treatment or for a common external tariff, although in practice all members accord each other unconditional MFN treatment.

[2] With the notable exception of the United States, which withdrew MFN from all Socialist countries (but not from Yugoslavia) during 1951–52. Poland was re-accorded MFN in 1960, but during 1962–63 it was temporarily withheld (from Yugoslavia as well).

[3] Cuba has been a full member. Yugoslavia after 8 years of 'special' and 'provisional' membership was admitted as a full member in 1966.

7 Weapons of Trade Policy

A. GENERAL FOUNDATIONS

APART from the institutional forms discussed in Ch. 5, governments have a large number of direct and indirect means at their disposal to translate their foreign-trade policies into effect. These means, which include various methods, procedures and more or less specific instruments are labelled here simply as 'weapons'.

There is an intriguing common feature of the weapons used under each system. Apart from certain isolated exceptions (such as strategic export controls), their working is generally so designed as to promote exports and inhibit imports. However, this is done for different reasons under each system. In a free enterprise economy exports have traditionally received exaggerated attention. The high level of exports promotes profits of the domestic producers and a higher level of employment. It is conducive to a more 'favourable' (or less 'unfavourable') balance of trade. It improves the state of international reserves and the strength of the nation's currency. It may enable foreign investments or foreign aid, and these can be used as weapons of foreign policy in other spheres than foreign trade as well. Even though relatively high exports may lead to rising prices, there is generally less opposition to these than to falling prices caused by excessive imports. Protectionist groups are usually well organized and they are adept in exerting pressure on governments.

There is a general impression in the West that under Socialism separate weapons of trade policy are superfluous. It is thought that the quantitative planning of imports and exports and the State monopoly of foreign trade afford such a complete system of arrangements that there is no need for further specific means. In fact this naïve view was held even in Socialist countries for a time.[1] Even in a highly centralized

[1] J. Zieleniewski and S. Szczypiorski, *Zasady organizacji i techniki handlu zagranicznego* (Principles of the Organization and Conduct of Foreign Trade), PWE, Warsaw 1963, p. 106.

variant of a centrally planned economy (a 'command economy') certain decisions must unavoidably be entrusted to the trading and producing undertakings. In fact experience has shown that too much centralization is not conducive to maximum performance and efficiency. 'This being the case', it is stated in a Socialist textbook, 'the degree of the centrally planned structure of imports and exports depends quite considerably on the decisions made by all those concerned – from the worker producing for export or requiring imported raw materials or equipment to the top government officials.'[1]

It is perhaps worth observing that in an economy under planned accelerated development there are inherent forces militating against exports but at the same time exerting pressure for excessive imports. Planned production targets, in general, emphasize quantity rather than quality. Further, owing to a variety of reasons, it is mostly sellers' markets that prevail in Socialist countries. Consequently, there is an in-built tendency to produce for the domestic market rather than for the highly competitive export markets. Similarly, the using enterprises are inclined to press for imported rather than domestically produced articles. Imports are usually of higher quality; they often carry the benefits of the latest foreign technology; and there is a wider choice in the buyers' world markets. To this, one must add the unsatisfied domestic market for consumer goods and the compelling yearning for Western luxuries. As a result, the Socialist producing enterprises prefer to sell in the domestic market, and for the foreign-trade corporations it is less troublesome to import than to export.

It must be noted that the in-built export-import tendencies in Socialist countries do not operate so strongly in relation to other Socialist markets. Trade among Socialist countries is carried on on the basis of mutual commitments agreed in advance in the atmosphere of sellers' markets. The weapons of trade policy employed by the Socialist governments are in fact mostly directed at trade with free enterprise economies, especially with the highly industralized countries of the West. Socialist countries badly need hard Western currencies, with which they can command purchases of indispensable equipment and industrial raw materials anywhere. But exporting to the West is most arduous. Quite apart from discriminatory practices against the Socialist

[1] *Ibid.*

CH. 7 §A PRICES, EXCHANGE RATES AND TARIFFS 105

Bloc, Western markets are highly competitive buyers' markets. To face the highly entrenched local producers, protected by various means by governments, as well as other highly sophisticated Western suppliers, Socialist governments have to devise specific weapons to spur and stimulate exports.

B. DIRECTIVE AND MOTIVATIONAL MEANS

In examining the weapons of trade policy in East-West trade, it is appropriate to distinguish between direction and motivation. Directive means are those which primarily rely on compulsion, and they are essentially administrative devices. Motivational means, on the other hand, are designed to operate as incentives or disincentives, even though some of them (such as tariffs and exchange rates) are mandatory as well. The types of such weapons and their relative importance in East-West trade are presented in a simplified form in Table XIV.

It will be realized that some of these weapons can be used to affect trade directly, as is the case with licensing and tariffs; others, such as administrative formalities and domestic economic activity, though operating with indirect effects, can also be used to promote the government's policy objectives. The means can be employed to produce either positive or negative effects. Each weapon is, naturally, exercised in a different manner under Capitalism and under Socialism, and usually for different specific reasons. Those which deserve special attention are briefly discussed below.

(a) Bilateral Trade Agreements

These agreements, concluded between two countries (as distinct from multilateral agreements, such as GATT), are an important feature of East-West trade. They are made between two governments (but occasionally semi-official or unofficial bodies may be the parties) for periods ranging from two to six years. The agreements stipulate the overall value of trade and the broad classes of goods. They may also regulate the method of payment, the application of tariffs, arbitration, transport, exchange of trade missions, etc. Besides, within the frame-

TABLE XIV THE ROLE OF THE MAIN WEAPONS OF TRADE POLICY IN EAST-WEST TRADE

MEANS	The Role Played in the West*	the Bloc*
A. *Directive Means*		
1. Bilateral trade agreements	X (x)	X
2. Licensing	X (x)	x
3. Quotas	X (x)	X
4. Administrative formalities	x	x
5. Administrative directions	x	X
6. Directive plan indicators	—	X
7. Listed prohibitions	x	x
8. Exchange control	x	X
9. Insulation of the domestic market	—	X
B. *Motivational Means*		
10. Tariffs	X	x
11. Subsidies	x	X
12. Material incentives	x	X
13. Credit terms	X	x
14. Credit guarantees	X	—
15. Domestic economic activity	X	x
16. Foreign investments	— (X)	— (x)
17. Foreign grants and aid	x (X)	x (X)
18. Changes in exchange rates	x	x
19. Multiple exchange rates	—	X
20. Publicity	X	x

* x/X – the role played in East-West trade is small/large (in brackets: in intra-Capitalist or intra-Socialist foreign trade only).

work of the trade agreement, there are annual (occasionally for eighteen months) trade protocols specifying or amending lists of commodities, and perhaps modifying other provisions of the agreement.

There were about 150 bilateral trade agreements between Western and Socialist countries in existence in 1968 (of the total number possible of 300). Ireland, South Africa and the United States are the only

CH. 7 §B   PRICES, EXCHANGE RATES AND TARIFFS   107

Western countries which have no bilateral trade agreements with any of the Bloc countries, but there is no Socialist country which has no trade agreement with at least one Western nation. The number of the agreements in East-West trade is not much greater today than it was ten years ago. On the other hand, the number of such agreements between Socialist and Developing countries has more than doubled in the last decade. For details, see Table XV.

Trading on a bilateral basis presents more advantages to a centrally planned than to a developed market economy, because imports and exports can be more definitely planned and integrated with the general economic plan (this subject is pursued further in Ch. 10 C). But there is no simple answer to the question as to in whose hands it is a more powerful weapon. On the one hand, a Socialist country usually has the advantage of initiative, one would expect it to have more experienced negotiators and it has a more developed machinery to ensure the execution (including non-completion) of trade agreements in the most effective ways suited to the government. Under certain circumstances, a Socialist government could exercise strong bargaining power with a predominantly one-crop economy, such as Iceland, Greece and Turkey.

However, Western countries also can and do use trade agreements as a defensive weapon – to prevent State trading countries from abusing their otherwise strong bargaining power with private traders and to prevent indiscriminate market disruption (see Ch. 9 D).[1] Besides, Western countries do not have to conclude bilateral agreements to be able to trade with the Bloc. Even where such agreements exist, trade can and does take place outside the proposed limit. Furthermore, trade agreements (unlike trade contracts) are not legally binding and they do not have to be fully honoured.[2]

[1] The attitude of the British Government was clearly described in 1963 by Mr F. Erroll (then President of the Board of Trade): 'We have established a framework of agreements within which trade can grow. These provide the essential safeguards for dealing with State trading countries. Since these countries are not subject to the discipline of the free open market, they could sell at prices which might disrupt our industries or unduly damage our traditional suppliers.' F. Erroll, 'East-West Trade in Perspective', *Board of Trade Journal*, 19/4/1963, p. 872.

[2] According to a study by Mikesell and Behrman, in 79% of the East-West trade agreements the actual trade balance differed from the target balance by more than $500,000. R. F. Mikesell and N. Behrman, *Financing Free World Trade with the Sino-Soviet Bloc*, Princeton 1958, pp. 85–86; also see M. L. Hoffman, 'Problems of East-West Trade', *International Conciliation*, 1/1957, pp. 266–84.

TABLE XV EAST-WEST BILATERAL TRADE AGREEMENTS
EXISTING IN 1968

(*With Comparative Totals for 1957*)

	ALBANIA	BULGARIA	CZECHOSLOVAKIA	EAST GERMANY	HUNGARY	MAINLAND CHINA	MONGOLIA	NORTH KOREA	NORTH VIETNAM	POLAND	RUMANIA	USSR	TOTAL
Australia		×		×						×	×	×	5
Austria		×	×	×	×	×				×	×	×	8
Belgium-Lux.		×	×	×	×					×	×	×	7
Canada		×	×	×	×	×				×	×	×	8
Denmark		×	×	×	×	×				×	×	×	8
Finland		×	×		×	×				×	×	×	7
France	×	×	×	×	×				×	×	×	×	9
Germany, West		×	×		×	×				×	×	×	7
Greece		×	×	×	×					×	×	×	7
Iceland		×	×		×					×		×	5
Ireland													0
Italy	×	×	×	×	×					×	×	×	8
Japan		×		×	×	×	×			×		×	7
Netherlands		×	×	×	×	×				×	×		7
New Zealand		×											1
Norway		×	×	×	×	×				×	×	×	8
Portugal			×	×	×					×			4
South Africa													0
Spain		×	×	×	×					×	×		6
Sweden		×	×	×	×					×	×	×	7

CH. 7 §B WEAPONS OF TRADE POLICY

TABLE XV (*Continued*)

	ALBANIA	BULGARIA	CZECHOSLOVAKIA	EAST GERMANY	HUNGARY	MAINLAND CHINA	MONGOLIA	NORTH KOREA	NORTH VIETNAM	POLAND	RUMANIA	USSR	TOTAL
Switzerland			×		×	×				×			4
Turkey		×	×	×	×					×	×	×	7
United Kingdom		×	×	×	×	×		×		×	×	×	9
United States													0
Yugoslavia	×	×	×	×	×	×	×			×	×	×	10
TOTAL IN 1968													
With Western Countries	3	20	19	15	21	10	3	2	1	21	17	17	149
With Developing Countries	3	18	38	22	28	34	1	6	2	37	30	45	264
Total	6	38	57	37	49	44	4	8	3	58	47	62	413
TOTAL IN 1957													
With Western Countries	5	16	18	17	18	6	0	2	1	18	15	16	132
With Developing Countries	1	2	21	12	16	15	0	2	2	17	9	15	112
Total	6	18	39	29	34	21	0	4	3	35	24	31	244

Sources. The details for 1968 were compiled from Capitalist and Socialist official and unofficial periodical literature. Although probably complete, they should be treated as minimum. Commercial understandings and treaties of limited scope are not included. The figures for 1957 are based on R. F. Mikesell and J. N. Behrman, *Financing Free World Trade with the Sino-Soviet Bloc*, Princeton UP, 1958, pp. 103–109.

To Socialist countries, trade agreements with Western nations are of limited value; in contrast to the agreements with other Socialist, and many Developing, countries, these agreements are unreliable and not specific enough. A Socialist economist summed up his view of East-West bilateral trade agreements thus: 'The bilateral basis of negotiations is partly a result of traditional East-West relations and mostly a consequence of individual Western countries endeavouring to secure maximum advantages and concessions from Socialist countries.'[1]

(b) Licensing and Quotas

Although these administrative restrictions were largely dropped in Western trade in the later 1950s, they are still important in trade with Socialist countries. When used in trade with other Capitalist countries quotas are generally global and unilateral, but with Socialist countries they are mostly bilateral. However, a growing proportion of imports from the Bloc is being freed from quota restrictions.[2] Through import licensing it is possible to ensure that quotas are not exceeded. Besides, licensing and, on some items, quotas are also used to administer strategic export controls.

Of the directive means, licensing is the most direct, flexible and effective weapon in a market economy. Quotas are direct and effective, too, but as they are determined in advance (a year or more) they are not so flexible. With the growing liberalization of imports from the Bloc, and of exports under the strategic embargo regulations, the role of these weapons to the West has been declining.

In Socialist countries licensing plays a different, and minor, part. It is not used to regulate trade, but rather to validate import and export contracts. However, it is occasionally used as a retaliatory or coercive

---

[1] S. Toczek, *Handel zagraniczny* (Foreign Trade), Warsaw, 3/1967, p. 12.

[2] For example, in the early 1960s only 10% of the British imports from the USSR, 30% from China and 50% of those from Eastern Europe were subject to quotas, the remainder entered Britain under the Open General Licence; see *Board of Trade Journal*, 23/6/1964, p. 1,373, 19/2/1965, p. 383, 24/12/1965, p. 1,501. However, it must be realized that quotas are usually fixed for those imports which otherwise would increase considerably (such as textiles, certain foods), whilst there is not much damage from non-quota imports, and in addition some imports are completely barred. France practically removed quotas on imports from the USSR and Eastern Europe (Albania and East Germany excepted), and West Germany did likewise, during 1966–68.

CH. 7 §B WEAPONS OF TRADE POLICY 111

weapon at short notice.[1] Similarly, as a rule, quotas are not used to regulate trade, as this is done more economically and effectively through directive plan indicators. However, in a sense quotas are used by Socialist countries when concluding trade agreements in which the upper limits of the reciprocal quotas of specified commodities may be negotiated (but this is only an expression of planned targets).

(c) Administrative Formalities and Directions

Administrative formalities in Capitalist countries can be used by governments in a variety of ways to discourage trade with Socialist countries. This is done by insisting on unnecessary forms, sanitary certificates, authenticity verifications, long periods of waiting and other time-consuming and costly procedures. In free enterprise countries, where the scope for direct controls is limited (except in relation to State trading enterprises) such formalities may be used unobtrusively and yet in effect they may be as powerful weapons as administrative directions.[2]

In centrally planned economies there is little need for relying on administrative formalities as a weapon. The Socialist formalities in foreign trade, as many Western traders know from experience, are often formidable. However, they mostly stem not from calculated designs but from the bureaucratic system of economic administration. To attain negative objectives, the government has the power and machinery to do it more effectively and cheaply through direct administrative controls – such as ministerial circulars to the foreign-trade corporations, conferences with their directors, confidential instructions, etc. Nevertheless,

[1] The case that aroused most comment in the West was that of the Soviet Foreign Trade Ministry's refusal to validate *Soiuznefteksport's* contract for the export of crude oil to Israel in 1956. This was at the time of the Israeli–Egyptian border incident and the Soviet Government's decision was obviously influenced by political-military calculus. The Israeli firm (Jordan Investments Ltd) sued the *Soiuznefteksport* for $2·4 m. damages, but the Soviet Foreign Trade Arbitration Commission (to which the dispute was referred) rejected the claim on the grounds that the act of the Ministry had been *force majeure* as far as the *Soiuznefteksport* was concerned. See S. Pisar, 'The Communist System of Foreign Trade Adjudication', *Harvard Law Review*, June 1959, p. 1,413.

[2] For Socialist views on the use of administrative formalities by Capitalist countries see, e.g., Zieleniewski and Szczypiorski, *op. cit.*, pp. 176–79; Z. Kamecki, J. Sołdaczuk and W. Sierpiński, *Miedzynarodowe stosunki ekonomiczne* (International Economic Relations), Warsaw 1964, pp. 453–85.

to tactfully rationalize government decisions unfavourable to Western traders, administrative formalities may be resorted to as well.

(d) Directive Plan Indicators

This weapon is peculiar to centrally planned economies and it is the most fundamental and direct means of laying down the concrete elements of foreign-trade policy. The indicators are targets set by the ministry of foreign trade, by which the foreign-trade corporations are bound. The degree of compulsion implied in the indicators depends on the length of the period which the plan covers. The targets in the 'perspective plans' (10–20 years) are in fact indicative only, although general tasks have a mandatory character. The targets in the medium (5–7 years) and annual plans are more specific and directive. The quarterly, or 'executive plans', are most definite and are clearly compulsory. 'Of the directive weapons', it is concluded in a Socialist study, 'the target indicators must be considered to be the most efficacious. The fact that they can be applied most effectively in a collectivist economy markedly strengthens the position of Socialism in competition with Capitalism in international economic relations.'[1]

In general, in the earlier stages of central planning in each Socialist country target indicators displayed a tendency towards increasing detail and compulsion. However, in all Bloc countries the trend has been reversed (with occasional setbacks) since the middle 1950s. But a truly revolutionary approach, evident in all the leading trading countries of Eastern Europe, dates only since 1963–66. Planning of foreign trade is in fact becoming what some Socialist economists now like to call 'anticipatory market research'.[2] In the interests of better performance and efficiency, the indicators tend to be less prescriptive, and greater reliance is being placed on motivational means.

(e) Subsidies and Other Incentives

Both Capitalist and Socialist countries subsidize at least some of their exports, including those in East-West trade. In Western countries

---

[1] Zieleniewski and Szczypiorski, *op. cit.*, p. 140.
[2] H. Ehrlich, *Aussenhandel*, East Berlin, 4/1964, pp. 1–4, and 5/1964, pp. 7–13; also by the same author, *Handel zagr.*, 11/1965, pp. 544–49.

mostly primary products are involved; and the most important of these exported to the Socialist Bloc are grains. All Western nations which have been exporting wheat to the Bloc (Australia, Canada, France, West Germany, Italy, Sweden, USA) subsidize this industry in one way or another.[1] Subsidies (in whatever form they may be) apply equally to exports whether destined to Capitalist or Socialist countries.[2]

In the case of one leading exporter, Australia (where it is possible to make reasonably reliable calculations), the actual amount of subsidiztion of the wheat exported to the Bloc over the period 1960/61–1966/67 amounted to more than $A90 m., or US$100 m. (see Table XVI, p. 142). Other primary products exported to the Bloc which have enjoyed subsidization in some form include barley, maize, rice and cotton. Besides, manufactured exports often receive government assistance too, mostly in camouflaged ways, through export bounties, payments to exporters' associations for 'trade promotion', exemptions from taxes, etc.[3]

In Socialist countries, subsidies are used not so much as an active weapon but rather as an *ex post* means of recompensing foreign-trade corporations and other exporting enterprises for 'losses' incurred, mostly as a consequence of the over-valuation of their currencies at the official commercial exchange rate. Payment of enormous export subsidies in the past was demonstrated in a United Nations study on the example of East Germany and Hungary.[4] However, there has been a tendency in the Bloc in recent years to bring prices closer to production costs and world market prices so as to reduce the amount of subsidization. This move has been most pronounced in Bulgaria, Czechoslovakia, East Germany, Hungary, Poland and Rumania.

At the same time, most Bloc countries have devised intricate systems of material incentives to encourage optimum trade performance. It has been found that 'plan, directives, propaganda and patriotic appeals are

[1] For details, see Ch. 6 A, footnote 1, pp. 90–91 and Ch. 9 A.
[2] However, up to 1963 the US Government barred subsidized exports to the Socialist Bloc (except to Poland after 1956), and apparently in certain cases the French Government did the same. In 1966 the US Agriculture Appropriation legislation was amended to forbid concessional surplus food sales to any nation trading with North Vietnam, on the strength of which a shipment of wheat was blocked to Yugoslavia.
[3] For a Socialist view of these forms of assistance see Zieleniewski and Szczypiorski, *op. cit.*, esp. pp. 132–36.
[4] United Nations *Economic Survey of Europe 1957*, Geneva 1958, p. vi, 22–29.

just not enough' to produce high-quality exports for the highly competitive Western markets.¹ Various schemes of premiums and bonuses have been devised which apply not only to the personnel of the foreign-trade corporations but also to factories producing for export.

The incentive funds are now based in most European Socialist countries on profits, i.e. on the efficiency of the foreign-trade corporations and relevant domestic enterprises. They are so designed as to make the corporations and enterprises reduce the costs of imports and the costs of production on the one hand, and to ensure the highest possible export prices. Risk is no longer borne wholly by the State budget, as losses arising from the corporations' or enterprises' negligence are deducted from profits.² It appears that these incentive payments are being applied to a greater extent in foreign trade than in domestic trade.³

In contrast to the more developed European Socialist countries (including Yugoslavia), other Bloc members have never developed such elaborate systems of *material* incentives. In fact in some of them, notably in China, a trend in the opposite direction can be observed under the name of 'anti-economism'. The 'Cultural Revolution' is partly a reaction against economic liberalism which for many years has been advocated by a number of Chinese economists led by Sun Je-fang (former vice-president of China's Central Statistical Office and the director of the Institute of Economics of the Chinese Academy of Sciences), who hold similar views to Liberman in the USSR.⁴ Instead,

¹ Zieleniewski and Szczypiorski, *op. cit.*, p. 173.
² For further representative sources see especially: A. Czepurko, *Handel zagr.*, 9/1966, pp. 392–97; M. Stefanski, *Finanse* (Finance), Warsaw, 2/1967, pp. 31–35; G. Grote, *Aussenhandel*, 3/1967, pp. 7–15; P. Gondos, *Külkereskedelem* (Foreign Trade), Budapest, 5/1967, pp. 134–36. An example of a scale of incentives and penalties introduced in Bulgaria in 1967 can be found in English translation in: (E. Silyanov, 'Foreign Trade Enterprises under the New System of Management of the National Economy', Vunshna turgoviya, Sofia, 3/1967) US Dept. of Commerce, Joint Publications Research Service, *Translations on East European Foreign Trade*, 4/5/1967, esp. p. 8. For further details see Ch. 14 C.
³ For example in Poland in 1955 the gross average monthly earnings of the personnel employed in domestic trade was 910 złotys, whilst of that in foreign trade 1,286 złotys (i.e. 29% higher) was recorded. The respective figures for 1965 were: 1,750 złotys, 2,710 złotys and 55%. Based on: Central Statistical Office of Poland, *Rocznik statystyczny 1967* (Statistical Yearbook 1967), Warsaw 1967, pp. 350, 399.
⁴ See, e.g., 'Resolutely oppose Economism', *Hung-ch'i* (Red Flag), Peking, 16/1/1967 (translation in: American Consulate General in Hong Kong, *Selections from China Mainland Magazines*, 30/1/1967, pp. 1–4); 'Rebellion for the Revolution not for Money',

CH. 7 §B   WEAPONS OF TRADE POLICY   115

there has been a drive to develop a wide range of non-material inducements, such as the award of titles of labour hero, Red Flag pennants, certificates and medals, the offer of the membership of the Communist Party, emulation campaigns, etc.

(f) *Foreign Investments and Aid*
In intra-Capitalist and intra-Socialist foreign trade, investment and aid programmes play an important part. However, in East-West relations these vehicles of trade have been practically absent.[1] One would hardly expect a flow of investment and aid from the capital-hungry East to the affluent West. In actual fact these weapons could be of use only to a Western government and, in effect, their importance has consisted in denials of such flows to the Socialist Bloc.

However, foreign grants, loans and investments (the latter by Western countries only) are important instruments used by both the East and the West to strengthen their influence in the uncommitted nations of the 'Third World'. In this case such grants, loans and investments are employed not merely as vehicles of trade but chiefly as weapons of foreign policy in general (see Ch. 11 D).

Other important weapons of trade policy are discussed elsewhere in this study: the insulation of the domestic market – Ch. 7 A, exchange rates – Ch. 7 B, tariffs – Chs. 7 C and 8 A, C, credits – Ch. 10 E and publicity – Ch. 15 E (viii).

Jen-min Jih-pao, Peking, 20/1/1967 (translation in: Am. C.G. in H.K., *Survey of China Mainland Press*, 31/1/1967, pp. 9–10); 'Circular Telegram Sent to Finance and Trade Centers to Combat Economism and Material Incentive Problems', *Kuang-ming Jih-pao*, Peking, 22/1/1967 (translation in: US Dept. of Commerce, Joint Publications Research Service, *Translations on Communist China: Economic*, 7/3/1967, pp. 5–8). Also see E. R. Lim, 'The Role of Profit in China's Industrial Planning', *China Mainland Review*, Hong Kong, March 1966, pp. 6–15.

[1] The following exceptions may be mentioned. Relief and rehabilitation grants by the United Nations and the United States in the early post-war period, the US aid to Poland since 1957 (and to Yugoslavia since 1950), and some small direct investments in joint East-West ventures (see Ch. 15 D). Some Socialist countries (the USSR, China, Czechoslovakia, Poland, Hungary, East Germany) have been extending modest (by Western standards) economic assistance to the Developing nations of Asia, Africa and Latin America (see Ch. 11 D).

C. A GENERAL APPRAISAL OF THE WEAPONS

It can be concluded from the preceding discussion that the differences in the weapons of trade policy, with the exception of the directive plan indicators and the insulation of the domestic market, are those of degree rather than of kind. As one would expect, directive means play a greater part in centrally planned economies, whilst in free enterprise countries governments depend more on motivational devices.

In Western countries, changes in trade policy are usually preceded by a period of warning and, in most cases, they have to be sanctioned by a legislative body. The response of private traders is often unpredictable and, besides, private interests are constantly at work undermining the execution of government policies – much more so than in a predominantly collectivist economy.

By virtue of the State monopoly of foreign trade, the weapons at the disposal of a Socialist government are more flexible and reliable. They can be used swiftly and unobtrusively, and with little interference. The instructions are transmitted to trading or industrial undertakings which are State-owned, and whose personnel (State-employees) is not adversely affected by changes in government policy or tactics.

Trade policy is, of course, only one aspect of government policy, and not even under extreme *laissez-faire* is it pursued in isolation from other facets of national life. But under Socialism trade policy is integrated more intimately with other policies. On the one hand, foreign-trade targets are dovetailed organically into the general economic plan. A failure to attain planned targets may, in certain cases, cause a whole chain of upsetting repercussions. Consequently, the instruments of trade policy may have to be used with greater determination to attain the desired economic objectives. This would apply particularly to the smaller countries which have moderate and less varied resources and thus are more dependent on foreign trade, as is the case with Eastern European countries. Moreover, owing to the monolithic nature of the State, there is a natural temptation to use the weapons of trade policy to achieve not merely goals of commercial value, but also objectives of ideological, political and military significance (see Ch. 11 for further details).

Whilst a Socialist government has more direct and flexible weapons at its disposal, it does not necessarily follow that they can all be easily utilized to good effect in East-West trade. On the whole, the West is less dependent for trade on the East than the other way round, and the Socialist Bloc stands to lose more from a denial of trade (see Ch. 14 D). It is also evident that Socialist countries are anxious to preserve the good commercial reputation which they have been patiently building up. With the Cold War tempered with the desire for peaceful co-existence (China excepted), there is less propensity to wield the weapons which may secure short-run successes with self-defeating effects in the long-run.

As far as commercial practices and usages in East-West trade are concerned, Socialist countries conform to the rules developed by Western nations. With some exceptions, this conformity applies even to intra-Socialist foreign trade (however see Ch. 15 C, E, F).

PART III

Major Issues in East-West Trade

8 Equality of Trading Opportunity

A. THE MFN RECIPROCITY

GOVERNMENT intervention and the existence of imperfect competition, factors which can probably never be eliminated from international trade, create favourable conditions for charges of 'unfair treatment'. One of the fundamental principles accepted in trade amongst both Capitalist and Socialist countries is that of non-discrimination, and the instrument through which it is normally put into effect is the reciprocity of the Most-Favoured-Nation treatment. The MFN clause carries two major rights for each contracting party. On the one hand, it means equal participation in concessions, i.e. any advantage granted to a third country must be immediately accorded to the contracting party. On the other, it implies a guarantee of non-discriminatory treatment, i.e. a treatment no worse than to any other trading partner.

The MFN reciprocity encounters practical difficulties even in trade between free enterprise countries. But the problem presents itself on a different scale of magnitude in East-West trade, where fundamentally different economic systems are involved. Prejudice and mistrust, nourished by the differences in political and social philosophy and attitudes, further tend to distort particular trade regulations and decisions in the eyes of the trading partner. Irregularities which may often be an innocent consequence of inefficiency or unforeseen circumstances may naturally be looked upon as premeditated acts of discrimination.

The meaning of MFN reciprocity as well as that of non-discrimination have been given different interpretations under free enterprise and under central planning. To ensure equality of trading opportunity between different economic systems, the concept of MFN must be broadened to include *equality of access* to each other's market. Thus full MFN reciprocity in East-West trade should guarantee the following to the contracting party:

(a) the application of the lowest tariff rates, including various charges associated with customs clearing;

(b) participation in other concessions accorded to third countries (such as travelling, protection of traders and ships, etc.);

(c) absence of discriminatory treatment in administering various trade controls, such as licensing, quotas, foreign-exchange allocations, credit terms, etc.;

(d) an equally favoured access to the market on a commercial basis, i.e. not only as favourable as that enjoyed by any other most favoured third country, but also with a reasonable *equivalence* of opportunities for traders *between the two contracting parties*.

All Capitalist member countries of GATT accord each other unconditional MFN;[1] similarly all CMEA, and other Socialist, countries do the same to each other. In East-West trade, most Capitalist countries accord MFN *tariff* treatment to the European Socialist countries, and many of them to China as well. This reciprocal concession is negotiated bilaterally in commercial treaties or trade agreements.

However, when different economic systems are involved, extending full MFN treatment – whether under GATT, in bilateral negotiations or by participation in tariff reductions such as those under the 'Kennedy Round' – some intractable problems are raised. Accusations of discriminatory treatment, meted out by Capitalist to Socialist countries and vice versa, can be traced back to the early 1920s. But the problem has become more acute since about the mid-1950s, since the revived export drive by Socialist countries, followed by economic integration in Western Europe. The role of MFN has been further enhanced in attempts to extend multilateralism in East-West trade. Besides, MFN in East-West relations is an example of coalescence of economics and politics. Apart from the conventional economic calculation, political motives play their role, firstly in according (or not according, or withdrawing) formal MFN, and secondly in giving effective reciprocity (or evading it) to the concessions received.

In 1956 the USSR, supported by other Socialist members of the

---

[1] Article I (1) of the General Agreement on Tariffs and Trade reads: 'any advantage, favour, privilege or immunity granted by any contracting party to any product originating in or destined for any other country shall be accorded immediately and unconditionally...'.

Economic Commission for Europe, moved for the inclusion of an unconditional MFN clause in a draft of an All-European Agreement of Economic Co-operation.[1] This move has been repeated several times since. But the Western European countries rejected the proposal, arguing that the clause is out of place in East-West trade, as tariff concessions would in effect operate unilaterally in favour of the centrally planned economies.

B. POSSIBILITIES OF EVASION OF EQUAL OPPORTUNITY

Socialist countries have traditionally been most anxious to place East-West trade on an MFN basis, and they have been quite eager to accord this treatment to imports from any reciprocating country. They can do this by undertaking: (a) if they have two-column tariffs, to apply minimum duties on imports from the contracting party, (b) if they have no tariffs, to admit imports duty-free. The latter treatment is compatible with the MFN principle because the contracting party is treated no worse than other trading partners. But Western countries have been highly sceptical of the *effective* reciprocity.

When tariff reductions are reciprocated between free enterprise countries, they usually lead to an expansion of imports by both contracting parties to mutual benefit. However when tariff concessions are reciprocated in East-West trade, owing to the operation of the market mechanism imports are increased by the free enterprise country, but not necessarily by the centrally planned economy. The increased foreign-exchange earnings by the Socialist country, if they are convertible, may be used instead to make purchases from another Socialist country or be converted into gold.

A particular concession accorded by a Socialist country can, in effect, be more nominal than real, because other actions can cancel the expected advantage to a Capitalist trader:

    (i) A tariff concession by a Socialist country to a free enterprise economy can be nullified by fixing an appropriate exchange rate (amounting to devaluation). It is much easier to do this in

[1] See European Commission for Europe, United Nations Document E/ECE/270, Parts I and II, Geneva, 12/3/1957.

Socialist countries because they are not bound by the rules of the International Monetary Fund. As arbitrage operations are illegal, even an *ad hoc* disorderly cross-rate applicable to the country in question is feasible. In fact the official exchange rate does not have to be changed. Discriminatory effects can be achieved by requiring the importing agencies, in their foreign-trade profitability calculations, to apply appropriate 'shadow' exchange rates or other coefficients in which differentiation is made between various countries or products (see Chs. 6 B and 14 B). Although normally in such calculations differentiation is based on purely economic grounds, there is nothing to prevent the authorities from fixing appropriate coefficients by reference to other considerations as well.

(ii) Pricing practices can be pursued in camouflaged ways for protectionist purposes. Reduced import duties do not necessarily lead to lower domestic prices and increased demand for imports, because imported commodities are sold at the same prices as domestically produced substitutes. A reduced import duty may simply be offset by a corresponding increase in the turnover tax. Similarly, the system makes possible the setting of abnormally low prices for exports, thereby causing injury to established competing producers in the partner country.

(iii) There is implicit preference for intra-Bloc, especially intra-CMEA, trade through the co-ordination of economic plans. Import and export commitments are treated seriously, and it is unlikely that tariff concessions to a Capitalist country would be allowed to upset such pre-determined trade patterns. For various reasons CMEA members find themselves paying higher prices for imports from each other than from free enterprise economies. Yet this does not deter them from giving preference to intra-CMEA trade (see Chs. 9 C and 14 D).

(iv) The planning and operational set-up under which imports are determined and admitted amounts to quantitative restrictions, and as such it is against the spirit of GATT and indeed difficult (in Western minds) to reconcile with a trade liberalization programme. For a variety of reasons, Socialist countries plan for the output in Department I (means of production) to grow faster than in Department II (means of consumption). Consequently, planners assign low priority to imports of consumer goods and of raw materials and equipment needed for their production, usually irrespective of the cheapness of such goods in the partner country and low import duties that may be applicable to them. Even in Czechoslovakia (a highly trade-oriented country and one enjoying a high standard of living) the import of manufactured consumer goods represents less than 4% of total imports, whilst the proportions for EEC and Austria have recently been 18% and 24%.[1] Tariff reductions *per se* will not increase the total amount of imports, unless planners decide to do so. It is difficult to see how planners can be expected to give much weight to tariff changes in the face of the distorted domestic prices and exchange rates.

(v) The fact that Socialist countries conduct a large proportion of their trade on a bilateral basis, means in effect that such countries are committed to making purchases from each other, not necessarily in the cheapest markets, thus by-passing the most deserving (low-cost) suppliers.

(vi) In each Socialist country there is a State foreign trade monopoly exercised as a rule through foreign-trade corporations. So far as a given class of goods is concerned, the corporations represent the only channel of access to the market in the Socialist country and the only avenue for exports (disregarding minor exceptions). Thus, corporations are usually much larger entities than the Capitalist traders they confront.[2] Under these conditions discrimination is the most rational behaviour for any importer or exporter which is in a monopsonistic or monopolistic position.

(vii) Finally MFN cannot be fully reciprocated by a centrally planned to a free enterprise economy because of what Holzman calls the inherent lack of 'equivalence' in East-West trade.[3] Socialist countries have a much wider range of choice in selling

---

[1] *Nowe drogi* (New Paths), Warsaw, 11/1966, p. 145.
[2] For the average value of trade handled by Socialist foreign trade corporations, see Ch. 5 B, pp. 78–79.
[3] F. D. Holzman, 'Foreign Trade Behavior of Centrally Planned Economies', *Industralization and Foreign Trade*, H. Rosovsky (ed.), John Wiley & Sons, New York 1966, p. 263.

and buying a given volume of goods in the Capitalist markets than the free enterprise countries have in the Socialist Bloc. This inability of a Capitalist trader to purchase what he wants in a Socialist country has been aptly described as 'commodity inconvertibility' (as distinct from 'currency inconvertibility').[1] Besides, there is not equal access to know-how in East-West relations. The Socialist Bloc benefits from a large 'implicit import surplus' of Western know-how for which no proper payment is made.[2]

As a result, a free enterprise country cannot help but regard a centrally planned economy as an extreme case of protectionism. A Capitalist exporter is not given full opportunity to compete in the Socialist market and he is not necessarily able to make a sale merely because he is more efficient than other suppliers. Even if there were no premeditated discrimination on the part of the authorities, under central planning of the type in force a foreign-trade corporation just cannot be given complete freedom to buy where it might otherwise wish to (i.e. in the cheapest market).

So much for the Western view of the actual or potential unfair treatment by Socialist countries to which free enterprise economies are exposed. But unfair treatment in East-West trade is not unilateral, in fact there is quite a 'reciprocity' in this respect. For the sake of symmetry we shall now examine the Socialist view of the different forms of discrimination.

(i) Even though the majority of Western countries accord the MFN tariff treatment to most Socialist countries, its benefit is partly cancelled by the discriminatory quantitative import restrictions still administered by most Western countries.

(ii) Other specific forms of discrimination have included prolonged and arbitrary anti-dumping procedures (see Ch. 9 F), less favourable credit terms (see Ch. 10 E), organized boycotts (such as those in the USA[3]), the application of discriminatory

[1] Holzman, *op. cit.*, p. 243; O. Altman, 'Russian Gold and the Rouble', *Staff Papers*, International Monetary Fund, April 1960, esp. pp. 430–31.
[2] Holzman, *op. cit.*, p. 263.
[3] For example in the USA, such boycotts were sponsored by the 'Committee to Warn of the Arrival of Communist Merchandise on the Local Business Scene'. As reported in 1965, it publishes *Index of Communist Imports* 'to combat, sidetrack and

transport requirements (as was the case of American wheat exports to Poland and the USSR which had to be transported in US flag ships, which doubled the cost of freight), not to mention strategic embargo.

(iii) Socialist countries also have to face a form of qualitative discrimination. Through various subtle means, the West avoids importing highly processed manufactures from Socialist countries, such as consumer durables, machinery and industrial plant. The proportion of manufactures in Western imports from the Bloc is only one-third, but in the Bloc's imports from the West it is two-thirds (see Ch. 2, esp. Tables IV and VI, pp. 35 and 38). The structure of Socialist countries' exports to the West does not reflect the high degree of industralization already attained under Socialism. These countries cannot help but think that the West still endeavours to treat the Bloc as a source of food and raw materials and a market for its manufactures.

(iv) Western countries are quick to accuse Socialist countries of extreme protectionism of manufacturing industries. But the same Western countries over-protect their agriculture. And yet it is mostly agricultural products that Socialist countries are capable of exporting to the West. On the average, agricultural subsidies in Western Europe represent some 15% of agricultural production.[1]

---

eventually wreck the economic efforts of the Communists to bleed and destroy our Nation.' A number of municipalities have passed ordinance requiring merchants who sell articles produced in Socialist countries to obtain an official licence (costing up to several thousand dollars) and to warn prospective customers of the origin of such goods. Penalties for non-compliance include $500 fines and 6 months imprisonment. According to a Socialist source, the Federal Government did nothing in the past to discourage such boycotts (however, in 1966 the Government declared these boycotts to be 'contrary to national interest', and it appears that the courts have held such ordinances illegal). See 'Ordinances Restricting the Sale of "Communist Goods"', *Columbia Law Review*, Feb. 1965, pp. 310–18, esp. pp. 310–11; H. Więckowski, *Handel zagraniczny* (Foreign Trade), Warsaw, 3/1966, p. 88; Mutual Defense Assistance Act of 1951, *The Battle Act Report 1966*, GPO, Washington, Dec. 1966, p. 5.

[1] According to a Socialist source (based on United Nations data), the percentages for the leading Western European countries were (averages over 1960–62): the United Kingdom: 53%, Switzerland: 15%, Austria: 13%, Finland: 12%, the Netherlands: 11%, West Germany: 8%, Sweden: 7%, Denmark: 4%, Norway: 4% and Belgium: 2%. E. Harasim, *Handel zagr.*, 1/1967, p. 14.

(v) Some three-quarters of the number of Western countries belong to preferential trade groupings, such as the EEC, EFTA and the British Commonwealth. Thus tariff treatment as applied to Socialist countries means *higher* tariff rates. Of all the economic groupings, the tariff policies of the EEC appear to be producing the most discriminatory effects on the Socialist Bloc.[1]

(vi) Although Capitalist countries are hasty to point out the discriminatory capacity of the Socialist foreign trade corporations, they overlook the restrictive practices of the Western national and international cartels in such commodities (affecting Socialist countries) as oil, tubes, copper, chemicals, etc.[2] Socialist countries can point out that GATT actually legitimizes discrimination by trading firms.[3]

(vii) In many cases, what Capitalist countries regard as discriminatory practices are not in fact *a priori* premeditated actions by

[1] A Socialist source gave the following examples of tariff discrimination: France, on cotton goods: 19% (from the Bloc) and 4% (from other EEC members); West Germany, on radios: 18% and 3%; Italy, on metal-working machinery: 14% and 4%; Benelux countries, on tractors: 11% and 1%. The EEC countries impose quantitative restrictions of food imports only from the Bloc. See especially V. Pavlat, *Mirovaya ekonomika i mezhdunarodnye otnosheniya* (World Economy and International Relations), Moscow, 11/1963, pp. 101–07; S. Bolski, *Życie gospodarcze* (Economic Life), Warsaw, 3/7/1966, p. 10; G. Kück, *Aussenhandel*, East Berlin, 9/1966, pp. 25–28; W. Bukowski, *Handel zagr.*, 11/1967, pp. 448–50, 12/1967, pp. 505–08 and 1/1968, pp. 6–9.

[2] For example, Western oil companies refused on several occasions to handle the distribution of Soviet and Rumanian oil in such countries as Australia, Ceylon, India and Italy, and they exerted pressure on independent distributors and even governments to prevent these Socialist countries from establishing their foothold (or increasing their share) in Capitalist markets. It is understood that the EEC countries have reached (a secret) agreement to restrict their oil imports from the USSR and Rumania not only to protect internal commercial interests (such as those of the French oil companies) but also for security reasons, lest they become too dependent on supplies from the Soviet area. For details see G. Adler-Karlsson, 'Does E.E.C. Discriminate?', *Economics of Planning*, Oslo, vol. 4, no. 2, 1964, pp. 105–12; B. Rachkov, *Vneshnaya torgovlya* (Foreign Trade), Moscow, 3/1964, pp. 12–16; T. Belous, *Vnesh. torg.*, 2/1965, pp. 17–23.

[3] It is interesting to note that in the Charter of the proposed International Trade Organization of the early post-war period, price discrimination was to be strictly regulated (under Articles 44–51). But the leading Western countries never ratified the Charter (partly because in their opinion the Charter was too hard on Western cartels and too lenient on State trading). See *Report of the Second Session of the Preparatory Committee of the United Nations Conference on Trade and Employment*, Geneva, August 1947, Ch. V, Articles 44–51.

Socialist countries. Some of these actions are rather acts of defence, such as discrimination between different currency areas or between countries with a differing incidence of import and export controls. Such 'induced discrimination' would disappear if Western countries removed their quota restrictions and limitations on currency transferability. Other practices, such as the quantitative planning of imports, are often autonomous, i.e. natural and legitimate processes under the economic system in operation. It cannot be hoped that Socialist countries will relinquish central planning, any more than it can be expected that the West will drop free enterprise.

(viii) Tariff concessions to Socialist countries do benefit Capitalist economies. It is true that Socialist exports are likely to increase. But the higher foreign exchange earnings will be spent on imports, mostly from the same Western country either directly (if there is a bilateral trade agreement) or indirectly (through multilateral dealings). Socialist countries do not want foreign exchange for its own sake. They spend their earnings pretty rapidly, judging by the low levels of their reserves (see Ch. 10 B). They do not want gold for its own sake either – in fact on ideological grounds they are contemptuous of it.[1] Socialist countries' demand for imports from the West is almost insatiable, limited only by their capacity to earn foreign exchange.

(ix) Capitalist countries often like to refer to the Articles of GATT as absolute standards by which to judge the trading policies and practices of any country. But the rules of GATT cannot be accepted as universal truths because they were worked out to suit the interests of the highly developed countries of the West, often at the expense of the Socialist as well as Underdeveloped countries. GATT is, in fact, an 'exclusive club of the wealthy'.[2] Only two Bloc countries, Czechoslovakia and

---

[1] After World War I Lenin wrote: 'When we conquer on a world scale I think we shall use gold for the purpose of building public lavatories in the streets of several of the large cities of the world. This would be the most "just" and educational way of utilising gold...'. V. I. Lenin, *Selected Works*, Lawrence & Wishart, London, vol. IX, p. 299.

[2] See, e.g., J. Wierzbolowski, *Handel zagr.*, 6/1961, pp. 275–80; R. Klockman, *Aussenhandel*, 11/1963, pp. 4–5.

Poland, are members of it.[1] But even though Czechoslovakia is a full member, the USA unilaterally withholds the MFN tariff treatment whilst many other GATT members apply discriminatory quantitative restrictions, on imports from the two Bloc countries, all in contravention of the principles of GATT.

Discrimination in East-West trade is, on the whole, easier to detect if pursued by a free enterprise economy. The details of tariff schedules, excise duties, subsidies, price and income supports, as well as information on licensing arrangements and quantitative controls are available to the public and the measures are administered as published.[2] But under central planning, considering the institutional set-up under which foreign-trade decisions are made and the predilection for secrecy for which most Socialist countries are noted, 'unfair' practices can be carried on and be hidden. It may be virtually impossible to either prove, or disprove, a particular act of discrimination.

C. THE QUESTION OF SAFEGUARDS

Owing to the operation of the market mechanism in free enterprise but not in centrally planned economies, the MFN tariff reciprocity without further safeguards works to the advantage of Socialist countries. This largely explains why Socialist countries are such enthusiastic proponents of liberalization in East-West trade via tariff reductions, although otherwise they have been traditionally opposed to the 'open door' policy. The pressure for safeguards has naturally come from Capitalist countries because, in contrast to centrally planned economies, they have no in-built protective devices. These safeguards fall into three categories: insistence on commercial considerations, quantitative regulation and limitation of currency transferability.

[1] It took 8 years for Yugoslavia to become a full member (in 1966) and Poland was not admitted to full membership until October 1967 although she had applied first in 1958. Full membership is conferred following the consent of a two-thirds' majority of the 75 full members; of these 71 are Capitalist countries (i.e. excluding Czechoslovakia, Cuba, Yugoslavia and Poland).

[2] The governments of the member countries of GATT are explicitly required to conform to this condition under Article X ('Publication and Administration of Trade Regulations'). However, private restrictive practices, such as the organized closing of outlets for certain imported articles, market sharing arrangements, etc., may be more difficult to detect.

(a) Commercial Considerations Clause

Charges of discriminatory practices against countries where, relative to private enterprise economies, there is considerable centralization of decision-making have been of long standing. Where trade is carried on by private firms motivated by own profit, imports are normally obtained from the cheapest source, whilst exports are sold in the most profitable market. But a State trader can naturally be influenced by a variety of considerations when making a particular import (or export) decision – ideological, political or military. Thus a prospective exporter to a Socialist country may not be given a fair opportunity to compete for the share of that market merely on the basis of his efficiency and prices.

The earliest formal attempt by a free enterprise country to prevent discrimination in East-West trade was the British–Soviet Commercial Agreement of 1930. On Britain's insistence, the Agreement was supplemented with a 'commercial and financial considerations' clause. This principle also found its way into GATT. Article XVII 1(b) ('State Trading Enterprises') reads:

> such enterprises shall ... make any such purchases or sales solely in accordance with commercial considerations, including price, quality, availability, marketability, transportation and other conditions of purchase or sale and shall afford the enterprises of other contracting parties adequate opportunity, in accordance with customary business practice, to compete for participation in such purchases or sales.

Where State trading is carried on in a non-Socialist country, it is easier to ensure the primacy of commercial considerations in trade decisions because in such countries the market mechanism still basically exists and State enterprises are normally run on commercial lines. As most of these countries are members of GATT and IMF, they are subject to a comprehensive code of commercial conduct. But in Socialist countries trading corporations operate on a different basis, and no Socialist country belongs to IMF or (except Czechoslovakia and Poland) to GATT.

The clause has often been inserted in trade agreements, but experience has shown that it is most difficult to enforce.[1] There is no way of

---
[1] It is worth noting that the 1930 British–Soviet Agreement was denounced by Britain. It was concluded that State trading and the MFN principle were funda-

determining whether it is complied with as the bids submitted to a corporation are not made public. But even if they were, a corporation could always give the plausible explanation that acceptance of the higher-priced bid was justified on the grounds of better quality, packing, delivery date, credit facilities, etc. In addition, it should be observed that even if the corporation did fully adhere to the clause, manipulation on the principle of a discriminating monopoly could still legitimately occur. By the rules of GATT, discrimination by trading enterprises is permissible provided it is done on commercial grounds.

(b) *Quantitative Safeguards*

A free enterprise country may take precautionary measures of this nature on two fronts – by negotiating maximum import quotas from, and minimum export quotas to, a Socialist country. By exercising quantitative regulation over imports, a Western country can prevent 'market disruption' or dumping that may follow tariff reductions. The controls, apart from the conditional offer of MFN in the first instance, can also be used as a weapon to bargain for improved access to the Socialist market. The Socialist government is pressed to undertake to spend all or a portion of the increased foreign-exchange earnings on imports from the partner country.[1] The undertaking may be specific (when the structure of the import is agreed to) or global. To avoid disadvantages of bilateralism, such import commitments – instead of being tied to the one country – can be multilateralized. The Socialist country may be given freedom to make the undertaken purchases in a

---

mentally irreconcilable. However, the clause was again inserted in the 1934 Agreement, as it was considered to be the only legal guarantee and nothing better could be thought of in its place. M. Domke and J. N. Hazard, 'State Trading and the Most-Favored-Nation Clause', *Am. Jour. of Intern. Law*, Jan. 1958, pp. 58–59.

[1] The solution of the problem along these lines can be traced back to 1927, when in a Latvian–Soviet trade agreement a supplement was added to the MFN clause. The USSR had to commit herself to import an agreed amount of Latvian goods each year. If the commitment were not honoured, Latvia would suspend MFN. This method was also adopted in the first US–Soviet commercial agreement in 1935 and, with minor modification, the system operated till 1951. Other Capitalist countries had already resorted to this method in the 1930s with the USSR, and since World War II with other Socialist countries as well. For further details see Domke and Hazard, *op. cit.*, pp. 55–68; J. E. S. Fawcett, 'State Trading and International Organization', *Law and Contemporary Problems*, Spring 1959, pp. 341–49.

CH. 8 §C   EQUALITY OF TRADING OPPORTUNITY   133

group of countries, such as the Sterling Area, EEC, OECD or GATT. Thus the USSR spends the balance of her earnings from Britain in Malaysia and Australia. Poland, for being admitted to the full membership of GATT in 1967, committed herself to a 7% annual increase in her imports from member countries.

Although quantitative safeguards are regarded in most Western circles as the only equitable basis for the MFN tariff reciprocity, in reality they are far from satisfactory.[1] The central feature of the quantitative safeguards is that the government of the Socialist country should guarantee a minimum amount of imports from the free enterprise country (or a group of them). But to place such a pledge on a fair basis, the guarantee would have to be similarly reciprocated by the Capitalist government(s). Otherwise, the Capitalist country's exports would be guaranteed but not those of the Socialist country.[2]

However, in a free enterprise country, where there is no State trading, the government cannot compel private traders to purchase their imports in a particular country to a specified amount. The most it can do is to undertake to issue licences up to the agreed maximum *if* traders are interested in importing that much from the Socialist country in question. But even where the Western government is in a position to issue mandatory directives to private traders and State enterprises, such a solution amounts to a bilateral commitment, and as such it contradicts the very spirit of MFN. The idea behind MFN is not to regulate and restrict, but to facilitate and increase trade.

(c) Limitations on Currency Transferability

Owing to the inconvertibility of Socialist currencies, the appreciation of the obvious advantages of multilateralism, the export effort of the Socialist countries naturally tends to be concentrated in hard currency

[1] At the Havana Conference, at which a genuine effort was made by Capitalist countries to fit State trading into world trade, the question of fixed global purchase undertakings by State trading countries being negotiated annually was debated at length. But the idea was finally discarded as unworkable, and was not included in the proposed ITO Charter. General elimination of quantitative restrictions has, of course, been one of the goals of GATT (under Article XI) or at least a non-discriminatory administration of such restrictions (under Article XIII).

[2] E.g., the USSR demanded such a reciprocity from Switzerland in the 1948 trade agreement. See Domke and Hazard, *op. cit.*, p. 64.

areas, especially in Western Europe and (by China) in Hong Kong. The concern of a Capitalist country is that whilst MFN enables a Socialist country to earn more foreign exchange, there is no assurance that the proceeds will be spent on purchasing imports from the same country. When such earnings are made fully convertible, purchases could be made elsewhere, or the proceeds could be converted into gold and hoarded. It has also been feared that if Socialist countries were in a position to accumulate large reserves of hard currencies or gold, by unexpectedly varying the size of their imports they could (intentionally or not) markedly contribute to the instability of the Capitalist markets.

For these reasons, Western European countries have operated varying degrees of restrictions on currency transferability. Although sterling has become fully convertible to Socialist countries since 1958, the continental Western European countries and Japan have continued their restrictions. Since about 1963 there has been a marked tendency towards liberalization of transferability as a result of negotiated mutual concessions in renewed trade agreements with several Eastern European countries (see Ch. 10, p. 211).

Apart from the three direct safeguards discussed above, the authorities in Western countries have given encouragement to the formation and work of various associations of traders dealing with the Socialist foreign trade corporations (see Ch. 5, pp. 77 and 87). Such associations help to strengthen traders' bargaining power by discouraging competitive bidding, by circulating information on Socialist foreign trade corporations and economies, and providing useful hints on the most effective techniques to deal with Socialist countries. Many proposals were made at one time or another in most Western countries, including the USA, to establish (or to extend the scope of the existing) State trading corporations to handle trade with other State trading countries (see Ch. 15 C, pp. 362–64). There were also several moves in the past to create a common organization (e.g. under OECD or NATO) to co-ordinate Western trade regarding the Socialist Bloc, but so far no such body has been formed (except for co-ordinating strategic export controls).[1]

[1] See especially, M. L. Hoffman, 'Problems of East-West Trade', *International Conciliation*, 1/1957, pp. 306–307; European League for Economic Co-operation, *East-West Commercial Relations*, Brussels 1965, p. 59; Committee for Economic

Although Western countries tend to regard the measures considered above as merely protective safeguards, Socialist countries cannot but see them as premeditated discriminatory devices designed to cause injury 'in order to apply brakes on the economic development of Socialist countries'.[1] It is for this reason that the Bloc countries (Bulgaria, Czechoslovakia, Hungary, Poland and the USSR) which participated in the United Nations Conference on Trade and Development in Geneva in 1964, submitted a draft resolution for setting up an International Trade Organization.[2] The rules of ITO were to be worked out by representatives of not only Developed nations but also Developing and Socialist countries. Membership of ITO was to be open to any country, irrespective of its economic and social system. The proposed Organization was to be part of the United Nations (whilst GATT is outside the United Nations). ITO's main responsibilities were to include 'the elimination of artificially-created restrictions and obstacles to trade in raw materials, semi-manufactures and manufactures' and 'the elimination of the adverse effects of the activities of closed economic groupings on the trade of third countries'.[3]

The attitude of the Socialist economists who are genuinely interested in placing East-West trade on an equitable basis appears to be the following. They concede that under multilateral conditions MFN accorded by Capitalist to Socialist countries is not equivalent to MFN extended by the latter to the former. To be reciprocally effective, MFN must (i) be negotiated bilaterally, and (ii) include not only purely commercial but also political conditions. The best safeguard that can be given is an obligation by the Socialist country to increase its imports *pari passu* with increasing export to the Western partner country or

---

Development, *East-West Trade. A Common Policy for the West*, New York 1965, pp. 20–21.

[1] R. Chwieduk et al., *Ekonomia polityczna* (Political Economy), PWN, Warsaw 1966, vol. II, p. 484.

[2] This proposal can be traced back to 1962. Early in that year, Khrushchev called for the formation of such a body. In June 1962, the idea was backed by the representatives of the Communist and Workers' Parties at the meeting of CMEA. In June 1963, the USSR presented a memorandum to the United Nations Economic and Social Council on establishing such an organization.

[3] The complete Draft Resolution can be found in *Proceedings of the United Nations Conference on Trade and Development*, Geneva, 23 March–16 June 1964, vol. V, pp. 424–27.

countries. This obligation must be such as not to undermine the operation of central planning. The idea entertained by many GATT members that Socialist countries should undertake not to increase import subsidies and make them into an instrument of negotiation, is generally considered in the Bloc as unjustified. It is maintained, not unreasonably, that these countries, in pursuing stable price policies at home, have to vary such subsidies according to changes in Capitalist markets.[1]

It appears that academic searching alone is not fruitful in providing solutions to the problem of equality of trading opportunity, because neither side is willing to meet the other half-way to make ideological concessions. So far, experience has shown that the most productive approach is on a practical basis through negotiations. By mutual *quid pro quo* concessions and undertakings, the contracting parties can arrive at workable arrangements to ensure what has come to be known in recent years as 'effective reciprocity'.

One of the most fruitful discussions on East-West trade problems so far was that contained in a report furnished by an *Ad Hoc* Group of Experts appointed by the Economic Commission for Europe in 1963. The Group, which included representatives from Western as well as Eastern Europe, analysed the problems associated with tariffs and access to markets in East-West trade. The Group concluded that in negotiations aimed at the expansion of East-West trade it was necessary to take into account 'not only tariffs and the discrimination which might exist in this regard but also other forms of State policy determining access to markets, and to seek to attain equality of treatment on the basis of undertakings which would have mutually advantageous and equivalent trade effects in both types of economy.'[2] The Group further agreed that: 'Effective reciprocity/mutual advantage should be measured in terms of concrete and comparable results, i.e. the increase in the volume and composition of trade between countries with different systems which would satisfy the trading partners and would serve as a basis for its further development on a long-term and balanced basis.'[3]

---

[1] Z. Kamecki, J. Sołdaczuk and W. Sierpiński, *Międzynarodowe stosunki ekonomiczne* (International Economic Relations), PWE, Warsaw 1964, p. 558.
[2] United Nations Document E/CONF./46/PC/47, para. 12.
[3] *Ibid.*, para. 24 (b).

It seems that in further developments towards ensuring non-discrimination and equality of trading opportunity efforts should proceed along the following lines. The free enterprise countries should accord the centrally planned economies non-discriminatory treatment in respect of not only tariffs but also the administration of quantitative controls and currency transferability. Judging by recent trends, this will probably be done by continued gradual liberalization of quotas and further multilateralization of transferability.

On the other hand, the centrally planned economies – apart from undertakings to expand and diversify their imports – might perhaps provide more information on the criteria on which they base their foreign-trade plans and more details of the commodity composition of their plans. Many Western anxieties would be dispelled if the foreign-trade corporations were given freedom to decide themselves on the geographical distribution of their imports and exports on the basis of commercial considerations only. Should the government use direct controls or manipulate the criteria of profitability, perhaps – with due regard to State secrets and without prejudice to the commercial interests of the corporations – it makes public the details of departures from conventional commercial considerations. It has also been suggested that when convertibility of balances is achieved within the CMEA group, to provide for flexibility perhaps these countries might undertake import commitments from the West as a group rather than individually.[1]

[1] *Proceedings of the United Nations Conference on Trade and Development, op. cit.,* vol. VI, p. 142.

9 Dumping

THE question of dumping in East-West trade usually conjures up sinister reflections on each side. In the West, dumping by Socialist countries is often viewed as a deliberate conspiracy to disrupt Capitalist markets and discredit free enterprise. In the Socialist Bloc, dumping is essentially regarded as a hallmark of Capitalism, whose monopolies and international cartels are bent on indiscriminately unloading surplus products on the economically weaker countries.

The concept of dumping lends itself admirably to different interpretations, depending largely on which side one's interests or emotions rest. In its broadest and vaguest meaning it implies any foreign competition, especially when imports are sold (after import duties) below the prices normally charged in the importing country by competing domestic and other foreign suppliers. This form of dumping, particularly when the degree of price undercutting is such that it produces sharp and substantial increases in imports, is sometimes described as 'market disruption'.

However, from the standpoint of economic theory and policy three more precise concepts of dumping warrant serious consideration.

(a) *The broad Vinerian definition.* 'Dumping is price discrimination between two markets.'[1] Haberler points out that this definition is preferable to others for three reasons: (i) price laws underlying dumping are the same as those applying to price discrimination in the domestic market; (ii) it includes 'reverse' dumping (when the foreign price charged is higher than the domestic price); (iii) dumping may occur as a result of price discrimination between two foreign markets.[2]

[1] J. Viner, *Dumping: a Problem in International Trade*, University of Chicago Press, 1923 (quoted by G. Haberler, *The Theory of International Trade*, Hodge & Co, London 1936, pp. 296–97).

[2] Haberler, *op. cit.*, p. 297; also see T. O. Yntema, 'The Influence of Dumping on Monopoly Price', *Jour. of Pol. Econ.*, Dec. 1928, pp. 686–98.

CH. 9 DUMPING 139

(*b*) *The popularly accepted meaning*. Dumping is 'the sale of a good abroad at a price which is lower than the selling price of the same good at the same time and in the same circumstances at home'.[1] This is the definition which is now pretty well established and accepted in the Western world.

(*c*) *The GATT definition*. This is still narrower than the preceding one. It includes two elements: when 'products of one country are introduced into the commerce of another country at less than the normal value of the products' *and* 'if it causes or threatens material injury in the territory of a contracting party or materially retards the establishment of a domestic industry.'[2] This definition, with certain minor national variations, has been adopted in principle by the members of GATT in administering anti-dumping legislation. GATT sets out three alternative criteria for 'normal value', i.e. a fair value in the exporting country:

(i) cost of production in the exporting country plus a reasonable addition for selling costs and profit;
(ii) domestic price in the exporting country;
(iii) the highest price for export to a third country.[3]

The decision as to what constitutes 'material injury' is left open by the GATT rules.

In this chapter we shall first examine to what extent the West has practised dumping in the Socialist Bloc. This will be followed by a study of market disruption and similar forms of dumping by Socialist countries in the West; it will include an analysis of price discrimination and of the conditions which may enable and prompt Socialist countries to pursue such discrimination. Then we shall consider the problem of protection against dumping originating from a different economic system. We shall conclude with an enquiry into the gains (or losses) from trade associated with dumping, including an examination of the weaknesses in the anti-dumping arrangements in East-West trade.

[1] Haberler, p. 296.
[2] GATT, Article VI, paragraph 1 of the General Agreement.
[3] For the full text see GATT, Article VI, para. 1 (a), (b)(i), (ii).

A. DO WESTERN COUNTRIES PURSUE DUMPING IN THE SOCIALIST BLOC?

Although it may be surprising to many Westerners, most highly advanced Capitalist countries have practised forms of dumping in their exports of primary and manufactured goods to the Socialist Bloc. The basic condition which makes this possible is the monopolistic position of marketing bodies or manufacturers in the domestic market and the keen competition prevailing in world markets. This situation is created chiefly by price (or income) support schemes in favour of certain rural industries and the economies of large-scale production operating in many manufacturing industries in Western countries, further reinforced by policies of protection (for further discussion see Section E of this chapter and Ch. 11 E, pp. 176–86, 262–64).

If dumping is understood in the broad Vinerian meaning, or even in the popularly accepted sense, the most obvious case of Western dumping in the Socialist Bloc is represented by wheat. This can be illustrated by reference to Australian wheat exports. Australia is the most suitable country to select because Australian wheat is fairly homogeneous and is marketed on an f.a.q. basis.[1] All wheat exported to the Bloc has been on purely commercial terms. It may also be added that Australia does not trade with any of the Socialist countries on a bilateral balancing basis, and all payments for imports from Australia are made in convertible sterling.

Table XVI, p. 142, shows the normal values of Australian wheat according to each of the three criteria laid down by GATT (and accepted by Australia as a member) and the average prices charged to the Socialist countries concerned since the big sales to the Bloc began in 1960.[2] It will be noted that in each of the six years the prices charged

[1] 'fair average quality' – representing the average quality of the season. The Australian basis of marketing differs from that of other countries, which sell according to sample, or (as in Canada) according to grades which are fixed and do not vary from year to year.

[2] The Australian Wheat Board, a semi-governmental marketing body which has the exclusive right of acquisition and disposal of wheat, does not publish the terms of sale (prices and interest rates on credits extended). This intriguing secrecy has frequently been criticized but to no avail. However, it is possible to calculate the average unit

CH. 9 §A DUMPING

to the Bloc countries were below the cost of production, the home consumption price and the *average* price obtained from third (Capitalist) countries. Credits would not account for the price differences. In fact, apart from minor amounts to Egypt, India and Pakistan, China is the only country to which credits have been extended, and yet the prices obtained from China have been almost consistently the lowest. Indeed, this fact has been officially acknowledged.[1]

The lower prices can be partly explained by quantity discounts and chiefly by the fact that the Bloc (up to 1960 traditionally only a marginal market for Australian wheat) unexpectedly appeared as a windfall buyer capable of absorbing cumbersome surpluses. The prospect of accumulating stocks was an embarrassment to the Liberal Party Government, critically dependent on the Country Party for support. To retrench the generous government guarantees to the wheat industry, so as to prevent increases in the wheat acreage and production, has proved an impossible task, given the recent constellation of the political parties in Australian politics.

---

prices obtained in each financial year from official sources published by the Commonwealth Bureau of Census and Statistics. On occasions, the Board announced that some shipments to China included quantities of 'off-grade' wheat. This explanation for the lower prices obtained from Socialist countries is not entirely acceptable to the author. To be valid, the AWB would have to demonstrate that the *proportion* of off-grade wheat sold to the Bloc was *higher* than to the Capitalist World; in spite of a challenge made by the author to this effect, the Board has never given details on this matter. The author has published several articles on this subject in reputable Australian journals and his findings have not been disputed by the AWB. The point is that the prices obtained from the Bloc have so consistently been lower, year after year since 1960. The argument of the 'off-grade' quality was also used by other Western countries in 1964/65 at the time of the 'wheat price war' to justify their price undercutting in competitive bids for the Chinese and Soviet contracts. See the author's 'Dilemmas in Australia's Trade with the Communist Bloc', *Australian Quarterly*, March 1964, esp. pp. 14–16; 'The Economics and Politics of Wheat Exports to China', *Australian Quarterly*, June 1965, pp. 44–55; 'Trade between Market and Centrally Planned Economies: Australia's Experience with the Communist Bloc', *Economic Record*, Dec. 1965, esp. pp. 591–93; 'Sino-Australian Trade, and Defence', *Australian Outlook*, August 1966, esp. pp. 161–62; 'Dumping in Sino-Australian Trade', *Economic Record*, Sept. 1966, esp. pp. 411–14.

[1] For example see statement by Mr McEwen (Deputy Prime Minister) in 1961, reported in *Commonwealth Parliamentary Debates (House of Representatives)*, 12/10/1961, p. 2,076. Senator Henty (representing the Minister of Trade and Industry in the Senate) stated in 1964 that over the two years 1961/62–1962/63 India paid about $A 4, and in 1963/64 $A 2, more per ton than China did; *CPD (Senate)*, 27/10/1964 p. 1,276.

TABLE XVI NORMAL VALUES, AND PRICES OBTAINED FROM THE SOCIALIST COUNTRIES FOR AUSTRALIAN WHEAT, 1960/61–1967/68 ($A per bushel[1])

Crop Year	Normal Values in Australia			Average f.o.b. Export Prices Obtained from:				
	Cost of Production[2]	Home Consumption Price[3]	Average f.o.b. Export Price Obtained from Non-Socialist Countries[4]	Albania	China	N. Korea	USSR	The Socialist Bloc (Weighted Averages)
1960/61	1·52	1·53	1·37	1·33	1·26	1·37	—	1·27
1961/62	1·57	1·58	1·43	—	1·36	1·37	—	1·36
1962/63	1·58	1·60	1·47	1·34	1·38	1·40	—	1·38
1963/64	1·44	1·46	1·50	1·36	1·37	1·43	1·42	1·39
1964/65	1·46	1·47	1·45	—	1·38	1·38	1·39	1·38
1965/66	1·52	1·53	1·42	—	1·36	1·45	1·38	1·37
1966/67	1·55	1·57	1·45	—	1·46	1·53	—	1·46
1967/68	1·64	1·67	1·48	—	1·36	1·31	—	1·36

[1] A$ 1·00 = US $1·12 = £0·47 (sterling).
[2] Official cost of production f.o.r. ports, as calculated by the Australian Bureau of Agricultural Economics under the Wheat Industry Stabilization Plans.
[3] Bulk f.o.r. ports.
[4] Strictly speaking by the GATT rules (and by the Australian legislation) it is the *highest* price charged to *a third country*, not the average price to a group of countries, that should be taken. If we did this, it would further strengthen our argument. However, it was thought desirable not to give too much weight to abnormalities.

Sources. Based on: Commonwealth Bureau of Census and Statistics, *Oversea Trade Bulletin*, Nos 59–65, Canberra; *Australian Exports*, Bulletins 4–10; Bureau of Agricultural Economics, *The Wheat Situation* (Canberra), Nov. 1968, pp. 11, 50–51.

The amount of subsidization, if we take the home-consumption price as the normal value in Australia, is indicated for each year in Table XVII, p. 143. The total value of the wheat exported to the Bloc over the period was over $A. 1,000 m. (US $1,140 m.) and the extent of subsidization amounted to over $A. 120 m. (US $135 m.), i.e. the degree of 'price undercutting' below the Australian domestic price was about one-

TABLE XVII SUBSIDIZATION OF THE AUSTRALIAN WHEAT EXPORTS TO THE SOCIALIST BLOC, 1960/61–1967/68

(*By the criterion of the Home Consumption Price*)

Crop Year	Home Consumption Price	Average f.o.b. Price Obtained from the Socialist Bloc	Quantity of Wheat Exported to the Socialist Bloc	Amount of Subsidization
	$A per bushel		Million bushels	$A million
1960/61	1·53	1·27	44·1	11·5
1961/62	1·58	1·36	73·0	16·1
1962/63	1·60	1·38	78·8	17·3
1963/64	1·46	1·39	146·7	10·3
1964/65	1·47	1·38	117·0	10·5
1965/66	1·53	1·37	98·6	15·8
1966/67	1·57	1·46	83·5	10·9
1967/68	1·66	1·36	90·2	27·1
			731·9	119·5

Source. Derived from Table XVI and its sources.

tenth. Thus in 1962/63 Albania, China and North Korea, were they to abide by the Australian anti-dumping legislation,[1] would have been entitled to impose countervailing duties amounting to 16%, 14% and 13% respectively on Australian wheat.

This price discrimination is made possible by the Wheat Industry Stabilization Plan. Under this scheme, by guaranteeing a suitable 'cost of production' and fixing an appropriate 'home consumption price' each year, the Government protects the wheat growers' income. The marketing of wheat is monopolized by the semi-governmental marketing board – the Australian Wheat Board. The Board sells wheat abroad at whatever the world market (or otherwise agreed) prices happen to be. If world market prices are low, to honour the guarantee the Government meets the deficiency out of the budget. It must be pointed

[1] Commonwealth of Australia, *Customs Tariff* (*Dumping and Subsidies*) *Act 1961–1965*, Section 9 (1), (3).

out that there has been nothing sinister about the Australian wheat prices charged to the Socialist countries. They were the prevailing world prices for that grade of wheat. The AWB had been saddled with mounting surpluses (except the relatively 'poor' season of 1965/66) which could not have been disposed of at better prices elsewhere.

As a result of the Kennedy Round of negotiations in Geneva which ended in May 1967, it seems that the world market price of wheat will be closer to the domestic costs of production in the leading wheat exporting countries, and thus the extent of subsidization of such exports to the Bloc may be smaller in the future.

The set-up in the case of other Australian exports to the Bloc is not so favourable to the practice of dumping. But it is possible to detect price discrimination in favour of Socialist countries in those exports which are reasonably homogeneous. Thus in 1964/65 the average price obtained per ton of oats exported to Capitalist countries worked out at $A. 43·50, but the price charged to Poland was only $A. 41·83.[1] In 1965/66 the average price of barley obtained from non-Socialist countries was $A. 51·62 per ton, but the price secured from Poland was only $A. 50·95 per ton.[2]

Similar subsidization of wheat and other grain exports to the Bloc has been practised by Canada, France, the USA and others. But in the case of these countries, the proof is more involved because the different prices obtained are complicated by the differing grades of wheat exported and by an element of aid (as for example in the case of the US wheat exports to Poland after 1957) and by bilateral deals.[3] There have been reports in the last five years of 'unfair' competition amongst the leading wheat exporters to the Bloc – Australia, Canada, France and Argentina. There have certainly been cases of competitive price undercutting and the extension of more and more favourable credit terms to China.

[1] Based on: Commonwealth Bureau of Census and Statistics, *Oversea Trade Bulletin 1964–65*, Canberra, p. 751; *Australian Exports 1964–65*, Canberra, p. 325.
[2] Based on: *Oversea Trade Bulletin 1965–66*, p. 784; *Australian Exports 1965–66*, p. 275.
[3] For example, upon examination of Canadian exports, the average price per bushel of durum wheat (except for seed) obtained from Capitalist countries in 1963 works out at Can. $2·31, whilst that charged to Socialist countries was only $2·05. In 1965 the respective figures were $1·96 and $1·87. Based on: Dominion Bureau of Statistics, *Exports by Commodities*, Ottawa, Dec. 1963, p. 31, and Dec. 1965, p. 36.

CH. 9 §A DUMPING 145

It is more difficult to demonstrate the dumping of manufactures because a particular statistical item is not necessarily homogeneous, so that price differences may be due to variations in quality, specifications, etc. However, there are many indications suggesting that Western price discrimination is not limited to primary products. It was revealed in a parliamentary enquiry recently that France had undertaken a contract delivery to Mainland China of 3 m. tons of nitrogen fertilizer at an average price of 16·66 francs per double centner. The precise degree of dumping is rather difficult to determine because several grades were involved, but the Minister for Economic Affairs confirmed that the export price to China was below the French domestic price. This transaction was defended on the grounds that the capacity of the French nitrogen fertilizer industry had been increased by 65%, it was operating under decreasing costs and that there was tough competition between Western European and Japanese suppliers for Chinese orders.[1]

The case of competition between French and Japanese fertilizer producing firms for Chinese contracts is not an isolated one. Reports of cut-throat competition amongst Western countries vying for the Socialist market are numerous. According to a survey carried out recently by the Japanese International Trade Promotion Association, Japan had lost much of her China market to the intensely competing Western European countries (especially in 1965–66).[2] Complaints have often been expressed in the United Kingdom that other Western European suppliers generally quote 5–25% lower than British prices to Poland.[3] Export rebates and various other more or less disguised forms of subsidization of exports – equally applicable to exports to the Bloc – which are operated by most Western countries, can also in a sense be looked upon as facilitating the dumping of manufactures.

We have demonstrated that Western countries have been pursuing dumping in the Socialist Bloc, but not in the sense laid down by GATT. To establish dumping in this latter sense we would also have to demonstrate 'material injury' to an industry in the Socialist country concerned.

[1] *Handelsblatt*, Düsseldorf, 2/3/1967, p. 6 (translated in: US Dept. of Commerce, Joint Publications Research Service, *Translations on Communist China: Economic*, 28/3/1967, pp. 1–2).
[2] *Far Eastern Economic Review*, 3/2/1966, p. 179; 16/6/1966, pp. 515, 569; 30/6/1966, pp. 628, 631.
[3] See, e.g., *The Economist*, 10/9/1966, p. 1,053.

However, the problem of injury does not arise in a centrally planned economy; this question will be considered further in Section D of this chapter, pp. 171–76.

B. WESTERN CHARGES OF SOCIALIST DUMPING

(a) *Reported Cases of Socialist Price Undercutting*
Complaints against Socialist dumping appeared first in the early 1930s when the Soviet Union dumped quantities of grains, oil, timber, furs, flax and coal in the world markets at unusually low prices, at a time when primary producing countries were already in difficulties. Apart from this isolated period, dumping by Socialist countries caused no concern until the middle 1950s. The relaxation of import and convertibility controls in the West coincided with the Soviet 'trade offensive', followed by export drives by Eastern European countries, China and even North Vietnam. The drive has been chiefly directed towards countries with convertible currencies in order not only to pay for increasing imports from them but also to earn sufficient surpluses to meet trade deficits elsewhere. Complaints of Socialist dumping in the West were most intense over the period 1958–62.

During 1957–58 the Soviet disposal of tin for sterling collapsed the price floor which the International Tin Council was desperately endeavouring to maintain. This led to angry protests in the United Nations by such countries as Indonesia, Malaya and Thailand.[1] During the same period the Russians also unexpectedly unloaded aluminium on the British market, undercutting Canadian prices by 4–12%.[2] Next, the Soviets 'invaded' the oil market (especially 1959–62) by selling crude oil and products in Western Europe, Africa, S.E. Asia and Latin America at prices up to 40% below those charged by Western oil companies. Later, Rumanians were matching the Russian price cuts in India and Ceylon.[3] Early in 1961 Soviet centre lathes were selling in Britain (after paying 10% import duty) 12% below the cheapest im-

[1] See, e.g., *FEER*, 26/1/1959, pp. 443–44; 28/5/1959, pp. 17–25.
[2] H. G. Aubrey, 'Soviet Trade, Price Stability, and Economic Growth', *Kyklos*, vol. XII, no. 3, 1959, p. 294.
[3] See S. C. Stolte, 'Oil as a Weapon in the Cold War', *Bulletin*, Munich, Sept. 1961, pp. 10–18; *FEER*, 21/7/1960, p. 127, and 15/3/1962, p. 593.

ported ones, and 30% below the domestically produced article of comparable quality.[1] At about the same time, the Soviet Union tried to establish a foothold in Singapore by selling cotton goods, undercutting the prices of identical Japanese fabrics by 15%.[2] In 1964 the Russians sent a consignment of aluminium sheet to Britain, undercutting the local price by 17%.[3]

The Chinese export drive was most intense in the latter 1950s. In 1958 the Malayan market was flooded with handkerchiefs at 60% below the price of the same-quality British product. In the same market knitted underwear, a wide variety of cotton goods, tyres, tools and other products were unloaded at price discounts ranging from 5% to 20% below the prices of identical articles sold by such a low-cost producer as Japan.[4] Similarly, the Chinese undercut the prices of comparable Japanese sewing machines in Indonesia by 15% in 1958[5] and South African methylated spirit in Singapore by 10% in 1959.[6]

In 1965 concern was expressed in the Australian Parliament that China had been endeavouring to undermine India as a traditional supplier of calico cloth by quoting to Australian importers not a firm price, but a price 10% below the Indian one, whatever that price might be.[7] In the same year, the Australian Tariff Board ascertained that China, France and West Germany had been dumping certain chemicals to the detriment of Australian manufacturers. But China 'underdumped' all other competitors by charging a price 37% lower than that of the next lowest-price supplier (France) and 73% lower than the British price. Even though the Australian producers reduced their price, the Chinese – after paying duties amounting to 102% – could still undercut the local price by one-third.[8]

In 1966 quantities of North Vietnamese cement were landed in Singapore. Even after paying heavy insurance against the risk of American air attack in the Gulf of Tonking, the price was far below that charged by local and such traditional suppliers as Britain and

---

[1] *The Economist*, 6/5/1961, p. 561.   [2] *FEER*, 9/2/1961, p. 269.
[3] *The Economist*, 23/5/1964, p. 861.
[4] *The Oriental Economist*, Tokyo, Sept. 1958, pp. 471–72; *FEER*, 14/5/1959, pp. 715–18.
[5] *FEER*, 18/6/1959, p. 843.   [6] *FEER*, 23/4/1959, p. 563.
[7] *Commonwealth Parliamentary Debates* (H. of R.), 18/3/1965, p. 111.
[8] Commonwealth of Australia, Tariff Board's Report on *Trisodium Phosphate Dodecahydrate*, Canberra, 12/3/1965, p. 4.

Japan, so that the Government had to impose quota restrictions. In fact there are several indications to suggest that much of the North Vietnamese cement was trans-shipped to Saigon where it was used for the construction of American air bases in South Vietnam.[1]

Other products sold in various parts of the world by Socialist countries at one time or another to the detriment of Western producers include: crockery, fancy goods, floor coverings, footwear, hardware, medicines, musical instruments, processed foods, silk and other yarns, sugar, transistors, watches and woodcarvings by China; cellulose, cement, diamonds, newsprint, platinum, rubber, school scientific equipment, timber and titanium manufactures by the Soviet Union; chemicals, cotton, woollen, rayon and synthetic textiles, hardware, hot-water bags, jewellery, laboratory glassware, leather and rubber shoes and wickerwork and basketwork goods by Czechoslovakia; cement, cotton goods, dairy products, industrial chemicals, machine tools, meats, rapeseed, rubber footwear and zinc by Poland; cameras and other photographic equipment, chinaware, fertilizers, office equipment, quality paper and rapeseed by East Germany; animal fodder, food preparations and pharmaceuticals by Hungary; chemicals and processed foods by Rumania; fruit and tobacco by Bulgaria. North Korea and North Vietnam are also reported to have sold coal, metalware and silk at cut-throat prices. Besides, the industrially more advanced Bloc countries have on many occasions undersold Western suppliers of industrial machinery, vehicles and complete plants, particularly in South-East Asia, the Middle East and Africa.

At one of the Tariff Board enquiries on Chinese competition in the Australian market, the Associated Chamber of Manufacturers of Australia pointed out that the tariff system can work logically only where the efficiency of an Australian industry can be rated against a competitive industry operating under similar free enterprise conditions basically powered by the profit motive. A doubt was expressed about the adequacy of tariffs to stop the 'progressive dismantling of the Australian industry' under the impact of competition from a centrally planned economy.[2] The cases which received the greatest publicity in the West

---

[1] *The Observer*, 18/12/1966, p. 1.
[2] *Tariff Board Inquiry Re Pillow Cases*, Official Transcript of Proceedings, Canberra, 24/1/1963, p. 57.

over the period 1957–68 are highlighted in a summarized fashion in Table XVIII below

TABLE XVIII EXAMPLES OF WESTERN ACCUSATIONS OF SOCIALIST DUMPING

The Most Publicized Cases Which Occurred During the Period 1957–68

Article Allegedly Dumped	Exporting Socialist Country	Importing Country or Region and the Year(s) of Occurrence[1]	Degree of Price Undercutting Below the Prevailing Level[2]
1. Tin	USSR	United Kingdom (1957–58)	up to 10%
2. Aluminium	USSR	United Kingdom (1957–58, 1964) Western Europe (1960...64)	5–20%
3. Flax	USSR	Western Europe, Argentina (1957...59)	5–20%
4. Cement	China, Poland, N. Vietnam, USSR	Western Europe (1957...65), USA (1962), S.E. Asia (1957...66)	5–40%
5. Tyres	China	Malaya (1958)	5–20%
6. Meats and processed foodstuffs	China, Hungary, Poland USSR	Western Europe, S.E. Asia (1957...66)	5–40%
7. Oil	Rumania, USSR	Western Europe, S.E. Asia, Japan, South America (1959...62, 1968)	up to 40%
8. Oil lamps	China, Czechoslovakia, Poland, USSR	S.E. Asia, the Middle East, North Africa (1958...63)	up to 25%

TABLE XVIII—*Continued*

Article Allegedly Dumped	Exporting Socialist Country	Importing Country or Region and the Year(s) of Occurrence[1]	Degree of Price Undercutting Below the Prevailing Level[2]
9. Hosiery	Czechoslovakia, E. Germany, Hungary, Poland, USSR	Western Europe, Canada, S. E. Asia (1959...65)	up to 30%
10. Haberdashery	China, Czechoslovakia, Hungary, Poland	Western Europe, Australia, Canada, S.E. Asia (1957...66)	up to 75%
11. Miscellaneous textiles (towels, pillow cases, piece goods, clothing, etc.)	China, Czechoslovakia, E. Germany, Hungary, N. Korea, Poland, Rumania, USSR	Western Europe, Australia, Canada, Japan, S.E. Asia, Middle East, Africa (1957...66)	up to 75%
12. Footwear	China, Czechoslovakia, Poland	Western Europe (1958...63, 1967–68) Australia (1959...65), Canada (1963...66), S.E. Asia (1959...66)	up to 70%
13. Glass and glassware	China, Czechoslovakia, Poland, USSR	Western Europe (1958...67), North America (1961...66), Australia (1960...66), S.E. Asia (1957...68), the Middle East (1958...66), South America (1958...61)	up to 50%
14. Pottery and fine porcelain	China, Czechoslovakia, E. Germany, Poland	Western Europe, North America, Australia, S.E. Asia, the Middle East (1958...68)	up to 40%

TABLE XVIII—*Continued*

Article Allegedly Dumped	Exporting Socialist Country	Importing Country or Region and the Year(s) of Occurrence[1]	Degree of Price Undercutting Below the Prevailing Level[2]
15. Newsprint and fine paper	China, Czechoslovakia, E. Germany, USSR	Western Europe, Australia, S.E. Asia, the Middle East (1957...65)	up to 40%
16. Furniture	China, Czechoslovakia, Poland, USSR	Western Europe (1958...62), Australia (1961...64), S.E. Asia (1958...66), the Middle East (1960...66)	5–25%
17. Ferrous metals	Czechoslovakia, Poland, USSR	E.E.C. (1960...63)	up to 20%
18. Iron and steel products	China, Czechoslovakia, E. Germany, Poland	Western Europe (1959...63), Japan (1959...66), S.E. Asia (1961...68), the Middle East (1959...68)	up to 30%
19. Zinc	Poland, USSR	Western Europe (1959...63)	up to 20%
20. Bicycles	China, Czechoslovakia, Hungary	Western Europe (1960...65), North America (1959...61), Australia (1962–64), S.E. Asia (1959...66)	up to 40%
21. Sewing machines	China, Czechoslovakia	Western Europe (1960...64), the Middle East (1958...66), S.E. Asia (1958...66)	up to 15%

TABLE XVIII—*Continued*

Article Allegedly Dumped	Exporting Socialist Country	Importing Country or Region and the Year(s) of Occurrence[1]	Degree of Price Undercutting Below the Prevailing Level[2]
22. Machine tools	China, Czechoslovakia, E. Germany, Poland, USSR	Western Europe (1958...68), South Africa (1959-61), Australia (1959...63)	up to 50%
23. Industrial machinery and vehicles	China, Czechoslovakia, E. Germany, Hungary, Poland, USSR	Western Europe (1960...64), the Middle East (1957...68), S.E. Asia (1958...68)	up to 40%
24. Complete industrial plants	China, Czechoslovakia, E. Germany, Hungary, Poland, USSR	Africa, the Middle East, S.E. Asia, Latin America (1957...66)	up to 20%
25. Methylated spirit	China, Poland, USSR	Western Europe, S.E. Asia (1959...65)	up to 20%
26. Various chemicals	China, Czechoslovakia, E. Germany, Hungary, Poland, Rumania, USSR	Western Europe (1958...68), Canada (1960...65) Australia (1961...64)	up to 75%
27. Watches and clocks	China, Czechoslovakia, E. Germany, Hungary, USSR	The Middle East (1959...66), S.E. Asia (1959...66), South America (1960...61)	up to 50%

TABLE XVIII—*Continued*

Article Allegedly Dumped	Exporting Socialist Country	Importing Country or Region and the Year(s) of Occurrence[1]	Degree of Price Undercutting Below the Prevailing Level[2]
28. Optical instruments	Czechoslovakia, E. Germany	Western Europe (1959...62)	up to 20%
29. Photographic equipment	China, E. Germany	Western Europe Canada, S.E. Asia (1962...66)	up to 70%
30. Musical instruments	China	S.E. Asia (1965–68)	up to 75%
31. Honey	China	UK (1967–68)	up to 15%
32. Titanium manufactures	USSR	USA (1967–68)	20%
33. Rapeseed	E. Germany, Poland	UK (1968)	up to 15%
34. Sand boots	China	Australia (1966–68)	up to 50%
35. Alarm clocks	China, Hungary	UK (1967–68)	up to 20%

[1] Including third (Western or Developing) countries where Western suppliers suffered substantial loss of the market. The dates marked with a hyphen (e.g. 1958–59) indicate continuous sales during that period; those with dots (e.g. 1958 . . . 62) denote intermittent sales at dumped prices.

[2] The prevailing price is taken as the base (e.g. £12). Thus 25%, 50%, 75% denote price undercutting amounting to a quarter, a half and three-quarters respectively below the prevailing price, i.e. the actual prices charged (including import duties) being £9, £6 and £3 respectively. 100% would mean that the article is given away free.

Source. Compiled from a variety of official and unofficial daily, periodical and irregular sources published in selected Western, Developing and Socialist countries.

(b) Accusations of 'Disguised Dumping'

In addition to price cutting, Socialist countries have also taken recourse to non-price competition, viz. better credit terms (no or small cash deposits, low interest rates, long periods of repayment), easier methods of payment (local inconvertible currency, barter exchange), early delivery, solid packaging (including useful containers), the provision of experts for the installation of the plant and the training of local operators, and generous commissions and privileges to agents.

Sometimes, Socialist products are of poorer quality so that a lower price is warranted. But buyers may not be able to make quality comparisons and lower prices, even though perfectly justified may, disrupt the market – in a sense Gresham's law operating in a mid-twentieth-century setting, with inferior articles driving out high-quality goods. Complaints have also been made of what may be described as 'component dumping', where some Western firms import low-priced components from the Bloc and thus are in a position to undersell other competing Western producers of the complete article.

(c) The Extent of Injurious Dumping – a Case Study of Australia's Experience

'Unfair' competition, whether through price undercutting below the prevailing levels or offers of other inducements, does not necessarily constitute dumping in its narrow sense, i.e. as defined by GATT. To be of concern to the authorities, dumping must *firstly* involve sales below normal value', and *secondly* it must cause substantial injury to a local industry. Two questions naturally pose themselves in this connection:

(i) What proportion of alleged Socialist dumping cases is in fact injurious to local industries?

(ii) Which countries – Socialist or Capitalist – are greater offenders?

Information on this technical aspect of dumping is not readily available. What we can do in the circumstances is to deal with this problem by sample studies. The two countries selected for the purpose are Australia and the USA. Australia in particular appears to be a suitable case study because she has well developed anti-dumping legislation and the machinery to implement it; she does not impose quantitative restrictions on imports from Socialist (or other) countries; Australian currency is fully convertible to them; and, as well, Socialist goods have to face not only the sensitive local producers but also well-established Western suppliers. Moreover, complete, precise and reliable source material covering a long period is available.

Until import licensing was abolished in 1960, competition from

Socialist imports caused no real concern to Australian industries.[1] However, since that time accusations of dumping have been numerous. Formal dumping complaints lodged with the Department of Customs and Excise (responsible for the administration of the anti-dumping legislation) now average over fifty a year. A notable feature of these complaints is that Socialist countries are charged more frequently than the size of their exports to Australia would justify. Of the total number of 291 separate complaints formally lodged in nearly 5 years (1 April 1961–31 January 1966), 24 were specifically directed against Socialist countries, and 19 others also included Socialist countries in addition to Capitalist nations. Even if we disregard the 19 cases, more than 8% of the complaints were levelled against the Socialist Bloc although it supplied only 1% of Australian imports.

Of the 43 dumping complaints in which Socialist countries were mentioned, chemicals, textiles and paper products appeared most frequently (see Table XIX, p. 156). The number of complaints against each Socialist country was – China: 14, Poland: 14, Czechoslovakia: 13, East Germany: 6, Hungary: 3. Albania, Bulgaria, Mongolia, North Korea, North Vietnam, Rumania and the USSR[2] (whose exports to Australia are insignificant anyway) were never accused of dumping in Australia up to the end of the period under consideration.[3]

Under the Australian anti-dumping set-up, the Government (i.e. the Department of Customs and Excise) cannot normally take anti-dumping action unless it refers the alleged dumping complaint to the Tariff Board (a permanent independent body) and a dumping case is established. The Government finds in practice that most dumping complaints are trivial or otherwise unjustified, and only roughly one in nine is referred to the Tariff Board. In the six-year period, covering 1 April

---

[1] Between 1945 and 1961, although there were several dumping complaints against Socialist countries, upon investigation it was shown that no injury had been caused to Australian industries, so that not one dumping case was officially established over that period (but there were 7 cases of dumping by Capitalist countries during the period in question).

[2] In 1960 the Soviet *Soiuznefteksport* took steps to market oil and products in Australia at up to 15% below the prevailing prices, but owing to the hostile attitude of the oil companies and a lack of co-operation from the Government the attempt failed.

[3] Based on data supplied directly by the Department of Customs and Excise, Canberra.

TABLE XIX AUSTRALIAN DUMPING COMPLAINTS AGAINST THE SOCIALIST BLOC BY COMMODITY GROUPS, 1961–67*

Type of Product	Number of Separate Complaints	Socialist Countries Mentioned
Chemicals	12	Poland, China, E. Germany, Czechoslovakia
Textiles	10	China, Czechoslovakia, E. Germany, Hungary, Poland
Paper and products	7	China, E. Germany, Czechoslovakia
Foodstuffs	2	China, Poland, Czechoslovakia
Gliders	2	Poland, Czechoslovakia
Other products	10	China, Czechoslovakia, Poland, E. Germany
	43	

* Formal complaints as lodged by the affected industries with the Department of Customs and Excise, Canberra, between 1 April 1961 and 31 January 1966, under the new anti-dumping legislation in force since 1 April 1961.

Source. Based on data supplied directly by the Department of Customs and Excise, Canberra.

1961–31 March 1967, the Board established 31 dumping cases, i.e. imported goods were sold in Australia 'below the normal value in the country of export' and 'a not insubstantial injury' was caused to Australian industries.[1]

Of the 31 cases, 8 involved Socialist countries. The relevant details are shown in Table XX, p. 157. Even if we disregard the two cases (of trisodium phosphate dodecahydrate and felt-based floor coverings) in which both Socialist and Capitalist countries were involved, the Socialist Bloc was responsible for 20% of the dumping cases, although it supplied only 1% of Australia's total imports. The value of the Socialist

[1] In 4 other cases, the Tariff Board declared 'no injury'; in one of these (*Phosphorus and Its Derivatives*, 31/1/1964), it was concluded that East Germany had sold tripolyphosphate at about 13% below normal value, but as it did not cause injury to the Australian industry no dumping was established.

goods dumped was $A. 2·8 m. In relation to Australia's total imports from the Bloc over the period, this sum represents a small amount (1·4% of the total). The extent of Socialist subsidization, if we accept the normal values adopted by the Tariff Board (based on values in Capitalist countries with similar production costs, see Section D of this chapter below), was less than $A. 0·8 m. By this token, the degree of 'subsidization' of the dumped articles by the Socialist countries reached on the average 27%.

It is possible that the extent of injurious dumping by Socialist countries was greater than the eight cases suggest. First, until September 1965, importers handling several products could circumvent the legislation by declaring a higher value for duty of the article under

TABLE XX ESTABLISHED CASES OF SOCIALIST DUMPING IN AUSTRALIA, 1961–67[1]

Articles Dumped (Period of dumping in brackets)	Socialist Countries Involved	Degree of Price Undercutting[2]	Total Value of the Article Dumped[3]	Amount of Subsidization Involved[4]
			$A[5]	
1. Woven Cotton Tape (1961–63)	Czechoslovakia	10–40%	20,000	5,000
2. Bicycles (1961–64)	Czechosl., Hungary, Poland	up to 40%	175,000	75,000
3. Trisodium Phosphate Dodecahydrate (1962–64)	China[6]	20–35%	20,000	9,000
4. Hot-Water Bags (1961–65)	Czechoslovakia	40%	69,000	28,000
5. Felt-based Floor Coverings (1964/65)	China[6]	15%	2,700	300
6. Footwear (1962–65)	China, Czechosl.	12–58%	2,000,000	400,000

TABLE XX—*Continued*

7. Men's Dressing Gowns (1963–66)	China	15–65%	168,000	75,000
8. Hoods and Capelines (1963–66)	Czechosl., Hungary, Poland	up to 50%	330,000	150,000
			2,784,700	742,300

[1] As determined by the Tariff Board, Canberra over the period 1/4/1961–31/3/1967.
[2] Percentage by which the article was sold below the 'normal value' (the latter taken as a base) in the Socialist country. The normal values adopted by the Australian authorities (the Department of Customs and Excise and the Tariff Board) were based on 'fair values' in market economies with similar production costs: Woven Cotton Tape – Great Britain; Bicycles – Italy; Trisodium Phosphate Dodecahydrate – France; Hot Water Bags – Great Britain; Felt-based Floor Coverings – Canada and Great Britain; Footwear – Italy; Men's Dressing Gowns – Japan; Hoods and Capelines – Italy.
[3] Valued f.o.b. (because Australia records her imports on this basis).
[4] Assuming the normal values officially adopted for the Socialist countries to be correct.
[5] $A. 1.00 = £0.47 = US $1.12.
[6] Capitalist countries were also involved.

Sources. Based on: Tariff Board Reports, Canberra: *Woven Cotton Tape*, 30/1/1964, pp. 4–5; *Trisodium Phosphate Dodecahydrate*, 12/3/1965, pp. 4–5; *Bicycles*, 25/5/1965, pp. 3–6; *Hot Water Bags*, 21/4/1966, pp. 5–6; *Felt-based Floor Coverings*, 8/8/1966, pp. 4–5; *Footwear*, 12/8/1966, pp. 14–15; *Hoods and Capelines*, 3/11/1966, pp. 4–8; *Men's Dressing Gowns*, 28/11/1966, pp. 3–6. Commonwealth Bureau of Census and Statistics, *Oversea Trade Bulletins* for the years 1960/61 to 1966/67.

dumping suspicion and lower ones for others – a form of evasion that was apparently practised by importers of Chinese textiles.[1] Second, the difficulty of obtaining data of 'normal value' in centrally planned economies may act as a deterrent in lodging complaints with the Department of Customs, and furthermore it is possible that Socialist countries may be given the benefit of the doubt by the authorities in the course of investigation of the complaints lodged (the problem of determining normal value in Socialist countries is discussed in Section D of this chapter). Third, it is not known to what extent other related issues of trade policy are taken into account by the authorities concerned. But

[1] The amendment of the *Customs Tariff (Dumping and Subsidies) Act* in September 1965 has made this practice illegal [by Section 4 (1A)].

CH. 9 §B DUMPING 159

no doubt the Government must weigh possible repercussions of anti-dumping action on exports to the Socialist country concerned.

(*d*) *Experience of Injurious Dumping in Certain Other Western Countries*

In contrast to Australia, experience in the United States has shown that Socialist dumping 'is not a major problem'.[1] Over the period 1954–65, the US Treasury Department made numerous investigations of alleged unfair price undercutting by foreign suppliers. But it was found that only in five cases had Socialist exports been sold in the USA below 'normal value' (in brackets the year in which the complaint was lodged):

(i) Muriate of potash by East Germany (1954).
(ii) Montan wax in crude form by Czechoslovakia (1955).
(iii) Bicycles by Czechoslovakia (1960).
(iv) Sheet glass by Czechoslovakia (1961).
(v) Window glass by the USSR (1964).[2]

These five cases were referred to the US Tariff Commission to determine if local industries suffered injury from this 'unfair' competition.[3] But over this period covering eleven years, the Commission established that the import of only *one* Socialist product caused injury to an American industry.[4] It was the case of the bicycles from Czechoslovakia. In the remaining cases there were no detrimental effects on local producers.[5]

---

[1] US Senate, *East-West Trade*, Hearings before the Committee on Foreign Relations, Part I, March–April 1964, GPO, Washington 1964, pp. 233–34.
[2] US Senate, *A Background Study on East-West Trade*, Prepared for the Committee on Foreign Relations, GPO, Washington, April 1965, pp. 49–50.
[3] The Commission was granted statutory authority in 1954 to make such determinations; that is why the period beginning in that year is taken as a basis for this discussion.
[4] Between 1954 and 1965, the Commission rendered 43 decisions. Of these, injury was established in 7 cases and a 'likelihood of injury' was declared in 2 other cases; of the Capitalist countries involved, only one was a Developing country (and one a Socialist country, see the text further on), the remaining offenders having been Western nations: Australia, Belgium, Canada, Portugal, Sweden and the United Kingdom. In the 34 cases left, 'no injury' determinations were made. For further details see A. C. Coudert, 'The Application of the United States Anti-dumping Law in the Light of a Liberal Trade Policy', *Columbia Law Review*, Feb. 1965, esp. pp. 204–205.
[5] *A Background Study on East-West Trade, op. cit.*, p. 50.

British experience of Socialist dumping appears to have been somewhere between that of Australia and the USA. In 1963 Mr (as he was then) F. Erroll, then President of the Board of Trade, declared: 'In the last few years there have been only a handful of well-founded cases of dumping by Bloc countries, and in these cases the countries concerned have usually agreed to drop the practice complained of when we insisted on their doing so. In this respect their trading record is no worse than that of our closest friends.'[1] In the West German experience, it was pointed out that Socialist dumping, at least recently, was no problem; in fact the danger was greater from Japanese imports.[2] According to a United Nations source, during 1960–63 there were 17 alleged cases of dumping by Czechoslovakia in Western markets, but of these only 3 were ruled by the competent authorities in the countries concerned as dumping which caused injury.[3]

From the limited information available, it is difficult to determine the precise incidence of Socialist dumping in the West as a whole. But it seems that the available data warrant a few generalizations. The difficulties that have arisen in the West have differed widely in extent according to the country and product, and have varied at different times for the same product. So far, Socialist exports have not caused any widespread or lasting market disruptions. In the industrially less developed Western countries, such as Australia, local industries backed up by sympathetic governments are very sensitive to new sources of competition, owing to their infant stage and excess capacity in relation to the limited local market.

On the other hand in the highly industrialized countries, as in the USA, Western Europe and Japan, the well-established and efficient local industries can either easily withstand Socialist competition or (as in many Western European countries) governments reduce the danger by administering quantitative restrictions on sensitive items. The effects of Socialist export drives were quite irritating when they coincided with, and further aggravated, recessions in the competing Western industries, as was the case with Canadian aluminium in

---

[1] F. Erroll, 'East-West Trade in Perspective', *Board of Trade Journal*, 19/4/1963, p. 870.

[2] *Intereconomics*, Hamburg, 1/1967, p. 9.

[3] UNCTAD, *Trade Problems between Countries Having Different Economic and Social Systems*, Doc. E/CONF. 46/34, Geneva, 9/3/1964, p. 37.

1957–58, Australian textiles in 1959–62 and Japanese light industries in 1965–66. The Soviet oil export offensive (1958–62) came at a time when there was already over-production as a result of Saharan developments.

(e) Socialist Dumping in Perspective

Judging by the Western experience so far, the extent as well as the effects of Socialist dumping can easily be, and indeed have been, exaggerated. First of all, the Bloc supplies no more than 4% of Western imports. There is little doubt that the alleged dumping cases have been given an undue amount of publicity in the West, far in excess of the value and repercussions of these transactions. In most cases the amount of goods involved was small and the sales were not repeated.

Although a Socialist country is in a position to practise dumping on a large scale and for long periods, on strictly economic grounds its ability to do so is much more limited than is commonly thought in the West. There is a widespread belief that under central planning costs somehow do not matter. In fact, the Socialist economic system provides no magic short-cut solution to the basic economic problem. Socialist leaders are aware of the competing claims on the limited resources for the improvement of living standards, industralization, defence and foreign aid. To them (unlike to governments and private businessmen in the West) exports are essentially a sacrifice to secure the required imports. Price undercutting is resorted to only when necessary. In view of the continued low consumption levels at home and an acute shortage of foreign exchange, the amount of products that Socialist countries can afford to dump lightheartedly is still extremely limited.

Contrary to what is often thought in the West, Bloc countries are very sensitive to waste. The utmost importance is now attached to cost accounting and export efficiency studies, even though the critieria used may be open to objection by the standards accepted in a market economy (see Ch. 14 B, C). If the high rates of growth are to be maintained, if the long-promised Communist cornucopia is to be made a reality and if the 'peaceful competition' with Capitalist countries is to be won, waste must be avoided. Refuting Western accusations of Soviet dumping, Khrushchev said in 1959: 'By engaging in dumping a country deprives itself of the possibility of accumulating resources for further development and thus deliberately restricts the expansion of its economy.'[1] Market disturbances in the West have not been caused primarily by Socialist actions. Instability of supply and prices is a characteristic feature of a free market mechanism. This instability had existed long before Socialist exports to the West began, and will never be removed completely even if the Bloc turned to complete economic isolation from the Capitalist World.

There is hardly any evidence to suggest that Socialist countries have pursued dumping with a view to driving out local or other competing foreign suppliers or to disrupting markets. There were numerous occasions during the bitter stages of the Cold War when Socialist countries could have played havoc with Western markets for particular products, and yet they did not take advantage of the available opportunities. There is little doubt that their export drive in the West has been prompted almost exclusively by a dire need for foreign exchange. On many occasions Socialist dumping was caused by nothing else but ignorance of local markets and in many instances Socialist suppliers agreed to conform to the prevailing prices and terms of dealings. It is noticeable that Socialist countries now rarely undercut the prices of standardized commodities, the world prices of which are well known. In recent years, their erratic price quotations have mostly applied to manufactures (see Table XVIII, pp. 149–53).

C. PRICE DISCRIMINATION PRACTISED BY SOCIALIST COUNTRIES

In the preceding section, we considered different forms of dumping practised by Socialist countries but we did not specifically refer to price differences. However, price discrimination is also a type of dumping, and it warrants separate treatment.

To demonstrate price discrimination by Bloc countries between domestic and foreign markets is *prima facie* quite easy. It can be done by comparing domestic wholesale prices and the average f.o.b. export

---

[1] Quoted from V. Diatchenko, 'International Trade and Peaceful Co-operation', UNESCO, *International Social Science Journal*, vol. XII, no. 2, 1960, p. 242.

prices obtained.[1] Thus in 1956, the domestic wholesale price of caustic soda in the USSR was 1,500 roubles per ton, but the price charged to Iran was 400 roubles. In the same year, Soviet crude aluminium, priced at 4,800 roubles a ton domestically, was exported to Czechoslovakia for only 1,800 roubles.[2] To illustrate by reference to Poland, in 1965 the domestic wholesale prices and the average export prices obtained, shown in this order in złotys below, were:[3]

coke	700 and 95,
sulphur	1,680 and 142,
caustic soda	2,250 and 361,
benzol	3,500 and 249,
methylated spirit	4,000 and 251,
soda ash	10,250 and 128,
diochromate of soda	15,000 and 831.

The domestic price of trisodium phosphate dodecahydrate in China in 1964 amounted to $A 65 per ton, but the price charged to Australia in the same year was only $A 54.[4][5]

However, if we examine the problem further, it is most difficult to prove that the domestic price in a centrally planned economy is lower or higher than the export price. The official exchange rates do not reflect the purchasing power of the Socialist countries' currencies, and in addition domestic prices are not free market prices and do not reflect all costs

[1] The articles chosen in the examples to follow are those which are standardized and in which quality differences do not exist or are small. If there are quality differences, it is rather a higher grade that would be marketed abroad where – in contrast to Socialist domestic markets – buyers' markets prevail. In effect, the export price may be even lower than implied in the nominal figures.

[2] US Senate, *Foreign Commerce Study*, Hearings before the Committee on Interstate and Foreign Commerce, 5 and 6 May 1960, GPO, Washington 1960, pp. 53, 124.

[3] The domestic prices, in most cases rounded off, were obtained from a variety of official and unofficial sources and they should be treated with caution. The average export prices were taken from Table XXIV, p. 168.

[4] J. Wilczyński, 'Dumping in Sino-Australian Trade', *Economic Record*, Sept. 1966, pp. 404–405.

[5] In the case of the Czechoslovak Skoda 1000 MB car, wholesale prices are not available to the author. Nevertheless, the prices at which the car retailed in different countries in 1966, expressed in US dollars, indicate an interesting relation between the prices charged domestically and in Western markets – in Czechoslovakia: $3,040, in West Germany: $1,195, in Austria: $1,350, in Britain: $1,500 and in Australia: $2,000 (the different prices in Western countries are accounted for by varying rates of import duties, purchase taxes and transport costs). Reported mainly in *Time* (Sth. Pac. edn.), 10/3/1967, p. 68.

anyway. As by the official (commercial) exchange rates Bloc currencies are over-valued, it is easy to show that export prices, particularly those charged in markets with convertible currencies, are lower than the domestic ones. The method of fixing export prices by Socialist countries was clearly described in a Polish textbook on international economics:

> Under these conditions the prices of exported goods are in fact fixed in isolation from domestic prices, viz. in line with world market prices and, when the latter cannot be established, on the basis of the prices charged by competing suppliers from third countries. Generally, under present conditions export prices quoted by Socialist countries are below their domestic equivalents at the official exchange rates. This might suggest that Socialist countries subsidize their exports. Such an assertion would be completely erroneous.[1]

The fact that, at the official exchange rate, Socialist countries charge lower prices for export than for domestic consumption can also be demonstrated by a macro-economic approach, by calculating the subsidies paid by a Socialist country on its exports. This was done in a United Nations enquiry, in which the existence of enormous export subsidies was demonstrated on the example of Hungary and East Germany,[2] and can also be shown from Polish experience.[3]

Tables XXI and XXII represent the price discrimination amongst foreign countries practised by the two leading Bloc exporters, the Soviet Union and Poland, on the example of diesel fuel and black coal. Tables XXIII and XXIV, show the price ranges within which other selected products were sold by these countries in different markets. The prices charged for exports involving small quantities and those (to satisfy Soviet critics) involving long land transport (such as to Afghanistan, China, Iran, Iraq, Mongolia) are omitted. The Tables are based on official statistics published in the countries concerned. Soviet and Polish exports (as in the case of most other countries) are valued f.o.b., or free to the national land frontier. The sample lists include only those products which are reasonably homogeneous; accordingly, most manufactures had to be excluded. But there is no reason to believe that

---

[1] Z. Kamecki, J. Sołdaczuk and W. Sierpiński, *Międzynarodowe stosunki ekonomiczne* (International Economic Relations), PWE, Warsaw 1964, p. 548.
[2] ECE, *Economic Survey of Europe 1957*, Geneva 1958, p. VI – 22–29.
[3] See footnote 4 to Ch. 6 B, p. 97.

TABLE XXI PRICES OBTAINED BY THE USSR FOR DIESEL FUEL EXPORTED TO DIFFERENT COUNTRIES, 1965

Country	Quantity Exported	Average Price Obtained	Percentage of the Average Export Price
	000 tons	Roubles per Ton	%
1. Switzerland	49	8·67	46
2. West Germany	381	11·94	64
3. Belgium	22	13·38	71
4. Argentina	547	14·09	75
5. Japan	645	14·30	76
6. Sweden	278	15·25	81
7. Yugoslavia	31	15·45	82
8. France	411	16·45	88
9. Norway	191	16·57	88
10. India	531	17·05	91
11. Ceylon	250	17·06	91
12. Iceland	243	17·11	91
13. Turkey	45	17·14	91
14. Cuba	208	18·57	99
15. Greece	205	18·66	99
16. Finland	1,581	18·66	99
AVERAGE EXPORT PRICE	—	18·75	100
17. Syria	155	19·97	107
18. Guinea	22	20·81	111
19. Bulgaria	288	23·99	128
20. East Germany	336	25·25	135
21. UAR	18	25·78	137
22. Poland	451	26·79	143
23. Hungary	152	26·84	143
24. Czechoslovakia	16	27·33	146
25. North Korea	175	30·45	162

Source. Based on: Ministry of Foreign Trade of the USSR, *Vneshnaya torgovlya SSSR za 1965 god* (Soviet Foreign Trade in 1965), Moscow 1966.

TABLE XXII PRICES OBTAINED BY POLAND FOR BLACK COAL EXPORTED TO DIFFERENT COUNTRIES, 1965

Country	Quantity Exported	Average Price Obtained	Percentage of the Average Export Price
	000 tons	Foreign-Exchange Złotys per Ton	%
1. Denmark	2,466	23	47
2. Belgium	258	26	52
3. Pakistan	51	26	52
4. Finland	1,817	27	55
5. Netherlands	229	31	62
6. Portugal	181	31	62
7. Switzerland	139	31	63
8. Italy	428	33	66
9. Spain	228	33	67
10. France	469	35	71
11. Bulgaria	2	36	73
12. Ireland	351	41	84
13. Sweden	230	42	85
14. Argentina	140	43	88
15. Greece	70	44	89
16. Norway	31	46	92
17. West Germany	389	46	93
18. Yugoslavia	559	48	97
AVERAGE EXPORT PRICE	—	49	100
19. Cuba	9	53	108
20. Austria	1,505	55	111
21. Rumania	78	55	112
22. Czechoslovakia	1,649	60	122
23. East Germany	2,025	60	122
24. USSR	6,517	62	126
25. Hungary	1,161	65	131

Source. Based on: Central Statistical Office of Poland, *Rocznik statystyki handlu zagranicznego 1965* (Yearbook of Foreign Trade Statistics for 1965), Warsaw 1966.

price discrimination in other products is smaller; in fact in non-standardized articles it is likely to be greater.

It becomes evident from Tables XXI and XXII that the price disparities are quite substantial, and they cannot be explained merely by differences in the terms of dealings (although this element may be present in some cases). Thus the price charged for Soviet diesel fuel to

TABLE XXIII PRICES OBTAINED BY THE USSR FOR SELECTED PRODUCTS EXPORTED TO DIFFERENT COUNTRIES, 1965

Products (In descending order of the total value exported)	Average Export Price	The Price Range	Export Price Range Applying to Western Countries	
	Roubles per Ton		Roubles per Ton	% of the Average Export Price
1. Crude oil	13	8–20	8–12	63–99
2. Black coal	11	4–14	4–14	39–127
3. Pig iron	44	30–144	30–46	68–105
4. Barley	56	51–62	51–62	91–110
5. Aluminium	436	299–503	299–465	69–107
6. Coke	21	15–25	15–17	72–82
7. Anthracite	16	7–23	7–22	42–142
8. Refined sugar	73	54–114	55–83	75–114
9. Zinc	259	217–400	270–330	104–127
10. Maize	56	52–62	52–62	93–111
11. Asbestos	116	60–199	60–199	52–172
12. Lead	244	214–409	250–322	102–132
13. Cellulose	116	89–150	102–109	88–95
14. Newsprint	119	100–127	102–121	85–101
15. Cement	8	7–14	7–10	86–121
16. Benzol	55	45–81	45–50	81–91
17. Sulphur	31	24–40	28–32	88–102
18. Naphthalene	68	48–120	48–61	71–90
19. Soda ash	27	19–32	28–32	104–121
20. Methylated spirit	57	53–68	53–54	92–95

Source. Based on: Ministry of Foreign Trade of the USSR, *Vneshnaya torgovlya SSSR za 1965 god* (Soviet Foreign Trade in 1965), Moscow 1966.

TABLE XXIV PRICES OBTAINED BY POLAND FOR SELECTED
PRODUCTS EXPORTED TO DIFFERENT COUNTRIES, 1965

Products (In descending order of the total value exported)	Average Export Price	The Price Range	Export Price Range Applying to Western Countries	
	Foreign-Exchange Złotys per Ton		Foreign-Exchange Złotys per Ton	% of the Average Export Price
1. Coke	95	36–113	36–82	38–87
2. Refined sugar	274	230–362	238–340	87–125
3. Zinc	985	750–1,570	1,207–1,385	122–141
4. Sulphur	142	94–190	94–190	66–133
5. Potato flour	362	306–419	306–405	85–112
6. Soda ash	128	75–144	75–144	59–113
7. Cement	38	35–54	36–47	95–124
8. Carbide	347	272–367	294–346	85–100
9. Barley	287	270–317	270–304	94–106
10. Casein	2,914	1,553–3,200	1,553–3,165	53–109
11. Zinc white	1,050	753–1,191	753–1,191	72–113
12. Benzol	249	237–358	237–275	95–110
13. Newsprint	459	377–524	421–455	92–99
14. Egg powder	5,568	5,101–7,065	5,101–5,962	92–108
15. Caustic soda	361	256–445	276–405	76–112
16. Colophony	736	663–836	663–757	90–103
17. Methylated spirit	251	228–638	228–310	91–123
18. Rock salt	28	19–60	19–28	66–100
19. Sodium diochromate	831	721–1,000	721–961	87–116
20. Acetic acid	579	466– 750	466– 632	80–109

Source. Based on: Central Statistical Office of Poland, *Rocznik statystyczny handlu zagranicznego 1965* (Yearbook of Foreign Trade Statistics for 1965), Warsaw 1966.

Switzerland in 1965, involving only a small quantity, was a third of the price obtained from Hungary, even though the volume exported to the latter country was more than three times as large; the disparity is even greater when compared with the North Korean price and the quantity involved. The meagre credits that are occasionally extended would not account for such large price differences.

If we further examine Tables XXIII and XXIV, an important conclusion emerges. With some isolated exceptions, Socialist countries tend to charge lower prices to Western nations than to other Socialist or Developing countries.

It must be realized that these Tables understate the degree of price discrimination, because these prices were averaged on a national scale and on an annual basis for each country. To this extent they hide different prices that might have been charged to different buyers from the same country and at different times during the year. Where quality differences do exist, as in manufactures, exports to the highly competitive Western markets have to be of higher quality, thus in effect further accentuating the lower extreme of the price ranges. The fact of price discrimination in Socialist exports is indisputable. Ample evidence has also been provided in various studies explaining (or even in those refuting) exploitation in Soviet Bloc trade,[1] as well as in United Nations sources.[2]

The operational aspect of price discrimination can be explained by the institutional peculiarities under which foreign trade is conducted. A foreign-trade corporation in each Socialist country is a large entity and, as a rule, is vested with a national monopoly of a clearly defined category of exports and imports. It does not have to treat a particular item of export as a commercial proposition, as losses on exports can be

---

[1] E.g., A. Zauberman, *Economic Imperialism: The Lesson of Eastern Europe*, Phoenix House, London 1955; H. Mendershausen, 'The Terms of Soviet-Satellite Trade: A Broadened Analysis', *Rev. of Econ. and Stat.*, May 1960, pp. 152–63; F. D. Holzman, 'Soviet Foreign Trade Pricing and the Question of Discrimination', *Rev. of Econ. and Stat.*, May 1962, pp. 134–47, and 'More on Soviet Bloc Trade Discrimination', *Soviet Studies*, July 1965, pp. 44–65; A. Kutt, *Prices and Balance Sheet in 10 Years of Soviet-Captive Countries Trade 1955–1964*, Assembly of Captive European Nations, New York, March 1966, esp. pp. 18–20.

[2] *Economic Survey of Europe 1957, op. cit.*; 'Ways and Means of Promoting Wider Trade Co-operation among States', *Official Records*, Doc. E/3389, 13/6/1960, pp. 71–72; *World Economic Survey 1962*, Part 1, pp. 107–10.

offset by 'profits' on imports.[1] By virtue of the State planning of prices and the monopoly of State trading, there is practically complete insulation of domestic from foreign prices. Whilst domestic prices are generally set at such levels as to regulate consumption and to provide funds for the State, export prices are geared to the conditions prevailing in particular foreign markets, sometimes at a fixed differential below other competitive suppliers' prices. The loss (by whatever standards) thus sustained can be recovered by the State from the higher domestic price of the same article or other articles – a form of subsidization of exports that can be pursued on a large scale and for long periods.

Furthermore, being a large monopolistic organization, a foreign-trade corporation is in a position to pursue the price policies typical of a discriminating monopoly, treating different foreign importers separately and charging different prices to each according to their elasticity of demand. Thus 'losses' incurred in the more competitive markets may be recouped by charging higher prices where the bargaining power of the corporation is stronger. In fact a corporation is not an ordinary business enterprise guided merely by commercial considerations but a State instrumentality required to implement its government's policy. Losses can be absorbed by the State budget.

It would be incorrect to conclude from the foregoing account that Socialist countries are active discriminators driving hard bargains and exploiting each foreign importer according to the degree of his weakness. The price discrimination rather reflects the weak bargaining position in which Socialist countries usually find themselves when confronted with Western importers operating in highly competitive buyers' markets. The discrimination in the prices of Socialist exports does not tell us the whole story. As a by-product of bilateralism, low export prices may be matched by low import prices, and high prices obtained for exports may be paralleled by high prices of imports (this subject is pursued further in Section E of this chapter below, and in Chs. 10 C, 14 E, pp. 182–83, 203–7, 343).

---

[1] As, by the official exchange rates, Socialist currencies are overvalued, and because the prices of imported goods are not set at their foreign-exchange equivalents but in relation to the domestically produced substitutes (or otherwise arbitrarily), substantial accounting profits are usually made on imports. See Ch. 6 A, B, pp. 91, 97.

D. PROTECTION AGAINST DUMPING ORIGINATING FROM A DIFFERENT ECONOMIC SYSTEM

Marxist writers have traditionally regarded dumping as an inexorable consequence of 'monopoly capitalism' – a product of the 'anarchy of production', an adjunct to imperialism, a vehicle for exporting unemployment and an instrument of the economic domination of underdeveloped countries.[1] But Socialist countries have never complained of Western dumping in the Bloc.

In a Socialist economy the problem of shielding domestic industries against dumping, wherever it originates, hardly exists. Under central planning, the size and composition of imports are largely predetermined in the foreign-trade plan where price differentials are only one of several factors taken into account. If an article has its place in the plan and is available at dumping prices, it will only be snapped up by the importing agency, and its personnel is likely to be rewarded with bonuses for their 'smartness'. If on the other hand, the article is not vital in fulfilling the targets laid down, it will just not be imported, however drastic the price undercutting may be. The question of injury to a domestic industry simply does not arise. The planned structure of imports, the State monopoly of foreign trade and an almost complete insulation of domestic from foreign prices already ensure unqualified protection for home industries, not only against dumping but against any imports not regarded as socially necessary. There is no need for separate anti-dumping legislation, a ministry of customs or a tariff board.

However, it may be observed that the administration of controls on imports from market economies is much more complex than on those from other centrally planned economies. Foreign-trade plans involving other Socialist countries are more definite and agreed in advance. The fulfilment of commitments is reciprocally treated as being of the utmost importance. On the other hand, the uncertainty of imports from

[1] See, e.g., K. Marx, *Capital*, Foreign Languages Publishing House, Moscow 1959, vol. III, pp. 232–33, 563–75; V. I. Lenin, *Collected Works*, FLPH, Moscow 1960, vol. 3, pp. 64–67, 593–95; J. Stalin, *Works*, FLPH, Moscow 1954, vol. 10, pp. 278–87; A. Frumkin, *Vnesh. torg.*, 12/1959, pp. 17–25.

Capitalist countries is much greater, and unexpected favourable turns in prices or other terms of dealings in Western markets may call for a revision of import tactics.

Imports into a market economy are determined in essence by private profit considerations, where price differentials play the key role. Ordinary tariffs are not usually effective to prevent dumped imports, and most Western countries have found it necessary to introduce special anti-dumping legislation. To be effective, the administration of such legislation is difficult enough in application to Capitalist economies, but when imports come from Socialist countries extra difficulties arise. First of all, most Bloc countries do not belong to GATT,[1] and none to IMF, and thus they are not bound by the trading standards or other *ad hoc* obligations undertaken by member countries. Besides, private initiative, aware of the special problems facing the authorities and spurred by the prospects of substantial gains, is constantly at work undermining the official anti-dumping mechanism.

The problem facing the authorities responsible for the administration of anti-dumping legislation in application to goods originating from a centrally planned economy in its ultimate analysis consists in determining what is called in GATT terminology 'normal value', or sometimes described in different countries as 'reasonable price', 'going market price', 'fair market value', 'current domestic value', or 'constructed value'. Of the three alternative criteria of normal value laid down by GATT – production cost in the exporting country, domestic price in the exporting country, and the highest price for export to a third country – the first two are hardly appropriate to a centrally planned economy. The problem stems from two sources. First, there is the difficulty of obtaining information regarding costs and prices. About half the number of Western countries maintain no diplomatic relations with the majority of the Socialist countries, and where there are diplomatic relations permanent trade missions are rare (see Table XXVII, p. 247). Bloc countries are noted for their predilection for secrecy, and travels for businessmen or officials are not made easy. Second, even if such information is obtained, the problem is how to interpret it in terms of the standards accepted in a market economy. In particular,

---

[1] Czechoslovakia and Poland are the only two Bloc countries which are full members of GATT.

there is the justified suspicion that Socialist costs or prices do not fully reflect such factor costs as rent and interest.

The third criterion, the highest price to a third country, is more appropriate and it has been used by the authorities in some Western countries. Its disadvantages, however, are that it has to be obtained from the exporting Socialist country itself; there is no way of checking on what is given and, of course, there may also be the difficulty of interpreting the data. Thus the three GATT criteria for establishing normal value are pretty well useless[1] for the authorities in a Western country confronted with suspected dumping originating from a centrally planned economy.[2]

However, the intensified export drive by Socialist countries in the late 1950s called for a more workable yardstick of 'normal value'. Consequently, some Western countries, such as Australia, Sweden and the United States, decided to introduce a fourth (alternative) criterion specifically applicable to imports from State trading countries, viz. a fair market value in a third country – a market economy with similar production costs.[3] In some Western countries (e.g. in the USA) the normal value so arrived at is referred to as 'constructed value'.

Using this approach in the case of *Printed Cotton Piece Goods* from China in 1958, the Australian Department of Customs and Excise made calculations on the basis of costs in Pakistan, Japan and Hong Kong. It was concluded that the Chinese price was not below normal value, and consequently no dumping was established. On the other hand, on the basis of prices in Italy it was ruled in 1965 that Czechoslovakia, Hungary and Poland had exported bicycles to Australia below normal value, these sales caused injury to local industries, and consequently a case of

---

[1] In fact GATT recognized the need for supplementary criteria, and in the late 1950s an interpretative note was added to provide for the possibility of using other criteria than the three originally embodied in Article VI. See GATT, *Anti-Dumping and Countervailing Duties*, Geneva, July 1958, p. 165.

[2] This was certainly the conclusion to which the Australian Parliament came when considering an amendment of the existing anti-dumping legislation in 1957. The problem was obviously beyond the endurance of the legislators at the time, so that a provision was made in the Act whereby it was simply left to the Minister for Customs and Excise to 'fix such amount as he thinks fit as the cost of production'. Commonwealth of Australia, *Customs Tariff (Industries Preservation) Act*, No. 91 of 1957, Section 5 (5).

[3] For a full text see, e.g., Commonwealth of Australia, *Customs Tariff (Dumping and Subsidies) Act 1961*, Sec. 4 (1) (a), (b), (c), (d).

dumping was declared.¹ Similarly, production costs of woven cotton tape in Britain were taken as appropriate to Czechoslovakia, those of trisodium phosphate dodecahydrate in France to China and those of trypolyphosphate in West Germany as applicable to East Germany.

If it is established that the price is below normal value in the exporting country and if such import causes injury to a local (or a third country's) industry, a corresponding 'dumping duty' (or a 'countervailing duty' if the article is subject to direct subsidization) is imposed. These charges are in addition to ordinary import duties.[2]

An alternative, or additional, method employed by many Western countries (Canada, New Zealand, United Kingdom and most Western European countries) to protect themselves against disruptive dumping by Socialist countries is by the application of quantitative restrictions. This is done either by fixing appropriate import quotas on sensitive items in advance, or by curtailing the import of the product on an *ad hoc* emergency basis. In extreme cases certain items may be almost completely barred; e.g. an American law of 1959 prohibits the use of

---

[1] It may be noted here that in the *Bicycles* case, upon the request of the Australian Tariff Board, the Polish authorities agreed to provide detailed confidential information of production costs and prices in Poland. However, the Board was in doubt about translating the data supplied into categories meaningful in a market economy. Instead, it decided to adopt the Italian normal value as a yardstick. Similarly in the USA, in the case of *Sheet Glass* from Czechoslovakia, Czechoslovak authorities submitted details of production costs to the Treasury Department in 1962. But owing to the difficulty of interpretation, the Department did not accept the evidence provided; instead, on the basis of 'constructed value' it concluded that the Czechoslovak export price was below normal value (however, subsequently the Tariff Commission made a determination of 'no injury' and consequently no dumping case was established). See Tariff Board's Report on *Bicycles*, Canberra, 25/5/1965, p. 5; A. C. Coudert, *op. cit.*, p. 226.

[2] Under Article VI, para. 6 (b) of GATT, provision is made for safeguarding imports from other GATT member countries, which may have discriminatory effects on a Socialist country (Czechoslovakia excepted). Specific provisions for protecting industries in a third country exist in the anti-dumping legislations of Australia, Britain and New Zealand. In Belgium, special duties levied on imports from State trading countries are considered to be countervailing duties. At one stage Switzerland was reported to be administering countervailing duties on imports of textiles from Czechoslovakia, Hungary and Poland, and the proceeds were earmarked for the subsidization of Swiss textiles exported to these countries. In some Western countries, such as Australia and South Africa, no dumping duties are imposed if the difference between normal value and the import price is less than 5%. In Canada, dumping duty cannot exceed 50% of the value of the commodity. See *Anti-Dumping and Countervailing Duties*, esp. pp. 9, 11 and 22.

Federal funds for the purchase of school laboratory equipment originating in any Socialist country as long as these articles are available from other sources, and at one stage the import of Soviet crab meat into the USA was banned (because it was thought that it was produced under slave labour conditions by using Japanese prisoners of war). According to a Socialist source, special Price Control Boards have been established in the Benelux countries and in Switzerland for textile goods originating from Socialist countries.[1]

In recent years Western European countries have removed quota restrictions on most imports from Socialist countries. However, in the bilateral trade agreements it is now usual to insert clauses requiring Socialist countries to sell at 'reasonable prices' so as not to cause 'market disruption' or 'material injury' to local industries. Import licences may be refused if there is a danger of dislocation. Explicit quotas on critical items are still retained.

On several occasions the problem of shielding Western producers against disruptive sales was solved directly on an informal basis. There are known cases of competing Western firms having made direct representations to Socialist authorities whereupon the latter decided to increase their prices or restrict sales. This was exemplified by Soviet aluminium in Britain in 1964 and Polish hand tools in France in 1965.[2] Similarly, it is known from Australian experience that China and Czechoslovakia in particular have been anxious to avoid complaints and have been prepared to increase their prices when necessary.

The methods and determination to protect endangered industries against Socialist dumping have differed from one Western country to another. Except for some attempts under the Organization for European Economic Co-operation over the period 1959–62, little effort has been made in the West on a systematized basis to face Socialist dumping. At different times in the past there were proposals by responsible bodies to establish some sort of machinery under NATO or OECD to co-ordinate Western handling of 'unfair competition' from Socialist countries, but no such specific body was in existence at the time of writing.[3] The problem of anti-dumping action is particularly vexatious

[1] S. Toczek, *Handel zagr.*, 3/1967, p. 110.
[2] *The Economist*, 23/5/1964, p. 861, and 11/12/1965, p. 1,230.
[3] E.g. see US Senate, Committee on the Judiciary, *Problems Raised by the Soviet Oil Offensive*, GPO, Washington 1962, p. 13; European League for Economic Co-

in those Western countries which critically depend on exports of certain key products to the Bloc, such as Australia (wheat, wool), Austria (iron and steel, industrial equipment), Canada (wheat, barley), Finland (engineering products), Greece and Turkey (tobacco and dried fruits), and Iceland and Norway (herrings and whale oil).

E. GAINS FROM DUMPING

(a) Conditions of Gainful Dumping by Western Countries
Systematic under-pricing of exports under private enterprise is a consequence of large-scale production or government intervention. A firm may be faced with decreasing costs on the one hand, and on the other with differences in the elasticity of demand for its products in the domestic and foreign markets. Under such conditions, price discrimination is the most rational course to pursue up to the point where marginal revenue in each market is equated with the combined marginal cost. Thus a firm may find it profitable to sell in foreign markets at prices below its average cost.

To export at less than marginal cost amounts to immediate losses. However, even such a step may still mean gain if the long-run advantages secured (e.g. establishing a foothold in the market, eliminating competing suppliers, getting rid of surpluses for fear of spoiling the domestic market) outweigh the short-run losses. The existence of import duties reduces the possibility of re-imports.[1]

The gain considered above is of private benefit to the producers.

---

operation, *East-West Commercial Relations*, Brussels 1965, p. 61; Political and Economic Planning, 'East-West Trade', *Planning*, London, May 1965, p. 172; US Committee for Economic Development, European Committee for Economic and Social Progress, Japan Committee for Economic Development, *East-West Trade – A Common Policy for the West*, New York, May 1965, pp. 26–27.

[1] Socialist economists see a clear causal connection between big-business, protection and dumping by Western countries. It is pointed out that: 'Import duties have been evolved into a powerful accomplice in the [Western] export drive; from a defensive tool originally employed by less developed economies, they have been transformed into a weapon of economic offensive in the hands of highly developed Capitalist countries.' See Z. Kamecki *et al.*, *op. cit.*, p. 32.

CH. 9 §E DUMPING

Whether selling abroad below domestic prices increases or decreases the country's social benefit will depend on several circumstances. If the firm is operating under decreasing marginal cost, to maximize profits, it will reduce the domestic price (unless the elasticity of demand is zero) until the marginal revenue is equal to the marginal cost. In this case dumping increases both private and social benefit in the exporting country. But under increasing marginal cost conditions, the domestic price is likely to rise and the social benefit from dumping may fall below private benefit unless increased employment and external economies are sufficient to compensate for the apparent loss. The apparent social loss may also be compensated for by correspondingly low import prices (for example as a consequence of barter operations).

Under normal conditions, agriculture can hardly match the ability of manufacturing industries to pursue dumping, on account of its small-scale production and a lack of monopoly power. However, for a variety of reasons in most Western countries agriculture receives government support through various marketing schemes and even direct subsidization, which may make dumping possible.

Dumping of surplus agricultural products (i.e. in relation to the high domestic prices) is justified only if social gains, deriving from internal and external economies, social stability, etc., at least outweigh the apparent financial losses associated with the higher domestic price and/or direct subsidization.

In general, value judgments made by governments are considered to approximate social benefit closer than if made by private firms. But just how much governments in political democracies are genuinely guided by the society's benefit, as distinct from the sectional interests of shrewd pressure groups, is a question for speculation. Dumping made possible by government intervention may still mean social loss if it is done merely to court the floating rural vote.

Judging by Australia's experience, most of the Western wheat exports to the Bloc since 1960 have been made at prices not only below official domestic costs and prices but also below the prices charged to other Capitalist countries. This can be partly explained by the fact that these exports have been large windfall sales on a marginal market. The commercial wheat market in the Capitalist World being saturated, the wheat exporters were faced with the bogey of mounting surpluses and vexatious storage problems. Selling large quantities at lower prices appeared preferable to accumulating embarrassing stocks. In retrospect, this was probably the wise thing to do, as otherwise the world prices of wheat might have slumped to well below the prices obtained from Socialist countries. In this way, the dumping sales to the Bloc have perhaps, on balance, increased Western social benefit. However, the author doubts if the sales by the Western wheat boards, with the tacit approval of their governments, were based on carefully reasoned plans. Rather, the authorities have been doing the right things for reasons of doubtful validity, and stumbling each year from one *ad hoc* decision to another, mindful of the floating farmers' vote at the next elections.

(b) *Gains from Dumping under Socialism*

What conditions prevailing in the Bloc may make dumping gainful to Socialist countries? These can be summed up as follows: genuine low costs of production in certain industries, the peculiar treatment of certain factor costs, social cost-benefit considerations, bilateralism, disequilibrium exchange rates and errors of judgment. We shall now analyse each of these conditions in turn.

Many Westerners who are prone to lay indiscriminate charges of Socialist dumping seem to be unaware of the far-reaching economic developments that have taken place under Communist regimes. In these developments are included many branches of industries which (not unnaturally) have come to be most active in export trade – such as iron and steel, engineering, textile, chemical and woodworking industries. In many cases, these industries have the advantage of an ample supply of local raw materials, as for example iron ore (USSR, China), coal (USSR, Poland, China), cotton (USSR, China), flax (USSR, Poland, China), oil (USSR, Rumania, China), salt (USSR, Poland, Hungary, Rumania, China) and timber (USSR, Poland, Rumania, Czechoslovakia).

As the industrial developments in the Bloc are relatively recent, many Socialist countries – like any industrial late-comers – have been in a position to dodge some costs, profiting by Western achievements and mistakes. Bloc countries have also been less extravagant in the proliferation of models, and it is claimed that Socialist countries have had greater success in reducing costs through a consistent policy of rationalization and standardization of products and processes.¹ Largely for this purpose, the CMEA countries established two Permanent Commissions for Economic Questions in 1958 (one if its Working Parties is responsible for 'Investment Efficiency') and for Co-ordination of Scientific and Technical Research in 1962; in addition, in 1963 the Institute of Standardization was set up.² Most Socialist countries can derive substantial economies of scale owing to the large domestic market, further enhanced by assured sales in the CMEA, or perhaps the whole Bloc, market.

As centrally planned economies of the collectivist type, Socialist countries can claim cost advantages because interest, rent and profit do not enter the cost of production to the same extent as in a private enterprise economy. The prices of capital goods are relatively low, and either there is no capital charge or otherwise in the countries where it has been introduced (Bulgaria, Czechoslovakia, East Germany, Hungary, Poland, Rumania, USSR) it is still low as compared with the practice under free enterprise.³ Interest rates on bank loans, where they are charged, are roughly half the rates prevailing in the West (2–3% as compared with 5–7% p.a.). Natural resources (farming land, forests, minerals, business sites), with some notable exceptions, are State or collectively owned. Their use is not necessarily reflected in production costs in the form of rent indicating productivity differentials. Profit, even though it is receiving increasing recognition in most Bloc countries, is considered as essentially an indicator of performance by an enterprise, not necessarily as cost. Under the planned direction of resources, the 'normal

---

¹ See, e.g., J. Kołacz and K. Barakan, *Handel zagr.*, 7/1963, pp. 284–90; Hu Ma, 'Standardization', *K'o-hsueh Ta-chung* (Popular Science), Peking, 5/3/1962 (translation in: American Consulate General in Hong Kong, *Selections from China Mainland Magazines*, 9/4/1962, pp. 10–15).

² It was reported that in 1964–65 there were more than 700 designing bureaux under CMEA jointly elaborating solutions to over 40 crucial problems of interest to all member countries. See S. Yovczuk, *International Affairs*, Moscow, 11/1966, esp. p. 112.

³ Contrary to the Soviet and Eastern European practice in the past, China has not deliberately pursued a policy of depressing the prices of producers' goods in relation to consumers' goods. This has been prompted by a desire to avoid unwarranted subsidization of producers' goods and their substitution for the abundant cheap labour. See S. H. Chou, 'Prices in Communist China', *Journal of Asian Studies*, August 1966, esp. p. 656.

profit' mark-up is not needed to keep a particular enterprise in the industry. Furthermore, in State enterprises no mark-up is necessary for 'structural risk', i.e. compensation for uncertainty caused by the actions of the competing firms in the industry.

Bloc countries can also claim low production costs when it comes to certain labour-intensive articles, such as clothing, embroidered textiles, haberdashery, hardware, handicrafts, fancy goods, etc. China, of course, has an unquestionable advantage in several of these lines. A Chinese economic journal revealed that in 1957 labour costs in the State-operated cotton mills in Shanghai (the leading textile centre producing for export) constituted 8% of the value of output (35% of the value added).[1] At the same time (1957/58) the corresponding proportion in the Australian cotton mills was over 20% (over 52% of the value added).[2] Similarly, in 1965 in the Polish cement industry labour costs represented 10% whilst in the USA the proportion was more than 30%.[3] Wages in the Bloc countries are set by the State with a view to ensuring desired capital accumulation. There is also a variety of non-material incentives (medals, certificates, emulation campaigns, etc.) which lead to increased production at no extra cost to the producing enterprises.[4] In this respect China can probably outdo all other Socialist countries. The view sometimes expressed in the West that the marginal cost of labour in China approaches zero finds support in Australia's trade experience.[5]

---

[1] Ch'in Liu-fang, 'A Preliminary Analysis of Cotton Yarn Price in Our Country', *Chin-chi Yen-chiu* (Economic Research), Peking, 7/12/1959 (translation in: American Consulate General in Hong Kong, *Extracts from China Mainland Magazines*, 7/3/1960, p. 7).

[2] Commonwealth Bureau of Census and Statistics, *Manufacturing Industries 1957/58*, no. 10 *Cotton Mills*, Canberra, p. 3.

[3] Based on: J. Porowski, 'The Export of Polish Cement 1945-1966', *Cement-Wapno-Gips* (Cement-Lime-Gypsum), Warsaw, 12/1966, pp. 363-66 (translation in: US Dept. of Commerce, Joint Publications Resarch Service, *Translations on East European Foreign Trade*, 24/4/1967, esp. p. 15); US Dept. of Commerce, *Statistical Abstract of the United States 1966*, Washington 1966, pp. 701, 771.

[4] However, according to Socialist economists material incentives paid to foreign-trade corporations and domestic enterprises producing for export are not export subsidies, as their operation is different from that in Capitalist countries. The aim of Socialist incentive payments is not to lower but to secure the highest possible price, as the size of the bonuses depends on the difference between domestic costs of production and the export prices obtained. See Z. Kamecki *et al., op. cit.*, pp. 549-50.

[5] For example, it was testified in evidence before the Australian Tariff Board that, 'It is quite common for China to quote *exactly the same price* for piece goods and the

Another fact which may explain the low production costs of certain articles is the low procurement prices paid by the State to peasants for deliveries of foodstuffs and of such industrial raw materials as cotton, flax, hemp, silk, sugar beet (or sugar cane) and oil seeds.[1] This naturally lowers the nominal cost of production to the State of such exportables whether in crude or manufactured form.

Under private enterprise the ultimate rationale for exports is obscured by independent micro-economic decisions. But in a planned economy with a high degree of centralization of decision-making, exports are naturally treated in terms of macro-economic values instead of individual advantage. The social cost of the items exported is compared with the social value attached to the imports, and this is viewed not only by reference to static short-term commercial considerations, but also in terms of long-run economic, political, ideological and military objectives. Economic effort in the Socialist Bloc is directed towards attaining the maximum feasible rates of growth. Thus the meeting of targets set in the plan becomes all-important and the necessary imports must be secured at almost any cost to avoid a whole chain of reaction of non-fulfilment and the upsetting of the plan. An export that may appear a loss by private cost-benefit valuation may still be socially gainful by the criteria meaningful to the top policy makers. 'Capitalist countries', pointed out the Vice-chairman of China's State Planning Commission, 'have economic accounting only for enterprises but not for the entire

---

made-up article. . . . This indicates that China is prepared to export at prices which *contain no cost whatsoever* for making-up labour. We would like to emphasize that such quotations are *common and normal*. They do not occur only occasionally.' (Emphasis in the original.) Commonwealth of Australia, *Tariff Board Inquiry Re Pillow Cases*, Official Transcript of Proceedings, Canberra, 24/1/1963, pp. 65 and 74. Also see E. P. Reubens, 'Under-employment Theory and Chinese Communist Experience', *Asian Survey*, Dec. 1964, pp. 1,191–1,204.

[1] For example, the procurement and free market prices of certain grains in Poland in 1965 (in złotys per quintal) were:

	Compulsory delivery	Above the compulsory delivery	Free market
Barley	236	374	373
Oats	151	268	365
Rye	176	282	347
Wheat	229	379	442

Central Statistical Office of Poland, *Rocznik statystyczny 1966* (Statistical Yearbook 1966), Warsaw 1966, pp. 299–300.

economy.'[1] Establishing a foothold in a foreign market in competition with Western suppliers could also be justified on these grounds.

Exports may also be sold at dumping prices if import prices in the same market (or on the same barter deal) are correspondingly low, so that in effect the terms of trade to the Socialist country may still be quite satisfactory and comparable with those prevailing in world trade. However, a bargain operation of this type does not represent a complete picture. In such cases of what might be called 'reciprocal dumping', although the transaction may be gainful to each trading partner in the micro-economic sense, the gains from trade are not maximized owing to the misallocation of resources, i.e. the fact that they are not allocated in accordance with the equimarginal principle in each partner country.

An interesting peculiarity of Socialist dumping, also a consequence of bilateralism, is 'indirect dumping'. Occasionally a Bloc country may re-export a commodity at a lower price than that paid in the first instance when it was imported. A Socialist country may find it necessary to accept an article which it does not need itself but which may be the only one its partner – especially another Bloc member or a Developing country – can pay with. Thus in 1965 the USSR paid Poland 14 roubles per ton of black coal but charged Denmark only 5 roubles per ton.[2] In 1964 Poland paid 539 foreign exchange złotys per ton of *raw* sugar from Cuba, but the f.o.b. export price charged to Sweden in the same year was only 347 foreign exchange złotys per ton of *refined* sugar.[3] Similarly, in 1957–58 the Soviet Union dumped tin in Western Europe at lower prices than those paid to China in the first instance in spite of high additional transport costs; and before that she had been re-selling Argentine hides, Brazilian cocoa, Egyptian cotton and Indonesian rubber in the West for lower prices than those paid in the first place.[4]

---

[1] Hsueh Mu-ch'ao, 'On Socialist Economic Accounting', *Hung-ch'i* (Red Flag), 1/12/1961 (translation in: *SCMM*, 18/12/1961, p. 11). For further details also see, Pien Ching-chung, 'That Price Must Be Based on Social Value', *Chin-chi Yen-chiu*, 17/3/1963 (translation in: *SCMM*, 6/5/1963, pp. 1–8); W. Sztyber, *Gospodarka planowa* (Planned Economy), Warsaw, 8–9/1964, pp. 85–89.

[2] Based on: Ministry of Foreign Trade of the USSR, *Vneshnaya torgovlya SSSR za 1965 god* (Soviet Foreign Trade in 1965), Moscow 1966, pp. 162, 183.

[3] Based on: Central Statistical Office of Poland, *Rocznik statystyki handlu zagranicznego 1965* (Yearbook of Foreign Trade Statistics for 1965), Warsaw 1966, p. 116.

[4] However, since that time Socialist countries have been prepared to refrain from re-exporting goods without the consent of the parties (or governments) involved. Clauses to this effect are now often inserted in trade agreements or contracts.

To determine whether such operations are gainful to the Bloc country concerned is not an easy task. Socialist countries usually trade with each other and many Developing nations on the basis of long-term trade agreements where the negotiated prices remain fixed for long periods, whilst world market prices (at which sales are generally made to Western countries) may be sometimes below and at other times above the agreement prices. If in addition non-commercial considerations are taken into account, such apparently anomalous transactions may still prove gainful in the context of the long-run period as a whole.

A related case of dumping may be a product of clearing balances bought at a discount. For example, a French importing house may buy a depreciated clearing balance earned by a Dutch exporter to the USSR (which of course can be spent only in the latter country). The discount may range up to 50%, although in most cases now it is about 5%. Thus in effect the cost of the import from the USSR could turn out to be quite low to the French importer.[1] In such cases, the loser is either the reseller of the clearing balance (the Dutch exporter), or more likely: the Socialist country (the USSR) which may have to pay higher prices for its imports – e.g. the Dutch firm is likely to charge the Russians a mark-up price in the first instance.

Dumping in the form of price discrimination may simply reflect the different degrees of attractiveness of different foreign currencies from the point of view of the Bloc country concerned, as well as the varying incidence of the partner countries' import or export controls. And yet such differences may not be indicated in the official exchange rates. Thus, charging lower prices to certain Western countries may be justified on account of the full convertibility of the earnings and the easier access to such markets (see Tables XXI and XXII, pp. 165 and 166). This evaluation is now done on a systematic basis in those Socialist countries which carry on foreign-trade efficiency studies [see Ch. 14, esp. sec. B(e), pp. 322–24].

Some dumping cases must, no doubt, result from errors of judgment. Unexpectedly good harvests, exceeded production targets, or simply

---

[1] The value of such switch operations has been recently increasing by about 15% p.a. An unofficial estimate for Western Europe places them at about $500 m. annually. For further details see *The Economist*, 14/1/1967, pp. 143–44.

mistakes in planning may lead to surpluses which cannot easily be disposed of (or are not allowed to be) in the domestic market. The planners treat market economies as a cushion to absorb such surpluses at any price, particularly if targets in other sectors are not reached and they must be made good by imports. Dumping in such cases may still be gainful in the sense that long-run losses to the Socialist economy may be minimized. Sometimes it may be expedient for a foreign-trade corporation to offer price discounts on its exports in order to meet the agreed import bill, avoid penalties abroad provided for in the trade protocol and earn bonuses at home for plan fulfilment.

Socialist exports may also be under-priced simply as a result of the pricing confusion that still prevails in all Bloc countries. One also wonders to what extent dumping in Capitalist markets may simply be due to the sheer incompetence of the officials concerned, whether in establishing domestic costs or in quoting foolishly low prices in foreign markets.[1] The Bloc countries have never been great world traders, and under central planning their intercourse with the Capitalist World has been severely restricted. The rising volume and diversification of their exports are bound to increase further the element of irregularity. In such cases, Western buyers are likely to be the beneficiaries at the expense of the Socialist exporting country and perhaps the domestic and foreign competing suppliers.

It may thus be concluded that for several reasons Socialist countries may find it expedient to under-sell competing Capitalist producers. They may be in a position to do so by virtue of genuine low production costs made possible by the availability of abundant cheap raw materials, rapid industrialization, rationalization and the economies of scale. These cost advantages are genuine even by the criteria accepted in a market economy. Certain other advantages deriving from the peculiar treatment of interest, rent and profit, from the existence of disequilibrium exchange rates and from errors of judgment, may be regarded as legitimate in the context of central planning of the collectivist type, although

---

[1] At a Conference on Export of Agricultural Food Products held in Poznan in 1964, a Polish expert demonstrated a high degree of negative correlation between world prices of sugar and the volume of sugar exports from Poland. The reasons given were ignorance of world market conditions and the fact that Poland had hardly any regular customers. *Handel zagr.*, 2/1965, p. 65.

CH. 9 §E DUMPING 185

unwarranted from the standpoint of a free enterprise economy. On the other hand, the legitimacy of the practices arising out of bilateralism, non-commercial motives and ignorance can be disputed on several obvious grounds. The question of low labour costs is more complex. Low wages prevailing in an economy are not a proof of dumping. For many Socialist countries, China in particular, labour is the relatively abundant factor, and the consequent low wages give them a comparative advantage in labour-intensive products. But, to what extent are the low labour costs genuine under Communist regimes? Should one accept their 'rational wage policies', the non-financial rewards to workers, as well as the more or less compulsory unpaid services extracted from certain groups of people as being consistent with genuine low labour costs? Under the present political system, the function of trade unions is not so much to protect the worker but rather to implement the policy of the government.

(c) Dumping and Domestic Shortages

It is rather paradoxical but nevertheless true that dumping of a particular article may take place in East-West trade whilst there are shortages in the exporting country's domestic market. In fact dumping is likely to cause such shortages. When a Western producer (or marketing board) is in a monopolistic position in the home market and faces inelastic demand, and less elastic than in the Socialist Bloc, it will pay him to restrict domestic sales to force an increase in the price above that charged to a Socialist buyer. By restricting domestic, in favour of foreign, sales a discriminating monopolist may maximize his total profits.

A similar policy can be adopted by Socialist countries – in fact on a more ruthless basis – by fixing the quantities and prices for the domestic markets by planners' directives. Thus the Soviet dumping of grains in 1932–33 was carried on in Western markets in spite of the disastrous famine at home, which cost the country more than 5 million lives.[1] Similarly, Czechoslovak high-grade textiles, certain Hungarian pharmaceuticals, Polish meats and Rumanian nuts have been dumped at one time

[1] Dana Dalrymple, 'The Soviet Famine of 1932–34', *Soviet Studies*, Jan. 1964, pp. 259, 271.

or another in the West in spite of domestic shortages, and Chinese textiles and rice in the face of rationing at home.

(d) Benefits from Dumping Accruing to the Importing Countries

Whilst dumping may be injurious to competing producers, it can normally be expected to bring benefits to the buyers in the importing country. However, when it comes to dumping in East-West trade, the benefit to buyers does not necessarily follow.

Buyers of the dumped goods are more likely to reap benefit in the West than those in Socialist countries. Not only are the dumped Socialist goods likely to be sold at low prices but, to counter the inroads of Socialist competition, other competing suppliers may respond by charging more reasonable prices. However, as experience proves in many Western countries, the lower prices of Socialist goods are not necessarily passed on to the end-user. For several reasons, the importers or retailers may prefer to gear their prices to those prevailing in the domestic market and pocket abnormal profits themselves. Sometimes they are forced to do this under the threats of being blacklisted as 'Communist agents'. Undue adverse publicity may also deter the public from taking advantage of the available Socialist bargains. Preliminary investigations and temporary dumping duties, even if the authorities subsequently establish no case of dumping, are often sufficient to act as a deterrent. There are numerous examples of Western suppliers increasing their prices as soon as Socialist competition is removed.

In Socialist countries, the prices of imported goods are not set at their foreign-exchange equivalents, but at levels in relation to the prices of domestically produced goods or their substitutes. If the 'dumped' imports are consumer goods, their quantity is likely to be limited and thus they will normally carry heavy turnover taxes to adjust the demand in the retail market to the available supply. However, there is no doubt of the benefit accruing to society in a broader sense, viz. a saving of foreign exchange, an increase in the State's revenues and a reduction in the demand pressure on the domestically produced articles.

F. WEAKNESSES IN THE ANTI-DUMPING ARRANGEMENTS IN EAST-WEST TRADE

Anti-dumping arrangements, like other weapons of protection, tend to favour the interests of the industries concerned at the expense of the users. In Capitalist countries producers represent more organized and active groups than consumers. In Socialist countries the planned industrialization drive presupposes giving priority to industries rather than to consumers. Thus under each system, the preoccupation of the authorities is with the injury to the existing industry, or one to be established, whilst the detriment to the consumer, caused by withholding low-priced imports, receives only residual attention.

There are no internationally acceptable criteria by which to judge detriment to the domestic industry. The decision in Western countries as to what constitutes 'material injury', or 'socially undesirable imports' in Socialist countries, must be largely arbitrary.[1] Neither Western nor Socialist countries provide for possibilities of appeal against their decisions.

From the macro-economic point of view dumping is harmful only if it is temporary or occurring intermittently. In such cases, the offending foreign exporter either aims to drive out the competing producers in order to exercise monopoly power later, or otherwise he unintentionally causes the temporary or recurrent closing down of a domestic industry competing with the imported article, or relying on it as an input. Western exporters cannot, of course, pursue these forms of dumping in Socialist countries where the flow of imports is centrally planned and controlled. There is hardly any evidence of this type of price undercutting by Socialist countries in the West, and it appears that they are, at least on principle, against this kind of dumping.[2]

However, if low-priced imports continue, no anti-dumping action is justified. It should make no difference how the cheapness is caused –

[1] In the case of one Western country (the USA) injury is not essential, mere subsidization in the exporting country is sufficient to justify the imposition of countervailing duties. See GATT, Report of Group of Experts, *Anti-Dumping and Countervailing Duties*, Geneva 1961, esp. p. 21.

[2] See, for example, Soviet assurances to this effect: United Nations, *World Economic Survey 1958*, New York 1959, p. 165; V. Diatchenko, 'International Trade and Peaceful Co-operation', UNESCO, *Int. Soc. Sc. Jour.*, vol. XII, no. 2, 1960, p. 242.

be it by abundant capital, entrepreneurial ingenuity and advanced technology, or by cheap labour, the disregard of certain costs and sheer stupidity in fixing low export prices. These reasons merely explain why a particular economy may have a comparative advantage in some products. The fact that an industry in the importing country suffers injury indicates that in the interest of the maximization of production from a given batch of resources, such producers should transfer their resources to some other industry where their comparative disadvantage is less. The ability to obtain cheap articles from imports ('indirect production') is the very – and the only valid economic – justification for international trade. If there is a loser at all, it is rather the exporting, not the importing, country.

Trade is the more gainful to a country the higher its export prices and the lower the prices it pays for its imports. It is amazing that this simple truth is lost in the muddle of the East-West dumping controversy. The absurdity of the farcical dumping and anti-dumping game is particularly obvious on the part of certain Western nations which subsidize Socialist wheat consumption at the expense of their own consumers and taxpayers and which at the same time, in effect, impel Socialist countries to charge higher prices for certain 'sensitive' items exported to the West.

Anti-dumping machinery in Western countries is, on the whole, more preoccupied with low costs in the exporting countries than with high costs in the domestic industries affected. To the writer's knowledge, no explicit distinction is made in the Western countries' anti-dumping legislations between intermittent and continuous dumping. In the Socialist Bloc, generally speaking, the law of comparative costs is not accepted as the basis for international trade (see Ch. 4 C). In a limited sense, the principle of comparative advantage in foreign trade has been receiving increasing recognition in the past decade, as is reflected in the foreign-trade efficiency calculations. However, the efficiency indices used have been devised and applied mostly to determine the optimum structure of *exports*. Their application to define the most gainful size and structure of imports is still in its infancy (see Ch. 14 B). It is unlikely that advantage would be taken of 'luxury' consumer goods, however cheap and however reliable their continuous supply might be.

In attempting to appraise the Western anti-dumping arrangements a

CH. 9 §F DUMPING   189

fundamental question arises: by whose standards is 'normal value' to be judged – by those accepted under free enterprise or those prevailing under central planning? Whether the present practices in the West, based largely on the rules of GATT, are appropriate to imports from centrally planned economies, is questionable. Socialist countries could point out that GATT is a mouthpiece of the developed market economies and its members are not favourably disposed to central planning of the collectivist type. To establish normal value for a centrally planned economy by adopting production costs in a third (i.e. a Capitalist) country as a yardstick is a convenient expedient, in essence probably unfair to a Bloc country. Such obvious advantages, which most Socialist countries enjoy, as a plentiful supply of raw materials, substantial economies of scale, low labour costs and certain advantages deriving from central planning and the socialization of the means of production, are ignored. It is a pity that owing to this approach these undoubted advantages cannot easily be passed on to the West through trade.

At the same time, it must be pointed out that Socialist countries do not take full advantage of foreign-trade opportunities with the West either. They have no clearly identifiable criteria for decision-making. So much depends on the judgment of top policy makers, and when they make errors the resulting losses, or missed gains, are likely to be on a large scale.

When low-priced imports originate in a different economic system, the complexity and uncertainty add to mutual suspicion. Although this anxiety can probably never be eliminated from East-West trade, it seems that long-term trade agreements could relieve it to a degree.[1] Admittedly, much of East-West trade is already covered by fairly long agreements (about three years), but they are considered by both sides as vague intentions rather than firm commitments to be honoured or to be relied upon. If, instead, the prevailing practice of the fairly firm annual trade protocols were placed on a long-term basis (say, five

[1] Such proposals have occasionally been made in several Western and Socialist countries. For example see East-West Trade Group, *Expansion of East-West Trade*, London, July 1963, esp. p. 39; United Nations, *Proceedings of the United Nations Conference on Trade and Development*, Geneva March–June 1964, New York 1964, vol. VI, p. 141; resolution passed at the Tenth East-West Round Table Conference, held in Belgrade in June 1965, reported in *East-West Commerce*, London, 1/10/1965, p. 14.

years), they could promote greater continuity and confidence in East-West trade.

In such an agreement, the Western country should guarantee not to arbitrarily block imports from the Socialist country by a unilateral decision where the Socialist exporter has no means of redress. On the other hand, the Socialist partner country should undertake not to pursue intermittent dumping likely to cause injury to an industry in the importing Western country. Furthermore, instead of treating trade with the West as of residual significance, Socialist countries ought to assign due importance to it in their economic plans.

At the same time, Capitalist countries should actively welcome Bloc nations participating in long-term international commodity agreements. Socialist countries, like Developing nations but in contrast to some Western countries, are favourably disposed to such agreements because stability of prices and orderliness of marketing conveniently fit into central planning. One wonders if, after all, long-range planning on each side is not the ultimate answer to an orderly course of East-West trade in the future.

In due time, with the benefit of the long-term bilateral experience, a more determined effort should be made, ideally under the auspices of the United Nations, to work out a code of fair and reasonable practices acceptable to both sides on a multilateral basis. Such a code would then be automatically regarded as part of East-West trade agreements, and perhaps one day it might be included in the charter of the proposed International Trade Organization.

10 Payments and Finance

A. TRADE AND PAYMENT FLOWS

DIAGRAM B, on p. 192, shows the flow of trade between the Socialist Bloc on the one hand and major areas in the West and in the Developing World on the other. Although Socialist countries are noted for their preference for bilateral balancing of trade, this is not necessarily the case in reality, even if the Bloc's trade with major areas is considered.

The Bloc earns the largest surpluses with Developing Asia (i.e. Japan and the four Socialist countries excluded) and with the European Free Trade Area. Apart from the EEC, the largest deficits are incurred in trade with Canada and with Australia, chiefly on account of large wheat purchases. In the Bloc's trade with the Capitalist World, different countries of the Sterling Area play an important complementary part. The CMEA group regularly earns substantial trade surpluses from the United Kingdom (see Diag. C, p. 193) and China from Hong Kong.[1] However, the Socialist Bloc incurs considerable trade deficits with Malaya, Australia and New Zealand. Thus roughly one-third of trade earnings from the United Kingdom is spent on imports of rubber and tin from Malaya, wheat from Australia and wool from Australia and New Zealand. In fact the Bloc usually earns an overall trade surplus with the Sterling Area. In the past this well established pattern of trade was quite satisfactory from the British point of view. The United Kingdom earned trade surpluses with Malaysia, Australia and New Zealand. This flow of trade through London brought Britain handsome earnings on invisible account – income from financial, insurance, forwarding, transport and other services.

---

[1] One-third of China's earnings of foreign exchange from the Capitalist world comes from Hong Kong. In the late 1960s the net trade balance (allowing for re-exports) averaged £100 m. annually, plus nearly £50 m. from remittances, investments, water sales and various services.

Diag. B. Flow of Trade between the Socialist Bloc and Major Areas of the World

Annual Averages of Exports and Imports in US $ Millions, 1966–1967

The size of the Areas shown is in proportion to the Bloc's trade turnover with them (stated in brackets).
The Bloc's trade balance with each Area is indicated within arrows.

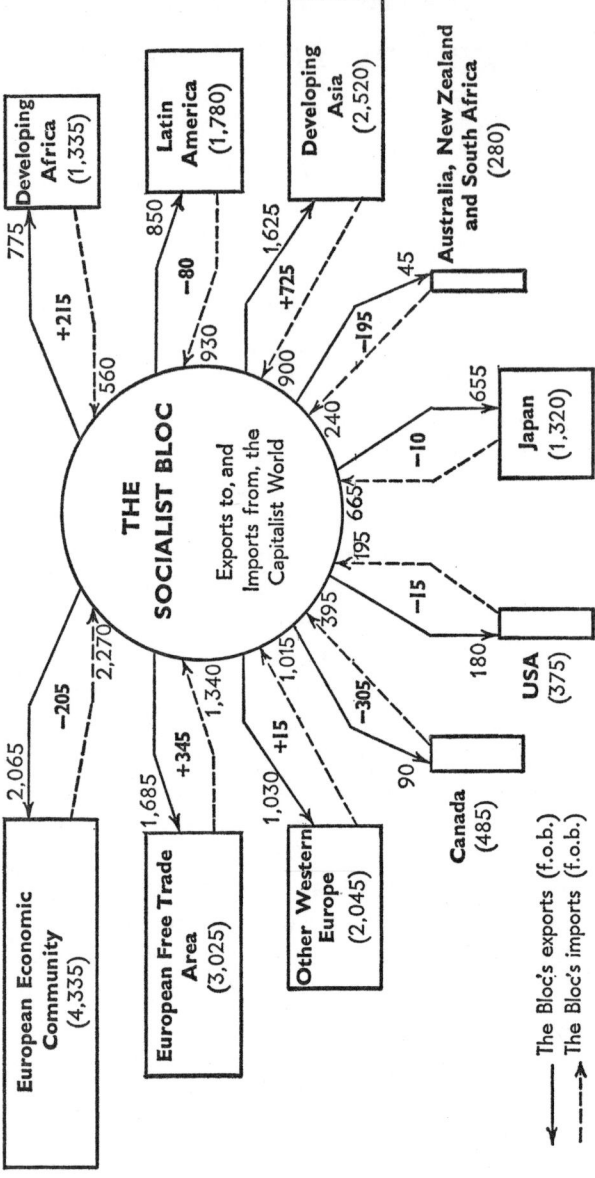

Source. Based on: United Nations *Monthly Bulletin of Statistics*, June 1968, pp. xii–xv.

Diag. C. Flow of Trade between the United Kingdom, the Socialist Bloc and the Oversea Sterling Area

*Annual Averages of Exports and Imports in £ Millions, 1966–1967**

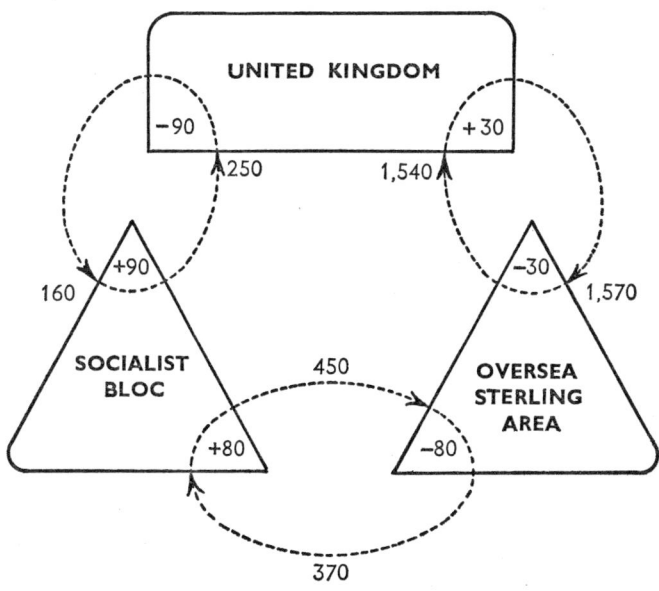

The figures in the angles show a trade surplus or deficit with the trading area faced

* Both exports and imports are valued f.o.b. The totals of trade between the Socialist Bloc and the Oversea Sterling Area are based partly on estimates.

Source.: Based on: United Nations *Monthly Bulletin of Statistics*, June 1968, p. xii; Central Statistical Office, *Economic Trends*, HMSO, June 1968, p. xxi; IMF and IBRD, *Direction of Trade* (monthly issues).

However, the recurring balance of payments difficulties which have faced Britain in recent years place the question of her deficits with the Bloc (see Table XXV) in a new light. The continuous loosening of commercial ties within the Sterling Area and the expected British entry into the Common Market are likely to upset the traditional flows of trade, with adverse effects on Malaysia, Australia and New Zealand.

TABLE XXV UNITED KINGDOM'S BALANCE OF TRADE WITH
THE SOCIALIST BLOC, 1938, 1948, 1953–67
(In million current £)

YEAR	Exports to the Bloc (f.o.b.)	Imports from the Bloc (c.i.f.)	BALANCE	UK's Trade Balance with:		
				E. Europe*	USSR	M. China
1938	30	43	− 13	−11	− 2	− 2
1948	30	52	− 22	− 2	−20	+n
1953	27	74	− 47	−19	−28	− 4
1954	34	74	− 40	−13	−27	− 2
1955	51	105	− 54	−23	−31	− 4
1956	78	99	− 21	−21	+ 1	− 2
1957	78	109	− 31	−13	−17	− 2
1958	76	102	− 26	−18	− 8	− 9
1959	97	136	− 39	−16	−28	+ 5
1960	136	171	− 35	−23	−22	+ 7
1961	154	192	− 38	− 6	−16	−18
1962	143	188	− 45	+ 1	−34	−15
1963	149	203	− 54	− 8	−31	− 5
1964	131	220	− 89	−32	−51	− 7
1965	156	256	−100	−32	−73	−39
1966	190	280	− 90	−16	−75	−n
1967	210	280	− 70	−21	−60	+10

* I.e. the 7 Socialist countries, the USSR excluded.

n = negligible, less than £500,000.

Source. IMF and IBRD, *Direction of Trade* (annual and monthly issues). The values were converted from US dollars to sterling at the official exchange rate applicable at the time.

B. THE BLOC'S RESERVES AND INTERNATIONAL LIQUIDITY

Without exception, all Socialist countries have been permanently faced with an acute shortage of foreign exchange, in particular of the convertible currencies of the West. This is a natural consequence of the economic system in existence and the policies pursued. On the one hand, the drive for planned, rapid industrialization calls for heavy imports of capital equipment and industrial raw materials, not to mention the unsatisfied demand for consumer goods. Planners' errors of judgment, unexpected disasters and perhaps incompetence often lead to unfulfilled targets. To overcome such bottlenecks, emergency imports, not provided for in the original plans, are often essential at short notice. These, of course, can usually be obtained more easily from market economies.

On the other hand, the drive is not geared towards building up export capacity but rather to developing key industries vital to overall industrialization, often irrespective of the comparative disadvantage. Many of these industries are not competitive enough to be able to earn foreign exchange in Western buyer's markets. The prevailing seller's markets in Socialist countries further reduce both inclination and capacity to export, not only quantitatively but also qualitatively. Besides, in contrast to Capitalist countries, where for several reasons exports are viewed with favour, Socialist leaders regard exports as essentially a sacrifice.

Moreover in trade with the West, being largely exporters of raw materials and importers of manufactures, Socialist countries have suffered long-range deterioration in their terms of trade. Their poor marketing techniques plus the various forms of discrimination they have to face in the West further reduce their chances of earning convertible foreign exchange.

It may be observed that the Bloc's shortage of foreign exchange could not be alleviated by any significant inflows of foreign capital or loans. In fact since 1954 it is some of the Socialist countries that have themselves embarked upon various economic aid programmes to the Developing World (see Ch. 11 D). Some of the aid has been extended in convertible currencies, but even if the aid is in the form of deliveries of goods it reduces export earnings from elsewhere. This, together with spending on espionage and subversive activities, has been putting further strain on their own foreign-exchange resources.[1]

[1] According to NATO estimates, the annual cost to the USSR of propaganda and subversion abroad amounts to a sum ranging from $200 m. to $300 m. Quoted from Z. Brzezinski, *Alternative to Partition*, McGraw-Hill, New York 1965, p. 61.

The Bloc's International Liquidity Reserves

Socialist countries keep the level of their international reserves a closely guarded secret (the USSR has discontinued publishing her figures since 1935). Several individual researchers as well as private, governmental and international bodies have been speculating about the actual size of Socialist holdings, particularly the size of the Soviet gold reserves and production.[1] Estimates of the Soviet gold reserves have ranged from US $1,500 m. to $10,000 (£620 m.–£4,170 m.), but it appears that in the late 1960s the level must be pretty close to the lower level.[2] There are several indications that $2,000 m. is not far off the actual figure. To the gold hoard we must add the holdings of convertible exchange. Considering that she often sells gold for convertible exchange in the West, and the amount sold usually reflects unexpected changes in her import requirements (see below), it is unlikely that these holdings would be greater than a quarter of her gold stock, say about $500 m. The fact that the USSR has been so determined in recent years to obtain Western credits and is prepared to pay, what appears to her on doctrinaire grounds, exorbitant interest rates would appear to support this estimate. All in all, the Soviet reserves of gold and convertible exchange are likely to be about $2,500 m., roughly sufficient to pay for 3–4 months' imports. The capacity of the Soviet reserves to sustain imports is not far off the average Western capacity, which is 5–6 months (see this Section further on).

The Chinese reserves of gold and foreign exchange are estimated to be around $400 m.[3] These reserves are probably enough to pay for no more than 3 months' imports under normal conditions.

---

[1] Those who have established some standing in this field include: Oscar Altman of IMF, Paul Bareau of London, Michael von Berg of Stuttgart, Keith Bush of Munich, the bullion brokers *Samuel Montague and Co.* and *Sharps, Pixley and Co.* both or London, the *Mining Journal* of London, *Neue Zürcher Zeitung*, *Metallgesellschaft* of Frankfurt, *Minerails et Métaux* of Paris, *Pick's* of New York, the *US Bureau of Mines*, and the *US Central Intelligence Agency*.

[2] See O. Altman, 'L'or et le rouble', *Economie Appliquée*, July–Sept. 1962, pp. 345–72, esp. p. 358; US Senate, *A Background Study on East-West Trade*. Prepared for the Committee on Foreign Relations, GPO, Washington 1965, p. 21; K. Bush, 'Soviet Gold Production and Reserves Reconsidered', *Soviet Studies*, April 1966, pp. 490–93.

[3] Alexander Eckstein's estimate of $250 m. (US Senate, *US Policy with Respect to Mainland China*, Hearings before the Committee on Foreign Relations, Washington March 1966, p. 350) is, in this writer's opinion, too low.

CH. 10 §B PAYMENTS AND FINANCE 197

To estimate the reserves of the remaining Bloc countries it is proposed to use official data applying to Yugoslavia. Yugoslavia is roughly average in the size of her area, population, national income and foreign trade of the 7 (other than the USSR) CMEA countries. If her reserves (which are known as she belongs to the International Monetary Fund), oscillating around $115 m.,[1] are taken as the average for the 7 countries, then the latters' total reserves would amount to a sum around $800 m. It is unlikely that the combined reserves of Albania, North Korea and North Vietnam exceed $200 m.

Thus, in the case of the Socialist countries other than the USSR, their total reserves are likely to be in the vicinity of $1,400 m. representing about one-tenth of their total imports.[2] The actual proportion certainly differs from country to country. For example, East Germany and Czechoslovakia seem to be stronger in this respect than others. It would appear, therefore that the reserves of the 11 countries are sufficient to pay for their imports for 1–3 months. If these speculations are correct, then the Bloc's combined international liquid reserves amount to a total around $3,800 m. (about £1,625 m.), which would constitute 7% of Western reserves.

For the sake of comparison, the size of Western international liquidity reserves may be briefly reviewed. All the 25 Western countries regularly publish their liquidity figures and all of them, except Switzerland, belong to the International Monetary Fund. As of mid-1968 their officially held reserves of gold, foreign exchange and holdings with IMF amounted to $60,000 m. (£20,500 m.). This total represented 40% of these countries' annual import bill (c.i.f.), i.e. sufficient to pay for their imports for about 5 months.[3]

The relatively meagre size of international reserves held by the

[1] IMF, *International Financial Statistics*, 7/1968, p. 16.
[2] It may be observed that Yugoslavia's reserves normally constitute 7–10% of her annual import bill.
[3] The reserves (percentage of imports in brackets) of the 15 largest Western trading nations were: the USA: $14,300 m. (42%), West Germany: $8,400 m. (45%), the United Kingdom: $2,800 m. (15%), France: $6,700 m. (49%), Japan: $2,000 m. (16%), Canada: $2,700 m. (24%), Italy: $5,300 m. (53%), the Netherlands: $2,500 m. (27%), Belgium-Luxemburg: $2,500 m. (31%), Sweden: $950 m. (18%), Switzerland: $3,000 m. (70%), Australia: $1,400 m. (33%), Spain: $950 m. (28%), Denmark: $500 m. (16%) and Norway: $650 m. (23%). Based on: IMF, *International Financial Statistics*, 7/1968, pp. 16, 34–37.

Socialist countries carries important implications so far as fluctuations in East-West trade are concerned. The Bloc countries' export effort is generally concentrated on a relatively few staple products, the output of which is heavily dependent on the vagaries of natural conditions. This is particularly true of China in whose total exports agricultural products represent more than 70%.[1] Furthermore, unexpectedly large imports of a particular class of goods, such as grains in recent years, inevitably mean a corresponding decline in other imports. This certainly applies to China and Eastern European countries (unless imports are financed by generous credits) but not so much to the USSR which is a substantial gold producer and can draw on her reserves.

Each Socialist country administers the strictest form of exchange control. Imports of consumer goods and 'non-essentials' are curtailed to a bare minimum and, within limits, efforts are made to maximize convertible foreign exchange earnings from exports and other sources. The stress seems still to be laid more on import replacement than on the genuine development of export capacity.

Production of Gold and Silver

One of the obvious ways of alleviating the foreign-exchange problem would be to produce precious metals. However, of the Bloc countries only the Soviet Union is in a position to produce substantial quantities of gold (plus some quantities of silver, see below). Production figures, again, are not published. Western estimates used to place the annual value of the Soviet gold production within the range $300 m.–$700 m., but recent studies give the range for the mid-1960s as $150 m.–$175 m., i.e. enough to pay for at least 2% and no more than 9% of the annual import bill of the USSR (assuming that no gold is diverted to domestic uses). There are several indications to suggest that the lower range, put forward by the US Central Intelligence Agency and the US Bureau of Mines, may now be closer to reality. The average annual value of the reported Soviet gold sales in the West since World War II works out at $170 m., although the sales in the first half of the 1960s averaged more

---

[1] Liu Jih-hsin, 'On the Relationship between Agriculture and Heavy Industry', *Ta-kung Pao*, 2/2/1961 (translation in: American Consulate General in Hong Kong, *Survey of China Mainland Press*, 29/3/1961, p. 5).

than $400 m.[1] Production costs of gold mining are believed to be very high and probably increasing.[2]

Apart from the Soviet Union, North Korea, Mainland China and Rumania are also gold producers. The estimated value of the gold mined in 1965 in North Korea is $6·5 m. and in China $2·5 m.[3] Rumania's production is apparently insignificant. It may be thus concluded that the Bloc's annual gold production is around the mark of $200 m. (about £85 m.) and it is rather unlikely that it will rise appreciably in the near future (unless the US dollar is devalued in terms of gold).

Total gold production in the Capitalist World in 1967 amounted to $1,450 m. of which the West contributed $1,250 m.[4] Thus the value of the Bloc's gold mined, as of the late 1960s, runs at about 15% of the Western gold production. South Africa is the only country in the world that can rival the Soviet Union in gold production, whilst other significant Western producers, Canada, USA, Australia and Japan fall well behind. The respective figures for these five Western countries in 1967 were: $1,060 m., $100 m., $60 m., $30 m. and $20 m.[5]

Most Socialist countries also produce quantities of silver. Their combined production is estimated to be about US $42 m. (£18 m.) annually. To this total, the USSR contributes $31 m., East Germany: $6 m., Czechoslovakia: $2 m., China: $1 m., and Rumania, North Korea, Poland and Hungary (in that order) the balance[6]. Annual production in the Capitalist world is valued at $210 m. of which the

[1] For further details see O. Altman, *op. cit.*, esp. pp. 345–53; K. Bush, *op. cit.*, pp. 490–91; *International Financial Statistics*, p. 15.

[2] According to Theodore Shabad, a Western authority on Soviet geography, the cost of mining one ounce of gold in the USSR was $65 in the early 1960s (compared with the US official price of $35), although the figure may be exaggerated; see US Senate, *East-West Trade*, Hearings before the Committee on Foreign Relations, Part II, February 1965, GPO, Washington 1965, p. 106. Almost all Soviet gold is mined in the remote parts of Siberia under extremely difficult conditions. The abolition of forced labour camps (which had provided cheap labour up to the late 1950s) must have made gold mining more expensive. Recently the USSR reported large gold finds in Central Asia, but Western observers are rather sceptical about their value as an economic proposition for large exploitation.

[3] Based on: US Bureau of Mines, *Minerals Yearbook 1966*, Washington 1967, vols. I–II, p. 243.

[4] Based on: *Int. Fin. Stats, op. cit.*, p. 14.

[5] *Ibid.*

[6] Based on: *Minerals Yearbook 1966, op. cit.*, pp. 361–62.

Western share amounts to $130 m. (about £55 m.).[1] But although the Bloc's $42 m. represents one-third of the Western production, it is still a negligible amount in relation to the annual commodity imports of Socialist countries ($25,800 m. or £10,750 m. in 1967[2]).

Other Ways of Alleviating the Bloc's Foreign Exchange Problem

To increase their earnings of convertible foreign exchange, Socialist countries have often exported goods badly needed at home, as has been the case with Bulgarian edible oils, Czechoslovak eggs, East German fertilizers, Polish meat, Soviet timber and Chinese rice. They have not hesitated to resort to price undercutting, particularly in hard currency areas (see Ch. 9 B, pp. 146–53).

The Bloc countries are also noted for their predisposition to barter transactions. This practice is now less widespread than formerly, owing to the reluctance of Western traders to enter into them. But it is still common for the Socialist foreign trade corporations to insist that the Western exporter accepts 5–20% in counter-purchases from the corporation in question as part-payment. Poland and Rumania are reported to be the most insistent barter offerors.[3] The issue of import licences by the ministries of foreign trade in Socialist countries is often made conditional upon the corporation having earned a certain amount of foreign exchange.[4] In each Socialist country there is usually a foreign-trade corporation, such as the Polish *Dal*, Bulgarian *Bulet* and the North Vietnamese *Transaf*, whose specific function is to arrange or engage in barter transactions involving the so-called 'soft' exports which may be difficult to market otherwise.

Of all Socialist countries, China appears to have made the most determined strides towards increasing her foreign-exchange earnings. In the early 1950s the regime apparently extended the cultivation of the

[1] *Ibid.*; *Mining*, Annual Review, London, May 1968, p. 28.
[2] United Nations *Monthly Bulletin of Statistics*, 6/1968, p. xii.
[3] Political and Economic Planning, 'East-West Trade', *Planning*, May 1965, p. 134; European League for Economic Co-operation, *East-West Commercial Relations*, Brussels 1965, p. 42; *The Economist*, 29/1/1966, p. 429; *Board of Trade Journal*, 12/7/1968, p. 76.
[4] J. Zieleniewski and S. Szczypiorski, *Zasady organizacji i techniki handlu zagranicznego* (Principles of the Organization and Conduct of Foreign Trade), PWE, Warsaw 1963, p. 152.

opium poppy to expand the export of opium and other processed narcotics (heroin and morphine). According to a reputable Soviet source, by the mid-1960s, China was earning about $500 m. annually from illicit opium traffic,[1] and a Taiwan source gave an estimate of total earnings between 1950 and 1963 as $5,000 m.[2] Japanese narcotics agents estimate that some 90% of all illicit drugs sold in the Capitalist world is derived from Mainland China.[3] Chinese exports of narcotics even attracted the attention of the United Nations Narcotic Drugs Commission. China has also treated the continued large imports of wheat and barley partly as a foreign-exchange proposition. These relatively low-priced grains enable China to export high-priced and high-yielding rice and soya beans (see Ch. 12 C, p. 283).

A sizeable amount of foreign exchange has come from the Bloc countries' nationals or descendants, resident outside the Bloc, in the form of cash and parcel remittances. By an elaborate system of favourable exchange rates, import duties on parcels (which can be payable in foreign currencies by the senders) and various incentives, the Socialist countries have successfully tapped a lucrative source. This flow of foreign exchange is of particular importance to China which pockets some $100 m. annually (although in bad years the proceeds may be as low as $10 m.)[4] from Overseas Chinese resident in South-East Asia.[5] The important Chinese community in the United States is, of course, legally barred from making direct remittances.[6] The remittances to the

[1] V. Ovchinnikov, *Pravda*, 13/9/1964.
[2] *China Post*, Taipei, 2/6/1963 (quoted in Kao Hsian-kao, *Chinese Communist Foreign Trade Diplomacy*, APACL, Taipei, June 1964, p. 77).
[3] *The Australian*, Canberra, 24/5/1965.
[4] Alexander Eckstein, *Communist China's Economic Growth and Foreign Trade*, McGraw-Hill, New York 1966, pp. 196–97; *Far Eastern Economic Review*, 16/3/1967, p. 480.
[5] Almost all Hong Kong's and Macao's imports of food come from Mainland China and are paid for in convertible currencies. The Hong Kong and Macao Chinese send food parcels to their relatives in China. The parcels are subject to Chinese import duties which can be pre-paid in foreign exchange by senders.
[6] As a matter of curiosity rather than of importance, it may be observed that China has also developed a dollar pipeline from South Vietnam. Prostitutes, who apparently are mostly controlled by Vietcong guerrillas, are made to insist on payment in dollars. A portion of these proceeds, together with other extortions payable in dollars, are then used by the Vietcong to purchase supplies from China. It is estimated that in 1965 $150 m. seeped to China in this way. China converts the dollars for sterling (or gold) in Hong Kong. However, the tightening up of the system of pay to the American forces towards the end of 1965 has put a brake on this flow. See *The Economist*, 5/2/1966, p. 538; the *Observer*, 18/12/1966, p. 1.

European Socialist countries from nationals resident in North and South America, Western Europe and Australia probably exceed $100 m. annually.[1]

Other odd sources of the Bloc's foreign-exchange earnings include joint East–West business ventures (see Ch. 15 D) and various ingenious devices by which Western tourists, businessmen, diplomats and others are induced to spend their hard currency in the Socialist country. Most Bloc countries also operate special retail shops in their leading business centres, in which foreigners as well as residents can purchase high-quality goods (not otherwise available) for Western currencies only. To the above, we must add the pressure exerted by Socialist countries for Western credits.

The Bloc's Reserves and Western Liquidity

At the height of the Cold War in the 1950s, many Western financial and political leaders feared the possibility of an indiscriminate flooding of the Western markets with Soviet gold to shatter the Capitalist monetary and price systems. Whether the Soviets ever seriously considered using gold sales as a weapon of cold warfare is not known, but there has been no actual attempt so far.

Nor is there any evidence to suggest that the Bloc has tried to cause disruptions in the Western markets by designedly accumulating and then suddenly running down its gold and foreign-exchange reserves. Perhaps this fact can be taken as evidence of the limitation of the Bloc's reserves, too small a proportion of Western resources.

Even the substantial Soviet gold sales in the 1960s, far from causing disruption, actually contributed towards improving Western liquidity.[2] As is well known, the liquidity crisis of recent years has been largely caused by the fact that gold production has been falling short of the fast-increasing needs of trade. Between 1948 and 1967 visible stocks of

---

[1] However, in 1967 Albania issued a decree prohibiting Albanians from receiving parcels or cash remittances from persons who left the country since World War II. Reported in *East Europe*, 10/1967, p. 34.

[2] The value of Soviet gold sales in recent years was: 1958: $220 m., 1959: $250 m., 1960: $200 m., 1961: $300 m., 1962: $215 m., 1963: $550 m., 1964: $450 m., 1965: $550 m. There were no significant sales in 1966 and 1967; early in 1968 a sale of $11 m. in London was reported. See *Int. Fin. Stats, op. cit.*, p. 15; *American Rev. of East-West Trade*, 4/1968, 53.

gold in the Capitalist world rose by only 30% whilst the value of foreign trade increased by 300%. The Soviet gold sales in the first half of the 1960s were adding 1% *annually* to the officially held gold reserves in the West, and the total sales over the decade 1956–1965 accounted for a half of all additions to these reserves. There have also been some, irregular, sales of silver by China, the USSR, East Germany and probably by other Bloc producers as well, for convertible Western currencies. Chinese sales were concentrated in 3 years, 1960–62 when their total value reached $115 m.[1] After an interval of ten years, Soviet sales resumed in 1965 when $13 m. worth was shipped to the West; another shipment in 1966 was valued at $11 m.[2] Information on the sales by other silver-producing Socialist countries is fragmentary only, but allowing for the retention for domestic use, the amounts exported must have been very small.

C. BILATERALISM

The Socialist countries' preference for bilateralism[3] is well known.[4] Acute foreign-exchange difficulties after the last war made most

[1] A. Eckstein, *op. cit.*, p. 219.
[2] *Mining*, Annual Review, May 1967, p. 13.
[3] 'Bilateralism' has a variety of meanings; from the narrowest to the broadest they are:
- (a) a barter exchange without using a common unit of account;
- (b) barter with a common unit of account;
- (c) a bilateral trade and payment agreement whereby the value of imports and exports between the two partner countries is balanced annually, the periodical excess of imports over exports being financed and regulated by swing credits; at least one of the currencies is inconvertible;
- (d) as (c), but overall balancing is achieved over a longer period, say 3–5 years;
- (e) a trade agreement whereby the value of imports and exports between the two countries is fixed by specific or global quotas, but transactions are carried on in a convertible currency;
- (f) as (e), but only part of the trade is subject to quotas;
- (g) a trade agreement in which two countries signify their intention to exchange certain broad classes of goods;
- (h) a bilateral agreement (as distinct from a multilateral agreement, as e.g. GATT) not regulating the size of exports and imports between two countries but normalizing commercial conditions of trade, such as MFN, exchange of trade missions, method of payments, etc.

The meanings most frequently implied in East-West trade are those of (c) and (f).

[4] The most comprehensive pioneering study of bilateralism in East-West trade can be found in R. F. Mikesell and N. Behrman, *Financing Free World Trade with the*

countries in the world turn to this form of trading. However, although Western countries have virtually abandoned it in their trade with Capitalist countries since the early 1950s, all Bloc countries still show a certain predilection for trading on a bilateral basis.

There is no perfectly satisfactory method of measuring the degree of bilateralism owing to the lack of precise information of individual transactions. But a reasonable indication for comparative purposes can be obtained by calculating the proportion represented by the bilaterally balanced element in the total commodity trade. By one of the methods, used by the United Nations,[1] the degree of bilateral balancing in East-West European trade between 1956 and 1965 oscillated around 70% whilst in the early 1950s the figure was about 55%.[2]

Over the three-year period 1962–64, the lowest degree of bilateral balancing in trade with Western European countries was recorded in Albania's (41%) and Bulgaria's (63%) trade, and the highest in East Germany's (74%) and Czechoslovakia's (76%) trade. The degree of bilateral balancing represented by trade with the East European countries (including the USSR) was lowest in the case of Iceland (19%) and Portugal (55%) and highest in the case of Greece (82%) and West Germany (86%); the figure given for the United Kingdom was 61%.[3]

Bilateralism obviously commands several advantages in the context of Socialist economic conditions and objectives. First of all, it is considered to make for 'just' trade. In orthodox Marxian thinking, unbalanced trade is a form of 'non-equivalent exchange' resulting in international exploitation of the weaker by the stronger partner country.[4] Second, bilateral balancing of trade simplifies the planning process in several ways. 'Anarchical' world market forces tend to introduce fluctuations in

---

Sino-Soviet Bloc, Princeton 1958. Also see R. L. Allen, *Soviet Economic Warfare*, Public Affairs Press, Washington 1960, esp. chs. I, II and VII.

[1] The sum of the bilaterally balanced element in each trade exchange as a percentage of the total of: the sum of the bilaterally balanced element in each trade exchange *plus* the sum of import surpluses *plus* the sum of export surpluses. The higher the percentage figure, the higher the degree of bilateral balancing; the figure of 100% would indicate perfectly balanced exports and imports with each trading partner annually. See ECE, *Economic Bulletin for Europe*, vol. 12, no. 2, pp. 46–49.

[2] *Economic Bulletin for Europe*, vol. 12, no. 2, p. 47; vol. 17, no. 1, pp. 49–52.

[3] *Econ. Bull. for Europe*, vol. 17, no. 1, pp. 49–52.

[4] K. Marx, *Capital*, FLPH, Moscow 1959, vol. III, p. 571.

the size of exports and imports and the trade balance, which make it more difficult for planners to mesh foreign trade with each country into the general economic plan.

Third, the most important practical consideration is that bilateral trade minimizes the need for currency transactions. This fact, in the face of soft currencies and relatively small international reserves, is a definite advantage. Fourth, whether at the governmental negotiations level or in the case of individual transactions, bilateralism enables a Socialist country to use the level of its imports to facilitate its exports. Otherwise, the latter may not easily find buyers in the highly competitive Capitalist markets. Furthermore, in by-passing world markets, a Bloc country can deal with each trader according to his degree of bargaining power, a fact which may yield benefits deriving from the application of the principle of discriminating monopoly/monopsony.

Fifth, bilateralism, particularly in the hands of a large country not critically dependent on foreign trade, can be used as a weapon of economic and political coercion. A trading partner may be favoured for a time with an assured market, made dependent, and then forced to submit to a variety of conditions. Non-commercial concessions, not otherwise attainable, may be secured in a bilateral trade agreement. The case of Finland, sometimes referred to as a 'captive economy' of the USSR, comes to mind. Sixth, many developing countries, which also have soft currencies and suffer from foreign-exchange problems, favour bilateral balancing of trade with Socialist countries. Finally, as the doctrine of comparative costs commands little respect in Socialist economic thinking, the missed short-run gains from trade consequent on bilateralism are not obviously patent as compared with potential benefits that could be derived from trading on a multilateral basis.

Even when the size of exports and imports is planned in a trade agreement to be equal, due to a variety of circumstances the balance is not necessarily achieved at any time during the year, or even at the end of the period. Unless the transactions are carried on in a convertible currency, there is a need in the trade agreement to provide for a method of payment. During the year, import surpluses are financed in such cases by swing credits which have generally averaged about 10% (the range falling between 5–20%) of the value of the agreed trade. Such overdrafts are mostly interest-free but on occasions Western countries have insisted on interest payments to discourage Socialist countries from accumulating excessive import surpluses.

It may be agreed that the balance at the end of the period will be settled in extra deliveries of goods or, quite common now, in gold or convertible currencies. In some cases trilateral deals are planned whereby settlements are achieved through appropriate deliveries and purchases involving a third country. This method may be limited to individual deals or (more commonly) placed on a global annual basis (see next section of this chapter). Otherwise the balance may be transferred to the next trade agreement.

The hey-day of bilateralism in East-West trade was reached in the mid-1950s. Its disadvantages had, of course, been recognized by the West long before that, and more recently by the Socialist countries themselves. Bilateral balancing leads to a reduction of trade to the capacity of the weaker partner, i.e. usually the Socialist country, which imposes limits on the gains that could otherwise be derived from the international division of labour. Alternatively the 'stronger' partner has to take certain imports low on its priority list because the other partner has nothing else to pay with. Such trade distorts the directional pattern of trade and it leads to price distortions. A Socialist country is often charged higher than world prices by Western traders to compensate themselves for unwanted counter-purchases. Such reluctantly acquired Socialist goods are then resold, and perhaps re-exported, at low prices as 'soft' items, which may subsequently prove detrimental to the export effort of the same Socialist country.

Contrary to what might be expected, East-West bilateral trade is characterized by instability. The Bloc countries apparently do not attach sufficient importance to meeting their agreement targets. In contrast to exports to, and imports from, other centrally planned economies, trade with Capitalist countries is treated as unreliable and residual. In spite of the official form of negotiations, bilateral trade agreements are not legal contracts. Mikesell and Behrman concluded that 'not only has bilaterally planned trade with the Soviet Bloc been wide of the agreement targets but it has also been less stable and more subject to erratic fluctuations than unplanned trade among the Free World countries.'[1] Other disadvantages associated with bilateralism

[1] *Op. cit.*, p. 80.

include the high cost of negotiating long-term trade agreements plus the annual protocols, inflexibility and the fact that it may degenerate into an instrument of economic and political pressure.

D. MULTILATERALIZATION OF TRADE AND PAYMENTS

The recent discussions, experiments and reforms that have been sweeping Eastern Europe, the withering away of the Cold War and the fast-increasing volume of East-West trade, put the question of multilateralism in trade between market and centrally planned economies in a new light. An endeavour is made in this section to consider the degree of multilateral balancing in East-West trade and to review the elements of multilateralism in the past. The relevance of the recent reforms to the multilateralization of East-West trade is then discussed in some detail, and this is followed by an evaluation of the prospects.

(a) *The Degree of Multilateral Balancing of Trade*

It has been pointed out in this chapter (Section A, pp. 191–94) that the Socialist Bloc, even as a whole, regularly earns trade surpluses in some parts of the world and incurs deficits in others, and that in reality there is not as much bilateral balancing in East-West trade as one might be inclined to think. There are several (imperfect) methods of measuring the degree of multilateralism in trade.[1] What is in fact measured by these methods is the degree of multilateral balancing as reflected in the *ex post* annual statistical returns of trade. The method adopted in this study is a variant of those used by other researchers.

The degree of multilateral balancing in a country's trade is calculated as the sum of trade imbalances with each trading partner in a particular group (i.e. the West or the Socialist Bloc) expressed as a percentage of the country's foreign-trade turnover with each partner country in the group:

[1] For example see League of Nations, *Review of World Trade*, vol. 1933, p. 60; M. Michaely, 'Multilateral Balancing in International Trade', *Amer. Econ. Rev.*, Sept. 1962, p. 688; F. L. Pryor, *The Communist Foreign Trade System*, George Allen & Unwin, London 1963, p. 190.

$$Dm = \frac{\sum_{1}^{n} |X - M|}{\sum_{1}^{n} X + M} \cdot 100;$$

Dm = Degree of multilateral balancing of trade
X = Value of exports (f.o.b.)
M = Value of imports (c.i.f.).

If country A exports £10 m. to B and it imports £10 m. from B, the degree of multilateral balancing is nil, but if A imports nothing from B and obtains its imports from elsewhere instead, the degree is 100.

The degree of multilaterality, in the sense of multilateral balancing of trade, in East-West trade in selected years is brought out in Table XXVI. For the sake of comparison, figures for intra-Western and intra-Socialist foreign trade are also given.[1] In general, both in intra-Western and in intra-Eastern foreign trade, the size of imbalances in relation to the size of the trade has tended to decline. However, in East-West trade rather the reverse appears to be true.

The results in Table XXVI indicate that, particularly in recent years, the degree of multilateral balancing is not as high in the West and not as low in East-West trade as one would be inclined to expect. In fact the degree of imbalance in East-West trade is now greater than in either intra-Western or intra-Eastern trade.

Of the significant Western trading nations with the Socialist Bloc, the highest degree of multilateral balancing with Socialist countries was achieved (1965–67 averages) by Canada (70%), Australia (68%) and Spain (30%), whilst the lowest was shown in the trade of Yugoslavia (14%), Turkey (9%) and Finland (6%). On the East side of East-West trade (disregarding insignificant traders with the West), the highest degree was exhibited in the trade of Bulgaria (34%), China (31%) and Rumania (28%), whilst the lowest was in the case of Poland (19%), Czechoslovakia (17%) and Hungary (17%).

The following Western countries attained a higher degree of multilateral balancing in trade with Socialist countries than in trade with each

---

[1] It may be of interest to note that the highest and the lowest degrees of multilateral balancing in intra-trade were attained in the trade of the following countries (averages over the 3-year period 1965–67). In intra-Western foreign trade: the highest – Greece (54%), Spain (50%) and Australia (30%); the lowest – Canada (11%), Belgium–Luxemburg (11%) and the USA (11%). In intra-Socialist foreign trade: the highest – China (11%) and Poland (8%); the lowest – Czechoslovakia (4%) and the USSR (4%). The figures applying to Socialist countries are based on partly incomplete data.

TABLE XXVI THE DEGREE OF MULTILATERAL BALANCING IN
EAST-WEST TRADE, 1938, 1948, 1957, AND 1960–67

(Weighted Member-Country Averages)[1]

	THE WEST[2]		THE SOCIALIST BLOC[3]	
YEAR	In Intra-Western Foreign Trade	In Trade with the Bloc	In Trade with the West	In Intra-Bloc Foreign Trade[4]
1938	35	27	25	21 (20)
1948	32	32	31	5 (16)
1957	23	23	14	15 (16)
1960	19	20	20	7 (9)
1961	19	23	23	9 (10)
1962	18	18	20	10 (15)
1963	19	36	20	9 (12)
1964	18	29	27	7 (15)
1965	17	21	23	6 (14)
1966	15	26	24	6 (8)
1967	15	23	26	4 (7)

[1] For the method used, see the text; the higher the figure (i.e. percentage), the higher the degree of multilateral balancing. National figures of trade were brought to a common denominator (US dollars at the official exchange rate applicable to visible trade) to make weighting possible. Where necessary, rough adjustments were made to bring export figures to an f.o.b., and imports to a c.i.f., basis.

[2] The WEST includes the 25 Developed Countries of Western Europe, North America, Japan, Australia, New Zealand and South Africa.

[3] The SOCIALIST BLOC includes the 12 centrally planned economies (Yugoslavia is treated as part of the West; Cuba is treated as a Developing Country, excluded from both divisions).

[4] These figures should be treated with caution. They are based on incomplete sources. Data on inter-trade amongst Mainland China, Mongolia, North Korea and North Vietnam, as well as other trade figures involving small values are absent. The way the national totals are weighted (in effect) may be questioned; the figures in brackets show simple averages.

Sources. Based on: IMF and IBRD, *Direction of International Trade* and *Direction of Trade*, annual and monthly issues, supplemented with national statistical yearbooks of Albania, Bulgaria, Czechoslovakia, East Germany, Hungary, Poland, Rumania, USSR, and Far Eastern Economic Review, *China Trade Report* (monthly), Hong Kong.

other (averages over the period 1965–67, the first figure referring to trade with Socialist countries, the second to that with other Western countries):

Australia	68%–30%
Belgium-Luxemburg	21%–11%
Canada	70%–11%
France	22%–13%
Germany, West	24%–15%
Italy	19%–13%
Japan	18%–13%
Netherlands	21%–15%
United Kingdom	23%–13%
United States	26%–11%.

On the other hand, in the case of the Western countries listed below, the degree of trade imbalances with Socialist countries was lower than with Western countries:

Austria	16%–24%
Denmark	19%–20%
Finland	6%–20%
Greece	19%–54%
Norway	20%–25%
Spain	30%–50%
Sweden	18%–19%
Switzerland	17%–25%
Turkey	9%–25%
Yugoslavia	14%–25%.

The trade of the remaining 5 countries (Iceland, Ireland, New Zealand, Portugal and South Africa) with the Bloc was too small to warrant inclusion in the above lists.

The statistical evidence on the degree of multilateral balancing of trade conveys an incomplete picture of the extent of multilateralism in East-West trade. It does not reflect the operational aspect of trade, i.e. the figures conceal the method of the settlement of imbalances. Thus on the one hand, even if individual traders in countries A and B used convertible currencies and were free to import what and when they liked from the partner's country, but if the countries' annual exports and imports happened to balance then the degree of multilateral balancing would be nil. On the other hand, even though the trade of countries Y and Z were being settled through a bilateral clearing account but the imbalances were settled by extra deliveries of goods in the following year, the degree of multilateral balancing would be increased thereby, although this would not make payments any more multilateral. Triangular (etc.) settlements, even if made by deliveries of goods, also appear as multilateral. Similarly, gifts and loans in the form of commodity deliveries may make for increased trade imbalances, but not necessarily for multilateralization of payments. To this extent, the degree of the multilateral balancing of trade overstates the degree of multilateralism in a broader sense in the early post-war years in all countries, and in the Bloc countries' trade both among themselves and with the West.

(b) Elements of Multilateralism

The main factors which have contributed to the increasing multilateralization of East-West trade may be now briefly discussed. We shall consider the Western side first. It must be observed, first of all, that in the early post-war period highly specific and detailed quotas used to be embodied in East-West trade agreements. But after the Korean War the restrictive quotas were gradually replaced with commodity lists, and even these became very broad and liberal. Many Western countries have practically removed them by now, at least on imports from the USSR and Eastern Europe. This decreasing restrictiveness of bilateral agreements may, in a sense, be regarded as a step towards multilateralism.

The liberalization of quotas has been paralleled by a gradual extension of the transferability of the Bloc countries' earnings in the leading countries of the West.[1] The Sterling Area and Western Europe have

[1] As reported by the European Commission for Europe in 1964: the USSR enjoyed full convertibility of all earnings of the currencies of Denmark, France, West Germany, Italy, Switzerland, the United Kingdom, Canada, the USA, Japan and New Zealand (and Australia), and she had bilateral clearing arrangements providing for the full settlement of annual balances in convertible currency with Belgium, the Netherlands, Norway and Sweden; the USSR had bilateral clearings with no, or restricted, settlement of balances in convertible currency with Austria and Finland. Other European Socialist countries, in general, enjoyed unrestricted transferability of the currencies of Belgium, West Germany, Italy, the Netherlands, the United Kingdom and the USA. Other Western European countries were offering varying degrees of transferability to different Socialist countries. See UNCTAD, *Trade Problems between Countries Having Different Economic and Social Systems*, Doc. E/CONF. 46/34, Geneva, 9/3/1964, p. 21.

been treated by most Socialist countries as convenient multilateral areas where traditionally trade deficits with some countries are offset with surplus earnings from others. At the same time Western countries, even if they sign bilateral trade agreements, insist on settling balances in convertible currencies. Only those Western countries (such as Austria, Finland and Greece, not to mention Yugoslavia) which are substantially dependent on the Bloc market, still enter into clearing agreements with Socialist countries.

To a limited extent, the voluntary clearing scheme operated by the Secretariat of the Economic Commission for Europe has introduced an element of multilateralism in trade between twenty Eastern and Western European countries. Several Developing countries (Argentina, Brazil, Israel, Morocco, Tunisia, UAR, Uruguay) have also been included in the system. During the decade following the introduction of the scheme in 1957, multilateral compensation payments to the value of $126 m. were carried out.[1] Between July 1957 and September 1963 over 62% of the European Socialist countries' bilateral balances with the participating Capitalist countries were settled through ECE.[2]

Planned multiangular operations under which trade surpluses and deficits are settled by including a third or even a fourth country in the trading circuit, have been a feature of East-West trade ever since the late 1940s. A well-known network is represented by Poland-Finland-the USSR, in which a Polish trade surplus with the USSR is often used to pay for a Polish deficit with Finland, while Finland is compensated by a trade surplus with the USSR. Other well-established triangular channels in East-West trade include East Germany–Finland–USSR, Rumania–Finland–USSR, Denmark–East Germany–West Germany, Czechoslovakia–Japan–North Vietnam, and many others. Even the USA has been drawn into them.[3]

Several Socialist countries are producers of precious metals. The sale

---

[1] J. Siotis, 'ECE in the Emerging European System', *International Conciliation*, 1/1967, p. 35.

[2] Z. Królak, *Handel zagraniczny* (Foreign Trade), Warsaw, 2/1964, p. 82.

[3] For example, in 1964 a $1·5 m. deal was arranged by which the USA was to import Turkish chromium ore and pay for it in agricultural surplus products to Poland; the latter was to complete the triangle by sending Turkey an equivalent amount of specified machinery, chemicals and consumer goods. Reported in *East-West Commerce*, London, 28/1/1964, p. 12.

of gold or silver, usually made for convertible Western currencies, enables these countries to obtain imports from any country, not necessarily from where they are matched by exports. Production and sale figures are not published by the Socialist countries, but some fragmentary data and estimates made in the West are available (see Section B of this chapter).

The Soviet Union is an important focal trader, introducing a significant element of multilateralism in East-West trade. Quite apart from the multiangular operations, having sizeable liquid reserves and being a substantial gold producer, she is sometimes prepared to pay such countries as Czechoslovakia and Poland for 'hard' items in convertible Western currencies. On many occasions the Soviet Union has also extended loans to Socialist countries in convertible currencies. Such proceeds have assisted these countries in increasing their imports from the cheapest source in the West outside bilateral clearing channels. Multilateral flexibility is also increased in those cases where foreign-trade corporations, or enterprises producing for export (as in Czechoslovakia, East Germany, Hungary, Poland, the USSR and of course in Yugoslavia), are allowed to retain a portion of their convertible-exchange earnings to spend where and on what they wish.

Although the devices employed can be regarded as concessions to multilateralism, their remedial operation is rather limited. In particular, the ECE settlements scheme is no real solution leading to multilateralism. The $126 m. worth of clearing carried out over ten years is a drop in the ocean – less than 0·5% of the value of East-West European trade over the period. Only a small proportion of the cases referred for clearing settlements can be carried out because of the lack of consent of the parties approached. The larger the sum involved, the more difficult it is to clear it – some of the clearing claims had to include at least seven countries.[1] Some of the leading Western European countries, such as Belgium, Britain and West Germany, have been highly critical of the scheme. The enthusiastic support it has been given by Socialist countries is explained by the fact that the scheme *facilitates their bilateralism*, not necessarily because they are genuinely interested in multilateralism.

[1] E.g., in the third quarter of 1963 the value of clearing balances to be settled amounted to $160 m.; however, the value of the operations actually cleared was only $7 m. See Królak, *op. cit.*, pp. 82–83.

Under multiangular deals, the size and direction of trade are still distorted. Such operations are still only a *second best* solution; admittedly they must be gainful to the parties involved, but the gains from trade are not maximized. These deals often result in resales or even re-exports. It is obviously wasteful when goods have to be moved instead of monetary claims.

So far as the production of gold and silver in the Bloc is concerned, it can visibly contribute to multilateralism only in the case of Soviet trade. But even in the USSR, current production can normally pay for no more than 3% of imports. Taking the Bloc as a whole, the production of precious metals represents only 1% of its commodity imports. Moreover, the Bloc's international reserves have been too small to be able to face the extension of unscheduled multilateral payments.[1]

(c) *Relevance of the Recent Economic Reforms in Eastern Europe to Multilateralism*

To achieve full multilateralism, Socialist currencies would have to become convertible into gold or hard currencies. To attain this ultimate requirement, Socialist countries would have to adopt some far-reaching reforms shaking the very foundations of central planning. These reforms would necessitate changes in foreign-exchange policy, conduct of foreign trade, domestic production and pricing.

First of all, exchange control would have to be so modified as to allow non-residents to hold a Socialist currency and provide a possibility of exchanging it into hard currencies. This could work only if the supply of and demand for a Socialist currency were such as to ensure an equilibrium in the foreign-exchange market. This would necessitate a chain of other reforms. The authorities would have to create a state of what Altman referred to as 'commodity convertibility' and a Czechoslovak monetary expert called 'internal convertibility.'[2] Western holders of credit balances with a Socialist country would have to enjoy unrestricted access to the supply market in that country. They would have

---

[1] As a matter of fact, the West is not a large producer of gold and silver in relation to its total trade. In 1967 Western production amounted to $1,300 m., i.e. roughly 6 times the Bloc's amount, which also represented 1% of Western commodity imports.

[2] O. L. Altman, 'Russian Gold and the Ruble', IMF *Staff Papers*, 1960, pp. 430–34; V. Zahalka, *Hospodarske noviny* (Economic News), Prague, 17/5/1968, pp. 1, 4.

to be accorded freedom to purchase what, how much and when they wanted, and be able to take it out of the country without restrictions (beyond those customary in a market economy – strategic, quality, etc., controls).

Producing enterprises in Socialist countries would have to be able and willing to respond to foreign demand quantitatively and qualitywise. The system of material incentives to producing enterprises would have to be extended and designed with a view to making production for export no less profitable than that for the domestic market. But to provide a sound and lasting foundation for multilateralism the most crucial of all reforms would have to include a rational price fixing system. A rational price structure could be shaped either by market forces, or perhaps scientifically by planners along the lines put forward by Oskar Lange ('trial and error adjustment pricing')[1] or Leonid Kantorovich (computational 'objectively determined valuations')[2] – both so far untested. By whatever process, prices would have to correspond to scarcity-preference relations. Such prices could, and would have to be allowed to, perform the function of guidance both to producers, in their search for profit maximization, and to consumers striving to maximize their satisfaction.

The postulate of rational pricing naturally implies that the exchange rates of Socialist currencies would have to be fixed at such levels as to reflect their purchasing power as compared with convertible Western currencies. Furthermore, instead of being mere accounting devices, the exchange rates would have to be made relevant in making decisions as to the direction, size and composition of imports and exports. Finally, Socialist countries would have to accumulate reasonably large international liquid reserves and publish their figures.

[1] O. Lange, 'On the Economic Theory of Socialism', *Rev. of Econ. Studies*, 1936/37, vol. IV, no. 1, pp. 53–71, and no. 2, pp. 123–42; O. Lange and F. M. Taylor, 'Trial and Error in a Socialist Economy', in B. E. Lippincott (ed.), *On the Economic Theory of Socialism*, Minneapolis 1938, pp. 72–83.

[2] See the references available in English: L. V. Kantorovich, *The Best Use of Economic Resources*, Harvard UP 1965, esp. pp. 121–51, 262–342, and his 'On the Calculation of Production Inputs', translated in *Problems of Economics*, May 1960, pp. 3–10. Also see excellent background studies: R. W. Campbell, 'Marx, Kantorovich and Novozhilov: Stoimost versus Reality', *Slavic Review*, Oct. 1961, pp. 402–18; A. Zauberman, 'The Revisionism in Soviet Economics', in L. Labedz (ed.), *Revisionism*, George Allen & Unwin, London 1962, pp. 258–80; M. Bornstein, 'The Soviet Price Reform Discussion', *Quart. Jour. of Econ.*, Feb. 1964, pp. 15–48.

None of the Socialist countries is prepared to go ahead with such drastic departures from central planning. Serious discussions and proposals for reform had already started in the mid-1950s in Hungary, Poland, Czechoslovakia and East Germany, but little had been done in practice before the early 1960s. By this time, the economic stagnation that had set in practically throughout the whole Bloc had made the shortcomings of extreme centralization too patent, particularly in the more advanced Socialist economies. The actual reforms in the new spirit were initiated in East Germany and Hungary in 1963–64 and in Poland, the USSR, Czechoslovakia, Bulgaria and Rumania during 1965–68. The reforms, which are still being implemented, include the following changes relevant to multilateralism.[1]

There has been some improvement in contacts between Western firms and the enterprises in Eastern Europe, a tendency begun before the recent wave of reforms. This has been facilitated by a growing procession of trade missions, individual businessmen and officials, the exchange of managers and technicians and technical literature and an increasing use of advertising. In Bulgaria, Czechoslovakia, East Germany, Hungary, Poland and Rumania there is a number of enterprises, particularly those producing for export, which can by-pass the foreign-trade corporations and deal directly with Western firms (see Chs. 5 C and 14 C, pp. 83–86, 330–32).

The most publicized element of the reforms includes the fact that enterprise profit is accepted as the main indicator of performance. This, together with the decentralization of management and administration, should enable enterprises to respond, within limits, to market demand and to improve quality. Incentives paid to enterprises producing for export have been in operation in most Bloc countries for a long time, but now they are being strengthened and extended. New price structures have been, or are being, introduced in which costs are more realistically reflected. Virtually all European CMEA countries have introduced charges on fixed capital, and there has been a growing aversion to the use of subsidies in production, and turnover taxes in regulating consumption.

[1] For a detailed discussion contrasting the Eastern European economies in relation to convertibility before and after 1956 see M. R. Wyczalkowski, 'Communist Economics and Currency Convertibility', IMF *Staff Papers*, July 1966, pp. 458–89.

The basic objective behind the reforms in Eastern Europe is to increase the performance and efficiency of the economies in which command planning and administration in their extremes have long outlived themselves. It is now realized that in the more developed Socialist countries further rapid growth can be ensured only through a more efficient use of resources, and this can be attained by a greater participation in the international division of labour. A Socialist economist described the situation in the following words: 'in the past the growth of foreign trade was based on extensive factors. The transition to intensive sources of growth has opened new vistas for foreign trade.'[1] The question of efficiency of production in different CMEA countries is now treated with the utmost concern. To make comparisions of the effectiveness of investments relevant to foreign trade the CMEA Permanent Commission for Economic Questions recently undertook a thorough analysis of costs covering 800 commodity groups (embodying 15,000 articles).[2]

It must be observed that the reforms have not been specifically designed to steer these economies towards convertibility and multilateral trade. Even though several measures can be regarded as significant steps towards creating conditions for multilateralism, their implementation is rather coincidental.

In spite of several concessions, centralized planning and control are still largely retained. Exports and imports are still centrally planned, and the institutional set-up under which trade is conducted is essentially unchanged. Direct dealings, where they are permitted, are meant to promote exports, and not to give freedom to Western traders to buy what, how much and when they want. It is doubtful whether material incentives will be strong enough to increase and improve production radically for the highly discriminating buyers' markets in the West, as long as the less exacting, unsatisfied sellers' market is available at home. Recent experience in some of these countries, such as Czechoslovakia, has demonstrated that the (partial) freedom extended to enterprises to fix their own prices largely removes the economic pressure from producers to adapt their production to the needs of foreign markets.[3]

Fundamentally, no new price systems have been adopted, price

[1] J. Bielecki, *Handel zagr.*, 1/1967, p. 5.
[2] A. Zwass, *Życie gospodarcze* (Economic Life), Warsaw, 23/4/1967, p. 17.
[3] W. Przelaskowski, *Życie gosp.*, 1/7/1968, p. 10.

structures are only being improved. With minor exceptions (which partly existed even before the reforms), prices are still centrally fixed. In foreign trade, whether with other Socialist countries or with the West, Capitalist prices are still used. The basic policy with regard to exchange rates and exchange control remains unchanged.

(d) IBEC and Multilateralization of Trade and Payments

Independently of the economic reforms considered above, there have been some interesting developments designed to place intra-CMEA trade on a multilateral basis. We shall consider these developments and their relevance to a possible multilateralization of trade with the West.

Already since 1951 the rouble has been used as a unit of account in intra-Bloc trade returns. But the first real move towards multilateralism was made among CMEA member countries in 1957, when an agreement was reached whereby unplanned clearing balances were to be settled through an office of the *Gosbank* in Moscow. However, this attempt was too modest to meet the demands of intra-CMEA integration and to provide substantial opportunities for the division of labour. In 1962 a Permanent Commission for 'Currency and Finance' was established. The Commission was instrumental in establishing the International Bank for Economic Co-operation (IBEC) which started operations at the beginning of 1964 with its head office in Moscow.

The main declared function of IBEC is to settle the member countries' trade balances on a multilateral basis. Its authorized capital is 300 m. transferable roubles,[1] payable in the form of credit balances with member countries, convertible currencies and gold in five annual instalments. The value of the operations carried out by the Bank in 1966 reached 46,000 m. transferable roubles, of which nine-tenths concerned trade settlements amongst member countries.[2]

Trade within the CMEA area is still governed by five-year bilateral agreements, and protocols drawn up annually and quarterly. But the

---

[1] The 'transferable' (or 'clearing', or 'conversion', or 'foreign exchange') rouble is, of course, a form of currency distinct from the internal rouble in circulation in the USSR. It is divorced from the Soviet financial system, even though its 'gold backing' is the same (0·987412 grammes of fine gold). Both are inconvertible.

[2] *Vesnik Jugoslovenske investicione banke* (Reports of the Yugoslav Investment Bank), Belgrade, 1/1968, p. 17.

imbalances, whether planned or unplanned, are settled by IBEC in transferable roubles. A surplus with one member country can be used to offset a deficit with another, provided the countries involved agree, i.e. each country needs to balance its exports and imports only with the group as a whole, not necessarily bilaterally. Each member country is required to secure a balance of receipts and payments, taking credits into account, within a calendar year. To ensure that the settlements are carried out smoothly and without delay, IBEC grants credits to authorized banks in member countries. In 1966 the Bank extended 2,400 m. transferable roubles (60% more than in 1964) worth of credits[1] at interest rates generally not exceeding 1·5%–2·0%.[2] Thus the credits extended covered no more than 6% of the trade settlements carried out. These credits enable the exporting countries to receive transferable cash payments for deliveries exceeding the agreed annual quantities and to use the proceeds to buy in other CMEA countries, whilst the importing countries are able to receive the goods immediately and pay for them later.

Although the original plan was meant for the member countries of CMEA, it does not preclude the inclusion of other Socialist countries. At a meeting of the IBEC Council in October 1965, it was decided that it was 'advisable to make settlements in transferable roubles with Socialist non-member countries which have, as a rule, an equal level of foreign-trade prices and are bound by long-term agreements among themselves and with IBEC members.'[3]

It is still too early to evaluate the contribution of IBEC to intra-CMEA multilateralism. But in spite of the wide publicity associated with the formation of the Bank, it is obvious that as yet it has not fulfilled the hopes held out for it. So far, the member countries have dodged the essential requirement of any multilateral system worth its name – the *automatic* clearing of imbalances. The transferable rouble is in fact not convertible until the balance is allowed by negotiations to become a claim on a country's goods. The condition of a multilateral settlement is the unanimity of all countries involved. This is not easy

---

[1] *Ibid.*, p. 18.
[2] Seasonal credits: 1·5%, irregular credits: 2·0%; credits not repaid on maturity carry 3·0%. In practice, about one-half of the credits received by member countries is interest-free. See A. Zwass, *Finanse* (Finance), Warsaw, 9/1966, pp. 41–50.
[3] K. Nazarkin, *International Affairs*, Moscow, 8/1966, p. 66.

because claims against some countries are still less desirable than against others, at least from the point of view of a particular country. Owing to the very low interest rates charged by IBEC and the perennially unsatisfied demand for imports, there is not enough pressure on debtors to repay credits, which tends to depress the already meagre reserves.

There are still too many countervailing forces in CMEA militating against multilateralism. Similar economic structures and developmental ambitions mean that the member countries, with the possible exception of the USSR, have similar surpluses and suffer from similar shortages. The chairman of the Board of IBEC, Mr K. Nazarkin, complained in 1966: 'A desire to balance trade on a bilateral basis between countries still prevails in a number of cases concerning deliveries of equipment and raw materials which are in short supply.'[1]

The less developed member countries support multilateralism more in principle than in reality. At this stage, complete multilateralism would further enhance the importance of the richer countries – the USSR, East Germany, Czechoslovakia – who have a wider range of goods to sell and are, generally speaking, more efficient. They would tend to accumulate surpluses at the expense of the less developed member countries – Bulgaria, Rumania and Mongolia. This would hardly contribute to the 'evening out of the national economic levels', one of the fundamental objectives postulated in the CMEA Charter (Art. I, para. 1).

Of what relevance can the system under IBEC be to the multilateralization of East-West trade? There is no simple answer to this. On the one hand, there is no doubt that the purpose of the scheme is primarily to facilitate the operation of bilateralism among Socialist countries, and the period over which it may be necessary to do this may prove much longer than is vaguely envisaged at present. The scheme is supposed to promote the intra-CMEA division of labour and economic integration in general. It may be argued that if the whole system succeeds to the member countries' satisfaction, they will have less need to perfect their trade and payments with the West. On the other hand there are several indications that the system may promote multilateralism in East-West trade.

[1] *Ibid.*

CH. 10 §D   PAYMENTS AND FINANCE   221

Under Article IX of the 'Agreement',[1] by decision of the IBEC Council, the Bank may make multilateral settlements in transferable roubles with Western or Developing countries not formally participating in the scheme. Furthermore, credits can be granted from the fund of the Bank when settlements of Capitalist countries 'with all IBEC members are made on their entire trade'.[2]

IBEC carries out operations in Western currencies, such as sterling, dollars, Swiss and French francs, West German marks, etc. In 1966 these operations amounted to the considerable sum of 2,800 m. transferable roubles ($3,080 m.).[3] It has established correspondent relations with banks in Belgium, France, West Germany, Italy, Sweden, Switzerland, the United Kingdom and elsewhere. The Bank is striving to build up its resources of gold and convertible currencies. Member countries are encouraged to deposit such currencies, on which relatively high interest rates are paid.

At the same time, some member countries – notably Poland – have been pressing for a portion of their clearing balances to be paid to creditors in convertible currencies. It is not clear at present to what extent such convertible credit balances can be used to pay bills in hard currency areas. But most, if not all, IBEC member countries would like to earn convertible surpluses within the CMEA area and use them for obtaining imports from the cheapest source in the West. This brings us to the next likely development – in fact the crux of the problem in East-West multilateralism.

To prevent a drain of convertible reserves, the prices, quality and conditions of delivery of goods in intra-CMEA trade will have to be brought in line with those prevailing in Western markets. If this is done, it would be the very step essential for creating conditions for multilateralism in East-West trade. It is explicitly stated under Article X of the Agreement that IBEC member countries are free to develop direct payments and financial links with other countries. In fact Article XIII of the Agreement and Article 43 of the IBEC Charter go further – they provide for the admission of Capitalist countries as members. It is worth

---

[1] The text of the 'Agreement on Multilateral Settlements in Transferable Rubles and Organization of the International Bank for Economic Co-operation' and of the 'Charter of the International Bank for Economic Co-operation' can be found in translation in *The American Review of Soviet and Eastern European Foreign Trade*, Jan.–Feb. 1966, pp. 3–36.
[2] Nazarkin, *op. cit.*, p. 66.   [3] *Vesnik Jugoslovenske investicione banke, op. cit.*, p. 18.

noting that the Secretariat of ECE has shown considerable interest in the CMEA settlements scheme and that IBEC was registered with the United Nations in 1964 as an international institution.

(e) Conclusions and Prospects

We can now review and appraise the forces bearing on the prospective development of multilateralism in East-West trade. Those militating against multilateralization are the following. Those forms of multilateralism in which Socialist countries participate are not consciously designed as a move away from bilateralism. Rather they are resorted to in order to make their bilateralism workable with the minimum of inconvenience and inefficiency. Although the avowed objective of the intra-CMEA payments scheme is a gradual extension of multilateral trade and the full convertibility of the credit balances, there is no declared commitment to this effect in trade with the West.

Given the present ideological attitudes and developmental commitments, Socialist countries are not yet ripe for multilateralism. Under multilateral arrangements, when one is free to buy at the cheapest source and sell where it is most profitable, many of the newly established or modernized industries (such as iron and steel, engineering) would have little chance of survival when faced with Western competition. This, of course, would not be acceptable to a Socialist leadership committed to 'balanced developments', and which fears lest the Bloc countries be again reduced to (using Oskar Lange's phrase) 'an underdeveloped backward East serving as a raw materials and food reservoir' for the West.[1] Bilateralism not only offers a chance of effectively nursing such industries but it also enables the earning of foreign exchange from otherwise uncompetitive exports.

Multilateralism would necessitate a substantial degree of the operation of the market mechanism to shape the size, direction and composition of trade. Whilst there is a tendency to enlist market processes in the internal operation of the economy,[2] it does not mean that Socialist

---

[1] O. Lange, *Essays on Economic Planning*, Asia Publishing House, London 1961, p. 14.

[2] In the CMEA countries, of course. There is no likelihood in the near future that the non-CMEA Socialist countries will embark on economic reforms comparable to those in East Europe. See Ch. 7 B(e), pp. 114–15.

leaders are prepared to tolerate disruptive market forces originating in Capitalist countries. The market mechanism, fluctuations and multilateralism are a threat to central planning, and there is little evidence that the Socialist leadership is inclined to replace 'visible hand' with anonymous and 'anarchical' forces operating in world markets.

The smooth operation of multilateralism presupposes a reasonable size of convertible reserves. But the resources of gold and convertible exchange that the Bloc commands are pitifully meagre, and it is difficult to see how in the near future these countries can accumulate reserves large enough to be able to absorb the shocks of multilateral payments. There is little hope of the Socialist currencies becoming convertible in the near future.

There is still too much discrimination in East-West trade to enable multilateralism to operate effectively. On the one hand, many Western countries still place restrictions on imports from Socialist countries, on currency transferability, credits and strategic exports. On the other, there is hardly any evidence to suggest that Socialist countries are inclined to accord the West unrestricted access to their markets. They are likely to continue giving planned preference to intra-Bloc, or at least intra-CMEA, trade.

In fact, it may be observed that in one respect there is a danger of multilateralism in East-West trade suffering a setback. As is well known, the Socialist Bloc has treated the Sterling Area as its handy reservoir for multilateral settlements. The substantial trade surpluses earned in the United Kingdom by the Bloc as a whole could be used to pay for its deficits with Malaya, Australia and New Zealand, a pattern of trade which has suited Britain in the past. But the recent serious difficulties in her balance of payments and the gradual disintegration of the Sterling Area have made Britain press more and more for 'bilateral justice'. Similarly, the cause of multilateralism in East-West trade will not be improved should Britain enter the Common Market.

On the positive side, the undercurrents working towards the extension of multilateralism in East-West trade can be restated as follows. First of all, it would be wrong to assume that Socialist countries are inevitably wed to bilateral trade. Bilateralism, in fact, was first introduced by Capitalist countries in the 1930s, and as a matter of fact Soviet trade between the wars remained very largely multilateral. After the war,

Socialist countries embraced bilateralism more from necessity than conviction, just as many Capitalist countries did between 1930 and 1950.

Second, the advantages of bilateralism to Socialist countries are becoming less compelling now. Even in the context of central planning, it is not essential to balance trade bilaterally. It is quite feasible to plan trade surpluses with some countries and deficits with others. The need for more flexible planning, as contrasted with rigid command planning, is now generally recognized in the Bloc. Third, the increasing application of more rational pricing, material incentives and decentralized management is likely to lead to improved supplies, quantitatively and qualitatively, in the domestic market, which may pave the way for lifting restrictions on the Western traders' access to the Socialist market. The reforms undertaken so far are only a beginning. It can well be expected that forces will be progressively released pressing for further liberalization. If market processes can operate internally and exhibit good performances, there may be less reluctance to expose Socialist economies to world market forces.

Fourth, Socialist countries will be more favourably disposed to multilateralism when they have more viable economies to meet Western countries on a reasonably equal footing in the open market. Even Marx, when theorizing on 'international values' and 'non-equivalent exchange', recognized the gains that could be derived from the differences in comparative costs in trade among countries at approximately the same stage of economic development.[1] The more developed Socialist countries, such as the USSR, East Germany and Czechoslovakia, stand a better chance in this respect than other Bloc countries.

Fifth, the intra-CMEA system of settlements under IBEC, cautious as it has been so far, may prove a sensible evolutionary stage towards multilateral trade with the West during which Socialist economies are still partly protected against the inroads of world market forces. The scheme does not exclude the possibility of placing settlements with Western countries on a multilateral basis. Sixth, it is doubtful whether

[1] When he made a comparison between earnings of capital invested in foreign trade and a nation's gains from trade: 'The same may obtain in relation to the country to which commodities are exported and to that from which commodities are imported; namely, the latter may offer more materialized labour *in kind* than it receives, and yet thereby receive commodities cheaper than it could produce them.' K. Marx, *Capital*, FLPH, Moscow 1959, vol. I, p. 232.

the CMEA members will be content to confine themselves to their present scheme to the exclusion of the potential gains offering from trade with the West. There are too many well-known divergent economic and political forces. The pressure, especially among the smaller countries more dependent on trade, to be able to use their surpluses in CMEA trade to buy extra badly needed imports from the West, is likely to continue.

The balance of the forces working against and in favour of the extension of multilateralism in East-West trade in the near future appears to be roughly equal, with perhaps a slightly better chance towards the extension. What course further developments will follow may very well depend more on the West than on the East. With the Cold War on the wane and the growing trend towards liberalism in CMEA countries, the West may find that its interests could best be served by dismantling the discriminatory arrangements in its trade and payments with the CMEA group at least. The *Ad Hoc Group* of experts, consisting of representatives from Western and Eastern Europe, which considered this problem under the auspices of ECE in 1964, stressed the 'close link between the liberalization of trade and multilateralization.'[1]

Furthermore, if the West is genuinely interested in the convergence of the two systems – a comfortable theory that originated, after all, in the West – it may find it a sound investment to ease the most obvious weakness of the CMEA multilateral scheme: shortage of convertible reserves. This could be done by assisting IBEC with a fund of convertible Western currencies, similar to the contribution of $350 m. to the European Payments Union made by the USA in 1950.[2] Alternatively, or perhaps additionally, the West might consider increasing assistance to developing countries to enable them to buy more goods within the CMEA area. CMEA countries could build up respectable liquid reserves and would be in a better position to increase their imports from anywhere in the West outside the confines of bilateralism. Recently two

---

[1] ECE, *Report of Ad Hoc Group to Twentieth Session of the ECE*, Adopted on 11/12/1964, Doc. TRADE/1962, para. 9.

[2] Schemes along these lines have recently been suggested by Prof. Z. Brzezinski (*Alternative to Partition*, McGraw-Hill, New York 1965, esp. pp. 162, 166–67, 170) and by Prof. H. W. Shaffer ('An East European Payments Union?', *East Europe*, 3/1966, pp. 14–21.

prominent Hungarian economists put forward concrete proposals for East-West financial partnerships. Prof. J. Bodnar proposed the formation of an East-West Bank and Prof. I. Vajda an East-West Payments Union.[1]

E. CREDITS

Short and medium-term credits have played a considerable role in East-West trade.[2] They are largely one-way traffic, that is they are extended chiefly by Western countries on their exports to the Socialist Bloc. This is a reflection of the shortage of foreign exchange in the Bloc on the one hand and Western eagerness to promote exports on the other. Socialist countries are prepared to extend short- and occasionally medium-term credits on their exports,[3] but Western importers, particularly those in the industrialized countries, as a rule pay cash. However, Socialist credits – short-, medium- and long-term – play an important part in the Bloc's exports to the Developing countries of Asia, Africa and Latin America (see Ch. 11 D, pp. 253–56).

It is estimated that the total amount of Western credits on exports to the Bloc outstanding in 1968 was in excess of £700 m. (or about $1,700 m.). The exact amount cannot be easily calculated because of commercial secrecy, especially in respect of short-term commercial credits. This means that some one-quarter, or perhaps more, of Western exports to the Bloc is credit financed.

Of the total sum estimated, about a quarter is on exports of primary products, chiefly wheat, and smaller amounts for barley, wool and other farm products. The credits extended by Australia and Canada on wheat

---

[1] *East Europe*, 12/1967, p. 49 and 6/1968, p. 17.

[2] It is assumed in this study, as is common in the context of East-West trade, that credits up to 6 months (occasionally up to 12 months) are short-term, those for 6 months to 5 years are medium-term and those above 5 years are regarded as long-term.

[3] Examples of Soviet credits to Western countries: a loan extended to Iceland in 1958 for 12 years at 2·5% p.a. for the purchase of vessels from East Germany (repayable in deliveries of goods to the USSR); a loan of $125 m. extended to Finland in 1959 for 5 years at 2·5% p.a.; loans extended to Sweden in 1964 for 4 years at 2·5% p.a. on Soviet cars; a loan of $20 m. to Turkey in 1968 for 15 years at 2·5% p.a. on Soviet industrial equipment. See J. Rutkowski, *Światowy rynek kredytowy* (The World Credit Market), PWE, Warsaw 1964, p. 270; *East-West Commerce*, 28/8/1958, p. 10, 1/11/1964, p. 5 and 1/6/1968, p. 9.

exports to the Bloc have been on the following bases in recent years. Australia: 10% – cash on shipment, 20% payable in 6 months, 20% – in 9 months and the balance of 50% – in 12 months. Canada: 25% – cash, 25% – in 6 months, 25% – in 12 months and the balance of 25% – in 18 months; but on occasions more liberal terms are known to have been granted, e.g. to Bulgaria in 1963 – the cash deposit constituted only 10% whilst the remainder was spread over 3 years. The interest rates charged have been kept secret, but they are believed to be about 5% p.a., or (more likely) less on very large deals.[1] The remaining three-quarters of the credits extended involve manufactures. These include mostly capital equipment – complete industrial plants (for chemical, textile, steel and engineering industries), ships and items of machinery.

All the major Western countries have been extending credits to the Bloc: Australia, Canada, Britain, West Germany, the Netherlands, France, Italy, Japan and others, even the USA. Approximately one-half of the credits to the Bloc are extended to the Soviet Union (which claims only one-third of the Bloc's imports from the West), the balance being about equally shared by East Europe and Far Eastern Socialist countries.

If British government-guaranteed credits are representative of the West taken as a whole, then the Socialist Bloc is more favoured than the Capitalist World. The amount of government-guaranteed loans alone to the Bloc outstanding at the end of each of the six years 1960–66 ranged between £80 m. and £100 m.[2] These amounts represented as much as 15% of such credits owing to the United Kingdom, whilst the Bloc absorbed only 3% of British exports. The figures quoted do not include privately extended credits.

Credit Insurance and Government Guarantees

Western banks and other financial groups are quite willing to extend short-term credits for up to twelve months without government

---

[1] E.g., 4% p.a. was charged by Japan, up to 1967 at least, on ships exported to the USSR. See *The Oriental Economist*, 4/1967, p. 242.

[2] The figures for selected years were as follows (in brackets, loans to Capitalist countries): 1955: £115 m. (£316 m.), 1960: £95 m. (£303 m.), 1963: £86 m. (356 m.), 1964: £84 m. (£424 m.), 1965: £83 m. (£473 m.) and in 1966: £81 m. (£537 m.). Source: Central Statistical Office, *United Kingdom Balance of Payments* 1967, HMSO, London 1967, p. 23.

guarantees. Most Western European banks provide short-term finance on the basis of a guarantee by the Soviet-controlled *Garant Versicherungs A.G.* of Vienna, which offers both commercial and non-commercial cover.

Since about the mid-1950s Western governments have (reluctantly) displayed an increasing willingness to guarantee medium- and long-term export credits through designated or (mostly) specially established government credit insurance corporations. With partial exceptions in the USA and Australia, these guarantees cover credits to Socialist countries as well, and for periods of up to fifteen years. Private insurers are reluctant to underwrite such credits because they have no means of assessing the debtors' financial standing and the extent of the risk. Socialist countries do not publish any data on their holdings of gold and convertible foreign exchange, and a critical attitude to State trading and the vagaries in the East-West political climate add to their reluctance. According to Mr Luther Hodges, the then US Secretary of Commerce testifying before the Senate in 1964, approximately 80% of Western credits extended to the Socialist Bloc carried governmental guarantees.[1]

Politics v. Economics

Like many other aspects of East-West trade, credits have been a subject of political controversy in the West. It has been held in several quarters that credits to Socialist countries carry much more than ordinary commercial implications. Discrimination at the government level has been common, particularly up to the early 1960s, usually reflecting the state of the East-West political climate. In general, Western credit policy has been less discriminatory to the Eastern European countries than to the USSR, and most to the Asian Socialist countries.

The political factor conditioning the credit policy towards the Bloc has been most obvious in the USA and, to a lesser degree, in West Germany and Japan. Private banks and financial institutions in the USA, although prepared to grant short-term commercial credits to CMEA countries, are unwilling to underwrite risks on medium export credits. The Export-Import Bank (government-owned) is prohibited from guaranteeing such credits unless it is shown on the US President's

[1] *East-West Trade, op. cit.*, Part I, p. 111.

finding that it is in the national interest. In the past, US credits were virtually limited to the Eastern European countries (except East Germany) on surplus agricultural products.[1] Credit insurance and guarantees on manufactured exports have, of course, been extended to Yugoslavia for years now. Even the Rockefellers, who for decades were noted for their negative attitude to American trade with the Bloc, recently declared their interest in financing East-West trade deals.

For a long time (up to 1964) West Germany pursued a restrictive policy, when the express permission of the Bonn Government (as distinct from the Laender authorities) was required for medium credits to Socialist countries. It has been claimed in East Germany that the West German Government is using credit policy in Eastern Europe as a means designed to isolate the Ulbricht regime.[2] It was reported that the Japanese Prime Minister, Mr Shigeru Yoshida, had given an undertaking to the Taiwan Government in 1964 not to extend long-term credits on exports to Mainland China. This became sufficient reason for the Peking Government to break previously signed contracts and negotiations for other deals in 1965.[3] However, Japan has been quite generous with credits to other Socialist countries, especially the USSR.

Liberalization of Western Credit Policy since 1963

The marked liberalization of Western credit policy towards Socialist countries since 1963 has followed two lines – more favourable credit terms and extended government guarantees. A number of factors has contributed to the new attitude.

The increasing interest of the Socialist countries in imports from the West has mainly centred on complete, costly plants, the production and

[1] The most generous terms were those on credits extended to Poland in 1960 and 1964, involving $105 m. and $31 m. worth of agricultural products, interest-free, repayment to start after 10 years (the final instalment after 30 years). See *East-West Trade*, op. cit., pp. 41, 44; *Handel zagr.*, 4/1964, p. 171. However, by the 1968 legislation the Ex-Im Bank is prohibited from extending credits or guarantees on exports to any country which assists a nation being in armed conflict with the USA (as in Vietnam).

[2] Karl-Heinz Domdey, 'Economic Contacts Between the Socialist and Capitalist Countries of Europe', *Peace, Freedom and Socialism*, 9/1965, p. 10.

[3] But in 1966 Mr E. Shiina, Japanese Foreign Minister, stated that his Government was not necessarily bound by the Yoshida Letter. *Far Eastern Economic Review*, 30/6/1966. p. 628.

installation of which alone may take several years. The application of the Berne Union rules,[1] by which international credits are (in general) limited to a five-year period, is arbitrary and without economic justification. With the improving political climate between CMEA countries and the West, there has been an increasing reluctance to use credits as a political weapon, a reluctance that has been paralleled with the Western desire to expand exports. This attitude has been particularly prevalent in Britain which, in the face of her recurring balance-of-payments difficulties, has been endeavouring to reduce her mounting trade deficits with the Socialist Bloc. Many business leaders and statesmen in Western Europe also thought that unless the credit policy were liberalized, Socialist countries – owing to their agricultural failures and a need for large food imports – would have to cut their imports of manufactures drastically.

Even before 1963 some Berne Union members, and particularly non-members (such as Japan and ENI of Italy) had been exceeding the five-year limit on exports involving ships and other large orders. It was reported that Britain lost several big contracts because other countries had offered better credit terms.[2] As early as 1960 the British Export Credit Guarantee Department introduced a 'matching policy', when it announced that it was prepared to exceed the five-year period if other countries did so. The actual departure in East-West trade was first made in the latter part of 1963, when Belgium extended a ten-year credit to Hungary on a chemical plant. In 1964 Britain extended government-guaranteed credits to Czechoslovakia, the USSR and Hungary on fertilizer and chemical plants, worth more than £60 m. for periods up to fifteen years. Several other Western countries followed suit – Italy,

---

[1] The Berne Union (Union d'Assureurs des Credits Internationaux), established in 1934 with its head office in Paris, now includes 26 public and private export credit insurance institutions operating in 20 Capitalist countries (Australia, Austria, Belgium, Canada, Denmark, Finland, France, West Germany, India, Israel, Italy, the Netherlands, Norway, Pakistan, South Africa, Spain, Sweden, Switzerland, the United Kingdom and the USA). The Union is concerned with medium-term credits only – up to 5 years (although on ships longer periods are acceptable). Through consultations and the exchange of information on customers, its aim is to prevent cut-throat competition in credit terms. Its recommendations have no binding effect on members or anybody else. The Union has not specifically discriminated against Socialist countries, nor has it concerned itself with long-term credits or State loans to any country.

[2] Political and Economic Planning, 'East-West Trade', *Planning*, May 1965, p. 149.

Japan, the Netherlands and West Germany. Competition amongst these countries was so keen during 1964–65 that, in addition to the lengthening of the periods, interest rates appear to have been whittled down to roughly 4–6% p.a.[1] In 1966 the Japanese Foreign Minister pointed out that, although the government-owned Export–Import Bank was not allowed to extend long-term credits to China, she could now obtain such credits from a consortium of private Japanese institutions at comparable interest rates.[2]

The liberalization of the credit policy towards Socialist countries has met with strong disapproval in many Western circles, particularly in the USA. The US Government has been especially opposed to credits exceeding the five-year period. Testifying before the US Senate in 1964, Mr Dean Rusk pointed out: 'They [long-term credits] amount to an extended advance of resources to the purchasing country and, in that sense, they have some of the characteristics of foreign aid.'[3] Long-term credits assist the Bloc in pursuing its autarkic policies, at least in relation to the West. Socialist countries, it may be argued, should make internal adjustments by shifting their resources to consumer and export industries. Long-term credits from the West only enable these countries to 'avoid or postpone such decisions and shift the burden of adjustment to Western capital markets'.[4]

The US Government has also been annoyed by the fact that whilst the USA has been extending aid and credits to Western countries, some of them – in defiance of American pleadings – have been aiding the Socialist Bloc. Furthermore, Socialist countries, whilst pressing the West for long-term credits on generous terms, have been extending economic aid to Developing nations in the hope of turning the latter against the West. Thus in 1967 the Soviet Union's outstanding debts to the West amounted to more than £200 m.; she having committed herself to 3,500 m. roubles' worth of credits to Developing Countries between 1954 and 1968. In fact, the USA found that whilst she had been

---

[1] See *Board of Trade Journal*, 6/11/1964, p. 988; 20/11/1964, p. 1,110; 26/3/1965, p. 676. US Senate, *East-West Trade*, Hearings 1965, *op. cit.*, Part II, pp. 5, 269. *Wirtschaftsdienst*, Hamburg, 11/1965, pp. 573–80. *Handel zagr.*, 6/1963, pp. 227–29; 11/1965, p. 525. *Życie gospodarcze*, 25/6/1967, p. 7; *The Oriental Economist*, *op. cit.*

[2] *Far Eastern Economic Review*, 8/9/1966, p. 450.

[3] *East-West Trade*, Hearings 1964, Part I, *op. cit.*, p. 15.   [4] *Ibid.*, p. 16.

extending generous credits to Poland, Poland had herself extended loans on generous terms to Cuba.[1]

It has been further argued in some quarters that as long as there is East-West tension, the Socialist Bloc must not be treated as favourably as other parts of the world. The shortage of foreign exchange, further aggravated in recent years by agricultural failures, is a vulnerable flank of the Socialist economies. The West should capitalize on this providential opportunity and it should use credits as a bargaining weapon. Equally favourable terms should be accorded to Socialist countries only for political concessions.

To place this approach on a systematic and effective basis and to prevent 'credit wars' amongst Western countries competing for the Socialist market, several attempts have been made in recent years to co-ordinate Western credit policies through NATO and OECD. It has also been suggested that credit terms should be kept vague and unpublished to facilitate bargaining on a *quid pro quo* basis, and to prevent the Socialist foreign trade corporations playing off one Western exporter against another. However, owing to divergent national views on the matter, so far no agreement has been reached.

F. PAYMENT RECORD

There is no evidence to suggest that any Socialist country has ever defaulted on commercial transactions with the West, whether involving cash or credit. Private traders and financiers, as well as official spokesmen, all agree that Socialist foreign trade corporations are a gilt-edged payment risk. The actual trade negotiations may be long and arduous, but once the contract is signed by the corporation, payment is certain to follow.

It is, of course, possible that there were instances of non-payment. If there were such cases, they must have been rare and involving small amounts. Terms and execution of contracts in East-West trade, very large deals excepted, are usually kept confidential. It is feasible that defaults of small amounts are unknown to the public, but it is doubtful if those involving larger sums could escape publicity in the West.

[1] *East-West Trade*, Hearings 1964, Part I, *op. cit.*, p. 37.

There have apparently been cases of delays in payment by Yugoslavia and some Eastern European countries. Such delays have been caused by misunderstanding, bureaucratic inefficiency and unexpected shortages of foreign exchange.[1] But these cases are isolated and have not been followed by defaults. It may be observed that the Soviet Union and China often make payments ahead of the due dates. A Socialist economic weekly described China's payment record in the West in the following words: 'the Chinese only buy what they can pay for, and their payment is more likely to be 3 months early than one day late.'[2]

In view of the ideological contempt for bourgeois traders and the chronic shortage of foreign exchange, further aggravated by agricultural disasters and planning blunders in recent years, the impeccable payment record that Socialist countries have established must be regarded by Western traders, bankers and statesmen as most remarkable. A contract with a Socialist foreign trade corporation is, in effect, a contract with its government. This excellent payment performance partly explains Western liberalization of credits to Socialist countries since 1963. These countries are, in fact, regarded as a better risk than most Developing nations. It is not unusual for Western firms themselves to provide export credits to Socialist countries, without going to banks or to insurers.

No documented evidence is available as to Western traders' payment defaults to Socialist countries. But the inherent risk of such defaults is stressed in Socialist literature. Most trade in the West is conducted by private firms and in case of their bankruptcy the possibility of default is quite real, and there is little a Socialist payee can do about it.

So far as payments on the trading account are concerned, the West has less reason to complain than the Bloc. The position is reversed in respect of other forms of obligations, which mainly involve property claims and war debts. Of all Western countries, the USA lays the largest claims. As of mid-1963 the total amount claimed from the Socialist Bloc exceeded $2,500 m. (excluding credits and aid since World War II).[3]

[1] P.E.P., 'East-West Trade', *Planning*, May 1965, pp. 126, 140.
[2] W. Wowczyk, *Życie gosp.*, 20/11/1966, p. 10.
[3] Bulgaria (war and other claims of US nationals): $3 m.; Czechoslovakia (WWI indebtedness and surplus property credits): $265 m.; Hungary (WWI indebtedness and surplus property credits): $13 m.; Poland (WWI indebtedness, surplus property credits and claims of US nationals): $487 m.; Rumania (WWI indebtedness and claims of US nationals): $108 m.; the USSR (WWI indebtedness, Lend-Lease deliveries of

Most Western countries had some investments in the present Socialist countries before the Communist takeover, but which have subsequently been nationalized. Practically all European Socialist countries (Albania and East Germany excepted) have concluded compensation agreements with the leading Western nations – mostly with France, Switzerland, the United Kingdom and the United States, but also with Belgium, Canada, Denmark, Greece, Italy, the Netherlands, Norway, Sweden and others.[1] The first of such agreements were concluded already in the late 1940s and the total number signed so far is about fifty.[2]

The agreed compensation payments have taken the form of convertible currencies, local currency of the Western country, specified commodity deliveries and in some cases blocked Socialist assets in Western countries. As a rule payments are made half-yearly and the instalments are spread over long periods. East-West trade agreements sometimes include provisions for earmarked export surpluses from Socialist countries to compensate Western claimants.

The problem of East-West property claims and war debts is inherently a contentious one. Although in principle Socialist countries (with the possible exception of China) are prepared to pay compensation for

---

peacetime value and loans): $1,463 m.; Mainland China (a portion of the loan to Nationalist China during the Civil War used by the Communist régime): $170 m. The claims against Yugoslavia (WWI indebtedness): amount to $78 m. (this figure does not include $482 m. worth of AID development loans, P.L. 480 sales and Export–Import Bank loans, all extended since 1948) and against Cuba (Export–Import Bank loans and NICARO nickel property claim): $169 m. Based on: *East-West Trade*, Hearings 1964, Part 1, *op. cit.*, pp. 29, 192 and 212. However, it may be observed that the US Government still holds the Czech gold (worth over £20 m.) captured by American troops from the Nazis, although in 1961 a tripartite commission ruled that the gold should be returned to Czechoslovakia.

[1] For example, Poland concluded treaties of indemnification between 1948 and 1963 with 11 Western countries (Belgium, Denmark, France, Greece, Luxemburg, the Netherlands, Norway, Sweden, Switzerland, the United Kingdom and the USA). The total sum for indemnification agreed upon was $156 m., of which up to the end of 1963 $57 m. had been paid off. The remainder is to be settled by 1990. Other examples of indemnity treaties signed include: Bulgaria with Canada, France and the USA; Czechoslovakia with Belgium, France and the UK; Hungary with France, the Netherlands, Sweden, Switzerland and the UK; Rumania with France, Greece, the Netherlands, Norway, Switzerland and the USA; the USSR with the UK; and Yugoslavia with France, Italy and the USA. Based on: J. Konopka, *Sprawy międzynarodowe* (International Affairs), Warsaw, 4/1967, pp. 62–73; United Nations, *Statement of Treaties and International Agreements* (monthly).

[2] J. Konopka, *op. cit.*

nationalized Western property, differences have naturally arisen as to the value of such claims. The US claims for war debts are regarded as out-of-date and unreasonable, considering that the countries concerned were fighting in the same cause as the USA. The Soviet Union apparently offered to repay the USA $300 m. for the $2,000 m. worth of civilian supplies of peacetime utility obtained under Lend-Lease. But the American Government does not consider this amount to be adequate and insists on at least $800 m.[1]

[1] *East-West Trade*, Hearings 1964, Part I, *op. cit.*, p. 212.

11 Politics in Partnership with Trade

THE role of political considerations in East-West trade is dealt with co-incidentally throughout this study where appropriate. However, because the political factor has been such a characteristic feature, a separate chapter is warranted, in which the extent to which this trade has been conditioned by political forces is put into clearer focus and critically appraised. We shall, naturally, concentrate our discussion on those political aspects of East-West trade not specifically considered elsewhere in this study.

A. THE COLD WAR AND EAST-WEST TRADE

Historically, there is of course nothing new in politics competing with economics in shaping the course of foreign trade. Embargoes on ships and trade by belligerents were already known in ancient times, regulation of the trade between imperial powers and their dependencies goes back at least to mercantilism, and more recently policies of protection have been partly conditioned by political reasons. However, governments did not normally go beyond these confines, and it did not occur to them to question the primacy of commercial calculus in foreign trade and to use trade as an active instrument of foreign policy.

In the context of the Cold War trade has assumed such a degree of sophistication that even Colbert would appear an amateur if confronted with Rusk, Khrushchev or Chou En-lai. This is not surprising because Capitalism and Socialism represent not only different economic but also different political systems. The differences are in fact fundamental because they are based on differing ideologies.

The beginnings of the Cold War on the Western side can be traced back to Churchill's speech at Fulton, USA, in March 1946, to which

President Truman gave his wholehearted support. In the following year, the supremacy of the Communist parties as well as Soviet power in Eastern Europe were finally consolidated and in China an all-out civil war broke out; in the West the 'Truman doctrine' and the policy of 'containment' were launched. Led by the USA and the USSR, the two camps embarked upon building up their economic and military capacity. Exhaustion after World War II, followed by the nuclear and intercontinental missile developments, have produced a stalemate where trade appeared to be one of the suitable substitute fronts of warfare. Trade has been seized upon by each camp as a weapon for strengthening its own position and weakening the adversary, with reciprocal self-justifying effects following.

At the height of the Cold War, Khrushchev frankly told a group of American senators visiting Moscow, 'We value trade least for economic reasons and most for political purposes.'[1] Chou En-lai tried to impress upon a group of Japanese businessmen visiting Peking in 1962 that 'trade and politics are inseparable'.[2] Two years later the chairman of the China Council for the Promotion of International Trade, speaking at the British Industrial Exhibition in Peking, criticized the British view that trade could be divorced from politics.[3] The attitude of the American Government was best described by Dean Rusk when testifying before the Senate Committee on Foreign Relations in 1964: 'Our trade policy toward Communist countries is an integral part of our overall policy toward international communism, and we must view it in this framework[4]... trade with the Communist world cannot be effectively used as a blunt instrument. It must be flexibly adapted and flexibly applied on the basis of political, military and economic realities.'[5]

In the East-West political wrangling on trade, each camp has concentrated on a different approach, broadly reflecting the strength and weakness of each side. Socialist countries have stressed the need for the removal of the discriminatory trade policies pursued by the West, as a

[1] Reported in *New York Times*, 18/9/1955.
[2] Kao Hsiang-kao, *Chinese Communist Foreign Trade and Diplomacy*, APACL, Taipoi 1964, p. 2.
[3] *Far Eastern Economic Review*, 10/12/1964, p. 519.
[4] US Senate, *East-West Trade*, Hearings before the Committee on Foreign Relations, Part I, GPO, Washington 1964, p. 4.
[5] *Ibid.*, p. 18.

necessary precondition to the normalization of East-West political relations and a reduction of tension. On the other hand, Western countries have insisted that a political *détente* should precede Western liberalization of trade.[1]

Both camps have realized that the balance of East-West power is basically determined not only by military power but also by economic strength, technological standards and political cohesion. Western policy-makers have been conscious of the fact that whilst the West has had an economic and technological, and perhaps military, superiority, its margin is diminishing owing to the rapid progress in the Socialist Bloc. By denying exports of arms, certain equipment and technology, the Bloc countries can be hit where they are most vulnerable. Besides, at different times trade policies have been applied to promote divergent trends by encouraging individual Socialist countries towards greater national independence. The US policy of 'peaceful engagement' and of 'building bridges' and the West German 'active Eastern policy' pursued towards Eastern European countries since 1963 have been designed mainly to weaken Bloc cohesion.[2]

There has been no lack of initiative on the part of Socialist countries in using trade as a weapon, even though their actions have had to be largely on the defensive. To orthodox Marxists, as Lenin put it, 'politics is the most concentrated expression of economics' and trade is naturally

---

[1] These two approaches were epitomized in the statements by the two leading actors in the Cold War. Mr Khrushchev told an American publisher in 1958: 'Trade and economic ties create a good basis for the consolidation of international political relations.' Testifying before the US Senate in 1964, Mr Dean Rusk pointed out: '... peace can contribute to trade.' See *International Affairs*, Moscow, 5/1958, p. 3; *East-West Trade*, Hearings 1964, Part I, *op. cit.*, p. 21.

[2] See a statement by Mr Rusk, *East-West Trade*, Hearings 1964, Part I, *op., cit.* pp. 4–5. Professor Z. Brzezinski, who was appointed in 1966 as one of the top policy advisers to the American Government, bluntly wrote in 1965: 'Economic difficulties in the East stimulate intense power conflicts and thus tend to loosen the communist structure... American economic assistance policy with respect to East Europe should be guided by two basic criteria: whenever a country increases the scope of its external independence from Soviet control, it should be rewarded; whenever a country appreciably liberalizes its domestic system, it should be rewarded. And similarly whenever an opposite trend develops, the United States should be prepared to discontinue its assistance, withdraw special privileges, such as the most-favored-nation clause (a matter of vital importance to the East Europeans), and should not hesitate to indicate the political motivations involved.' *Alternative to Partition*, US Council for Foreign Relations, McGraw-Hill, New York 1965, pp. 153–54.

a reflection of class struggle on an international scale.[1] In fact, Lenin was more specific when he said: 'The bourgeois countries must trade with Russia; they know that without some form of economic relations their collapse will proceed further than it has gone up to now.'[2] On the one hand, the bogey of unemployment and the frustrations of Western businessmen irritated by export controls have often been played upon. On the other, no effort has been spared in painting rosy vistas of insatiable markets in the Bloc.

This was well illustrated at the Economic Conference held in Moscow in 1952 which was attended by 500 delegates from all over the world. The Chairman of the Conference, Mr Nesterov, offered dazzling prospects for exports to the Bloc. He even quoted actual figures, which came to be known as the famous 'Nesterov figures', by which East-West trade could increase. In such overtures as this it has often been difficult to separate the element of genuine interest in trade expansion from Cold War propaganda. Mr Nesterov very well knew the limits of foreign-exchange reserves in the Bloc and its limited capacity (and desire) to produce what the West wanted. The fact is that no spectacular orders followed the Conference and many Western businessmen then blamed their governments for depriving them of Socialist contracts. 'Some of them', noted a British observer at the time, 'joined organizations sponsored by the Communist Party to agitate for relaxations of controls'.[3] In 1958, Mr Khrushchev claimed that Soviet-American trade could be increased to several thousand million dollars. But recent American studies indicate that even by 1970 the Soviet capacity to pay for imports from the USA will be at best between $200 m. and $300 m. annually,[4] compared with actual imports worth $3 m. in 1958 and $60 m. in 1967.[5] There has been little hesitation in manipulating trade offers

---

[1] V. I. Lenin, *Selected Works*, Lawrence & Wishart, London, vol. IX, p. 17.
[2] *Ibid.*, p. 307.
[3] Jean Bird, *East-West Trade*, London 1954, p. 36. It was pointed out by Mr (as he was then) Eden in the House of Commons that, 'the British Council for the Promotion of Trade... were not solely or even primarily commercial and that this body which was founded after the last year's Moscow Economic Conference was a Communist front organization and was mainly concerned with the dissemination of Communist propaganda.' *Board of Trade Journal*, 14/11/1953, p. 1,000.
[4] M. L. Harvey, *East-West Trade and United States Policy*, National Association of Manufacturers, New York 1966, p. 160.
[5] United Nations *Monthly Bulletin of Statistics*, 6/1960, p. viii; 6/1967, p. xvi.

not only to break the strategic embargo and to foment conflict between businessmen and governments but also to nourish differences between Western countries in general.

Trade offers were also made at one time or another by the USSR, Mainland China and East Germany courting diplomatic recognition. The meetings of the European Commission for Europe (of which all European Socialist countries, except East Germany, are members) as well as other international conferences, have been used as a platform for denouncing Western trading policies. In this Socialist countries have been matched with due reciprocity by the West.

The machinery and methods by which Western countries put their foreign-trade policies into effect are by no means neat and tidy, and the set-up varies from country to country in spite of some co-ordination under the auspices of NATO and OECD. In contrast to domestic commerce, foreign trade is subject to a variety of controls, many of which are specifically directed against the Socialist Bloc. The system in each country is a hotch-potch of various measures designed to meet particular objectives, and on the whole they have proved quite adequate in each country (however, see Ch. 12 D).[1] In a limited sense, even the USA, the most outspoken champion of free enterprise, has taken recourse to

[1] For example, the system in outline in the USA, the leading Western country in the Cold War strategy, is as follows. There are 9 main Acts of Congress regulating trade with Socialist countries: *The Trading with the Enemy Act of 1917* (which has been invoked to prohibit all trade with M. China, N. Korea, N. Vietnam and Cuba), *The Johnson Act of 1934* (prohibiting long-term credits to countries which had defaulted payments to the USA in the past), *The Export Control Act of 1949* (all exports except those to Canada must be licensed), *The Trade Agreement Extension Act of 1951* (by which MFN has been withheld), *The Mutual Defense Assistance Control Act of 1951* (by which US aid can be denied to any country not observing controls on exports of primary strategic significance), *The Foreign Aid Appropriation Act of 1964* (by which credit guarantees are regulated), *The Food for Peace Act of 1966* (which has replaced the *Agricultural Trade Development and Assistance Act of 1954*, regulating the export of subsidized foodstuffs), *The Agricultural Appropriation Act of 1966* (by which the export of subsidized food is prohibited to any country supplying equipment or materials to North Vietnam) and *The Export-Import Bank Act* (as amended in 1968; regulating the financing of exports for use in Socialist countries). The main governmental bodies concerned are: the Council of Economic Advisers and the National Security Council, both attached to the Executive Office of the President; the Departments of State, Treasury, Defense, Commerce, Agriculture; several semi-independent bodies, such as the Central Intelligence Agency, the Atomic Energy Commission and the Export-Import Bank; the Economic Defense Advisory Committee. Besides these, there are numerous influential non-official organizations formulating sectional views on trade policy, such as the Committee for Economic Development, the National Association of

State trading (foreign aid, credits, marketing of primary products) as a weapon in the Cold War. In fact, at one stage the US Government was seriously considering the formation of an overseas trade monopoly to face Socialist countries in world markets;[1] even recently, in a study published by the National Association of Manufacturers, bilateral trade agreements between the USA and Socialist countries have been advocated which could be 'interrupted any time . . . to use trade with the East as a positive instrument of policy.'[2]

There is little doubt that basically Socialist countries have a more effective in-built capacity for enlisting politics and trade in each other's support. When one and the same State so thoroughly dominates the political scene and engages in foreign trade, it is only natural for it to regard politics and trade as being complementary in the totality of State actions. Given the institutional framework within which trade is conducted, a Socialist government can harmonize the course of trade with its political objectives. Unexpected changes in trade can be made by confidential memoranda to foreign-trade corporations quickly, without special legislative sanctions and concern for the electorate. Commercial losses need not be a deterrent because they are absorbed by the State budget and are regarded as being compensated for by political gains.

The use of trade for political ends may consist in either denying certain exports or imports, or otherwise in using politics and trade in a positive sense to assist each other. We shall next consider these two facets of East-West trade.

B. DENIAL OF TRADE

In normal trading relations each partner, although striving to reap the maximum benefit for himself, does not regard the gain derived by the other as detrimental to himself. However, this principle has not neces-

---

Manufacturers, the US Chamber of Commerce, and various *ad hoc* pressure groups either favouring (e.g. the '198 Group' of academics) or opposing (e.g. the Committee of One Million, Young Americans for Freedom, the American Legion, the Longshoremen's Union) commercial and political relations with Socialist countries.

[1] J. N. Hazard, 'State Trading in History and Theory', *Law and Contemporary Problems*, vol. 24, Spring 1959, p. 243.
[2] Harvey, *op. cit.*, pp. 152, 168.

sarily been accepted in East-West trade. Instead, the policy makers have been anxious to prevent the opponent from gaining too much lest he strengthen his position. In other words, the direct commercial losses to the country denying particular exports or imports have been treated as being more than outweighed by its gains in a wider, political, sense. The actual extent and forms of restrictions and prohibitions have varied from country to country, and in each case the emphasis has varied over the last two decades. The initiative in denying trade has rested mostly in Western hands. This appears to confirm the fact that not only is the West less dependent on the Socialist Bloc for trade than the reverse, but also that the West is more able to withstand the economic loss.

It has been felt in many Western quarters that trade assists the authorities in Socialist countries in covering up their planning mistakes and other shortcomings of the system. Normal trading relations with these countries 'would mean tacit approval of the regimes and giving no hoped to the common people longing for liberation from communism.'[1] The denials were most comprehensive during the 'frigid phase' of the Cold War, 1950–53, but since that time, with occasional reversals, there has been a gradual relaxation. Of the Western countries the USA has developed the most rigorous system of denials, as part of her general policy of 'containment' and 'isolation',[2] having banned all trade with Mainland China, North Korea and North Vietnam, and almost all with Cuba. In addition to Taiwan (which bars all trade with Mainland China), Australia, New Zealand, South Africa and West Germany have followed stricter policies than the remaining Western countries.

Refusal by Western countries to trade on a normal commercial basis had its beginnings already between the wars when the USSR had to face the gold blockade, credit bans and various discriminatory measures against Soviet imports and exports. Since World War II, the most obvious case of Western denial of trade to the Socialist Bloc has been the strategic export controls (see Ch. 12 for details) and quantitative import restrictions. The latter controls (as in the case of oil and certain metals)

---

[1] US Senate, *East-West Trade*, Hearings before the Committee on Foreign Relations, Part II, GPO, Washington 1965, p. 100.

[2] The concept of 'containment' and 'isolation' can be traced back to 1947 when it was first expounded in an article: X, 'The Sources of Soviet Conduct', *Foreign Affairs*, July 1947, esp. pp. 576, 580–82, attributed to Dr George F. Kennan.

have been partly dictated by the desire to avoid possible political pressure by not becoming too dependent on the Bloc. The withdrawal of MFN from Socialist countries by the USA in 1951 was not dictated by economic reasons, but by the political climate produced by the Korean War.[1] The US Government also frowns upon its export promotion organizations fostering exports to the Bloc.[2] The subsidiaries of American companies operating in other countries have been under pressure from the US authorities to observe the American version of strategic export controls.

In the later 1950s, there was a remarkably relaxed atmosphere between the USA and the USSR. The Soviet Union wanted to increase trade and licences were being freely issued by the US Department of Commerce. But the deterioration of the political situation following the Berlin Wall crisis immediately led to reprisals by the American Government. Export licensing was tightened in 1961 and 1962, MFN was withheld from Poland and Yugoslavia (1962–64) and American firms were discouraged from participating in Leipzig trade fairs. The period 1961–63 witnessed a most intense boycott of Polish, Czechoslovak and Yugoslav goods in the American market. The boycotts were organized and financed by anti-communist elements and, as a Socialist economist pointed out, 'the Government did nothing to indicate its disapproval.'[3]

The US Government has also exerted pressure on other Western countries to check their trade, particularly with China, North Korea, North Vietnam and Cuba, a fact which has not contributed to Western

---

[1] Withdrawal of MFN means that imports from Socialist countries are subject to tariffs about four times higher than those of other countries.

[2] At the symposium held in 1959, an American lawyer described the feelings prevailing in the business community in the USA in the 1950s as follows: 'American businessmen are, in fact, most reluctant to deal with Sino-Soviet-bloc corporations. They do not want to have to explain to a congressional committee why they sold something to the Soviets, whether or not they are required to have an export license. They do not want to be barred from contracts with the US Government because of sales to the Soviet Union or its satellites. They do not want to be subjected to unusual FBI checks. They want to be thought of as "good Americans".' (B. Fensterwald, 'United States Policies toward State Trading', *Law and Contemporary Problems*, vol. 24, Summer 1959, p. 380). Even as late as in 1968, the editor of a newly established journal, *The American Review of East-West Trade*, observed (March 1968, p. 19): 'In effect, U.S. firms are conducting their East-West trade activities in a semi-underground fashion, for fear of harmful political repercussions on domestic business.'

[3] H. Więckowski, *Handel zagraniczny* (Foreign Trade), Warsaw, 3/1966, p. 88. Also see, J. Werner, *Handel zagr.*, 7/1963, pp. 295–97, and Ch. 8 B, footnote 3, pp. 126–27.

unity. The American policy has also been designed to discourage smaller nations, especially those relying on one staple product for export income, from becoming too dependent on the Bloc market. In 1962, a plan was announced, by the Australian Wool Bureau, of technical assistance to the Mainland Chinese wool textile industry (to promote Australian wool exports to China in consequence). But owing to subtle diplomatic pressure, the plan has never been put into practice.

The ability of Socialist countries to harm or weaken the West by denials of exports or imports has been and still is negligible. Nevertheless, numerous cases can be quoted in which Socialist countries took recourse to restricting trade. In a general sense, the Socialist countries' reluctance to import consumer goods from the West can be partly explained in political terms. Such severe quantitative restrictions not only prevent 'contagious' consumption but also release foreign exchange for imports of machinery and industrial raw materials to promote the development of such economic structures as are considered essential on social and political grounds. The autarkic policies pursued by Socialist countries up to the mid-1950s and, otherwise, attempts to divert trade into intra-Bloc channels, as well as the schemes for intra-CMEA specialization in order to become less dependent on the Capitalist World, have had greater political than economic appeal.

In spite of some relaxations by several Eastern European Socialist countries, Western businessmen are still denied unrestricted travel and access to the using and producing enterprises. The Bloc countries are also noted for their limited, or complete lack of, participation in those international commercial and economic organizations (GATT, International Chamber of Commerce, IMF, IBRD, etc.) which are dominated by Western countries (see Table XXXII, pp. 368–72).

Now, to quote a few specific cases of denial of trade by Socialist countries. The Soviet Bloc broke off its trade with Yugoslavia following the political dispute and rift in 1948, as a result of which its share in Yugoslav trade fell from 50% to practically nil over the next five years.[1] Following the defection of V. Petrov, a member of the Soviet embassy in Canberra, in 1954 the USSR broke off diplomatic relations with

[1] Based on: United Nations *Yearbook of International Trade Statistics 1952* and *1955*, Statistical Office of the United Nations, New York, pp. 384 and 720 respectively.

Australia and practically discontinued wool imports until diplomatic relations were resumed in 1959. In the late 1950s, the USSR also cut off certain imports from Finland and Iceland when Communists were dropped from the governments in these countries. In 1964/65 Soviet imports from West Germany were reduced and the trade agreement was broken as a result of a dispute over the status of West Berlin. Socialist countries have frequently attacked South African racial policies in the forum of the United Nations, urging economic sanctions. Since 1964 (the USSR since 1960) the Socialist Bloc has virtually ceased importing wool from that country (although in the latter 1950s the Bloc absorbed one-tenth of her wool exports); other trade with South Africa is insignificant now, too.

Apart from the USSR, the greatest initiative in 'politicizing' trade has been displayed by China. Trading relations with Japan have pretty closely reflected the political climate between the two countries. To the 1956 trade agreement with Japan, the Chinese Government attached two political strings, viz. that a Chinese trade delegation be stationed in Japan and be accorded diplomatic privileges and that a flag of the Peking regime be hoisted over the headquarters of the delegation. These stipulations amounted to making Japan extend a *de facto* diplomatic recognition to Peking. After the 1957 flag-tearing incident in Nagasaki, China repudiated the $190 m. agreement, contracts were cancelled and trade evaporated to a trickle between the two countries for the next four years.

Although trade has been resumed since 1961 and has grown to remarkable proportions, China has refused to deal with those Japanese firms which are noted for anti-Chinese sentiments. Late in 1960, the Peking Government announced that China would deal only with 'friendly firms'. On the advice of the Japan Communist Party and the Sohyo Federation of Labour, she designated fifty such firms, mostly of small and medium size (several large Japanese companies set up dummy subsidiaries to pass for 'friendly firms'). In 1966 China broke off commercial relations with a number of the 'friendly firms' which were supporting the Japan Communist Party and becoming increasingly pro-Soviet.

C. POLITICS IN AID OF TRADE

In the earlier stages of the Cold War, both East and West endeavoured to manipulate trade chiefly for negative effects. But then, particularly since about the mid-1950s, increasing importance has been attached to securing positive effects by offers of trade to the other side. Besides, in many instances trade and economic aid policies have been designed to court the support of uncommitted nations. We shall consider Western policies and practices first.

Already before the Korean War, following the expulsion of Yugoslavia from Cominform, not only did many Western European countries and the USA extend substantial economic and military aid but also they opened up their markets and sources of supply to the defecting country. As a result, the share of the West in Yugoslav trade increased from 45% in 1948 to 90% in 1953.[1] One of the main considerations which prompted the British Government to extend diplomatic recognition to the Peking regime in 1950 was that of trade. After the events of 1956 when Poland sought improved relations with the West, the USA responded by extending MFN treatment to Poland, relaxing the licensing of exports and providing economic aid under Public Law 480.

Views have occasionally been expressed by primary producing and manufacturing interests in several Western countries, especially those more dependent on foreign trade, that exports to the Bloc assist in maintaining higher levels of employment. This reduces opportunities for Communist subversion which normally thrives wherever there is unemployment and dissatisfaction.

Up to the early 1960s, the use of trade by the West as a positive weapon was limited to isolated cases. However, since about 1963 a new approach has been foreshadowed in several Western countries. In that year, West Germany set out to isolate Ulbricht's regime by building up diplomatic and commercial contacts with East Germany's Eastern European friends. At the time of writing, with the exception of Albania, Bonn had trade missions throughout Eastern Europe (see Table XXVII, opposite). As a prelude to the exchange of ambassadors with Rumania in

[1] Based on *UNYITS 1955*, *op. cit.*, p. 720.

TABLE XXVII EAST-WEST DIPLOMATIC RELATIONS, 1968[1]

D = Diplomatic representation[2]
T = Trade representation (official or unofficial)[3]
C = Consular representation
N = No diplomatic recognition[4]

	Albania	Bulgaria	Czechoslovakia	East Germany	Hungary	Mainland China	Mongolia	North Korea	North Vietnam	Poland	Rumania	USSR
Australia		T	T	N	T	N		N	N	T	D	D
Austria	D	D	D	NT	D	NT	D	N	N	D	D	D
Belgium		D	D	NT	D	N		N	N	D	D	D
Canada		D	D	N	D	N		N	N	D	D	D
Denmark		D	D	NT	D	D		N	N	D	D	D
Finland	D	D	D	NT	D	D	D	N	N	D	D	D
France	D	D	D	NT	D	D	D	N	C	D	D	D
Germany, West		T		N	T	N		N	N	T	D	D
Greece		D	D	NT	D	N	D	N	N	D	D	D
Iceland		D	D	NT	D					D	D	D
Ireland				N		N		N	N			
Italy	D	D	D	NT	D	N		N	N	D	D	D
Japan		D	D	N	D	N	N	N	N	D	D	D
Netherlands		D	D	NT	D	D		N	N	D	D	D
New Zealand				N		N		N	N	T		D
Norway		D	D	NT	D	D		N	N	D	D	D
Portugal	N	N	N	N	N	N	N	N	N	N	N	N
South Africa				N		N		N	N			
Spain	N	NT	NT	N	NT	N	N	N	N	NT	C	T
Sweden		D	D	NT	D	D	D	N	N[5]	D	D	D
Switzerland		D	D	N	D	D	D	N	N	D	D	D
Turkey	D	D	D	NT	D			N	N	D	D	D

TABLE XXVII—*Continued*

	Albania	Bulgaria	Czechoslovakia	East Germany	Hungary	Mainland China	Mongolia	North Korea	North Vietnam	Poland	Rumania	USSR
United Kingdom		D	D	NT	D	D	D	N	C	D	D	D
United States		D	D	N	D	N	N	N	N	D	D	D
Yugoslavia	D	D	D	D	D	D	D	D	D	D	D	D

[1] The entries should be treated as minimal, as they may be incomplete.

[2] In some instances, the representation is handled indirectly by dual accreditation. E.g. Finland, Sweden and Switzerland are represented in Mongolia through their Moscow missions. In many cases, diplomatic representation includes trade (often handled by the First or Second Secretary or a Commercial Counsellor) as well as consular representation.

[3] In several cases, trade and consular representation of Socialist countries are combined (as e.g. by Czechoslovakia and Poland in Australia).

[4] Blank spaces indicate that either there has been no official declaration about recognition or non-recognition or that in spite of diplomatic recognition there are no diplomatic relations.

[5] It was announced in January 1969 that Sweden and North Vietnam would establish full diplomatic relations.

Sources. Compiled from a variety of official and unofficial sources. The assistance generously given by the Department of External Affairs, Canberra, is gratefully acknowledged.

February 1967, West Germany liberalized quotas on imports from that country. Early in 1964, American policy towards the Soviet Bloc was subjected to a thorough re-examination by the Committee on Foreign Relations under the chairmanship of Senator Fulbright, with a view to introducing greater flexibility in US policy towards the European Socialist countries. The hearings were continued in early 1965,[1] and a year later a similar reappraisal was made of Sino-American relations.[2]

In May 1964 President Johnson put forward a new policy with regard to the Eastern European countries, 'to build bridges across the gulf

[1] See *East-West Trade*, Hearings 1964, Part I, and Hearings 1965, Part II, *op. cit.*

[2] See US Senate, *US Policy with Respect to Mainland China*, Hearings before the Committee on Foreign Relations, GPO, Washington 1966.

which has divided us from Eastern Europe. They will be bridges of increased trade, of ideas, of visitors and of humanitarian aid.'[1]

The changing attitude in these two Western powers, whose rigid and unimaginative policies had for years contrasted with a more flexible and lenient approach by other Western countries, can be explained by two developments. On the one hand, owing to a variety of reasons (see Ch. 12) the policies of denying trade to Socialist countries had been proving ineffective. On the other, polycentric tendencies, divergent national interests and the adoption of some elements of free enterprise in the European CMEA countries have provided promising openings for the West. It came to be realized that the Socialist Bloc is in fact no longer a unified monolith. Instead, Socialist countries must be treated separately as acting independently of each other. In 1964 Mr Rusk clearly distinguished four variants of US trade policy toward the Socialist Bloc. In descending order of *rapprochement* they were those towards Eastern Europe, the Soviet Union, Cuba and the Far Eastern Socialist countries.[2] Thus the USA has been encouraging trade with the Eastern European countries 'where it helps promoting independent policies along national lines.'[3] He further stated:

> Through such measures we can hope over time to develop avenues of practical contact with the peoples and officials of the Eastern European countries. Trade carries with it more than commodities. It helps to bring the presence of the United States to the Eastern European peoples, to associate them in some measure with our economy, and to demonstrate American enterprise and efficiency. By these means, trade enables us to exert some influence on the evolution of policy and institutions in this period of accelerating change in Eastern Europe.'[4]

However, President Johnson's policy of 'building bridges' via liberalized trade, including his determination to press for Congress giving

---

[1] *New York Times*, 24/5/1964. Policies along these lines had already been advocated in these two countries several years before. In 1960 the West German *Bundestag* moved for 'an Eastern policy aiming at the restoration of a free all-German state that maintains friendly and prosperous relations with the Soviet Union and all Eastern European countries.' In 1961 Z. Brzezinski and W. E. Griffith argued for a policy of 'peaceful engagement'. See G. Schröder, 'Germany Looks at Eastern Europe', *Foreign Affairs*, Oct. 1965, p. 16; Z. Brzezinski and W. E. Griffith, 'Peaceful Engagement in Eastern Europe', *Foreign Affairs*, July 1961, pp. 642–54.
[2] *East-West Trade*, Hearings 1964, Part 1, *op. cit.*, pp. 5–18.
[3] *Ibid.*, p. 5. [4] *Ibid.*, p. 10.

him authority to extend MFN to the Eastern European countries (in addition to Poland), which was reiterated in 1965, 1966 and 1967, has run into political opposition. As these countries have declared determined support for North Vietnam, it has been feared that they could 'use American trade as a means of diverting their own resources to aiding Vietnam.'[1] This brings us to the other side of the Socialist Bloc.

There have also been some Western attempts to promote trade with China by political overtures in recent years. Early in 1964 France established diplomatic relations with Peking, but although commercial contacts have been improved the expansion of trade has so far been very modest. There have been several moves by different groups in the USA to change American policy towards China but with no practical results as yet. In 1961 President Kennedy offered to consider Chinese requests for the import of food from the USA. But the Peking regime denounced the offer of trade not only in food but in other commodities as well. At the 1966 hearings before the Foreign Relations Committee on US policy towards China, the majority of experts, whilst supporting military containment, advocated a political and commercial 'deisolation'. A similar policy has been urged by the '198 Group' of American scholars,[2] ARFEP (Americans for a Review of Far Eastern Policy) as well as by various business groups casting nostalgic eyes upon China's increasing interest in extra-Bloc trade.

So much for the Western side. In a general sense, the relaxed internal political atmosphere in most European Socialist countries since Stalin's death (1953), the declaration of the policy of peaceful co-existence (after 1956) and a gradual retreat from previous autarkic policies, have all favoured expansion of trade with the West. For most Eastern European countries, expansion of trade with the West is a means of some emancipation from 'Big Brother'. Similarly, China has exhibited a growing preference for extra-Bloc trade, prompted by the ideological dispute with the Soviets on the one hand, and the relaxation of Western strategic export controls on the other. Even many Stalinist diehards favour

[1] *US News and World Report*, 31/1/1966, p. 33.
[2] See their 'Position Paper – Recommendations for a Change in the United States – Chinese Relations and Policies', which appeared in the *New York Times*, 21/3/1966.

increasing trade with the West because it can be used to exacerbate bourgeois 'contradictions'. Socialist leaders also have their own theory that the Capitalist World is no longer a monolithic entity but a conglomerate with conflicting political and economic interests.

How politics can aid trade is illustrated by the following examples. As a gesture to the country which (at the time) had the largest Communist Party in the Capitalist world, the Soviets unexpectedly contracted in 1954 to buy the whole crop of almonds from Italy when the USA announced import quota restrictions on this commodity. To keep Finland out of Western alliances and to secure her co-operation in the maintenance of Soviet military bases against the West, the USSR has, in general, given very favourable trading terms. Some of the Finnish exports are high-cost articles produced by industries which had to be set up after World War II specifically to meet reparation deliveries to the USSR. These uneconomic industries (engineering and shipbuilding in particular) could not easily find markets in the West and they would have to be phased out if it were not for Soviet patronage.

The gradually improving political relations between the USSR and Yugoslavia since 1954 have been marked with Soviet offers of trade and aid and a partial admission of Yugoslavia to CMEA in 1964.[1] In 1958 Iceland, a member country of NATO, had a disagreement with Britain over fishing rights. When subsequently Britain cut off her imports of fish, the Soviet Union immediately undertook to purchase large quantities of this Icelandic staple export.

Whereas the West had capitalized on the Yugoslav case after 1948, the Socialist Bloc has found a parallel opportunity in Cuba since 1960. Close political contacts have been reinforced by trade agreements on very generous terms to Cuba, with economic and military aid thrown in. In 1959 less than 2% of Cuba's trade was with the Socialist Bloc, but the share has risen since to over 60%.

In some small ways, East-West trade is promoted by Western Communist parties which sometimes participate directly or indirectly in

---

[1] In 1967 the Bloc claimed 32% of Yugoslavia's trade. In this, the USSR's share was more than 13% (in 1953 trade between the two countries was nil), after Italy she is now the largest trader with Yugoslavia (although she is likely to be outstripped by W. Germany). Based on: *UNYITS 1955, op. cit.*, p. 720, and *Direction of Trade*, 4/1968, p. 179.

private companies which trade or finance trade with Socialist countries. It is known that in choosing agents for the sale of books and periodicals in Capitalist countries, the Soviet Union and China have given preference to Communist parties or their nominees. As was indicated in the preceding section of this chapter, in trade with Japan China prefers to deal with 'friendly firms'.[1] It may also be mentioned that in 1963–64 the Chinese authorities sent 1,700 letters to firms in seventy countries dealing with China urging ostracism of Brazil in protest against the arrest of nine Chinese journalists suspected of subversive activities.[2]

D. COMPETITION FOR SUPPORT IN DEVELOPING COUNTRIES

To strengthen its position each camp, led by the USA on the one side and the USSR and China on the other, has taken recourse to trade and aid with a view to enlisting the support of the uncommitted nations of Asia, Africa and Latin America. It is doubtful if these nations would be such an object of patronage merely on humanitarian grounds. In addition to the political goodwill, each camp has been striving to safeguard its sources of strategic raw materials, such as copper, rubber and tin, of which many Developing countries are important (or exclusive) world producers. The commercial and political goodwill of these countries has also been looked upon by each camp as a venue for reducing economic dependence on the opposing side.

First of all, the West has adopted a lenient attitude towards admitting Developing countries into GATT.[3] Various assistance schemes, such as the Colombo Plan and those under United Nations auspices have been instituted. To this we must add the large economic, technical and

[1] At the beginning of 1967 there were about 300 Japanese firms accepted as 'friendly' (roughly 100 being actively engaged in trade with China). In recent years they have handled from two-thirds to three-quarters of the total Sino-Japanese trade. Most of these firms have had some association with the Japan Communist Party, such as having JCP members as directors and employees, and themselves providing most of the funds needed by the Party. See Kyosuke Hirotsu, 'Trouble between Comrades', *Current Scene*, Hong Kong, 15/3/1967, esp. p. 9.

[2] Evidence cited in Commonwealth of Australia, *Commonwealth Parliamentary Debates* (H. of R.), Canberra, 23/4/1964, p. 1469 and 13/5/1965, p. 1,543.

[3] Numerically, Developing countries now outnumber Western countries – 55 to 24. See Table XXXII, p. 368.

military aid given by the leading Western powers, especially the USA. The aid has often been extended to strengthen anti-communist elements in expectation of pro-Western alignment or at least neutralism.

Socialist effort has been broadly directed at promoting the processes leading to the Socialist road to economic development (including State trading), expropriation of Western assets, anti-colonialist sentiments and non-alignment. There is plenty of evidence showing how trade can become an extension of diplomacy for the Soviet Union and China in particular in the Third World. To break the Western boycott of Iran, following the nationalization of the Anglo-Iranian Oil Company (1951), the USSR immediately agreed to make large barter deals with that country. During 1954 and 1955, when Burma was faced with difficulties in selling her rice, owing to a glut in world markets, China and the USSR agreed to buy the surpluses, even though they did not need the product and in fact had to re-export a portion of it later. In 1956 the two countries purchased Egyptian cotton and in addition the Soviets sent technical personnel to help Egypt in her dispute with Britain and France over the Suez Canal.[1] Similarly, the substantial Soviet purchases of cocoa from Ghana when Dr Nkrumah was in power were politically motivated.[2]

Since the early 1960s, China has carried her trade tactics further afield, courting ideological and political support, to the annoyance of both the West and the Soviet Union. China not only supported the war of liberation in Algeria against France by gifts of arms and food but soon afterwards signed a trade agreement (1962) and an accord on cultural exchanges (1963). China's trading interest with the Developing World cannot be easily justified on purely commercial grounds because their import and export capacities are more competitive than complementary.

Socialist interest in trade with Developing countries is reflected in the growth of the number of trade agreements – the respective figures for

---

[1] It is worth noting that Egypt was the first Arab country to have extended diplomatic recognition to China – in May 1956, i.e. 5 months before the Suez Canal affair.
[2] A detailed account of Socialist policies and practices in the 1950s can be found in US Department of State, *The Sino-Soviet Economic Offensive in the Less Developed Countries*, Washington, May 1958. For a more recent treatment see Carole A. Sawyer, *Communist Trade with Developing Countries 1955-65*, Praeger, New York 1966; M. I. Goldman, *Soviet Foreign Aid*, Praeger, N. York 1967; J. D. Montgomery, *Foreign Aid in International Politics*, Prentice-Hall, N. York 1967.

1953, 1957 and 1968 having been 49, 112 and 264.[1] It may be observed that trade agreements in themselves have a certain propaganda value for Socialist countries, associated with the visits by trade missions, the signing of contracts, etc. Socialist countries pride themselves that they accord better terms of trade to Developing nations than the Western countries do.[2]

Socialist aid schemes to Developing countries date only from 1954, i.e. six years after the US aid programme had been launched. From that time to 1968 the Socialist Bloc committed itself to about $12,000 m. in economic, military and technical aid. The USSR is the main contributor (about two-thirds of the total), followed by China (about one-fifth), Czechoslovakia, East Germany, Hungary and Bulgaria. This compares with the Western aid commitments (1949–68) totalling over $100,000 m., two-thirds of which has been contributed by the USA.[3] The aid distributed by different agencies of the United Nations is not included in the above figures, but most of such funds are contributed by Western countries.

The main features contrasting Socialist and Western aid schemes to underdeveloped countries may be briefly noted. First, the Socialist aid effort has been much smaller in size as compared with the Western aid programme, the ratio being roughly 1:8. Second, the Socialist Bloc has limited its aid to carefully chosen countries – 35 of them so far; Western aid is more widely spread – the USA alone has been aiding more than 90 countries. The keenest competition between the two camps has been observed in Afghanistan, Ceylon, India, Iraq, Syria, Ethiopia, Ghana, Guinea, Somali, Tunisia, Argentina and Brazil.

Third, the Bloc's effort is mostly concentrated on supplying equip-

---

[1] See Table XV, p. 109. The figure for 1953 was obtained from R. F. Mikesell and D. A. Wells, 'State Trading in the Sino-Soviet Bloc', *Law and Cont. Pr.*, vol. 24, Summer 1959, p. 443. This increase can, of course, be partly explained by the growing number of Developing countries capable of entering into trade agreements – their number in 1953 stood at less than 50 whilst in 1968 it was 90.

[2] Imre Vajda, *The Role of Foreign Trade in a Socialist Economy*, Corvina Press, Budapest 1965, p. 283.

[3] Agency for International Development and Department of Defense, *Proposed Mutual Defense and Development Programs FY 1966*, GPO, Washington, March 1965, pp. 175–81; Agency for International Development, *Proposed Foreign Aid Program FY 1968*, GPO, Washington 1967, pp. 60, 271–97; *International Affairs*, Moscow, 4/1966, p. 23; *Foreign Trade*, Moscow, 7/1968, pp. 5–7.

ment and technical advice for well-defined industrial projects, some large, but mostly small. This contrasts with the Western emphasis on humanitarian aid in the form of food, health and education programmes and the development of food and raw material production. There is little doubt that for show purposes, the Socialist approach is more effective. It also appears that the Bloc is more genuinely interested in promoting industrialization on ideological grounds. Not only does it lead to 'balanced proportionate development' but it also tends to produce an industrial class more amenable to Communist ideology than a conservative and suspicious peasantry.

Fourth, Socialist aid, whether economic or military, is mostly in loans rather than grants, the latter representing only 5% of the total. Loans are on generous terms; interest rates are low, mostly 2–3% p.a., whilst some loans are interest-free and others carry up to 5%;[1] they are for long periods – mostly for 10–15 years, but in some cases up to 50 years. Loans are repayable in local traditional commodities or local currencies. On the other hand, Western aid has come about half and half in grants and loans (slightly more grants than loans). Such aid has usually had some strings attached, and the terms on loans have not been as generous as those offered by Socialist countries.

On the whole since 1966, both Western and Socialist political enthusiasm in extending aid to the Third World has markedly cooled off. The West, in particular the USA, has found that political advantages gained in the Developing countries in most cases have been short-lasting, in others unreliable or downright negative. Of the Socialist countries, China already in 1965, in the famous Lin-Piao Declaration, hinted that the revolutionary elements in the Third World should rely on their own local means for social and economic advancement. At the second UNCTAD Conference in New Delhi in 1968, Mr N. Patolichev, the Soviet Minister for Foreign Trade, also urged the Developing nations to fall back upon their own resources for speeding up their development, and depend less on outside aid. The USSR and the Eastern European countries participating in the Conference voted against, or abstained from voting on, the resolution that 1% of the GNP

[1] Eastern European Socialist countries as a rule charge higher interest rates than the USSR does. See J. Rutkowski, *Światowy rynek kredytowy* (The World Credit Market), PWE, Warsaw 1964, esp. pp. 259–64, 273–84.

of the more developed nations be given in aid to Developing countries (but the resolution was passed because most Western nations supported it).

The way in which Socialist assistance schemes are handled yields distinct political and economic advantages to the Bloc which, as compared with Western aid, have been out of all proportion considering the relatively small amounts of aid involved.[1] The fact that Socialist aid is mostly in loans and in the form of deliveries of equipment repayable in local goods carries important implications so far as trade is concerned.

In their trade with the West, Developing countries are exposed to widely fluctuating demand and prices, and they have experienced difficulties in earning sufficient foreign exchange to finance their development. The willingness of the Socialist countries to provide markets by accepting repayments in primary products is welcomed with relief. This contrasts with the American practice. The USA in most cases requires repayment in foreign (convertible) exchange and is not willing to open up her markets because, like Developing nations but unlike Socialist countries, she has the problem of disposing of her own primary products.

A study of Western and Socialist competition in Developing countries would be incomplete without examining the trends in trade. Table XXVIII, p. 257, shows the value and relative importance of the trade with the Third World to the West and to the Socialist Bloc since 1938. Of particular interest to us are the tendencies since the Korean War. It will be noted that, relatively speaking, the West has been turning away from Developing countries. Whilst in 1953 trade with the Third World represented 29% of total Western trade, by 1968 the proportion had declined to 20%.

Trade between the Bloc and the Third World has never been large in absolute terms. However, the Third World is claiming an increasing share of the Bloc's total trade – the proportion having risen from 5% in 1953 to 12% in 1967.

Of what significance is trade with the West and with the Bloc to the Third World? This is brought out in Table XXIX, p. 258. The over-

[1] At the 1966 Hearings before the Committee on Foreign Relations, Senator Fulbright asked: 'Why is money that we spend, which amounts to far more than they [Russians] spend, so ineffective to buy people out of these situations? Is our money not as good as Russian money?' *US Policy with Respect to Mainland China, op. cit.*, p. 486.

TABLE XXVIII WESTERN AND SOCIALIST TRADE WITH THE THIRD WORLD,[1] 1938, 1948, 1953–67[2]

YEAR	Western-Trade Turnover with the Third World		The Bloc's Trade Turnover with the Third World	
	In £ Million at Current Prices	% of Total Western Trade with the World	% of the Bloc's Total Trade with the World	In £ Million at Current Prices
1938	1,570	24·3	12·7	110
1948	5,670	31·2	12·6	230
1953	10,540	28·5	4·8	260
1954	11,130	28·9	5·5	330
1955	11,840	27·7	6·6	430
1956	13,060	27·2	7·0	490
1957	13,930	27·0	7·6	600
1958	13,410	27·3	8·3	710
1959	13,590	25·8	7·3	730
1960	14,640	24·6	8·2	880
1961	14,790	23·6	10·4	1,150
1962	14,990	22·6	10·6	1,300
1963	16,140	22·1	11·3	1,480
1964	17,680	21·4	11·4	1,620
1965	18,880	20·8	12·3	1,880
1966	20,500	21·2	12·5	2,010
1967	21,550	20·0	11·5	2,010

[1] *The West:* Canada, USA, all Europe except the eight Socialist countries, Japan, South Africa, Australia and New Zealand.

The Socialist Bloc: Albania, Bulgaria, Czechoslovakia, East Germany, Hungary, Poland, Rumania, USSR, Mainland China, Mongolia, North Korea and North Vietnam.

The Third World: all the remaining countries, other than the West and the Socialist Bloc.

[2] All exports and imports are valued f.o.b. The world total includes shipments to unknown destinations, usually constituting less than 3% of world trade. No data are available on inter-trade among the four Asian Socialist countries (M. China, Mongolia, N. Korea and N. Vietnam), and thus to this extent the Bloc's as well as the world's totals are understated, but the amount involved is believed to be less than 1% of world trade. The values were converted from US dollars at the rate current at the time.

Sources. Based on: *United Nations Yearbook of International Trade Statistics* and *Monthly Bulletin of Statistics.*

TABLE XXIX THE THIRD WORLD'S TRADE WITH THE WEST
AND WITH THE SOCIALIST BLOC, 1938, 1948, 1953–67*

YEAR	Foreign-Trade Turnover with the West		Foreign-Trade Turnover with the Socialist Bloc	
	In £ Million at Current Prices	% of the Third World's Trade with the World	% of the Third World's Trade with the World	In £ Million at Current Prices
1938	1,570	70·1	4·7	110
1948	5,670	67·0	2·7	230
1953	10,540	72·3	1·8	260
1954	11,130	72·3	2·3	330
1955	11,840	71·9	2·6	430
1956	13,060	73·4	2·8	490
1957	13,930	73·1	3·1	600
1958	13,410	73·3	3·9	710
1959	13,590	73·3	3·9	730
1960	14,640	73·4	4·4	880
1961	14,790	72·5	5·6	1,150
1962	14,990	71·9	6·3	1,300
1963	16,140	71·5	6·4	1,480
1964	17,680	71·8	6·6	1,620
1965	18,880	71·7	7·1	1,880
1966	20,500	72·2	7·1	2,010
1967	21,550	72·9	6·8	2,010

* For explanations and sources, see Table XXVIII, p. 257.

whelming role of the West to Developing countries is unquestionable – more than two-thirds of their total trade is with the West, the proportion in fact being slightly higher than before World War II. On the other hand, although trade with the Bloc is small in absolute terms, its percentage share is increasing very fast; but even so, it represents a fraction (one-tenth) of the Third World's trade with the West.[1]

[1] According to Socialist forecasts, supported by United Nations sources, the share of the Third World in the Bloc's trade will rise to 15% by 1971 and the share of the latter in the Third World's trade to 10%. See B. Najniger, *Gospodarka planowa* (Planned Economy), Warsaw, 8–9/1966, esp. p. 17.

CH. II §E POLITICS IN PARTNERSHIP WITH TRADE 259

E. OIL, WHEAT AND TECHNOLOGY

These three items entering East-West trade deserve a separate discussion because they illustrate the different ways in which politics has expressed itself through trade. By value, oil is the most important item of the Socialist Bloc's export to the West, wheat has become a leading Western commodity exported to the Bloc, whilst technology, for long a controversial problem in East-West trade, is assuming an increasing importance.

(a) Oil

For several decades now, oil has been the most important single commodity entering world trade. Oil has loomed prominently in several national and international conflicts in the last decade or two in regions stretching from Brazil and Cuba through North and East Africa, the Middle East to Indonesia. To Socialist countries, especially to the USSR, these conflicts appear a clear proof of the power and interference of the 8 big Western oil companies (5 American, 1 Anglo-Dutch, 1 British and 1 French) constituting the 'International Oil Cartel'. A leading Soviet authority on oil marketing described them recently thus: 'there is hardly a group of monopolies that has displayed as much destructive energy, craft, intrigue and special inclination to international piracy as the oil business in its efforts to secure control both of domestic political relations in various countries and of the principal factors of world politics.'[1] In the Soviet view the oil concessions to the Western companies in the Middle East constitute the foundation of Western political influence there and a serious threat to the USSR on her doorstep.

It is against this backdrop that the Soviet Union has staged her rather spectacular oil offensive in the Capitalist World since the mid-1950s. In the last decade the volume of these exports has increased by more than ten times – from less than 4 m. tons in 1955 to 45 m. in 1967.[2] Of the

[1] B. Rachkov, 'Oil, Trade and Politics', *International Affairs*, Moscow, 4/1966, p. 20.
[2] So far as the total output is concerned, the USSR produces nine-tenths, the balance being contributed by Rumania, China, Hungary, Albania, Bulgaria, Poland and Czechoslovakia. Their total production in 1967 was 310 m. tons, or 18% of the world total (the Western share amounted to 30% and the Third World's to 52%); in 1950 the

other Socialist countries, only Rumania and Albania are significant oil exporters. The most rapid increase was recorded in the later 1950s and early 1960s when annual increments reached 50%.

It is during this period that there was a good deal of bitter competition between the Soviet *Soiuznefteksport* and Western oil companies. It led to Soviet price undercutting by 5–20%, and in some cases by up to 40%, below world market prices in Latin America, Western Europe, Egypt, India, Ceylon and Japan.[1] In the late 1960s the Bloc's export of oil and products to the Capitalist world worth over $600 m. annually represented about 5% of the latter's total requirements. In 1967 Western Europe and Japan each satisfied 4% of its oil needs from Socialist sources. But the percentage for Finland and Iceland has recently been as high as 80%, for Austria and Greece – 30% and for Italy and Sweden – 10%. Oil accounts for one-fifth of the Soviet income from exports to the West.[2] To emancipate herself from her dependence on Western shipping and oil companies for transport, the Soviet Union has launched an ambitious scheme to build and acquire tankships. She now has enough tankers to carry nearly all of her off-shore shipments.

The success of the Soviet oil offensive has been due to several reasons. Most Soviet oil is of low sulphur content and is reasonably priced. In contrast to the Western oil companies, which insist on payment in hard currencies, the USSR as well as Rumania are usually prepared to make counter-purchases of local machinery or raw materials – a fact of considerable weight in countries experiencing foreign-exchange problems. In view of the steadily rising demand for oil, many countries, especially Brazil, Italy, Egypt, India and Ceylon have welcomed more competition, which lessens their dependence on the Anglo-American oil dictatorship.

The Soviet oil export drive has caused a good deal of concern to

---

Bloc's share was less than 10%. By 1980 the USSR plans to overtake the USA by producing 700 m. tons annually (in 1967 the USA produced 420 m. tons, or about 25% of the world total). See B. Rachkov, *Vneshnaya torgovlya*, Moscow, 3/1964, pp. 12–16. *Petroleum Press Service*, London 1/1967, p. 8; 6/1967, pp. 233, 240; 2/1968, p. 66; 7/1968, p. 280.

[1] See *Far Eastern Economic Review*, 21/7/1960, p. 127; 19/1/1961, pp. 97–100; 6/4/1961, p. 76; 17/5/1962, pp. 339–40. S. C. Stolte, 'Oil as a Weapon in the Cold War', *Bulletin*, Munich, 9/1961, pp. 10–18. G. A. Vvedensky, 'Soviet Oil and the Export Market', *Bulletin*, 5/1963, pp. 30–39.

[2] *Petroleum Press Service*, 10/1964, pp. 367–69; 3/1967, p. 109; 4/1968, p. 138.

Western oil companies and governments. The oil companies have already suffered from over-capacity, made worse by the Saharan developments. The companies as well as other believers in free enterprise have viewed with alarm the Soviet assistance given to several countries (such as Ceylon, India, Indonesia, Egypt, Tanzania, Cuba) in setting up or strengthening State oil corporations. It has also been felt that the expanded export markets in the Capitalist world are providing the USSR and Rumania with extra capacity, beyond their normal peace-time needs. This in case of war could be turned to assist the Bloc's warfare whilst at the same time causing dislocation to the West. The fact that these countries have no refining and distributing facilities of their own in the West, makes it easier for them to withdraw their oil supplies unexpectedly even in peacetime.[1]

Since 1961 EEC has evolved an elaborate system of co-ordinating its policy on oil imports from the Socialist Bloc. It has been designed not only to protect the Community's oil interests but also, for security reasons, to prevent too much dependence on the Bloc.[2] Similar steps have apparently been taken elsewhere. According to a Soviet source:

> Diplomatic pressure in the interests of the British and American oil concerns – ranging from official notes and representations to calls by US and British ambassadors on heads of governments – has been applied in Italy, Japan, India, Ceylon, the UAR, Brazil, Uruguay and many other countries. Diplomatic action was frequently backed up by a suspension or threat of suspension of American aid.[3]

To what extent has the USSR really been motivated by political factors in her oil export drive? There is little doubt that her exports have been genuine surpluses. Consumption in the Soviet Union, and in fact in the rest of the Socialist Bloc, has been rising much more slowly than the production capacity, whilst consumption in the West has grown more rapidly. What the USSR has been doing in fact, is to try to regain her pre-war role in Western markets. It may be noted that between 1926

---

[1] But in 1968, the Soviet oil company *Nafta* proceeded to build oil storage facilities in Antwerp in co-operation with Belgian interests. See *Amer. Rev. of East-West Trade*, 5/1968, p. 69.

[2] G. Adler-Karlsson, 'Does EEC Discriminate?', *Economics of Planning*, Oslo, vol. 4, no. 2, 1964, esp. pp. 106–109.

[3] B. Rachkov, 'Oil, Trade and Politics', *Intern. Aff.*, Moscow, 4/1966, p. 19.

and 1935 Western Europe obtained 14% of its oil requirements from the USSR, whilst in recent years the proportion has averaged only 5%.[1]

On the other hand, the fact that the USSR has, on the whole, been charging lower prices to the West than to the 'fraternal' Socialist countries (see Table XXI, p. 165) seems to suggest that she is counting on other than immediate financial returns. Furthermore, it is difficult to see what the USSR and Rumania stand to gain *economically* by assisting oil exploration and other oil projects in several less developed countries (Turkey, Brazil, Algeria, Ethiopia, Egypt, Syria, Iraq, Afghanistan, India and elsewhere).[2]

(b) Wheat

In a general sense, politics is responsible for the direction in which wheat moves in East-West trade. On the one hand, in most Western countries, such as Australia, Canada, France, Sweden and the USA, wheat production is subsidized in a variety of ways. These policies are largely a result of internal party politics, the farmers' vote often deciding which political party gets into power. At the same time, rapidly rising standards of living lead to a relative decline in the role of starchy foods in favour of high-quality protein diets. In consequence, the West has tended to produce increasing wheat surpluses available for export.

On the other hand, in most Socialist countries the continued industrialization drive has produced adverse repercussions on agriculture. Besides, as a Socialist economist pointed out, the grains deficit is partly caused by faulty price structures which lead to excessive consumption of low-quality foods by humans and wasteful feeding of grains to animals.[3]

---

[1] It was pointed out in a Soviet source that up to 1901 Russia had held the first place in oil production and in the export of oil products. In 1931 Italy obtained 68% of her oil needs from the USSR, and the percentages for Belgium, France and Germany stood at 35%, 22% and 22% respectively in 1932. See B. Rachkov, *Vneshn. torg.*, *op. cit.*, pp. 12–16.

[2] Of these Turkey is the only Western country; in June 1967 an agreement was signed with the State-owned TPAO whereby the USSR is to build a large refinery at Izmir, to be financed by a Soviet loan at 2·5% p.a. for 15 years, repayable in Turkish agricultural commodities. Reported in *Petroleum Press Service*, 7/1967, p. 272.

[3] For example, Poland has about the highest *per capita* figure of grains consumption in the world, viz. 147 kgs. This figure could be reduced to 125 kgs. if consumption of proteins (meat, eggs) increased by 6 kgs. See M. Niesiołowski, *Gosp. plan.*, 4/1966, p. 35.

Up to 1963 the Soviet Union was one of the four leading world exporters of wheat, and between the wars Bulgaria, Hungary and Poland were substantial exporters of grains, whilst China's imports up to 1961 were quite small. The large wheat imports by the Bloc began in 1961, following the disastrous effects of the Great Leap Forward and extremely adverse seasons in China during the period 1959–61. Eastern European countries (except Rumania) and North Korea have also stepped up their imports, and the USSR joined in after 1963 with huge orders. It is rather paradoxical that almost all these imports have come from the West (and not from Developing countries) – from Canada, Australia, the USA, France, Italy, West Germany and Sweden. In the late 1960s the Bloc's imports of wheat from the West averaged 15 m. metric tons a year worth about £300 m., representing one-sixth of its total imports from the West.[1]

Maxim Litvinov, former Soviet Minister for Foreign Affairs, once said, 'Food is a weapon'. Judging by wheat in East-West trade, there is evidence to suggest that the Soviet Union and China have lived up to this assertion. In 1948 the USSR exported quantities of wheat to France and Italy at the time of food shortages preceding elections to bolster the Communist movement, in spite of serious deficiencies in several parts of the USSR. After 1963, part of the Soviet-purchased wheat was diverted to Cuba directly from Canadian ports. Similarly, in spite of the critical domestic food situation, after 1961 China re-exported Australian and Canadian wheat to Cuba, Albania, East Germany, Hungary, Morocco, Algeria, Tunisia, Egypt, Syria, North Korea, North Vietnam and probably elsewhere as well.[2] The Chinese apparently used gifts of flour and wheat in areas along the Indian border to subvert local tribesmen against the Indian Government. These re-exports or gifts have obviously been designed not only to spite Western powers (such as the USA, France, West Germany) but also to compete with Moscow for ideological support.

In their wheat purchase policies in the West, the Socialist countries

[1] Based on: International Wheat Council, *Review of the World Wheat Situation 1966/67*, London, Nov. 1967, p. 33.
[2] Commonwealth of Australia, *Commonwealth Parliamentary Debates* (H. of R.) Canberra, 8/4/1964, p. 885; Pauline Lewin, *The Foreign Trade of Communist China*, Praeger, New York and London 1964, p. 77; Far Eastern Economic Review, *China Trade Report*, 1/1967, p. 11.

have not been able so far to play off one exporter against another to secure political advantages.[1] However, owing to differences in the political climate in Canada and in Australia, the Bloc countries have favoured the former with long-term contracts instead of single or annual deals with Australia. In several respects, Canada has been pursuing a foreign policy more independent from the US line than Australia has been able to. Anti-Chinese feelings are less intense in Canada than in Australia, and Canada dropped the special China Embargo List long ago (in 1957) whilst Australia has not. No doubt, these facts must have carried some weight, considering that China, the USSR, Bulgaria, Czechoslovakia, East Germany, Hungary and Poland have all signed 2–5 year agreements with Canada since 1961. But the wheat deals with Australia have been on a single contract basis covering no more than 12 months. It may also be observed that Chou En-lai has been quoted recently as saying that Australia would have to withdraw her troops from Vietnam if she wished to continue wheat sales to China.[2]

(c) *Technology*

Accusations against Socialist countries of unfairly appropriating Western know-how go back to the 1920s. These charges have become more vocal after the mid-1950s, since when the number of Socialist countries has risen to twelve. However, of greater consequence has been the fact that as Socialist countries have been entering advanced and sophisticated stages of industrialization, they have been increasingly interested in the most up-to-date models and processes. In the past, their practice was often to import just one prototype plant or a specialized machine or instrument, to reproduce on a large scale, and perhaps to export them to other Socialist countries or even elsewhere. Alternatively or additionally, essential blueprints, processes or key components have been obtained illicitly through industrial espionage.

East-West misunderstanding on patent rights has, of course, been largely due to differences in the basic concepts of property. On ideo-

[1] But in 1964 China profited from a small 'price war' in which she skilfully played off Australia, Canada, France and Argentina against each other. See J. Wilczyński, 'The Economics and Politics of Wheat Exports to China', *Australian Quarterly*, June 1965, esp. pp. 45–46.
[2] *CPD (H. of R.)*, Canberra, 22/9/1965, p. 1,137.

logical grounds, the orthodox Communists regard inventions as a form of collective property from which the whole society is entitled to benefit. In their view royalties on industrial patents are essentially exploitation by Capitalist monopolies.

The irritation of the Western countries stems from three facts. First, by not paying due compensation to Western firms, Socialist countries are in fact cheating and thus they tarnish their own otherwise well-earned reputation. Second, Western firms are sometimes confronted with a type of disguised dumping in third markets, i.e. they have to compete with Socialist exports produced with the aid of poached patents. Third, concern at government level has centred on the Bloc's improved capacity to win the East-West economic race. It has been popular in some Western countries, especially in the USA, to attribute the high rates of growth attained by the USSR and other Socialist countries to the import of Western technology. Exploitation of Western know-how is a time and resource-saving device. Benefiting by Western mistakes and achievements, Socialist countries can narrow 'the gap' and divert more research resources for space and military purposes.

The attitude of Socialist countries to foreign patents has been undergoing a fundamental change in recent years. The prevailing attitude now is that it is fair that they should pay a reasonable amount towards the development costs of a particular invention. It is rather difficult to pinpoint the reason for this change of principle. The desire for peaceful co-existence, the trend towards more liberal 'economic revisionism' comprising as it does elements of capitalism and an increasing propensity to assimilate Western technical achievements on a more systematic basis to sustain high rates of growth, have provided a basis for the volte-face. But the fact that Socialist countries now, too, have technology to sell has probably carried the greatest weight.[1] Several Soviet economists have recently argued that the exchange of know-how even

---

[1] Now even the USA acquires know-how from the USSR. Already in the early 1960s more than 50 patents were being purchased by American firms from the USSR annually, e.g. a turbine chilling process, chirurgical sewing apparatus, a continuous steel extrusion process, smelting by electrodes and mould forming from self-hardening sands; see K.-H. Domdey, *Aussenhandel*, East Berlin, 2/1964, pp. 32–35. The Soviet foreign trade corporation *Litsensintorg* now circulates an inventions newsletter as well as pamphlets indicating inventions available for licensing. Czechoslovakia, East Germany, Hungary and Poland are also significant sellers of patents to the West.

within the CMEA area should be placed on a 'commercial basis at world market prices.'[1]

Since about 1962 most Socialist countries have established specialized foreign trade corporations, concerned with the acquisition and sale of designs, processes and prototypes. All European CMEA members now belong to the International Union for the Protection of Industrial Property and most of them to the International Union for the Protection of Literary and Artistic Works (see Table XXXII, p. 370).

However, membership of an international convention cannot prevent abuse. In Socialist countries the user of the patent and the authority supervising its enforcement are one and the same monolithic State. Owing to a variety of reasons, Socialist countries are as a rule reluctant to enter into arrangements which provide for royalties to be paid in proportion to the quantity produced, so that Western patent sellers can usually expect only single lump-sum payments.

It may be observed that in recent years, politics or not, East-West trade in technology has been booming, and it is likely to continue in the foreseeable future. Many Western firms are keen to sell patents to eager Socialist corporations and, with the exception of military technology, Western governments are not unduly perturbed now. It is thought that the rising income from patent sales helps the Western firms to finance new research and innovations, thus constantly keeping ahead of Socialist technological standards in the fields concerned.

A new approach to the East-West technological intercourse is represented by joint ventures. Since 1964, many Socialist and Western enterprises have embarked upon various forms of co-operation in industrial production. Thus a Socialist enterprise, using a Western partner's know-how, may produce certain equipment or components and then supply part of the production to the patent-holder as a payment and retain the rest itself. In other cases, Socialist and Western enterprises, both contributing their own know-how jointly, produce the agreed complete equipment to be subsequently marketed in the partner, or even a third, countries (for further details see Ch. 15 D, pp. 377–84).

[1] For example, O. Bogomolov, *Kommunist*, Moscow, 18/1966, esp. pp. 20–21.

F. CONCLUSIONS

The West and the East each represent well over 20% of the world's area and population and each some 40% or the world's industrial output (see Table I, p. 24). Yet the Western share in the Bloc countries' trade is only 25%. Similarly, the Bloc's share in Western countries' trade is less than 6%. Before the war the respective shares of trade were much higher, viz. 74% and 10% (see Table XII, p. 54).

The reasons for the low level of East-West trade are complex, but there is little doubt that the underlying cause has been chiefly political, for which each side has, hypocritically, blamed the other. The West has accused Socialist countries of autarkic tendencies and of an artificial diversion of trade into intra-Bloc, especially intra-CMEA, channels. The accusations by the Bloc have centred on the Western strategic embargo and various discriminatory quantitative import restrictions plus the Western European integration designed to isolate the Socialist Bloc.

The propensity of different countries in each camp to manipulate trade for political ends has varied. On the whole, the larger, the richer and the less dependent the country on foreign trade, the more it has been inclined to sacrifice trade to politics. This generalization certainly applies to the United States and the Soviet Union. The share of imports in the American and Soviet national incomes is less than 5%.[1] In relation to their national resources, the economic losses sustained by these countries have been small. They have been borne by them quite cheerfully considering that these countries have regarded themselves as messianic leaders of the respective camps in the Cold War.

On the other hand, the smaller member countries have been more and more reluctant to forgo economic gains for the sake of political objectives.[2] China represents an odd case. Her proneness to extend aid and to manipulate trade in her relations with Developing countries contrasts with her own poverty. The primacy of ideology and politics over trade has been further demonstrated in her case by the fact that she has not

---

[1] Based on: United Nations *Monthly Bulletin of Statistics* 7/1968.
[2] For the proportions represented by the foreign-trade turnover in the national incomes of these countries, see Ch. 1, p. 25.

hesitated to risk a dispute with the Soviets in spite of the disastrous consequences to her economic development.

Have the political manipulations of East-West trade fulfilled the hopes held out by their designers? It appears that the degree of effectiveness of trade as an adjunct to politics has been overestimated, each side having entertained an exaggerated view of the indispensability of its trade to the opponent. It is doubtful if the balance of East-West power has been altered to any significant degree by the denials or selective promotions of trade. Reflecting on the policies pursued by the two leading powers instigating the East-West conflict, a well-known historian concluded: 'Looking back over the history of the first twenty years of this Russo-American Cold War, we can now see that the two superpowers stalemated each other, and have done vast damage to the rest of the world as well as to themselves, because they have been acting under illusions.'[1]

Whilst Western denials in the 1950s, perhaps in some isolated cases of industries, slowed down the rate of development to a small degree in the Bloc, they have practically lost their effectiveness in the 1960s. Not only has the absolute size of the trade never been large, but the Socialist Bloc is a vast and varied area with a considerable degree of economic co-operation. Besides, the effectiveness of denials to the Bloc has been reduced by the Western failure to agree on a co-ordinated common policy. The insistence by the USA on uncompromising trade controls has generated a good deal of ill-will in Canada, Britain, France, Italy, Japan and elsewhere.

Testifying before the Committee on Foreign Relations in Washington in 1965, Dr G. F. Kennan, who probably understands the Soviet Bloc better than most other Western diplomats and scholars, concluded: 'Communist countries are not going to pay for normal trade with us by any specific political concessions... I think the denial of normal facilities for trade with us, especially in cases where we extend them to other countries, does have a definitely adverse effect on the behavior of Communist countries.'[2] And yet there are still naïve veiws held by many who believe that Western policies can be decisive in the polycentric tendencies and reformist trends in the Bloc. These developments are

[1] A. J. Toynbee, 'Russian American Relations. The Case for Second Thoughts,' *Journal of International Affairs*, vol. XXII, no. 1, 1968, p. 2.
[2] *East-West Trade*, Hearings 1965, Part II, *op. cit.*, p. 148.

endocrine processes consequent upon the political and economic evolution, in fact independent of trade or other policies pursued by the West towards Socialist countries.

What is the balance sheet of the East-West competition for political support in Developing countries? On the debit side the amount of aid commitments by the two camps up to 1968 exceeded $110,000 m. On the credit side? There is no doubt that both camps are disappointed. Few Developing nations have been bribed into lasting alignments. Many of them, such as (apart from Yugoslavia) Egypt, Pakistan, India, Laos and Indonesia have more or less skilfully played off one camp against the other to become beneficiaries rather than pawns of the East-West conflict. Containment of Communism in Developing countries has been achieved not so much by Western trade, aid or even military support, but almost wholly by the emergence of national regimes which do not particularly want to uncritically support or imitate Socialist ideas or practices, or for that matter those of the West either.

Although the Socialist Bloc now claims 7% of the Developing countries' trade (as compared with 2% in 1953) the share is still small. Much of this increase can be attributed to a natural tendency for the liberated countries to wish to diversify their regional distribution of trade away from the colonial powers. Besides, the Bloc's drive to expand its trade with these countries can be at least partly justified on purely economic grounds. Owing to rapidly advancing industrialization, Socialist countries (especially the European ones) whilst gradually developing a comparative advantage in manufactured goods, are faced with increasing costs in agriculture and extractive industries. There is no sounder economic basis for trade than complementary economies.

The fact that East-West trade could be divorced from the inroads of politics is illustrated by some developments in recent years. Owing to the inexorable polycentric tendencies within each camp and the fading away of the Cold War, trade is being increasingly dictated by economics rather than politics. Political non-recognition has not prevented remarkable increases in trade. In 1965 Japan became China's most important trading partner, having displaced Britain and the USSR, even though Japan maintains no diplomatic relations (whilst Britain and the USSR do). In August 1966, Prime Minister Sato stated that while Japan would not recognize the Peking Government she would actively further step up economic and personal relations.[1]

In spite of the Hallstein Doctrine, by which West Germany once pledged not to have diplomatic relations with any country recognizing East Germany, trade has been flourishing. Since 1962 West Germany has displaced Britain as the leading trader with the CMEA group of countries. The permanent trade missions – however unofficial – exchanged with most of these countries since that time, have not done a bad job after all.

Similarly, absence of diplomatic relations has not prevented an unprecedented growth of trade between Australia and Canada on the one hand and China on the other. Sino-Australian trade has been flourishing in spite of Australian troops fighting in Vietnam, and in spite of the Australian decision to re-open her embassy in Taiwan in November 1966. When recently the large Canadian wheat exports to China were handicapped by inadequate inland transport facilities, upon request the USA lent trains to Canada for the purpose.

The expansion of trade between Japan and the USSR in recent years has been most impressive, even though no peace treaty has been signed between the two countries since World War II. Similarly, the Nationalist regime of Spain has been trading most actively with Socialist Cuba for years, and more recently with most Eastern European countries. Following the Soviet and four other Warsaw Pact countries' military intervention in Czechoslovakia in 1968, in several Western countries (especially in Australia, Britain, France, West Germany, USA) trade sanctions were urged against the invading nations. However, parliamentary support for such measures was invariably small and the governments chose not to act. (For further details of the growing *rapprochement* via East-West trade, see Ch. 15, Sections A–E.)

[1] *Far Eastern Economic Review*, 29/9/1966, p. 614.

12 Strategic Embargo

A. DEVELOPMENT OF WESTERN STRATEGIC EXPORT CONTROLS

STRATEGIC embargo, which became the principal Western weapon in the Cold War, can be traced back to 1947, but the first concrete steps were taken in the following year. Early in 1948 talks were initiated amongst leading Western powers in an attempt to reach an agreement on a common policy on strategic trade with the Soviet Bloc. Without waiting for other countries, in March 1948 the USA introduced a comprehensive system of export licences on all goods intended for export to Socialist countries.

In November 1949 a body known as the Consultative Group, consisting of high-level diplomats, was formed by seven Western countries (Belgium, France, Italy, Luxemburg, Netherlands, USA and UK) with headquarters in Paris. The Group created a working committee called Co-Com (Co-ordinating Committee) to provide an informal forum for discussions and to maintain a multilaterally acceptable list of goods subject to embargo. The Committee started its operations in January 1950. Later the Group's membership increased to 15 – all NATO countries (except Iceland) plus Japan. Although Co-Com lists have never been binding on the co-operating nations, they have been regarded as minimum lists, any country being free to impose extra controls. The USA has administered more extensive lists than any other nation. Under the Mutual Defense Assistance Control Act of 1951 (the Battle Act), the USA made the extension of military, economic and financial aid conditional upon the recipient country (61 in all at the time) observing the embargo. The US Government also negotiated bilateral agreements with various countries (including those not receiving American aid, such as Australia and New Zealand) to widen the enforcement of the controls.

The scope and rigour of the controls reached their height during the Korean War (June 1950–August 1953). The international strategic controls embodied three lists:

(i) the complete 'embargo list' – comprising 260 listings;
(ii) the 'quantitative control list' – about 90 listings;
(iii) the 'surveillance list' – about 100 listings.

At the same time the US security lists included about 100 listings more.[1] Each listing included a number of separate articles.

In addition to a complete embargo on trade with North Korea, the USA has also discontinued all her trade with Mainland China since December 1950, after the Chinese entered the war.[2] In May 1951 Western nations managed to push a resolution through the General Assembly of the United Nations, recommending an embargo on exports of clearly strategic significance to China and North Korea, with which almost all Capitalist countries complied. The Co-Com and other co-operating nations, in addition to their controls applicable to the Soviet Bloc, introduced 'special China lists'. These controls were further reinforced in most Western nations by prohibiting ships from carrying embargoed goods from any country to China and North Korea.[3] For the sake of the co-ordination of different national policies the Paris Group established Chin-Com (China Co-ordinating Committee) in September 1952.

In spite of considerable agitation against the embargo after the Korean armistice, especially in Britain and Japan, the Co-Com nations decided to retain both the Co-Com and Chin-Com lists. However, the controls have been gradually relaxed since that time in six major stages: in 1954, 1957, 1958, 1962, 1964 and 1966. In 1954 the Co-Com 'embargo list' was reduced on balance by 90 listings (to 170), the 'quantitative list' by 70 (to 20) and the 'surveillance list' by 40 (to 60) listings.[4]

---

[1] Mutual Defense Assistance Control Act of 1951, *The Revision of Strategic Trade Controls*, GPO, Washington 1954, p. 21; MDACA, *The Strategic Trade Control System 1948–1956*, GPO, Washington 1957, p. 18.

[2] Small quantities of imports of crude feathers, bristles, etc., needed at the time for strategic stockpiling, continued to be imported up to 1953. Since 1958 a limited amount of trade has been allowed in newspapers, periodicals and books on a mutual exchange basis. The total trade embargo has been extended to North Vietnam since 1955.

[3] See MDACA, *World-Wide Enforcement of Strategic Trade Controls*, First Half of 1953, GPO, Washington 1953, esp. pp. 13–40.

[4] US Senate, *A Background Study on East-West Trade*, Prepared for the Committee on Foreign Relations, GPO, Washington 1965, p. 7.

In the face of strong disapproval by the USA, almost all Western nations dropped the China differential, which until then had applied not only to China (incl. Tibet) but also to North Korea, Macao and North Vietnam, following the British move in 1957.[1] As a result Chin-Com was dissolved. At the 1958 meeting of the Consultative Group, it was agreed to reduce further the coverage of the 'embargo list'. In addition, it was decided to abolish 'quantitative' and 'surveillance' lists and replace them instead with a new system of secondary controls in the form of a 'watch list'. All in all, the downward revision affected about two-fifths of the commodities.

In 1960 the USA began to restrict her trade with Cuba. These restrictions, following Cuba's increasing economic and military collaboration with the Socialist Bloc, soon developed into an embargo on almost all trade (US exports of medicines and unsubsidized foodstuffs excepted). Other Co-Com nations, whilst prohibiting exports of a clearly military value, have refrained from imposing such drastic controls, especially since the dismantling of Soviet nuclear missile bases in Cuba in 1962, in spite of American shipping sanctions and diplomatic exhortations.

In 1962 and in 1964 Co-Com made further substantial downward revisions of embargoed items. At the beginning of 1964 the Co-Com list covered about 10% of the total number of items entering world trade. In addition, the USA had restrictions on a portion of the remaining 90% of the items.[2] Since that time the strictness and scope of the controls have continued to decline, even though some additions have been made from time to time. At the time of writing, the controls still covered items of direct military value and a highly selective range of materials, machinery and instruments. As of mid-1968, the British strategic embargo schedule consisted of three lists, *Munitions*, *Atomic* and *Industrial*, containing 130 classes which embodied nearly 600 separate articles (see Table XXX, pp. 279-80).

[1] At the time of writing, the China differential was still observed by Australia and New Zealand. The USA and Taiwan ban practically all their trade with the three Asian Socialist countries, and similarly New Zealand decided to discontinue all her trade with North Vietnam, since 1964. If there is any trade between South Vietnam, South Korea and the Philippines on the one hand and the three Socialist countries on the other, it must be negligible.

[2] Statement by Mr D. Dillon (Secretary of the US Treasury) testifying before the Committee on Foreign Relations. See US Senate, *East-West Trade*, Hearings before the Committee on Foreign Relations, Part 1, GPO, Washington 1964, p. 220.

The administration of the controls on industrial equipment has been quite liberal, especially in application to the European Socialist countries with the exception of Albania and East Germany. In July 1965, on the proposal of the British representative supported by the USA, Co-Com decided that nuclear reactors needed for peaceful purposes by selected European Socialist countries could be exported, provided that the International Atomic Energy Agency in Vienna is allowed to make necessary inspections.[1] The US controls continue to be more comprehensive and stricter than those of any other nation.

It appears that continued relaxation of the embargo is inevitable. In July 1968 the USA signed an agreement with the USSR which includes co-operation in the peaceful uses of atomic energy, and at about the same time the (then) Vice-President H. Humphrey, campaigning for the presidential nomination, called for an end to the total embargo on US trade with the three Asian Socialist countries and Cuba. In the same year, Sweden decided to remove her restrictions on strategic exports to Socialist countries. The Prime Minister, Mr Sato, said in the Japanese Parliament in 1966 that his Government would seek a gradual lifting of the embargo, and a similar statement was made by the Minister for International Trade and Industry, Mr Shiina, in 1968. At the meeting of the International Chamber of Commerce in Paris in 1967 it was concluded that it was possible to lift all the restrictions immediately, but proposals were made for a gradual relaxation of the controls on non-military items over a trial period of three years.[2]

B. RATIONALE OF THE EMBARGO

The Western decision to adopt strategic export controls has been prompted by a variety of considerations. First, the West has been con-

---

[1] *Board of Trade Journal*, 20/8/1965, p. 433. However, it must be noted that the general embargo on reactors still applies. The member countries agreed to a procedure (in early 1965) by which exceptions to the embargo can be made with *unanimous* agreement *in each individual case*. See MDACA, *The Battle Act Report 1965*, Washington, February 1966, p. 5.

[2] See *Amer. Rev. of East-West Trade*, 7/1968, p. 8; Far Eastern Econ. Rev., *China Trade Report*, 8/1966, p. 8 and 4/1968, p. 9; *Soviet News* (issued by the Soviet Embassy in London), 16/7/1968, p. 34.

vinced that its exports are of greater strategic value to the Bloc than the other way round. It has been argued that the Bloc's demand for Western goods is not a genuine interest in international trade to improve living standards, but is designed to strengthen its military power and self-sufficiency in the industrial field. Neglect of consumer goods industries and of agriculture supports this argument.

Second, in a centrally planned economy bottlenecks, threatening the fulfilment of developmental programmes, are a familiar feature. In such cases, Socialist countries naturally turn to free enterprise economies, especially the inexhaustible Western buyers' markets, to obtain the critical items.

Third, in contrast to the centrally planned economies, exports from Western countries are handled predominantly by private trading firms. Consequently, special State controls must be instituted to safeguard the national interest. The imposition of such controls is no more than matching the Socialist in-built capacity for administering similar restrictions. Fourth, it has been hoped in the West that the denials would cause losses and dislocations to the Bloc countries' economies and consequently Socialist leaders would be more amenable to talk peace and, perhaps, make political concessions.

The concept of what is 'strategic' defies a clear-cut and universally acceptable definition. In the narrowest sense, it covers items of direct military use and such items are reasonably easy to identify and define. On the other hand, extremists – such as the late Bernard M. Baruch, a well-known American expert on war production and defence – would regard any item as being of strategic value because if the opponent country wants it it must strengthen that country in one way or another; a similar attitude was entertained by Dr Adenauer, who at one stage considered wheat as a strategic item. Others would take a stand somewhere between the two views. A general non-committal definition may be taken as: 'strategic items are those raw materials and manufactures (including munitions) which would increase the military strength of the Soviet bloc.'[1]

Taking the period since 1948 as a whole, the types of embargoed items can be judged by four specific objectives guiding the administration of the controls:

[1] *World-Wide Enforcement of Strategic Trade Controls, op. cit.*, p. 1.

(a) To slow down the military build-up of Socialist countries.
(b) To slow down the development of the military-supporting capabilities of Socialist countries.
(c) To slow down economic growth by causing dislocations in key Socialist projects.
(d) To pre-empt key materials in short supply considered necessary for the Western defence effort.

To attain these objectives over a period of rapid progress, the interpretation of what is 'strategic' has necessarily had to be dynamic, adapted to the changing concept of warfare and the supporting capacities in the Bloc as well as in the West. In a recent American study made for the use of the Congress, four criteria underlying the multilateral Co-Com embargo system were explicitly stated:

(i) the Bloc's dependence on a given import;
(ii) the contribution of the given import to the military and military-supporting industries;
(iii) the availability of substitutes;
(iv) the magnitude of the risk.[1]

However, neither Co-Com nor national lists could ever tell the full story, because each application for an export licence is considered on its merits according to a variety of circumstances. One wonders on how many occasions the decisions, one way or the other, were purely arbitrary. Some countries, such as Australia, have chosen not to publish any lists.

On many occasions military, scientific, technological and economic considerations were so evenly balanced that the decision on granting or refusing a licence was made vaguely on political grounds. For example, a large order for machine tools for the manufacture of trucks in the USSR was denied by the USA in 1962 owing to a threatening crisis over Berlin.[2] On the other hand in 1965 the US authorities issued a licence for the export of a nuclear reactor to Rumania to express political pleasure at her growing nationalism in defiance of Moscow. The application of the almost complete American embargo on trade with Cuba was justified by Mr Rusk in 1964 on four grounds: to reduce Dr Castro's will and capacity to export subversion to other American States,

[1] *A Background Study on East-West Trade, op. cit.*, p. 14.
[2] *Ibid.*, p. 13.

to convince Cubans that Dr Castro's regime cannot serve their interests, to demonstrate to Latin American Republics that Communism has no future in the Western Hemisphere, and to increase the cost to the USSR of maintaining an outpost in Cuba.[1]

The idea behind quantitative restrictions administered by the Co-Com nations up to 1958 was to allow marginal exports (such as vehicles and medicines) for civilian use in Socialist countries but not for strengthening their military and military-supporting base. Periodically, certain items such as rubber, tin and nickel, were barred because they were in short supply in the West and were needed for Western re-armament. Fissionable materials (uranium, plutonium and thorium) are still in this category.

The actual range of items embargoed has varied from time to time and in application to different Socialist countries. Western allies have never been in complete agreement even at a particular time or in their treatment of individual Socialist countries. The range tended to be greater in periods of acute East-West crises, such as the Berlin Blockade (1948-49), the Korean War (1950-53), the Berlin Wall and the Cuban missiles affairs (1961-63) and the military intervention in Czechoslovakia (1968). Whether the marked trend for a relaxation of controls in recent years is merely an interlude before another crisis, or a tendency towards a complete discontinuation of the embargo, it is impossible to judge at the time of writing.

The controls have been most stringent in application to North Korea, Mainland China and North Vietnam, reflecting these countries' underdeveloped economies and (as it appears to the West) aggressive policies. With these countries the USA has maintained no trading relations (exchange of newspapers, periodicals and books excepted), whilst other Co-Com nations administered a special China Embargo up to 1957 and some other countries (Australia and New Zealand) are still continuing it. The American treatment of Cuba has been much harsher than that of the CMEA countries. It may also be mentioned that the USA has banned imports of certain furs from the USSR and has barred using public funds for imports of science-teaching equipment from the Soviet Bloc. The most lenient treatment has been accorded to Yugoslavia (since 1948), to Poland (since 1957) and to Rumania (since 1964).

[1] *East-West Trade*, Hearings 1964, Part I, *op. cit.*, p. 13.

Of the Co-Com nations, Britain, France, Italy and Japan have led the way towards reducing the scope of the embargo.

C. THE BLOC'S VULNERABILITY

The Bloc's vulnerability relevant to Western strategic export controls can be pieced together from a variety of sources: (*a*) from a study of the Bloc's natural resources and the existing state of key secondary and tertiary industries, (*b*) from the Bloc countries' economic plans, (*c*) from these countries' scientific and technical literature which may indicate major deficiencies and needs for improvement and the steps taken towards overcoming them, (*d*) from patterns of these countries' trade enquiries and procurement effort, (*e*) from reports supplied by Western intelligence agents situated in the Bloc, and (*f*) from admissions by Socialist leaders in public statements.

From these sources strategic embargo lists are compiled. Such lists can be broadly taken as indicating the Bloc's vulnerability. An example of a recent list in a summarized form is given in Table XXX. However, the limitations of such published lists must be recognized. They are incomplete and the authorities are not bound by them. Some items are listed for the sake of Western pre-emption rather than because of the Bloc's vulnerability. Each application for a licence is considered separately in the context of a variety of considerations at the time.

Although the vulnerability varies from one Socialist country to another and it has, of course, been changing with time, certain generalizations applicable to the Bloc as a whole may be stated. Comprising a quarter of world area and spanning half the world, the Bloc has varied physiographic, geological and climatic features, so that it is nearly self-sufficient in natural resources. However, of one of the major metals, copper, it can produce only one-half of its requirements – the USSR, Bulgaria and Albania being the main Bloc producers. Since the embargo on this metal was relaxed in 1957, even the USSR has been importing it from the Capitalist world. The Bloc is also deficient in such strategic commodities as niobium, molybdenum, tungsten, tantalum, titanium, zirconium, berylium and lithium, and it produces no natural rubber.

TABLE XXX A RECENT STRATEGIC EMBARGO LIST
A Summary of the Goods Subject to Embargo by the United Kingdom to the Socialist Bloc, as of July 1968

Group (No. of classes in brackets)	Number of Separate Articles	Example of Articles
MUNITIONS LIST (21)	180	Small arms, machine guns, artillery, tanks, explosives, propellants, projectors, power-controlled searchlights, tear gas, armour plate, vehicles designed for military uses, specialized diesel engines.
ATOMIC ENERGY LIST (5)	80	Fissionable materials, fluorine, artificial graphite, zirconium metal, berylium metal, dosimeters, neutron generator tubes, nuclear reactors of potential military use.
INDUSTRIAL LIST		
A. Metal-Working Machinery (8)	21	Grinding heads and spindle assemblies, presses and specialized controls, numerical control systems, spin-forming machines.
B. Chemical and Petroleum Equipment (8)	25	Equipment for producing solid propellants, gas liquefying equipment, certain types of valve cocks and pressure regulators, ion vacuum pumps.
C. Electrical and Power-Generating Equipment (4)	20	Electric vacuum furnaces, electron beam equipment, electric arc devices, photovoltaic cells.
D. General Industrial Equipment (6)	27	Cable-making machinery, electronic valve-making machinery, stenters, vacuum metallizing machinery.
E. Transportation Equipment (6)	30	Warships, fast coasters, fast fishing vessels, certain aircraft, helicopters, buoyant electric conducting cable, certain compasses.

TABLE XXX—*Continued*

Group (No. of classes in brackets)	Number of Separate Articles	Example of Articles
F. Electronic Equipment (35)	90	Jamming apparatus, pulse modulators, radar equipment of certain types, location apparatus, radio transmitters and spectrum analyzers, amplifiers, cypher machines, electromagnetic waveguides.
G. Scientific Instruments and Apparatus (13)	60	Certain electronic computers, scientific control equipment, servometers, potentiometers, magnetometers, gravimeters, certain specialized photographic equipment.
H. Metals, Minerals and Their Manufactures (10)	22	Anti-friction bearings, certain magnetic metals, certain types of steel, tungsten, tantalum, titanium, zirconium, artificial graphite.
I. Chemicals, Metalloids and Petroleum Products (12)	35	Primary explosives, hydraulic fluids, boron, certain plastics, fluorocarbon compounds, high energy liquid fuels, synthetic lubricating oils.
J. Synthetic Rubber and Synthetic Film (2)	8	Synthetic rubber, synthetic film for dielectric use.
TOTAL: (130)	598	

Source. Based on: *Board of Trade Journal*, 19/8/1966, insert, and published amendments up to August 1968.

Although the Bloc produces some 40% of the world's industrial output, there is evidence that its military and military-supporting base, when compared with the West, suffers from weaknesses in several respects. The Bloc has been handicapped by inadequacies in the production of certain machine tools, highly specialized types of steel, synthetic rubber and fibres, a number of advanced chemicals, certain specialized types of vehicles, some aviation equipment, certain telecommunication apparatus, transistor manufacturing equipment, a group of appliances relating to space and missile operations, high-memory computers, highly sophisticated electrical and electronic apparatus, and a range of highly specialized scientific instruments. Even the more advanced Socialist countries have been lagging in several fields of applied research and industrial technology, although the lag has not of course, been uniform.

It is conceded in Socialist literature that even such well-established industries as machine tool construction, instrument making, electrical engineering and those producing equipment for power, chemical and petroleum industries are noted for their insufficient capacity.[1] Central planning and public ownership of the means of production have not proved to be easily adaptable to rapidly changing requirements for a wide variety of advanced articles. The fact is that a large proportion of industrial production is well below Western standards. It was estimated recently in a Socialist source that even in Czechoslovakia, probably the most advanced Socialist country industrially, only 40% of the products of the machine building industry matched world standards, 40% was partly obsolete and 20% completely out of date. The respective figures applying to the Hungarian machine building industry were 14%, 39% and 47%.[2]

Have the Western strategic export controls hit the Bloc at its most vulnerable sinews? The practical effects on the Bloc will be considered in the next section of this chapter, but some general observations on the appropriateness of the embargo may be put forward at this stage. The more one studies both sides of the embargo, the more one wonders to what extent the element of naïveté in the West has prevailed over common sense.

Although the Munitions and the Atomic Energy lists have comprised a large proportion of embargoed articles (nearly one-half), the Bloc's vulnerability on this score can easily be overestimated. No reasonably industrialized country, much less a bloc of countries, conscious of the hostility of the Developed world, would base its defences (or aggression) on supplies from a potential enemy. The Warsaw Treaty Organization and CMEA have taken appropriate measures to ensure the adequate production of required armaments. This purely military production in

[1] I. Oleinik, *Voprosy ekonomiki*, 9/1967, p. 130.
[2] *Ibid.*, p. 124.

reality is the Bloc's least vulnerable front. In fact, several Socialist countries, such as the USSR, Czechoslovakia, East Germany and China, have been important exporters of armaments to several Capitalist countries (especially to South-East Asia, the Middle East and Africa) for years. Some Socialist military equipment, such as certain types of small arms, tanks, artillery, fighter aircraft, rocket launchers and missiles, have proven their equality to, if not superiority over, Western equipment at one time or another.

The embargo on the remaining articles has been based on the assumption of the vulnerability of the Bloc's industrial base. Whether the traditional view that industrial power is of crucial moment, because in wartime it can be transformed into indispensable military support, still holds water is questionable. Whilst a viable industrial base is essential in localized conventional wars, it would not be decisive in the context of a global atomic war. The development of nuclear and missile weapons does not necessarily require a broad industrial base. Preparedness for such a war rests chiefly on scientific research and on only a few highly specialized branches of certain industries. Thus in terms of intercontinental nuclear warfare, embargo is more relevant on highly specialized and advanced Western scientific and technological achievements than on warships, tanks, guns, steel, machine tools and in fact all the other items combined.

Manufacturing industries are not the most vulnerable sector of the Bloc economies. In fact these industries, especially heavy and engineering branches, owing to the priorities assigned to them for such a long period now, are the strongest and most dynamic. The Bloc economy's soft under-belly has been and still is agriculture. If the West wanted to hit the Bloc where it would hurt most, an embargo on grains would be more painful than on armaments, steel and machinery. One is tempted to speculate what repercussions such a complete ban would have had on the common people, on their morale and confidence in the regimes in China, North Korea, Eastern Europe and the USSR.

Quite apart from rescuing Communist regimes from serious embarrassment and perhaps social unrest, it may be argued that the massive wheat imports from the West indirectly strengthen the Bloc's military potential in several respects. First, imports of food make possible a diversion of manpower and investment resources to manufacturing industries, thus strengthening the Bloc's industrial base in general. Second, in the case of China in particular, imports of wheat enable her to export rice and soya beans as a foreign-exchange-earning proposition. Thus, by exporting high-priced rice (about £70 per ton) and instead importing relatively cheap wheat (about £25 a ton) – to some extent subsidized by the West – valuable foreign exchange can be earned on balance; besides, the yield of rice per acre (40 bushels) is about three times that of wheat (13 bushels).[1] The foreign exchange thus earned can be used to import industrial equipment from the West and strategic materials from elsewhere.

Third, most of the wheat exported to the Bloc has been on credits. Since 1961 wheat credits extended to China alone have exceeded £600 m. In a sense, such continuous credits can be viewed as a form of economic aid. Finally, it is known that the Chinese policy of importing bulky foodstuffs to the coastal areas (where most of the population as well as foreign-exchange-earning industries are situated) is not of a temporary nature but is partly designed to release the meagre and overburdened internal transport facilities for military purposes and for the movement of industrial equipment and raw materials. A similar policy has been followed by the USSR in importing wheat to the Far Eastern provinces from Canada and Australia, even before 1963, to relieve the pressure on the Trans-Siberian Railway.

D. THE EFFECT OF THE EMBARGO ON THE BLOC

To calculate the total damage to the Bloc, and to the West, inflicted by Western strategic export controls is well-nigh impossible with the present tools of analysis, quite apart from the difficulty of obtaining full and precise information from each side. It was aptly concluded in an American document on the subject that, 'Social sciences have not yet developed an acceptable objective measurement of either the strategic

[1] In the late 1960s, China exported 1,000 tons worth £70 m. annually and she ranked the third largest (after the USA and Thailand) rice exporter in the world. Her main customers are: Ceylon, Cuba, Hong Kong, Japan, Malaysia and Pakistan. See Far Eastern Econ. Rev., *China Trade Report*, 7/1968, p. 18; FEER, *Yearbook 1967*, Hong Kong 1966, p. 161.

impact or economic impact of East-West trade on either the East or the West.'[1] Subject to these obvious limitations, we shall attempt to estimate the effectiveness of the controls by bringing the effects of the embargo on the Bloc and on the West into clearer focus – in those respects where it is possible.

Between 1947 and 1953 the Bloc's imports from the Co-Com countries fell from US $900 m. to $450 m. (about £220 m. and £160 m. at the exchange rates applying at the time). Whilst before the embargo was imposed the Socialist countries had been obtaining more than 25% of their import requirements from the Co-Com nations, the proportion fell to less than 7% in 1952 and in 1966 it stood at 20%.[2] The Bloc's need for imports from the West has been much greater than the Western need of imports from the Bloc. The goods and technology required from the West are much more advanced and sophisticated, they are more closely related to military and military-supporting industries and to the fulfilment of other planned targets of crucial significance. In most cases there are no alternative sources of supply of equally efficient substitutes, whether from intra-Bloc sources or from uncommitted nations.

Referring to the effects of the embargo on the USSR (the least vulnerable of all Bloc countries) Mr Khrushchev stated in Leipzig in 1959 that it

> has cost us a great deal, because we were forced to introduce a great number of branches of industries to manufacture new products which, if there were no restrictions on trade, we could obtain from other countries where these products have been manufactured efficiently for a long time, and which one could buy at a mutually advantageous price.[3]

An experienced high official of the US Department of Commerce concluded in a study on the subject that the embargo has had 'an adverse impact on the Communist countries ranging from substantial in the early years – to limited though important in recent years.'[4]

---

[1] *A Background Study on East-West Trade, op. cit.*, p. 15.
[2] The proportion was 65% in 1938. These calculations are based on United Nations sources: *Yearbook of International Trade Statistics, Monthly Bulletin of Statistics* and *Direction of Trade*.
[3] Quoted with permission from Frank O'Brien, *Crisis in World Communism*, Committee for Economic Development, New York 1965, p. 148.
[4] Cited from *A Background Study on East-West Trade, op. cit.*, p. 42.

CH. 12 §D STRATEGIC EMBARGO   285

The extent of the adverse effects on the Bloc can, however, be easily overestimated. First, East-West trade has never been large. In 1948 its value was only about $3,000 m. or 2·5% of the world foreign trade turnover. In 1953, when the Korean War ended, its value dropped to $2,150 m. or 1·3% of world trade (see Table XI, p. 52). Some of this fall was due to the initiative of the Socialist countries endeavouring to reduce their imports of consumer goods and to re-direct their trade towards friendly Developing countries and otherwise into intra-Bloc channels (see Table X, p. 46). This brings us to the next point.

A large bloc of countries is less vulnerable to trade embargoes than a single country would be. A Socialist economist pointed out that the creation of the foreign-trade monopoly in the Bloc countries was accelerated by the strategic embargo.[1] Western controls have simply tended to drive these countries into autarky on national or intra-Bloc bases. In this the USSR and China, the main objects of the embargo, have suffered less than the smaller Socialist nations.[2] The USSR has the largest resources and she is the most developed of all Socialist countries; in fact of all civilized countries in the world she is the most self-sufficient.

When the embargo was most rigorous against China up to 1957, her vulnerability was mitigated markedly by deliveries of military (including nuclear blueprints) and industrial equipment, designs and technical advice from the Soviet Union and her Eastern European associates. She also obtained loans from the USSR totalling some £480 m. Considering her underdeveloped economy, China was content with importing from the West simpler equipment not on strategic lists. Otherwise, trans-shipment of China-embargoed goods through neutral countries, through various devious channels in South-East Asia and through European Socialist countries (of goods on the Chin-Com but not on the Co-Com list) further reduced the impact on China. Soviet cancellation of a defence technology agreement in 1959, withdrawal of specialists in 1960 and the consequent Sino-Soviet rift have increased China's vulnera-

[1] Imre Vajda, *The Role of Foreign Trade in a Socialist Economy*, Corvina Press, Budapest 1965, esp. p. 153.
[2] For example see the Polish views on the subject: B. Łączkowski, *Handel zagraniczny* (Foreign Trade), 6/1961, pp. 198–99; Z. Kamecki, J. Sołdaczuk and W. Sierpiński, *Miedzynarodowe stosunki ekonomiczne* (International Economic Relations), PWE, Warsaw 1964, p. 78.

bility. However, these moves have been paralleled by a gradual liberalization of Western controls and, indeed, more recently by a feverish race for Chinese contracts.

On the other hand, Western denials have tended to force the smaller Socialist countries, Cuba included, into Soviet and Chinese arms. This fact has done no good to anybody except the USSR and China, whose dominant position has been further strengthened in the Bloc.

Third, collective ownership of the means of production, central planning and co-ordination of economic plans, especially within the CMEA group, have made it much easier for Socialist countries (than would be possible in the West) to face the embargo. Socialist countries have not been simply waiting as sitting targets but have usually been determined to make swift adjustments by shifting resources away from the industries producing unembargoed goods to the endangered flanks. As a result of the sudden West German ban on the export of large-diameter welded pipes to the USSR in 1963, the Soviets constructed necessary plants at Cheliabinsk, Novomoskovsk and Shadnovsk in a few months.[1] The Soviet Union now claims to be the world's leading producer (600,000 tons annually), and a plan has been announced to build another factory at Volgograd.[2]

Fourth, scientific and technical progress in countries with a solid industrial base, responsible after all for two-fifths of the world's industrial output, facilitates making adjustments to overcome shortages produced by denials of particular items. During World War II the Allied bombing of Germany was based on the so-called 'bottleneck theory'. It was thought that the military-supporting base would collapse if industries producing certain strategic components, such as anti-friction bearings, were destroyed. The futility of that denial was demonstrated in surveys carried out after the war. They showed that even under blockaded wartime conditions, substitutes for the materials denied or destroyed were rapidly developed and factories were quickly reconstructed by transfers of machinery from other less essential industries. It was concluded that denials, whether by bombing or embargoes, to be really effective must be very broadly based and near-complete.[3] There is

[1] See *The Economist*, 30/3/1963, p. 1212; *Intern. Affairs*, Moscow, 8/1965, p. 13.
[2] *Życie gospodarcze* (Economic Life), Warsaw, 21/5/1967, p. 11.
[3] *A Background Study on East-West Trade*, op. cit., p. 15.

little reason to believe that the selective nature of the strategic export controls, as administered particularly by nations other than the USA, has done any better than the wartime 'bottleneck' approach.

Fifth, Co-Com countries have disagreed on what is 'strategic' – the very object of the embargo. On many occasions the items embargoed by the USA were supplied by other allies, as was the case with the British buses and French locomotives (and Spanish fishing vessels) sold to Cuba in 1964. Similarly, the special China List, still observed by some Western countries, is just a joke when other Western nations are falling over backwards in vying for the Chinese market. Since the relaxation of the embargo in 1964, China has been supplied with no less than forty complete factory plants, most of which have at least a moderate strategic value (steel rolling mills, steel tubing plants, an ammonia factory, oil refineries, etc.). There is a large body of opinion in the West, steeped in *laissez-faire* philosophy, which regards strategic embargoes in peacetime as fundamentally wrong.

Finally, there have been other minor factors weakening the impact of the embargo. First of all, taking advantage of shortages of certain commodities in the West at various times, Socialist countries agreed to export selected items only in exchange for strategic goods, and in such cases Western governments often had to issue export licences. This was the case in the early 1950s with Soviet timber, asbestos and chromium, Polish coal and Chinese rice and oil substances. A large number of the really badly needed items found their way to the Bloc through illicit trans-shipment. Thus in 1952, by ingenious manipulations embargoed (at the time) diamond tools, diamond dust and ferrotungsten slipped through quite legally to Czechoslovakia. In the same year Dutch authorities uncovered an international ring engaged in shipping strategic goods to Eastern Europe. It is also known that similar rings were doing booming business through Burma, Hong Kong, Macao, Singapore, Thailand and elsewhere.[1]

In many cases the effect of the embargo has been weakened by the loophole provided for in the tacit Co-Com understanding, viz. that of 'special national interest or hardship'. Through this escape clause, many

[1] See, for example, *World-Wide Enforcement of Strategic Trade Controls, op. cit.*, p. 10; Kao Hsiang-kao, *Chinese Communist Foreign Trade and Diplomacy*, APACL, Taipei 1964, p. 21.

Western countries (especially France, Japan and the United Kingdom) have smartly exported ships, jet planes, automated equipment, communications apparatus, computers and other items on the strategic lists. Besides, Socialist countries have turned to uncommitted nations for articles which for several years were on the Co-Com lists, such as rubber from Ceylon and copper from Latin America and Africa.

How ironical Western strategic embargo can be is illustrated by the case of China and steel. It is now pretty well agreed in the West that China has made tremendous progress in her iron and steel industry, prodded largely by the embargo. China turns out a very wide range of steel rods, bars, sheets and plate, and apparently she has recently started producing new varieties of steel.[1] In fact, it is reported that in 1966 the American forces in South Vietnam purchased a substantial quantity of Chinese steel for military installations (see Ch. 15 B, p. 361).

In a recent comprehensive and authoritative study, a Swedish scholar produced some quantitative estimates of the effect of the embargo on the Soviet Union, the main target of the controls. His conclusions are that the overall effect has been very small, especially in the 1960s. In the decade of the 1950s, the rate of economic growth in the Soviet GNP was slowed down by no more than one year, probably by about as much as in the West. At the most, 5% of Soviet defence and investment resources was affected and the retardation effect in these sectors was less than four months.[2]

Trade embargoes in the past never achieved their expected results. Similarly, Western strategic export controls have not visibly weakened the military potential of the Socialist countries. Nor have these countries been deterred from pursuing policies they had committed themselves to. Far from becoming intimidated, their attitude often hardened. The *détente* in East-West relations (however modest in scope) in recent years is not a product of the tightening up of trade controls by the West but rather of their relaxation.

---

[1] *Far Eastern Economic Review*, 31/3/1967, pp. 623–27.

[2] G. Adler-Karlsson, *Western Economic Warfare 1947–67*, Almqvist & Wicksell, Stockholm 1968, pp. 190–91, 200.

E. EFFECTS ON THE WEST

After the peak of the strategic controls was reached, a group of American experts summed up the effects of the embargo on both camps in the following statement:

> In military and industrial terms, both sides are slightly hurt by the controls and the Soviet Bloc is probably hurt more than the free world. However, the cost of maintaining these controls in the free world must also be measured in other terms as well. The controls clearly strain somewhat the political ties among free-world countries and contribute slightly to balance of payments and employment difficulties on our side.[1]

The cost to the West has consisted in loss of exports, the burden of the administration of the controls and adverse effects on Western cohesion.

Statistically, the effect of the embargo on Western exports to the Bloc is brought out in Table XXXI. It will be noted that the loss of exports has been greatest to the USA, whose trade with the Socialist Bloc has not yet regained even its *nominal* pre-embargo level. The enhanced role of the Developing countries to the Socialist Bloc in 1952 stands out.

No complete figures of the costs of administration of the controls are available. A rough estimate of the *direct administrative costs* borne by the Western co-operating nations (including the cost of liaison) suggests a figure of about £50 m. *a year*. The costs must have been greater when in addition to the Co-Com, the Chin-Com list was administered (one of the important reasons for dropping it in 1957). It was disclosed in evidence before the Foreign Relations Committee of the US Congress in 1964 that the Department of Commerce alone[2] was employing over 300 persons handling export controls and the annual cost amounted to some $4 m. In the early 1960s the Department was receiving 500–700 export licence applications a day, of which about 15 were proposed shipments to

---
[1] Commission on Foreign Economic Policy, *Staff Papers*, Washington, Feb. 1954, p. 450.
[2] The Department of Commerce is the main body concerned with the operational side of the controls. But in addition, there are at least 19 other Agencies, Committees and Working Groups concerned with the controls, See *Strategic Trade Control System 1948–1956*, MDACA, Ninth Report to the Congress, GPO ,Washington 1957, p. 16.

TABLE XXXI EXPORTS TO THE SOCIALIST BLOC IN SELECTED YEARS[1]

(In £ million at current prices, and percentages of total exports of each country or group)

Countries	1938	1948	1952	1958	1966	1967
United States						
Value	38	99	n	40	71	70
%	6·0	3·2	n	0·6	0·7	0·6
United Kingdom						
Value	26	28	20	71	190	210
%	5·2	1·8	0·8	2·3	3·8	4·1
Co-Com Countries[2]						
Value	223	223	161	554	1,570	1,600
%	8·6	3·0	1·2	2·8	3·6	3·4
Western Countries[3]						
Value	253	368	1,082	811	2,050	2,270
%	8·0	4·0	1·6	3·2	4·1	4·2
All Capitalist Countries[4]						
Value	289	486	1,238	1,118	2,925	3,080
%	6·7	3·8	4·7	3·7	4·5	4·5

[1] *Socialist Bloc* – Albania, Bulgaria, Czechoslovakia, East Germany, Hungary, Poland, Rumania, USSR, Mainland China, Mongolia, North Korea, North Vietnam.
[2] *Co-Com Countries* – Canada, USA, Belgium, Denmark, France, West Germany, Greece, Italy, Luxemburg, Netherlands, Norway, Portugal, Turkey, United Kingdom, Japan.
[3] *Western Countries* – Developed Countries, as defined in United Nations sources: North America, Europe (except Socialist countries), Japan, Australia, New Zealand, South Africa.
[4] *Capitalist Countries* – all countries except the 12 Socialist countries.
n = negligible, less than £1 m., or 0·1%.
Sources. Based on United Nations sources: *Yearbook of International Trade Statistics, Direction of Trade and Monthly Bulletin of Statistics* (values converted from US dollar, at the official exchange rate at the time).

the Bloc. To be processed, the applications for export to Capitalist countries were taking 5–10 days, and those to the Bloc up to 30 days.[1] The number and value of approvals and denials, of course, varied from

[1] US Congress, Select Committee on Export Control, *Investigation and Study of the Administration, Operation and Enforcement of the Export Control Act of 1949 and Related Acts*, GPO, Washington 1964, p. 9; *East-West Trade*, Hearings 1964, Part I, *p. cit.*, p. 77.

year to year, the proportion of denials declining in recent years. As handled by the US Department of Commerce in the early 1960s the value of the approvals and denials was:[1]

	Approvals	Denials
1960	$95 m.	$24 m.
1961	$58 m.	$36 m.
1962	$50 m.	$49 m.
1963	$139 m.	$5 m.

In 1966 5,500 export licences were sought by American firms doing business with the Bloc countries, of which 98% had been granted.[2]

Even recently, a prominent West German industrialist described the feelings of the business community in his country in the following statement: 'The possibility that an embargo may be imposed at any time hangs like the sword of Damocles over the head of German industry.'[3] Although in several Western countries there is a possibility of insurance against the vagaries of government policy on the embargo, it still adds to the cost of trading with the Bloc.

One of the curiosities of the American strategic embargo is a complete ban on the importation of seven types of furs from the USSR (ermine, fox, kolinsky, marten, mink, muskrat and weasel). It was pointed out by the American Fur Merchant Association in 1965 that this ban had contributed to the decline of New York as an international centre for fur trade in favour of London.[4]

Co-Com nations, much less other Western nations, not to mention Developing countries, have never been in complete agreement as to what constitutes 'strategic significance'. The decisions of the Consultative Group have had to be based on unanimity, and the Group has never been able to institute sanctions against a member country not observing the agreed lists and other rules, whether by omission or commission.

From the very inception of the controls, the American approach has been more comprehensive and rigorous than that of other Co-Com

---

[1] *Investigation and Study, op. cit.*, p. 32; *East-West Trade*, Hearings 1964, *op. cit.* p. 237.
[2] Reported in *East Europe*, 4/1967, pp. 38–39.
[3] Reported in *Intereconomics*, Hamburg, 1/1967, p. 7.
[4] As compared with 1947–51, the fur trade turnover passing through New York and London over the period 1952–62 showed a 17% decrease for New York but an 85% increase for London. See *East-West Trade*, Hearings 1965, Part II, *op. cit.*, pp. 221–27.

countries. This led to serious frictions on several occasions, as was the case at the time of the dropping of the Chin-Com list in 1957 and of supplies of transport equipment to Cuba in 1963/64. In 1958, in an atmosphere of East-West *détente*, Khrushchev made a definite offer to the USA to expand trade in a wide range of goods. Upon refusal, the Soviets went to Britain, negotiated virtually the same list of goods and signed a five-year trade agreement. In several cases Britain and France saw nothing wrong in disposing of their obsolete lines of ships, aircraft and computers to the Bloc whilst replacing them with new models at home.

Some other specific sources of irritation which have contributed to the weakening of Western unity may be mentioned. The US Battle Act of 1951, by which American aid can be withheld from any country not observing strategic embargo is an instrument without precedent in international economic relations (even though moderated by the US President's liberal interpretation of the Act). The legislation was based on the conviction, of doubtful validity, that other countries could be made to conform to US policies. The point is that the countries which are capable of producing and exporting embargoed items have recovered economically and are no longer dependent on American aid, or otherwise are too proud to be blackmailed. High-level admonitions to various Western countries were often met with resentment, or at least were regarded as excessively moralistic and naïve. The fact that the USA expects her subsidiary companies in foreign countries to observe the American version of the embargo, has produced bitterness in several countries, especially in Canada, Belgium, Britain and France.[1] Similarly, since 1954 foreign licencees of US-owned patents and technical data have been prevented from exporting any article so produced to China and North Korea without the US Government's permission.

During the Korean War while Britain was restricting the export of certain medicines of military value, West Germany and other European countries were doing lucrative business by freely exporting such drugs.[2]

---

[1] Over the 5 years 1959–63, 70 applications were received by the US authorities from American foreign subsidiaries to export to the Bloc. Of these, 57 were approved and 13 denied. *Investigation and Study, op. cit.*, p. 12.

[2] For details see *Board of Trade Journal*, 20/12/1952, p. 1,200; 27/12/1952, p. 1235; 9/5/1953, p. 938. However, in mid-1953 these countries agreed to impose similar restrictions (*ibid.*, 27/6/1953, p. 1282).

On the other hand, when West Germany suddenly barred the contracted sale of 163,000 tons of large-diameter steel tubes to the Soviet Union in early 1963, other Western countries (mainly Sweden and Japan) supplied the USSR, according to a Soviet source, with 262,000 tons in the same year.[1]

[1] N. Lyubimov, 'Soviet Foreign Trade Problems', *International Affairs*, Moscow, 8/1965, p. 13. It may be observed that the NATO council, on the recommendation of the Economic Committee of NATO lifted the embargo as from 10/11/1966; see *Pravda*, 13/11/1966, p. 5.

13 Trade Disputes

A. SETTLEMENT OF FOREIGN-TRADE DISPUTES

DISPUTES are liable to arise over a very wide field of foreign-trade dealings, such as prices, late shipment, non-delivery, quality of merchandise, specifications, damage in transit, refusal to accept the delivery of goods, differing interpretation of commercial terms, conditions of payment and many other technicalities associated with commercial transactions.

The organization and methods of settling foreign-trade disputes are not uniform in the West, or even in each Western country. Sometimes disputes are handled by ordinary courts. In the majority of cases, however, *ad hoc* arbitration tribunals are established under the auspices of the chamber of commerce or a trade association (such as the Liverpool General Produce Association, or the Scandinavian Board of Hides and Skins). Otherwise, there may be permanent arbitration courts in existence which may have established an international reputation (such as the London Court of Arbitration, the Netherlands Arbitration Institute, or the Arbitration Institute of the Stockholm Chamber of Commerce).

In some parts of the world, a group of countries with close commercial links may form a regional agreement to facilitate the speedy settlement of disputes by arbitration. The Inter-American Commercial Arbitration Commission, based on agreements amongst the chambers of commerce of interested countries, is of this type. The only truly international body is the International Court of Arbitration attached to the International Chamber of Commerce in Paris.

In the Socialist Bloc the institutional set-up is more uniform, although the system in each Bloc country has been partly fashioned on some Western models. In the early stages of Communist regimes, settlement of foreign-trade disputes was handled either by ordinary domestic courts or by courts or tribunals in other countries. However, later, permanent arbitration courts, concerned with foreign trade only, were established in almost all Socialist countries: in the USSR – in 1932, Poland – 1949, Bulgaria – 1952, Czechoslovakia – 1952, Hungary – 1953, Rumania – 1953, East Germany – 1954, Mainland China – 1954, North Korea – 1955 and in Albania in 1959.[1]

The Socialist foreign trade arbitration courts are attached to their respective national chambers of commerce. The fact that these courts' jurisdiction extends only to foreign trade and to the exclusion of ordinary domestic courts, contrasts with the practice in Western countries, where ordinary courts are not excluded from handling foreign-trade disputes, whilst the tribunals concerned with foreign trade only are under the auspices of some international body. In Mongolia and North Vietnam, the disputes are probably referred to ordinary courts or to arbitration courts in other Socialist countries; at any rate, their trade with the West is negligible.[2]

In intra-Bloc trade, the settlement of disputes is regulated by several multilateral treaties, the main one being the *General Conditions of Delivery of Goods in Intra-CMEA Trade*, effective since January 1958 and revised in 1967. This treaty provides for arbitration by a permanent arbitration court (to the exclusion of ordinary courts) in the defendant's country, unless the parties agree to an arbitration court in a third CMEA country. This being the case, specific arbitration clauses in intra-CMEA contracts are as a rule superfluous. Within the CMEA organization there is a Sub-committee on Arbitration attached to the Permanent Commission on Foreign Trade established in 1956, with a head office in Moscow.

There are also several specialized arbitration bodies of an international nature, patronized by several Socialist countries: the International Court of Arbitration for Maritime and Inland Navigation of Gdynia established by Poland, Czechoslovakia and East Germany in 1959,[3] the

[1] K. Grzybowski, *The Socialist Commonwealth of Nations*, Yale UP, New Haven and London 1964, p. 226.

[2] But North Vietnam has the Maritime Arbitration Board (established in 1964). Yugoslavia established the Foreign Trade Arbitration Board in 1946, but in 1954 it was replaced by a system of economic courts, which were further re-modelled in 1958. In trade with Capitalist countries, the Yugoslav Federal Economic Chamber of Commerce systematically recommends arbitration by the International Court of Arbitration at the International Chamber of Commerce. See Karl-Heinz Böckenstiegel, 'Arbitration of Disputes between States and Private Enterprise in the International Chamber of Commerce', *American Journal of International Law*, vol. 59, 1965, p. 581.

[3] The USSR, China and North Vietnam have separate national Maritime Arbitration Boards.

Gdynia Cotton Association (established in 1938),[1] and the Polish Arbitration Commission for Hides and Skins (established in 1963) also of Gdynia.[2] This co-operation in Eastern Europe is further supplemented with bilateral agreements between Eastern European chambers of commerce and those in Asian Socialist countries.

In general, the settlement of trade disputes with Capitalist countries does not differ in form from that in intra-Bloc trade. An eminent Polish lawyer observed that, 'the law of external trade of the countries with planned economies does not differ in its fundamental principles from the law of external trade of other countries, such as e.g. Austria or Switzerland. Consequently, international trade law specialists of all countries have found without difficulty that they speak a "common language".'[3] However, minor differences of an operational nature do exist and where significant they will be brought out in the subsequent discussion.

Each Socialist arbitration court (or commission, or board) includes a panel (or 'college') of arbitrators whose number varies from court to court. In Albania there are 7 members; in the USSR – the Maritime Arbitration Board has 15 whilst the Foreign Trade Arbitration Court has 21 members; in Bulgaria and Rumania – 15 members in each; in China – the Arbitration Court has 15–21 and the Maritime Board has 21–31 members.[4]

In the remaining Socialist countries there appear to be no fixed numbers on the arbitral panels, but Czechoslovakia and Poland seem to have the largest numbers of all Socialist countries.[5] The arbitrators are drawn from commercial, industrial, legal and academic circles.[6] It would

[1] In its membership the following countries are represented in addition to Poland: Bulgaria, Czechoslovakia, East Germany, Hungary, Rumania, Yugoslavia and several cotton exporting countries (Iran, Sudan, Syria). For details see H. Senkowski, *Handel zagraniczny* (Foreign Trade), Warsaw, 4/1967, pp. 169–70.

[2] In addition, on request the International Bank for Economic Co-operation (head office in Moscow), conducts arbitration in matters relating to finance and payments. See K. Nazarkin, *International Affairs*, Moscow, 8/1966, p. 66.

[3] H. Trammer, 'The Law of Foreign Trade in the Legal Systems of the Countries of Planned Economy', *The Sources of the Law of International Trade with Special Reference to East-West Trade*, C. M. Schmitthoff (ed.), Stevens & Sons, London 1964, p. 42.

[4] Grzybowski, *op. cit.*, p. 227.

[5] Czechoslovakia has about 100 whilst Poland has about 50. *Hospodarske noviny* (Economic News), Prague, 17/5/1968, p. 12; *Handel zagr.*, 11/1962, p. 510.

[6] Of the 46 members of the College of Arbitrators in Poland in 1962, 16 were university professors and associate professors, 14 – managers of enterprises, 12 – lawyers and 4 were described as 'experts'. *Handel zagr., loc. cit.*

be most unusual for judges to be represented on the panels because 'judges of state tribunals in centrally planned economies are not generally qualified to examine matters pertaining to external commerce'.[1] So far as is known, no Socialist country now prevents nationals of Western countries from being appointed as arbitrators or to provide expert evidence, although up to 1957–59 foreigners had been excluded from Bulgarian, East German and Polish arbitral panels.

From the arbitral panel, each party to the dispute selects one arbitrator.[2] The two arbitrators then select a third member to act as the chairman. The arbitrators can be challenged on the grounds of prejudice. The three members form what is known as the 'arbitration tribunal'.[3] The arbitrators are required to act as judges, not as prosecuting or defending counsels for the disputants by whom they are nominated.

As in the West, arbitration proceedings are generally open, but they can be held *in camera* upon request of one (or both) of the parties or if the tribunal considers it in the public interest to do so. Conciliation is the first step attempted, and it is in order even if arbitration proceedings have already begun.[4] The awards by the tribunals are final, i.e. as a rule there is no possibility of appeal.[5]

In contracts with Capitalist traders, foreign-trade corporations insert clauses in which the country of arbitration is stipulated. In general, a Socialist country insists that possible disputes be handled in its own foreign-trade arbitration court. However, like any arbitration court its jurisdiction is conditional upon the voluntary consent of the parties concerned and no foreign trader is forced to submit to Socialist arbitration. Thus it may be agreed that a dispute arising before shipment

[1] Trammer, *op. cit.*, p. 45.
[2] The Rules of the Czechoslovak and Hungarian Foreign Trade Arbitration Courts permit selection of arbitrators who are not on the panel.
[3] The rules in some countries (as e.g. in the USSR) provide for a tribunal to consist of one arbitrator only, should both parties request it.
[4] For example, 60% of the disputes involving Soviet and other Socialist foreign trade corporations referred to the Foreign Trade Arbitration Court of the USSR between 1947 and 1954 were settled by conciliation. See J. Zieleniewski and S. Szczypiorski, *Zasady organizacji i techniki handlu zagranicznego* (Principles of the Organization and Conduct of Foreign Trade), PWE, Warsaw 1963, p. 768.
[5] But in the case of certain specialized arbitration bodies appeals are allowed: from the Soviet Maritime Arbitration Board to the Supreme Court of the Soviet Union, and from the Gdynia Cotton Association to the Cotton Arbitration Chamber in Le Havre. See Zieleniewski and Szczypiorski, *op. cit.*, p. 291; Senkowski, *op. cit.*, p. 170.

be settled in the country of dispatch and after that in the country of receipt of the goods. If contract is made by correspondence, the practice in some countries (e.g. the USSR) is to handle the dispute in the country of the offeror, whilst in others (e.g. Poland) in the country of acceptance of the offer.[1] Alternatively, it may be agreed to have the dispute settled in the defendant's country to ensure a speedy enforcement of the award, or otherwise in a 'neutral' country such as Sweden or Switzerland.

Although settlement of disputes in East-West trade poses several problems, up to the mid-1950s there had been little genuine attempt to provide a common basis for co-operation. Since that time, considerable progress has been made between the Western and Eastern European countries under the auspices of the United Nations in working out multilateral arrangements for the international co-ordination of foreign trade litigations. This work has led to two important international agreements. By the *Convention on the Recognition and Enforcement of Foreign Arbitral Awards*, concluded in New York in 1958, not only Western *ad hoc* and permanent arbitral bodies, but also permanent arbitration institutions in Socialist countries are internationally recognized and accepted. As of mid-1966, 9 Western (Austria, Finland, France, West Germany, Greece, Japan, the Netherlands, Norway and Switzerland), 6 Socialist (Bulgaria, Czechoslovakia, Hungary, Poland, Rumania, the USSR, including Byelorussia and Ukraine) and 14 Developing countries were adherents to the New York Convention.[2]

The other agreement is the *European Convention on International Commercial Arbitration*, concluded in Geneva in 1961. It contains a number of provisions regulating certain controversial problems, such as the organization of arbitration bodies, the appointment of arbitrators, the competence of the tribunals, the applicability of national laws, etc. The Geneva Convention, which came into force in January 1964, has been very well received by the European Socialist countries. At the time of writing it has been ratified by Bulgaria, Czechoslovakia, Hungary, Poland, Rumania and the USSR (and Yugoslavia), but by only a few Western European countries (Austria and West Germany among them).

[1] Trammer, *op. cit.*, p. 44.
[2] Based on data supplied directly by the Secretariat of the Economic Commission for Europe in a letter dated 4/10/1966.

B. SOURCES OF CONFLICT

As long as there were only Capitalist countries, the task of international law was relatively simple, confronted as it was with essentially similar societies based on the institution of free enterprise and private property. This has not been the case with the emergence of Socialist countries. The existence of political, social and economic systems, basically antagonistic to each other, naturally creates an inherent predisposition for suspicion and conflict. It is doubtful if the concept of law and justice can ever be completely divorced from the accepted social values. At any rate, neither the East nor the West has particularly wanted to achieve this. In Socialist countries it is explicitly acknowledged that the law is an instrument of the policy of the State.[1]

The orthodox Communist approach to international law was unequivocally described by a Chinese jurist in the following words:

> International law is one of the instruments of settling international problems. If this instrument is useful to our country, to Socialist enterprise or to the peace enterprise of the people of the world, we will use it. However, if this instrument is disadvantageous to our country, to Socialist enterprises or to peace enterprises of the people of the world, we will not use it and should create a new instrument to replace it. Today we have a majority of the old international jurists who still adhere to the purely legalistic viewpoint by restricting themselves to the limited area of international law and thus they subject themselves to the disposal of imperialism.[2]

Although the attitude in the CMEA countries is now less dogmatic,[3] they

---

[1] A Hungarian expert on international law, writing in a Western journal, pointed out that, 'It is of primary importance... that for many Western lawyers law is equalised with the bourgeois concept of law. Socialist lawyers, however, are free from this misconception, owing partly to the Marxist historical view recognizing as many types of law as social systems exist.' Gyula Eorsi, 'Comparative Analysis of Socialist and Capitalist Law'; *Co-existence*, Ontario, Nov. 1964, pp. 140–41, 146. Mao Tse-tung, emulating Marx and Lenin, stated more bluntly: 'The state apparatus, including the army, the police and the courts, is the instrument by which one class oppresses another. It is an instrument for the oppression of antagonistic classes, it is violence and not benevolence'; quoted from Hungdah Chiu, 'Communist China's Attitude Toward International Law', *Amer. Jour. of Int. Law*, April 1966, p. 247.

[2] Quoted from Hungdah Chiu, *op. cit.*, pp. 248–49.

[3] At the 22nd Congress of the CPSU in 1961, it was declared that there were no longer any opposing social classes in the USSR and thus no need for class suppression.

are still firmly committed to the Marxist-Leninist philosophy, the supremacy of the Communist Party, collective ownership of the means of production and central planning.

The concepts underlying world commerce today were developed when international trade was conducted between private traders. Most of the established usages and institutional forms developed by Capitalist countries have been adopted by Socialist countries. Many of the practices have been adopted with reluctance, some of them with appropriate adaptations especially designed to accommodate Capitalist traders. Nevertheless, this has not removed the inherent mutual suspicion. Grounds for conflict have increased since 1953, with the Bloc's intensification of the trade drive in Capitalist countries. Western criticism of the Socialist system of handling foreign-trade disputes has centred mainly on the relation of the State to the arbitration courts, insistence on the domestication of litigations and on certain aspects of procedure. These are treated in the subsequent discussion.

(a) *Juridically Incestuous Relation between the Socialist State and the Arbitration Bodies*

Doubts have been entertained in the West as to whether the foreign-trade arbitration bodies are really independent courts of justice or merely government administrative agencies. These bodies are attached to their respective national chambers of commerce. This set-up, modelled on the Western practice, gives the appearance of their independence from the State. Admittedly, the chambers' operations are not official acts of government.

But fundamentally it is difficult not to see the chambers as government instrumentalities. They are not free associations of traders in the traditional Western sense but products of State legislation. They are an integral part of the monopolistic foreign trade structure, and as their activities fall within the scope of government operations they cannot escape the general supervision by the ministries of foreign trade. In the

---

The dictatorship of the proletariat was reaffirmed as a 'state of the whole people' (see *The Road to Communism*, Documents of the 22nd Congress of CPSU, Foreign Languages Publishing House, Moscow 1961, p. 251). The same attitude has been adopted in other CMEA countries as well.

West, tribunals with exclusive jurisdiction over international disputes are rare, but where they do exist their operations are carefully regulated by some international body. However, in Socialist countries, with minor exceptions of little consolation to Western traders, each tribunal – in spite of its exclusively international function – is under national auspices.

The arbitrators are naturally persons of distinction. Many of them would be members of the Communist Party, or otherwise owe their success to the regime in power. Most of the arbitrators are employees of some organization owned and controlled by the State and concerned with economic administration. They would naturally be inclined to uphold the decisions made by higher authorities and perhaps the 'reason of the State', rather than to decide issues on their merits as viewed by private traders in the West.

Since the reforms of 1957–59, there has been a tendency towards restricting the size of the arbitral panels, so that disputants now have a limited choice of arbitrators. A precondition of a sound arbitration system is that it must ensure the equality of the disputing parties before the tribunal; but the Socialist system does not exclude the possibility of bias. It is widely held in Western legal and business circles that the chairman of the arbitration tribunal handling a trade dispute of an international nature should be of a nationality other than that of either of the disputants.[1]

When in effect the same ubiquitous State, even though appearing under different guises, is both a party to the dispute and, even though indirectly, an arbitrator of it, it is difficult for the Western trader to be reassured that his case is not prejudiced.[2] But in most cases it would be impossible for the injured private trader to prove any prejudiced intention on the part of the Socialist country, because a particular act may be

---

[1] Safeguards to this effect are embodied in the arbitration rules, for example, of: the International Chamber of Commerce, the American Arbitration Association, and the Japan Commercial Arbitration Association. See M. Domke, 'Arbitration of State Trading Relations', *Law and Contemporary Problems*, Spring 1959, esp. 326.

[2] Socialist countries would naturally be inclined to take advantage of the doctrine of 'absolute sovereign immunity', for long accepted in some Western legal circles. By this doctrine, a foreign sovereign (or State) cannot be sued regardless of its activity. However, owing to the development of State trading since World War I, the old doctrine has been replaced by a 'restrictive theory', by which a foreign State is not immune if the activity in question is of a commercial nature, as distinct from a public or governmental activity.

merely a logical and legitimate outcome of the political and economic system in force.

Under these conditions, should an unexpected change in government policy, leading to breaches of contracts by the foreign-trade corporations, be accepted as *force majeure*? This question is a sore point in East-West trade, as was illustrated by the publicity given in the West to the dispute between the Israeli *Jordan Investment Ltd* and the Soviet *Soiuznefteksport* of 1956-58. In the Arab-Israeli conflict at the time of the Suez Canal crisis, the Soviet Government took the side of the United Arab Republic, and in consequence the Soviet Ministry of Foreign Trade cancelled the export licence for crude oil. The *Jordan Investment's* claim for $2·4 m. damages was referred to the Foreign Trade Arbitration Court in Moscow. The *Soiuznefteksport* opposed the claim on the grounds that the Ministry's cancellation of the licence was a *force majeure*. The Court accepted the validity of this argument and rejected the claim.[1] A similar case occurred in 1956 involving two Socialist foreign trade corporations. By a decree of the Presidium of the Council of Ministers in Poland a change was made in the economic plan, which made it difficult for the Polish *Weglokoks* to supply the contracted quantity of coal to the East German *Bergbau Handel*. The Foreign Trade Arbitration Court of Poland which handled the dispute ruled that the governmental decree constituted a *force majeure*, and consequently the *Weglokoks* was not liable.[2]

(b) *The Socialist Insistence on Domestication of Foreign-Trade Litigations*

Until the late 1950s, Socialist countries had been content to have disputes in East-West trade handled in their Western partner's country, or in a neutral country, or by bodies under the patronage of some international institution. But since that time there has been a noticeable tendency for all Bloc countries to insist on the domestication of foreign-trade adjudication. They have endeavoured to introduce clauses into

[1] S. Pisar, 'The Communist System of Foreign-Trade Adjudication', *Harvard Law Review*, June 1959, p. 1413.
[2] J. Jakubowski, 'The Settlement of Foreign Trade Disputes in Poland', *International and Comparative Law Quarterly*, vol. 11, 1962, pp. 815-16.

trade contracts with Capitalist traders stipulating that controversies must be submitted to the arbitration court in the Socialist country.

Domestication of litigations gives several advantages to the Socialist party to the dispute. As was pointed out in Socialist sources, it is easier to nominate the most appropriate arbitrator and to maintain contacts with him; it is also easier and less expensive to attend hearings and supply evidence.[1] To this we must add the question of national pride.

The Western trader does not, of course, have to agree to such a stipulation. But the question arises of whether he really has a free choice. By refusing arbitration in the Socialist country he may lose not only the contract but in fact the custom of the foreign-trade corporation, the only access channel to the market in the Socialist country in question. The fact that a foreign disputant has the right of choice of the arbitrators is of little consolation to him. There is not enough intercourse between the East and the West, and still too great a predisposition for secrecy in Socialist countries in general, to make the arbitrators known personalities outside the Bloc. In practice, when the case is handled in a Socialist country, most Western traders forgo the right of selection.

With the exception of the Soviet Maritime Arbitration Board and the Polish Cotton Arbitration Association the tribunals' awards are final, so that the impossibility of appeal adds further to the Western trader's discomfort. If the West embarked on a trade drive in the Bloc, Socialist countries would be in a stronger bargaining position regarding the place of settlement of disputes.

(c) *Other Grounds*

In the settlement of trade disputes, a good deal of attention is paid in Western countries to accepted usages, procedures and practices which have been developed over centuries and which have become an integral part of the commercial system in the West. It is true that in some Socialist countries arbitration rules provide either explicitly (as in Bulgaria and Poland) or implicitly (in the USSR) for trade customs to be taken into account. But even if the willingness of the Socialist arbitrators is granted, are they really capable of sitting in judgment over

---

[1] Zieleniewski and Szczypiorski, *op. cit.*, p. 767; J. Mazal, *Hospodarske noviny*, *op. cit.*, p. 12.

trade customs which have grown out of freedom of enterprise and devotion to private property – categories which are essentially alien to them? They are more likely than not to stick to the formal letter of the law rather than to substantive justice.

In some Socialist countries, as for example in Poland, members of the Council of the Arbitration Court (as distinct from the selected tribunal) are empowered to participate in proceedings *in camera*. This fact does not ensure the independence of the tribunal, and in fact it is against the law of some Western countries (such as Switzerland). In some Bloc countries, notably in the USSR, the rule of prohibiting the administration of oaths to witnesses often makes the awards unenforceable by Western standards. Finally, contrary to Western practice, there are practically no specialized arbitration facilities available on a commodity basis.

So much for Western criticism of the Socialist arbitration set-up. Socialist mistrust of the Western system of settling East-West trade disputes has been of longer standing. The efforts by Socialist countries to establish their own arbitration machinery, and their insistence on the domestication of litigations have been dictated more by defensive than offensive considerations. Socialist legal and commercial circles have been critical of the Western hotch-potch system which lacks uniformity and, in their eyes, does not exclude the possibility of prejudice.

They are aware of the fact that disputes handled by ordinary courts are time-consuming, expensive and too legalistic to answer the needs of international trade. In the orthodox Marxist view, judges in Capitalist countries would tend to come from the higher social classes. This being the case, their capacity for impartiality may be questioned when confronted with a disputant representing a social order for which they would have little sympathy.

C. A GENERAL APPRAISAL

The most obvious questions that pose themselves in studying disputes in East-West trade are: Is East-West trade more liable to disputes than trade among Western or Socialist countries? What proportions of the

East-West trade disputes are handled in the Western and in the Socialist disputants' countries, and in third countries? Is there a recognizable pattern of bias in awards made in these different countries? To provide complete answers to these questions would be more in the sphere of competence of a lawyer than of an economist or a political scientist.

So far as is known, no comprehensive study of the problem has been made so far. The absence of complete and officially authorized reports of the courts' or tribunals' cases and awards, particularly of those in Socialist countries, covering a long period, makes the assessment of the incidence of disputes and the impartiality of awards impossible at present. The CMEA group of countries has a committee on foreign-trade arbitration, but it is not known if it systematically studies cases of dispute in East-West trade. There have been several proposals in the West to establish some form of machinery under NATO or OECD or EEC to co-ordinate Western policies, or at least exchange information, on trade disputes with Socialist countries, but no permanent agency has yet been established to that effect.[1]

Some idea of the disputes handled by the Socialist tribunals may be gathered from the available information concerning the Polish, Czechoslovak and Soviet Foreign Trade Arbitration Courts. It does not necessarily mean that these data would equally apply over long periods or be representative of the Bloc as a whole.

In the first six months of 1962 the Polish Foreign Trade Arbitration Commission had 60 disputes under consideration, of which 22 cases involved Capitalist and 38 Socialist countries. Thus Capitalist countries were involved in 37% of the cases, which is the same proportion as these countries' share in Poland's foreign trade turnover in 1961–62.

Of the 22 cases, 12 cases involved 8 Western countries: West Germany (4 cases), USA (2), Belgium (1), Canada (1), Iceland (1), Italy (1), Switzerland (1) and Yugoslavia (1). The most important reasons for the disputes were listed as follows: (*a*) delays, (*b*) non-delivery, (*c*) bad quality, (*d*) prices. Other minor causes concerned payments, storage charges, commissions, damage in transit and transport costs. Of the total

[1] For evidence see Political and Economic Planning, 'East-West Trade', *Planning*, London, May 1965, p. 172; Committee for Economic Development, *East-West Trade – A Common Policy for the West*, New York 1965, p. 36; US Senate, *East-West Trade*, Hearings before the Committee on Foreign Relations, Part II, GPO, Washington 1965, p. 132.

of the 60 cases, 35 were completed during the period in question, the average period of duration having been six and a half months. The awards made in the 35 cases were distributed as follows: in 35% of the cases in favour of the Polish disputants, in 35% – in favour of foreign disputants, whilst in the remaining 30% of the cases awards were partly in favour of the Polish and partly the foreign parties.[1]

In Czechoslovakia, on the average 150–200 cases are submitted to the Arbitration Court annually. Of these, one-third involves Capitalist countries, the proportion that corresponds to these countries' share in Czechoslovak foreign trade (31% over the period 1966–68). The most frequent cause of the disputes was late delivery and failure to rectify the defects of the goods concerned. The total value of the claims under consideration at the beginning of 1968 amounted to 45 m. foreign-exchange korunas (about $6 m.).[2]

The Soviet Foreign Trade Arbitration Commission considered over 500 cases over the period from 1957 to 1967, and the number of disputes submitted in 1967 was 150. Over this period *Eksportles*, the Soviet foreign-trade corporation exporting timber, which is well known in Western markets, was involved in 155 disputes with British, West German, Italian, Czechoslovak and East German trading partners; of this number, 53 cases were settled by mutual agreement, 65 in favour of foreign firms and 37 in favour of *Eksportles*.[3]

Although many Western traders are hesitant to submit to arbitration in a Socialist country, others have found the system quite satisfactory. After all, the Socialist tribunals' jurisdiction is conditional upon voluntary submission, and the foreign-trade corporations now appear to be less insistent in contracts stipulating arbitration in their own country.[4] Foreign nationals are now allowed as arbitrators and expert witnesses in all European Socialist countries at least. There are provisions for proceedings to be held in foreign languages and for adjudication

[1] *Handel zagr.*, 11/1962, p. 510.
[2] J. Mazal, *op. cit.*
[3] *Foreign Trade*, Moscow, 5/1968, pp. 24–25.
[4] For example, when the Czechoslovak *Centrotex* sued the Pakistani *Fqrid & Sons Ltd*, referring the case to the Czechoslovak Foreign Trade Arbitration Court. But the Pakistani firm objected to the dispute being heard in Czechoslovakia because there had been no clause in the contract to this effect, and the Czechoslovak Court upheld the objection. See D. F. Ramzaitsev, 'The Law Applied by Arbitration Tribunals', *The Sources of the Law of International Trade*, *op. cit.*, p. 141.

to be based on foreign law. In contrast to the awards made by Western tribunals, once a Socialist tribunal makes a favourable award to a foreigner, performance follows automatically without additional uncertainty, delays and expense.

It is generally conceded in Western legal and commercial circles that settlements of foreign-trade disputes by permanent arbitral bodies is the most appropriate method. This is so particularly when disputes involve parties from different social systems.[1] Foreign arbitration awards are more readily enforceable than foreign judicial decisions, because in many national legislations there is no distinction made between domestic and foreign arbitral awards and the arbitrators are private persons not representative of foreign States.[2] On the operational side, arbitration is less formalistic, less expensive and less time-consuming than litigation in ordinary courts.

There appears to be a consensus of opinion in the West that, in retrospect, the procedures and awards of the Socialist tribunals have been on the whole fair and reasonable. In fact, their tribunals are acquiring a growing degree of acceptance from Western traders, courts and governments.[3] The enthusiasm of the European Socialist countries for multilateral co-operation in international commercial arbitration under the auspices of the United Nations and the policy of peaceful co-existence are bound to further strengthen this confidence.[4]

---

[1] See, e.g., *The Sources of the Law of International Trade, op. cit.*, esp. pp. 25, 222. The countries of the ECAFE Region came to a similar conclusion at a conference held on commercial arbitration in Bangkok in 1966; see P. Sanders, 'Trade Arbitration between East and West', *International and Comp. Law Quart.*, July 1966, esp. p. 744.

[2] L. Kos Rabcewicz-Zubkowski, 'The Legal Aspects of Trade with Communist Countries', in *East-West Trade*, A Symposium, P. E. Uren (ed.), Canadian Institute of International Affairs, Toronto 1966, p. 97.

[3] For example see S. Pisar, *op. cit.*, p. 1,478; A. Nove and D. Donnelly, *Trade with Communist Countries*, Hutchinson, London 1960, pp. 113–14; London Chamber of Commerce, *Trading with the Soviet Union*, A Guide for the Importers and Exporters, 2nd ed., London 1961, pp. 8–9; K. Grzybowski, *op. cit.*, p. 237; H. J. Berman in US Senate, *East-West Trade*, Hearings before the Committee on Foreign Relations, Part II, GPO, Washington 1965, p. 132.

[4] The Committee on Peaceful Co-existence of the Soviet Association of International Law declared in 1962: 'The principle of peaceful co-existence is a universally recognized principle of modern international law; ... whereas international law of the past was a law of war and peace, it has today become a law of peace and peaceful co-existence.' Quoted from L. Lipson, 'Peaceful Coexistence', *Law and Contemporary Problems*, Autumn 1964, p. 871.

14 Gains and Waste

A. GAINS FROM TRADE UNDER FREE ENTERPRISE AND UNDER CENTRAL PLANNING

IN the most general sense, gains from international trade consist in the increase in social welfare as a result of the savings in costs as measured by the difference between what it would cost the country to supply its needs from domestic sources and the cost of obtaining such supplies from imports.

Such gains can be differently interpreted. They can be taken as profits made by the enterprises engaging in foreign trade, or they can be understood as benefits accruing to the whole economy. They can be looked upon as immediate returns, or viewed in terms of the long-run advantages. They can be treated narrowly as those benefits which are measurable in terms of money, or broadly as those including non-monetary advantages (and disadvantages) as well.

In the ultimate analysis, the question of gains from trade must be considered in terms of the aims of the social system in force. Is trade to ensure maximum profits for traders or maximum satisfaction for consumers or the maximum rate of economic development? This naturally raises the question of who the judge of the gains is to be – the trader, the consumer, the government or the Party.

Under free enterprise, the working of the market mechanism is conducive to the maximization of commercial gains in the microeconomic sense. Trade is fundamentally conducted in accordance with the principle of comparative advantage, i.e. the size, structure and direction of trade are basically determined by price differentials. Prices in these countries normally include all costs (plus varying amounts of profit, according to the degree of monopoly power). Prices also perform an allocative function, i.e. factors of production tend to be put to such uses and up to that point where marginal cost is equated to the marginal revenue of the product. In all Western countries, governments, guided roughly by long-run social cost-benefit considerations, intervene in the operation of the mechanism mainly through tariffs and subsidies. Under these conditions, the interest of individual traders and of the country as a whole coincides, i.e. as long as trade is profitable to individual exporters and importers, it is gainful to the economy.

Under central planning of the Socialist type, the accounting 'profits' (or 'losses') made by the foreign-trade corporations do not indicate the economic gains accruing to the economy. Prices do not necessarily reflect all costs fully (rent, interest, and in some cases even wages), nor do they indicate scarcity. The price structure differs substantially from world market prices, and the official exchange rates further exaggerate the distortions between domestic prices and those in different foreign markets. Settlements between foreign-trade corporations and domestic producing and using enterprises are made as a rule in accordance with domestic prices, not foreign-exchange equivalents (however see Section D of this chapter below). The predisposition of Socialist countries to bilateralism can be partly explained by their desire to maximize gains in a visible, direct way; e.g. in the case of barter the gain is indicated by the terms of trade of the transaction, and so the problem of finding the profitability of the items exported and imported can be by-passed.

Priorities assigned to investment, to promote rapid economic growth and 'balanced' development at the expense of current consumption, lead to a size and structure of trade which would not be considered optimal by Western standards. Besides, the constraints imposed by bilateralism militate against the optimum direction of trade, i.e. imports are not necessarily obtained from the cheapest source and exports are not sold in the most profitable market.

There is, of course, no absolute criterion of the gains from trade. The gains can be appraised only in terms of specific objectives explicitly or implicitly pursued by the government. Under free enterprise, where self-interest is accepted as legitimate, foreign trade is conditioned ultimately by consumers' preferences. In the centrally planned economies, foreign trade is chiefly considered as one of the important ways of speeding up planned economic growth. A Polish economist and administrator summed up the Socialist view of trade in the following way: 'There is no such thing as absolute gain from foreign trade, one can only speak of the effectiveness of foreign trade in the context of the given or desired rate of economic development, and for different levels of national income there are different degrees of gains from foreign trade.'[1]

The authorities in Socialist countries are cheerfully prepared to sacrifice short-term commercial gains to long-run macro-economic advantages, and it is accepted that the less developed a country is, the more it should disregard the temptation of short-term benefits.[2] Some Socialist economists have expressed the view that a country can benefit from trade only if its labour productivity is higher than the average productivity in the world market, i.e. it is not gainful for a relatively underdeveloped economy to engage in foreign trade. However, this thinking, based on a misinterpretation of Marx, is not generally accepted. It is conceded that a less efficient country has to forgo more in social labour costs than a more efficient one, but trade can still be gainful to the former.[3]

Does each system achieve its objectives in the most efficient way? A market economy has a mechanism which, in general, ensures the most efficient flow of trade. However, monopolistic trading interests, in their quest for profit maximization, may distort the flow of trade and exploit consumers (see Ch. 9 E). Besides, not all consumer wants (e.g. narcotics) are in the best interest of the society. Where the government intervenes, private traders in their desire to maximize their own profits, tend to undermine government policies.

A centrally planned economy of the Socialist type has no automatic or simple mechanism to ensure maximum gains from trade. Even though in several Socialist countries determined efforts have been put into foreign-trade efficiency studies, no satisfactory system has yet been evolved (see Sections B and C of this chapter).

---

[1] J. Wierzbołowski, *Gospodarka planowa* (Planned Economy), Warsaw, 6/1966, p. 18.
[2] See G. Shagalov, *Voprosy ekonomiki*, 6/1965, p. 94; M. Maneli, *Nowe drogi* (New Paths), Warsaw, 4/1967, pp. 82–91.
[3] Shagalov, *op. cit.*, p. 91.

B. FOREIGN-TRADE-EFFICIENCY CALCULATIONS IN THE SOCIALIST BLOC[1]

The need for devising methods of analysis of foreign-trade efficiency[2] in Socialist countries derives from the peculiar organic features of their economies discussed in the preceding section – distorted price structures, insulation of the domestic from foreign markets and disequilibrium official exchange rates.[3] This need has become more pressing since the mid-1950s, owing to the growing size and proportion of foreign trade in the Socialist countries' national income, which means that the efficiency or inefficiency of foreign trade is producing increasing repercussions on their economies.[4]

Of all Socialist countries, Poland, East Germany, Czechoslovakia and Hungary have been most active in the studies of foreign-trade efficiency and the implementation of their findings, whilst the USSR, Bulgaria and Rumania have been mostly adopting the ideas and practices of the former. The efficiency of foreign trade is one of those fields of economics which has received the most widespread attention in these countries. Efficiency analysis in the remaining Bloc countries is carried on on a modest scale and with a limited degree of sophistication.

[1] This section is partly based on the author's article published in the *Economic Journal*, March 1965. However, substantial modifications have been introduced in respect of methodology, scope and terminology to fit this section into the broader setting of this study, and to reflect developments since the time the article was written.

[2] In the subsequent discussion, distinctions are made between efficiency, effectiveness and profitability. The term 'efficiency' is used in a general sense as a relation of input (costs) to output (receipts), when all conditions underlying supply and demand as revealed by the market are taken into account. The concept 'effectiveness' is specifically used in application to the Socialist studies of the efficiency of exports, imports or investment, computed by reference to the variables laid down by policy makers. 'Profitability' is a micro-economic term indicating the degree of financial performance whether of a Western firm or a Socialist trading or producing undertaking.

[3] Cf. the case of Yugoslavia which has decided to introduce a considerable degree of market mechanism and to fix equilibrium exchange rates.

[4] An illustration of the absurd situations that often arose is provided by the Polish metallic sodium, which in the mid-1950s was exported for $200 a ton whilst for the amount of coal alone used up in the process of production one could obtain $700. See J. Krynicki, *Problemy handlu zagranicznego Polski* (Problems of Poland's Foreign Trade), PWN, Warsaw 1958, p. 316.

(a) *Historical Background*

Apparently already before the war, rough indicators of the profitability of exports and imports were used in the USSR,[1] but their application and worthiness were extremely limited. Since World War II it is possible to distinguish four stages in the development of foreign-trade efficiency analysis.

(i) *1945–1953*. Little of permanent value was done during this period. Crude calculations of the profitability of exports were attempted in isolated cases by some foreign-trade corporations, with practically no guidance from theoretical studies. The usefulness of the calculations increased when they were applied to gauging the profitability of processing imported components for re-export, in which case the task was relatively simple as they were expressed in foreign currencies.

(ii) *1954–1957*. During this period, the problem attracted the attention of professional economists in the atmosphere of the reaction against autarky and in view of the normalization of trading relations (made possible by the completion of post-war reconstruction and the termination of Eastern European reparations). Widespread interest was particularly aroused by the contributions of such writers as Liska and Marias of Hungary, Rolow of Poland and V. Černiansky of Czechoslovakia.[2] The governments, although interested in the results of the discussions, were still sceptical about their value, and were not yet prepared to translate theory into practice. Towards the end of 1957 an important intra-Bloc *International Conference on Foreign Trade Efficiency* was held in Czechoslovakia.

(iii) *1958–1963*. This crucial stage was noted for governments' active participation in the studies on an organized basis and their practical applications. At first, the ministries of foreign trade made it mandatory for the foreign-trade corporations to establish special cells to carry on the calculations of effectiveness of the most important exports along the

[1] Shagalov, *op. cit.*, p. 95.
[2] T. Liska and A. Marias, 'Optimum Returns and International Division of Labour', a summarized translation can be found in United Nations, *Economic Survey of Europe 1954*, pp. 131–34; A. Rolow, *Handel zagraniczny* (Foreign Trade), Warsaw, 12/1956; V. Černiansky, *Aussenhandel*, East Berlin, 15/1957. For further details of the early bibliography on the subject see A. Rolow, *Rachunek ekonomiczny w handlu zagranicznym* (Economic Calculations in Foreign Trade), PWG, Warsaw 1960, pp. 175–80.

improved lines. Further research to broaden the theoretical foundations were undertaken by government departments and research institutes. These efforts have been designed to evolve comprehensive models with a large number of variables, so as to bring the analysis of the effectiveness of exports and imports to a common basis. The authorities have undertaken the calculation of norm-setting marginal exchange rates and of the relative value of foreign currencies in order to issue them to the foreign-trade corporations and the relevant industrial enterprises.

(*iv*) *Since 1963* the efficiency analysis has assumed a broader role in sympathy with the economic reforms initiated in the countries most active in these studies. Greater attention is being given to the effectiveness of imports and to the overall gain from foreign trade. Efficiency calculations are taken into account in the overall planning, thus to some extent influencing the structure of the economy, and the new approach was applied in working out the 1966–70 plans. Steps have been taken to place foreign-trade planning on a value basis (as distinct from the quantitative approach followed in the past). Attempts have also been made to rationalize the relations between the foreign-trade corporations and the domestic enterprises by making the material incentives of the personnel of both directly dependent on their foreign-trade effectiveness in terms of foreign exchange.

The actual efficiency calculations are carried out by the foreign-trade corporations and more recently also by the industrial enterprises producing for export, whilst the ministries of foreign trade undertake studies of a broader nature. In the more foreign-trade-oriented countries, there are also other bodies pursuing research on particular aspects of the problem. Thus in Poland these bodies include: the Finance Department of the Ministry of Foreign Trade, the Committee for Foreign Trade Efficiency Affairs (attached to the Ministry of Foreign Trade), the Institute for the Study of Economic Fluctuations and Prices in Foreign Trade, the Research Institute Attached to the State Planning Commission, the Polish Academy of Sciences, the Polish Chamber of Foreign Trade; to these must be added *ad hoc* study groups or Commissions (such as the one appointed in 1963 under the chairmanship of Prof. M. Kalecki) as well as numerous individual researchers who have an impressive record of high-quality publications.

The essential feature of the efficiency methods devised consists in indices in which different forms of domestic costs are related to foreign-exchange values (receipts or expenditure). The indices fall into three categories: those to measure the effectiveness of exports, of imports, and of relevant investments. In addition, there are coefficients of the relative value of foreign currencies, marginal exchange rates and econometric models of the overall efficiency of foreign trade.

There is no one universal index used in all Socialist countries pursuing the calculations. The number of different indices counted in one Socialist country alone (Poland) in existence at one time or another exceeds a hundred, most of them variants used for some specific purpose. In each country, naturally, there are differences in approach, reflecting differences in domestic conditions, in the objectives postulated, in the definitions of terms and in the peculiarities of its pattern of trade. Only those indices are considered in this study which represent some significant principle or stage of development. Other indices used, some of which are extremely complex, are variants of those discussed below.[1]

(b) Indices of the Relative Effectiveness of Exports

The greatest progress has so far been made in devising various types of indicators of the effectiveness of exports. This is calculated by comparing the domestic price or cost with receipts of foreign exchange.

[1] The symbols used in the indices to follow have been adapted by the author to English terminology. The ratios shown here indicate costs in domestic currency divided by foreign-exchange values (the procedure followed in Bulgaria, Hungary and Poland) as this approach appears more logical to the author. But in some Socialist countries (Czechoslovakia, East Germany, the USSR) the ratios are reversed and the results must be interpreted accordingly. The discussion in this section is based mainly on: A. Rolow, *Rachunek ekonomiczny w handlu zagranicznym, op. cit.*; J. Nykryn and K. Herman, *Effektivnost a rentabilita v zahranicnym obchodie* (Effectiveness and Profitability in Foreign Trade), SNTL, Prague 1962; P. Glikman, *Efektywność investycji zwiazanych z handlem zagranicznym* (Effectiveness of Investment Relevant to Foreign Trade), PWE, Warsaw 1965; G. L. Shagalov, *Ekonomicheskaya effektivnost tovarnogo obmena mezhdu sotsialisticheskimi stranami* (Economic Effectiveness of Commodity Exchanges between Socialist Countries), Mysl, Moscow 1966; the following periodicals: *Aussenhandel* (Foreign Trade, published in East Berlin), *Czechoslovak Foreign Trade* (Prague), *Ekonomista* (The Economist, Warsaw), *Gospodarka planowa* (Planned Economy, Warsaw), *Handel zagraniczny* (Foreign Trade, Warsaw), *Planovoe khoziaistvo* (Planned Economy, Moscow), *Vneshnaya torgovlya* (Foreign Trade, Moscow), *Voprosy ekonomiki* (Problems of Economics, Moscow), *Die Wirtschaft* (The Economy, East Berlin), *Życie gospodarcze* (Economic Life, Warsaw).

CH. 14 §B GAINS AND WASTE   315

The order in which the indices are discussed roughly indicates an increasing degree of complexity and, in general, indicates the main evolutionary stages in their development.

(*i*) *Market Effectiveness of Export.* This index was used by foreign-trade corporations to indicate the profitability from the point of view of the domestic market. The prevailing domestic price is compared with the export price that can be obtained:

$$mEX = \frac{dP + mC}{FPd} \;;$$

mEX – market effectiveness of export;
   dP – domestic price (including turnover tax) at which the foreign-trade corporation obtains the articles from a domestic enterprise;
   mC – domestic portion of marketing costs, including the commercial mark-up allowed to the corporations (the costs are also known as 'circulation' costs);
   FPd – current export price that can be obtained in a foreign market, expressed in domestic currency at the official exchange rate.

But in this index the effectiveness is obscured by the differing rates of turnover taxes, and it does not show the most important fact in which the government is interested, viz. the foreign-exchange-earning capacity of different exports in relation to costs.

(*ii*) *Index of the Gross Foreign-Exchange Effectiveness of Export.* This index relates the domestic factory cost price of the exportable article to the foreign-exchange price that can be received:

$$GfeEX = \frac{C + mC}{FPfe} \;;$$

GfeEX – gross foreign-exchange effectiveness of export;
   C – factory cost price (including factory profit mark-up, but not including the turnover tax);
   FPfe – net current export price obtainable in a foreign market, expressed in foreign exchange (marketing costs incurred in foreign exchange per unit of the article are deducted).

As in this index turnover taxes, which are normally imposed on consumer goods to provide investment funds, are not included, by exporting such goods the treasury suffers loss of revenue. A special variant index has been devised to evaluate the relative value of the foreign-exchange gain against the loss of revenue to the government.

(iii) Index of the Net Foreign-Exchange Effectiveness of Export. In the preceding index no account is taken of the import content on which foreign exchange was expended. In the 'net' index adjustments are made on behalf of important components included in the exportable commodity. It is essential to make these deductions from the production cost (and the foreign-exchange price) as domestic prices of imported materials do not necessarily reflect the actual monetary expenses in acquiring such materials:

$$NfeEX = \frac{C - iS + mC}{FPfe - iSfe};$$

$NfeEX$ – net foreign-exchange effectiveness of export;
    iS – value of the imported component supplies used up in the article, expressed in domestic currency;
  $iSfe$ – value of the imported component supplies used, expressed in foreign exchange at world market prices.

This type of index is of particular use to those Socialist countries which mostly import raw materials but export finished products, as is the case with Czechoslovakia, East Germany, Hungary and Poland.[1]

A simplified form of this index is expressed as a percentage ratio of the foreign-exchange cost of the imported component supplies to the foreign-exchange price of the exportable article:

$$NfeEX' = \frac{iSfe}{FPfe} \; 100.$$

The lower the percentage, the more profitable is the processing in terms of foreign exchange.

[1] For example, nearly one-half of the work force employed in manufacturing industries in Poland depends on imported raw materials. The proportion is higher for Czechoslovakia, East Germany and Hungary. See R. Chwieduk (ed.), *Ekonomia polityczna* (Political Economy), PWN, Warsaw, 1966, vol. II, 441.

CH. 14 §B GAINS AND WASTE   317

(*iv*) *Index of the Pure Net Foreign-Exchange Effectiveness of Export.* The preceding index overrates the foreign-exchange earning capacity of an article containing (domestically produced) components which, if exported, can earn foreign exchange in their own right. Therefore an index has been worked out to show the extent to which further processing of exportable commodities is worth while from the point of view of earning additional foreign exchange:

$$pNfeEX = \frac{C - iS - eS + mC}{FPfe - iSfe - eSfe};$$

pNfeEX – pure net foreign-exchange effectiveness of export;
    eS – value of exportable components in domestic currency at domestic prices;
  eSfe – value of exportable components in foreign exchange at world prices.

(*v*) *Index of the Foreign-Exchange Equivalent of Labour.* The indices discussed so far do not clearly bring out the 'value added' by domestic labour over and above the value of materials used in the process of manufacturing. In an attempt to remove this deficiency, an index of the 'foreign-exchange equivalent of labour' was devised:

$$feEl = \frac{C - S + mC}{FPfe - Sfe};$$

feEl – foreign-exchange equivalent of labour;
  S – value of all supplies used (imported and domestic) in domestic prices;
 Sfe – value of all supplies used (imported and domestic) in foreign exchange at world prices.

A variant of this index is employed to show how many units of current ('live') labour it is necessary to expend in an industry where there is idle export-producing capacity to earn one unit of foreign exchange:

$$feEXw = \frac{Wd}{FPfe - Sfe};$$

feEXw – foreign-exchange export effectiveness of wages;
  Wd – wages (in domestic currency) per unit of the exportable article.

Another variant of this index is frequently used to determine the material intensity of exports.

(vi) Partial and Global Indices of the Foreign-Exchange Effectiveness of Export. The problem naturally arises of how far back in the production process of the exportable article one should go to calculate the effectiveness of export. For this purpose 'partial' and 'global' indices have been applied. In the 'partial' index only the labour costs in the 'last phase' of production are taken into account, whilst in the 'global' index labour costs through all stages of production are included:

$$feEXg = \frac{pC^1 + pC^2 + \ldots pC^n}{R^1 + R^2 + \ldots R^n} = \frac{\Sigma pC}{\Sigma R};$$

$feEXg$ – global foreign exchange effectiveness of export (according to the phases of production);

$pC^1, pC^2 \ldots pC^n$ – processing costs in the analysed phases of production, expressed in domestic currency;

$R^1, R^2 \ldots R^n$ – net foreign-exchange receipts obtainable consequent on the cost of processing at each phase.

In practice, the analysis does not go beyond a major branch of industry.

(c) Indices of the Relative Effectiveness of Import

The Bloc countries did not attach much importance to import efficiency analysis in the past. The import structure is mainly established by the developmental needs of the national economy in the general economic plan, largely within the ramifications and objectives laid down by the Party guided by political and macro-social considerations. In general, it is assumed implicitly that the import of articles not produced domestically is gainful if they are essential to fulfil developmental plans or to enable gainful export production.

However, in the countries more dependent on foreign trade and where efficiency studies are more advanced (Poland, East Germany, Czechoslovakia, Hungary) calculations of import effectiveness have been carried on for years, and increasing significance is being attached to them.[1] Where such calculations are carried on, the methods are broadly similar to those applied in exports. But such analyses cover a narrower range of

---

[1] In Poland, calculations of the directional effectiveness of imports were made compulsory in 1965. For details see S. Humin, *Handel zagr.*, 9/1965, p. 417.

items, fewer variables are taken into account and the number of variant indexes is smaller.

(*i*) *Index of the Foreign-Exchange Effectiveness of Import.* In this general index, the domestic price is compared with the foreign-exchange price:

$$feEM = \frac{dwP - mC}{FPfe};$$

feEM – foreign-exchange effectiveness of import;
  dwP – domestic wholesale price at which the imported article is sold by the f.t.c. to domestic enterprises;
  mC – domestic marketing cost of the f.t.c. per unit of the article imported, including the allowed commercial margin;
  FPfe – average (c.i.f.) foreign exchange price of the imported article.

It must be observed that owing to the traditional dichotomy between the price level of consumer goods (which include turnover taxes) and producer goods, this index if applied to imports of producer goods would not indicate comparable results because the latter, although being high-priority imports, would be far less profitable than the former. Consequently, either corrections are made on behalf of turnover taxes or the same index is used for both – to establish the relative effectiveness of imports *within each group*. As a rule, the proportions between imports for consumption and for investment are determined autonomously, not on the basis of effectiveness calculations.

(*ii*) *Index of the Foreign-Exchange Effectiveness of Import for the Retail Market.* A similar index to the above is used in application to consumer goods. Its purpose is to determine a structure of imports yielding the highest revenue for the government and at the same time absorbing the highest amount of consumers' purchasing power:

$$feEMrm = \frac{drtP - D}{FPfe};$$

feEMrm – foreign-exchange effectiveness of import for the retail market;

drtP – domestic retail price of the imported article, minus wholesale and retail mark-ups, expressed in domestic currency;

D – the margin by which the imported article deteriorates (e.g. in the case of perishables such as fruits).

The scope for using this index is rather limited because it applies to articles of second and third priority.

(iii) Index of the Foreign-Exchange Effectiveness of Import-Replacement Production. Anti-import production is a well-known ambition in Socialist (as well as in Capitalist) countries. In this index an attempt is made to establish the relative effectiveness of such production from the point of view of saving foreign exchange:

$$feEMr = \frac{dC}{FPfe} ;$$

feEMr – foreign-exchange effectiveness of import-replacement production;

dC – average domestic prime cost of production in domestic currency.

Using this index, in which the distortion of the turnover taxes is removed, it is possible to weed out unprofitable imports and uneconomic domestic production.

(iv) Index of the Foreign-Exchange Effectiveness of Labour in Import-Replacement Production. In this index component supplies are deducted. The calculation can be based on a partial or a global basis:

$$feEMl = \frac{dC - S}{FPfe - Sfe} ;$$

feEMl – foreign-exchange effectiveness of labour in import-replacement production.

(d) The Foreign-Exchange Effectiveness of Investment

The indices discussed so far are employed to analyse the current effectiveness of foreign trade, that is their purpose is to achieve a more rational utilization of the existing production possibilities. Up to about

1960 constant capacities were postulated in the calculations. However, modifications in the size and structure of exports and imports call for changes in investment. Thus in medium and perspective planning it is essential to examine the effectiveness of the relevant investment outlays bearing on the balance of payments. Such outlays can be viewed as enabling to earn additional foreign exchange (in export industries) or to save expenditure of foreign exchange (in import-replacement industries). In each case, extra imports are likely to be needed not only for components to be used in production but also for the implementation of the investment projects.

(i) *Index of the Capital Intensity of Foreign-Trade Production.* To evaluate the effectiveness of the proposed investment programmes involving single outlays, an index has been evolved in which the capital outlay needed to increase the production capacity is related to the amount of foreign exchange gained in a year:

$$feEI = \frac{Id}{\Sigma Afe - \Sigma Sfe};$$

feEI – capital intensity of investment in export or import-replacement production;
Id – investment outlay, expressed in domestic currency, needed to attain a given increase in production capacity;
ΣAfe – amount of foreign exchange that can be earned or saved in a year as a result of the investment;
ΣSfe – the foreign-exchange value of the material supplies used up in the project in question in a year.

In its reversed form, the index shows the direct effect of the contemplated investment project on the balance of payments. In whichever form, the index is satisfactory in application to those investments which command about the same period of useful life. If periods differ, from the point of view of the effect on the balance of payments, then the time factor must be taken into account:

$$feEI' = \frac{Id}{(\Sigma Afe - \Sigma Sfe)n};$$

n – expected number of years of exploitation of the investment projects.

Several variants of this index are in existence to provide for cases where production of a complex finished article involves investment in several industries.

(ii) Synthetic Index of the Foreign-Exchange Effectiveness of Foreign Trade. A combined index of the foreign-exchange effectiveness of export, can be obtained only when in addition to prime costs capital outlays are also accounted for. An attempt to achieve this is made in the so-called 'synthetic' index. E.g. a synthetic index of the net foreign-exchange effectiveness of export assumes the following form:

$$sNfeEX = NfeEX + (feEI \cdot d);$$

d – coefficient of investment discount.

The coefficient of investment discount is a figure fixed for the whole industry or for the whole economy. E.g. in Poland a uniform coefficient, 0·2 or 20% p.a., was used in working out the investments in the 1966–70 plan (previously the coefficients applied ranged from 0·07 to 0·15). The coefficient introduced in Hungary in 1964, applicable to manufacturing industries (with exceptions) was fixed at 0·05, i.e. 5% p.a., of the value of the fixed and circulating capital used.[1] The lower the value of the synthetic index, the more effective is the production in terms of foreign exchange.

(e) Relative Value of Foreign Currencies and the Marginal Exchange Rate

Foreign values in the indexes discussed so far were expressed in a foreign currency. Such values, of course, must be brought to a common denominator. The official-parity exchange rates do not usually indicate the relative desirability of different foreign currencies from the point of view of the socialist country, owing to the elements of bilateralism, different degrees of currency transferability, etc.

---

[1] See Rolow, *op. cit.*, p. 155; Humin, *op. cit.*, p. 420; S. Balazsy, *Gosp. plan.*, 8–9/1964, pp. 89–93.

To overcome this disability and to provide a rational basis for determining the effectiveness of the direction of trade, the ministries of foreign trade (or ministries of finance) fix the so-called 'coefficients of the relative value of foreign currencies.' In working out these coefficients, the prices in trade with a country with a fully convertible currency are studied first and the exchange rate established is taken as a basis. The relative values of other currencies, from the point of view of the Socialist country in question, is arrived at by taking into account export and import prices in trade with the country (or currency area) considered, the size and composition of exports and imports, the ease of access to the market, etc.[1] The coefficients are fixed annually (or more frequently) and are issued to the foreign-trade corporations, industrial branch associations and enterprises carrying on efficiency calculations.

The indices of effectiveness and the coefficients of the relative value of foreign currencies make it possible to establish a scale of exportable articles in a descending order of effectiveness for each foreign country or currency area. The degree of effectiveness is indicated by the rate showing how much it costs the economy to earn (or save) one unit of a comparable unit of foreign exchange. The higher the rate the less gainful is the export. E.g. by exporting article A it may cost the Hungarian economy 5 forints to earn 1 foreign-exchange forint, whilst exporting B the respective figures may be 8 to 1. This means that each transaction in fact carries a different exchange rate, according to the domestic cost of production of each article and the degree of desirability of the foreign currency. The actual transaction exchange rate indicates the degree of gain from the point of view of the Socialist economy, given the institutional set-up and policy objectives.

Each year the ministry of foreign trade, in consultation with the ministry of finance and the state planning commission, fixes what is known as a 'limiting' exchange rate, above which exports are not allowed. In altering this marginal exchange rate, the authorities are

[1] For details and theoretical foundations, see the pioneering work by W. Trzeciakowski, *Metody wyznaczania kursu granicznego i uproszczone metody analizy efektywności handlu zagranicznego* (Methods of Determining the Marginal Exchange Rate and Simplified Methods of Analysis of Foreign Trade Effectiveness), Institute for the Study of Economic Fluctuations and Prices in Foreign Trade, Warsaw 1964. On the more recent view of the role of the marginal exchange rate see S. Polaczek, *Gosp. plan.*, 7/1966, pp. 25–28; J. Wesołowski, *Finanse* (Finance), Warsaw, 2/1968, pp. 65–71.

guided chiefly by changes in the level and structure of foreign prices, domestic retail prices, domestic real wages and the structure of domestic production. Many Socialist economists think that for each foreign market a separate rate should be fixed, but in practice the authorities adopt one rate only and its applicability to each market is made possible by multiplying it by the coefficient of the relative value of the foreign currency concerned.[1]

The limiting, or marginal, exchange rate marks the least effective parcel of exportables (or of import-replaceables) which must still be exported (or imports replaced by home production) to balance the import bill postulated in the plan. Thus the main consideration behind fixing the level of the rate is in fact to ensure a balance-of-payments equilibrium. A higher marginal rate would be fixed in the case of an anticipated balance-of-payments deficit, as such a rate would make an additional parcel of exportables profitable and would stimulate import-replacement.

(f) *Relative and Absolute Effectiveness of Foreign Trade*

The indices which we have considered bring out the relative effectiveness of exports or imports. However, once the marginal exchange rate is known, it is possible to calculate the absolute value of the gain to the economy by the following formula:

$$aE = R^m(V - C - dI);$$

aE – absolute effectiveness of export (or import-replacement);
R^m – marginal (or limiting) exchange rate;

---

[1] The last-known marginal exchange rate in Poland, as reported in application to the cement industry at least, was 17.50 domestic złotys to 1.00 foreign-exchange złoty, i.e. export was considered unprofitable if, to earn 1 foreign-exchange złoty, the cost of production exceeded 17.50 domestic złotys; in such cases, exports are prohibited unless special permission is granted. Thus, with the official published rate of 4.00 foreign-exchange złotys to US $1.00, the marginal cost of earning one dollar was 70 domestic złotys. In Czechoslovakia in 1967, the cost of earning $1.00 ranged from 14 to 57 korunas (the weighted average being about 30), and apparently the marginal rates applicable to different export industries have had to be steadily extended upwards since 1955; the published official commercial rate is $1.00 = 7.20 korunas. According to Joseph Szabados, the marginal rate introduced in Hungary at the beginning of 1968 was set at $1.00 to about 60 forints (compared with the official commercial rate of $1.00 = 11.73 forints) and this 'devaluation' effect is 5 times greater in relation to hard currencies but only 3 times to soft currencies (such as the Soviet rouble). See J. Głowacki, *Handel zagr.*, 1/1967, p. 41; V. Zahalka, *Hospodarske noviny* (Economic News), Prague, 17/5/1968, p. 1; J. Szabados, *East Europe*, 6/1968, p. 16.

CH. 14 §B   GAINS AND WASTE   325

V – net foreign-exchange value of the exportable (or import-replaceable) article expressed in domestic currency using the coefficient of the relative value of the foreign currency concerned;

C – domestic social cost of the production of the article in domestic currency, including marketing costs and assuming a constant capacity;

d – discount rate on the investment outlay;

I – supplementary investment outlay in domestic currency necessary to attain the required scale of production.

(g) The Problem of a Generalized Model of the Optimization of Foreign Trade

Up to about the mid-1960s the foreign-trade-efficiency analysis was focused on its effectiveness within clearly defined limits. The large numbers of indexes devised in the leading CMEA countries probably well served the particular function they were designed for at the operational level. But the inadequacy of this approach at the top planning level was apparent to many thinkers long ago. It was recognized that the ultimate aim of the efficiency analysis should be to determine the repercussions of foreign trade on national income and the rate of growth. Consequently, the question of the effectiveness of foreign trade is an integral part of the problem of the efficiency of the whole economy.

To evolve a general model of the efficiency of foreign trade in the context of central planning, it is essential to analyse all factors relevant to the country's foreign trade, such as domestic costs, export and import prices in each foreign market, the composition of trade with each market, the elasticities of demand and supply in foreign and domestic markets, the incidence of restrictions on access to each market, currency transferability, rights and obligations arising from commercial treaties and trade agreements, the requirements of the balance of payments and of the domestic monetary equilibrium, not to mention the anticipation and execution of socially desirable developments.

The task amounts to working out a scientifically substantiated model revealing all the main variables pertinent to foreign trade, and determining their interrelationships, whereby the optimum combination of possibilities can be discovered. W. Trzeciakowski, one of the talented

Polish economists, attempted to work out such a complete system of foreign-trade efficiency. His econometric 'model of the optimization of foreign trade' was constructed with the aid of inter-branch balances and linear-programming techniques. From his tables it is possible to determine the optimum solution to the tasks set in a plan. More complicated, dynamic models have been attempted in Hungary by J. Kornai, T. Liska and B. Martos.[1]

However, these models are of immense complexity. Owing to the large number of factors to be taken into account, a determination of the optimum planning variants is feasible only with the application of highly sophisticated mathematical methods and modern computing techniques. In the meantime, less ambitious models of the partial optimization of foreign trade have been designed. For example in East Germany in the mid-1960s three such models were being elaborated and perfected: (i) the optimization of the regional structure of trade (by the Ministry of External Trade), (ii) the optimization of the commodity and regional structure for certain related commodity groups (by the foreign-trade corporations in co-operation with the State industrial associations and large enterprises producing for export), and (iii) the optimization of the geographical structure of exports and imports (by the foreign-trade corporations).[2]

(h) The Effectiveness Calculations and Gains from Trade

After some two decades of searching, a centrally planned economy still has no simple mechanism for ensuring the most gainful flow of trade. The frequent repetition of similar regulations, the proliferation of the indexes, the upsurge of critical writings on the subject and the reformist undercurrents prevalent in Eastern Europe in recent years attest to this fact.

In five of the twelve Socialist countries no systematic analysis of foreign-trade efficiency has been carried out, and in the seven where it has, some exports are not covered and only small proportions of imports

---

[1] See A. Zauberman, 'The Criterion of the Efficiency of Foreign Trade in Soviet-type Economies', *Economica*, Feb. 1964, pp. 5–12.

[2] G. Grote, 'Problems of Foreign Trade in the German Democratic Republic', *Economics of Planning*, vol. 6, no. 1, 1966, p. 76, and his *Aussenhandel*, 2/1967, pp. 23–30.

CH. 14 §B   GAINS AND WASTE   327

are included. Due to a variety of reasons, the import side has been neglected in all these countries. No satisfactory methods have been worked out for calculations of the effectiveness of those imports which cannot be produced at home and those not used in export production.

And yet, the efficiency of foreign trade in its ultimate analysis can be determined only in the context of a combined evaluation of exports and imports. In the traditional Marxist fashion, the yardstick for measuring the effectiveness of exports is based on 'production-value' (social cost of production) whilst imports are defined essentially by reference to 'use-value' (measure of social utility). As long as imports are largely predetermined it is difficult to see how the problem of foreign-trade optimization and equilibrium can be conclusively analysed.

Where the efficiency calculations are carried out, it is also difficult to see how in many cases arbitrary or subjective decisions can be avoided, as for example which articles should be classed as 'exportables' or 'import-replaceables' to start with. In some cases, no objective measure of costs exists, or the basis is vague – the average cost of the industry or the average or marginal enterprise, the current or anticipated costs, or perhaps the marginal cost after all?[1] The actual decision made by the persons concerned is likely to be biased by the desire to maximize bonuses. The system of material incentives has stressed the performance of targets rather than efficiency. It is conceded in Socialist literature that the centrally fixed coefficients and rates, relating foreign currencies to each other and to the domestic currency, lack accuracy and the calculations are certainly unreliable so far as marginal exports are concerned.[2]

Owing to the conflict between ideology and reality, there is still no sound system of calculating domestic costs. Labour is the only factor cost reasonably fully reflected (if we ignore non-material incentives) in

[1] Although the concept of marginality is rejected in orthodox Communist economics, some reputable economists (e.g. in Poland) have argued for years that marginal costing should be applied to calculations in foreign trade. It is maintained that production associated with foreign trade is marginal to the economy in the sense that it is surplus (for export) or substitution (import-replacement) production. Consequently, a failure to take the marginal cost into account may result in losses or missed gains to the economy. The official opposition to this view is not as strong now as it was in the past. See, for example, H. Fiszel, in *Zagadnienia ekonomii politycznej socjalizmu* (Problems of Socialist Economics), O. Lange (ed.), PWN, Warsaw 1958, pp. 345–46; Rolow, *op. cit.*, p. 95.

[2] See, for example, Shagalov, *op. cit.*, *Vop. ekon.*, 6/1965, pp. 98–99; J. Wierzbołowski, *Handel zagr.*, 3/1966, p. 91.

production costs. It is doubtful if the uniform capital charges and turnover tax mark-ups, as e.g. introduced in Poland, can remove cost distortions. It may be observed that in the USSR turnover taxes are excluded from the calculations of export effectiveness but included in imports, even though world market prices are closer to true economic values.

Even in Poland, where of all Socialist countries the system of foreign-trade analysis is probably most developed, it is conceded that there is a lack of integration between effectiveness calculations, the planning process and the functioning of the financial order.[1] A Polish expert pointed out in 1966: 'The present methods of analysis of the effectiveness of foreign trade, just as previous methods irrespective of their theoretical foundations, are burdened with the same error: ... they result in a confusion between the aims of the central planners and those of the trading and producing undertakings.'[2] In consequence, there is a basic conflict between three related but not overlapping objectives: the maximization of foreign-exchange earnings (or savings), the maximization of the profits of the trading and industrial undertakings (and thus bonuses to the personnel) and foreign-trade efficiency.

Even where the calculations demonstrate a high degree of effectiveness or unprofitability of certain articles beyond doubt, it does not mean that the authorities immediately respond by planning for the expansion or the discontinuation of the relevant production. 'The economic plan', it has been complained, 'is realized, in general, in the way originally worked out, irrespective of changes in domestic or foreign markets during the year.'[3] The possibility of acting on the strength of the effectiveness calculations at the operational level is limited too: 'export decisions are, in fact, not taken independently by the trading and producing undertakings but are largely planning decisions.'[4]

Foreign-trade transactions may still take place, even if clearly unprofitable by the effectiveness calculations. They are apparently not rare, because there are official regulations providing for such possibilities. In some cases, approval of the ministry of foreign trade must be

[1] See statement by Prof. Trąmpczyński, Polish Minister for Foreign Trade, in *Handel zagr.*, 9/1965, p. 413.
[2] Wierzbołowski, *op. cit.*, *Gosp. plan.*, 6/1966, p. 16.
[3] Wierzbołowski, *op. cit.*, *Handel zagr.*, 3/1966, p. 91.
[4] Wierzbołowski, *op. cit.*, *Gosp. plan.*, 6/1966, p. 16.

sought, but in others conditions are clearly listed where the permission of higher authorities is not necessary.[1] Besides, the government – guided by its own considerations – may override the decisions based on the calculations, whether at the planning or the operational level.

Finally, there must be a large number of people engaged in these studies on an organized basis and in the actual calculations. In Hungary, whose total population is 10 m., the figure runs into tens of thousands.[2] One wonders how many highly skilled people must be tied up in this sort of work in other Socialist countries whose combined population exceeds 1,000 m. The cost to the economy, in terms of operational inefficiency, is further increased by the lack of competent personnel.[3] Publications are mostly theoretical and highly technical, and the methods of analysis are becoming more and more complex.

So much for the debit side. Although the practical results of the effectiveness analysis have been rather disappointing, one must not overlook the contribution it has made towards the improved capacity of the Socialist countries to increase their gains from trade. Methodological foundations have been laid down and the search for improvement is continuing. The analysis has helped in improving the structure and direction of trade and foreign-currency earnings in general.

As a result of the analysis, in many instances production methods were rationalized or clearly uneconomic articles were eliminated from trade. At the same time, the study of Western markets has been placed on a systematic basis. It is, in fact, easier in Socialist countries to say now what is economical from the point of view of foreign trade than from the point of view of internal economic relations.

Some of the present deficiencies of the analysis will, no doubt, be overcome with the application of economic cybernetics and high-speed, high-memory electronic computers, which are already revolutionizing economic planning and administration.[4] Although at present the

[1] J. Głowacki and B. Wojciechowski, *Handel zagr.*, 2/1965, p. 71.
[2] S. Balazsy, 'Some Timely Questions Relating to the Economic Efficiency of Foreign Trade', translated from Hungarian in *Eastern European Economics*, vol. I, no. 4, 1963, IASP, New York, p. 34.
[3] See Wierzbołowski, *op. cit.*, *Handel zagr.*, 3/1966, p. 91; Trąmpczyński, *Handel zagr.*, 9/1965, p. 413.
[4] In 1964 a CMEA Conference on the Economic Efficiency of Foreign Trade was held at which the main emphasis was placed on the application of mathematical models and modern computational techniques. In the following year, a seminar was held in

Socialist countries are well behind the West in the production and use of computers, rapid progress is being made, which is aided by the gradual relaxation of the strategic embargo on their export to the Bloc.

The basis of the effectiveness calculations and their application to planning changes in the structure of trade and domestic production are being approached in a more radical way in the economic reforms initiated in Eastern Europe, to which subject we shall now turn.

C. RECENT REFORMS IN EASTERN EUROPE AND GAINS FROM TRADE

The central features of the recent reforms which are relevant to a possible improvement in these countries' gains from trade are the following: (*a*) price reforms, (*b*) the reformulation of material incentives, (*c*) decentralization, and (*d*) a changing approach to imports.

These reforms, which were still being implemented at the time of writing, have been most far-reaching in East Germany (begun in 1963), Poland, Czechoslovakia, Hungary, Bulgaria and Rumania, and less so in the USSR (and absent in Albania) – at least in application to foreign trade.

In the price reforms initiated, greater attention is paid to the conditions underlying supply and demand. The scarcity of capital and natural resources, and the need for its reflection in costing, is recognized. In all European CMEA countries capital charges are now explicitly included in costs. The use of 'computational' or 'basic' or 'shadow' prices (as in Poland, E. Germany and Czechoslovakia), in which adjustments are made to domestic prices to bring them closer to all-inclusive social costs, is a step towards creating price structures reflecting true economic costs.

The declared or implied purpose of the price reforms is to phase out gradually the equalization payments between the state treasury and the foreign-trade corporations (particularly subsidies). Of likely major

---

Budapest on creating State computing systems in the European CMEA countries, and in 1966 an International Computer Exhibition was staged in Prague (at which, among others, American, British, French and Swedish firms exhibited and did booming business). See G. Otto, *Aussenhandel*, 6/1964, pp. 11–13; J. Hunsicker, Parts I and II, *Aussenhandel*, 1/1965, pp. 11–13 and 3/1965, pp. 12–15; L. Babashkin, *Planovoe khoziaistvo*, 6/1966, pp. 30–40; K. Szwarc, *Życie gosp.*, 18/2/1968, p. 5.

consequence, is the reform of the method of settlements between the foreign-trade corporations and enterprises producing for export. The latter are to be paid for their goods delivered to the corporations not at the domestic prices but in accordance with the prices actually secured in foreign markets. The next logical step is simply to bring domestic prices closer to world market values. This appears to be closer to reality in the goods exportable than the possibility of pricing imports in the domestic market at their foreign-exchange equivalents.

A new approach is being adopted to material incentives payable to the personnel of the foreign-trade corporations and export-producing enterprises. Their bonus funds are not now based merely on the quantitative fulfilment (or over-fulfilment) of targets but on profits expressed in value terms. Profit is now accepted as the most important indicator of the efficiency of the foreign-trade corporations and the enterprises producing for export. What is more significant, their profitability is based on net foreign exchange earnings actually received from exports. Claims for damages for poor quality, delays, faulty consignments, etc., are deducted from bonus funds.[1] Both the enterprises and the corporations have a joint interest in producing and supplying exactly what the foreign customer wants.

Moreover, under the new system of accounting it is in the interest of the corporations to exert pressure on the producing enterprises to reduce costs, while the latter prod the corporations to secure the highest prices possible. Special reserve funds of foreign exchange have also been established to finance the expansion of the exports showing the highest degree of foreign-exchange effectiveness. It is claimed that under this system of incentives, micro-economic profitability coincides with the gain to the economy.

Under the new system, some of the previously centralized planning, administrative and management powers have been transferred to industrial branch associations and enterprises. Planning of foreign trade is now to be focused on long-range indicators, whilst for shorter periods

[1] For an example of the new scale of incentives operating in foreign trade see E. Silyanov, 'Foreign Trade Enterprises under the New System of Management of the National Economy', *Vunshna turgoviya* (Foreign Trade), Sofia, 3/1967 (translation in: US Dept. of Commerce, Joint Publications Research Service, *Translations on East European Foreign Trade*, 4/5/1967, p. 8). For an account of the Polish experience see *Handel zagr.*, 4/1968, pp. 151–52.

the targets are set in broad commodity groups. Instead of the previously highly specific quantitative targets, there is a trend towards defining tasks – which are still directive – in value terms.[1]

This decentralization allows greater freedom of initiative to the corporations and industrial enterprises which can carry out the details of the tasks in the manner most profitable to them. There is an increasing number of enterprises producing for export which are allowed to carry on their own marketing, especially in Western markets (see Ch. 5 C, pp. 83–86). This, combined with the new system of bonuses, means that export industries are now in a better position to influence foreign-trade contracts according to their view of profitability.[2]

Traditionally, considering the relatively undeveloped Socialist economies, certain minimum imports were treated as indispensable to make planned, rapid development possible, and the role assigned to exports was simply to pay for these imports. But in the more developed European Socialist countries there is now scope for choosing between domestic production and imports, and more attention is being paid to the size and structure of imports so as to attain the economies of social labour. Methods for calculating the effectiveness of certain types of imports and applied in practice are: the directional effectiveness of imports, the effectiveness of outlays on import replacement, on components for export production and on consumer goods imports.

The present tendency is to enable industrial branch associations, industrial enterprises and even domestic trading enterprises to participate in the calculations of the effectiveness of imports, as it is considered that they are in a better position to make analyses of the profitability of imports in their respective fields of responsibility.[3] There is a growing body of opinion, most vocal in Czechoslovakia and Hungary, favouring a

[1] On this important subject see an interesting article by H. Kosk, *Gosp. plan.*, 6/1966, pp. 23–28.

[2] For further details see E. Faude and W. Maier, *Aussenhandel*, 4/1964, pp. 18–22, 6/1964, pp. 8–11; 7/1964, pp. 6–11; A. Nagy, *Közgadasági szemle* (Economic Review). Budapest, 2/1965, pp. 204–17; Z. Zdyb, *Finanse* (Finance), Warsaw, 3/1967, pp, 24–30; 'Action Programme for the Development of Foreign Trade', *Noviny zahranicniho obchodu* (Foreign Trade News), Prague, 19/6/1968 (this important document, laid down by the Czechoslovak Communist Party in 1968, can be found in English translation in: US Dept of Commerce, JPRS, *Translations on East Europe: Economic and Industrial*, 19/7/1968, pp. 47–73).

[3] For the changing views on imports see M. Rakowski, *Gosp. plan.*, 8–9/1965, pp. 28–37; Humin, *op. cit.*, pp. 416–22; W. Maier and E. Faude, *Aussenhandel*, 3/1966, p. 6–9.

gradual liberalization of import policy to create a mild form of competition as a stimulus to the efficiency of the domestic enterprises. The (then) Czechoslovak Minister for Foreign Trade pointed out in 1967: 'The solution of the question of efficiency of foreign trade calls for the removal of barriers between the home and foreign market because in foreign trade economic relations do not affect the economy separately, but in reciprocal relation with general financial, income and price policies.'[1]

The avowed aim of the reforms is to ensure the identity of the microeconomic interest at the operational level of foreign trade with that of the national economy. It is hoped that the profitability of the trading and industrial undertakings associated with foreign trade and the maximization of foreign-exchange earnings will be consistent with increasing foreign-trade efficiency.

> Central planning in a Socialist economy [concluded a Polish economist] does not exclude the possibility of the enterprises making their own decisions independently (within broadly-set plans); on the contrary, planned goals are or rather should be realized through such decisions. Material incentives should be so designed as to make the enterprises' independent decisions consistent with the planners' assumptions and preferences.[2]

But the reforms are bringing many problems in their trail, imposing breaks on departures from traditional policies and practices. To what extent should the enterprises producing for export be remunerated according to foreign-exchange earnings in the uncertain and widely fluctuating Western markets? One of the traditionally accepted responsibilities of central planning is to shield the economy against the excesses of Capitalist booms and recessions.

There is still disagreement as to whether the domestic 'goal prices',[3] which deviate from costs as understood by Socialist standards, are appropriate for foreign-trade effectiveness calculations. The analysis of import effectiveness cannot be based on a sound footing until far-reaching changes are made in the systems of fixing the domestic prices of imported articles and the limits placed on foreign-exchange allocations.

[1] F. Hamouz, *Czechoslovak Foreign Trade*, 7/1967, p. 3.
[2] Wierzbołowski, *op. cit.*, *Gosp. plan.*, 6/1966, p. 16. Also see I. Konnik, *Vop. ekon.*, 5/1966, pp. 18–30.
[3] Prices fixed centrally roughly in accordance with (desirable) supply and demand conditions, to act as economic levers.

The solution of these and other problems inexorably presenting themselves is not easy if central planning is to be workable. It is likely to be retarded by the anti-liberalization forces which reassert themselves from time to time. The reformist tendencies are, of course, still inoperative in Albania and Asian Socialist countries.

D. WHICH SIDE GAINS MORE FROM EAST-WEST TRADE?

It is impossible to estimate the overall gains from trade accruing to partner countries with any degree of precision. Apart from the impossibility of obtaining information on costs, prices and the character of production that would prevail without trade, some of the gains deriving from trade do not lend themselves to quantification. The social sciences have not yet evolved satisfactory tools of analysis to enable a precise evaluation of statistically unmeasurable factors.

Any trade, as it takes place, must obviously be gainful to both partners. But quite likely it is of greater benefit to one side than to the other. It is endeavoured in this limited space merely to bring out the respects in which the balance of gains in East-West trade differs.

As was discussed in Ch. 2 (see especially Tables IV–VII), some two-thirds of Western exports to the Bloc consists of machinery, capital equipment and other manufactures, whilst about the same proportion of imports from the Bloc is made up of food and crude materials. The composition of the Socialist countries' trade with the West contrasts with that with Developing nations, to which the Bloc exports mostly manufactures but from which it imports chiefly food and raw materials.

So far as its structure is concerned, trade with the West is regarded by most Bloc countries as highly unsatisfactory. Their exports to the West embody a low proportion of value added by labour, whilst their imports chiefly consist of high-priced items of low-material intensity but with a high percentage of value added. From the point of view of the Socialist countries, to which, on doctrinaire grounds at least, the labour theory of value has a great appeal, this fact is of grave concern.[1]

---

[1] See, e.g., G. Rubinshtein, *Vop. ekon.*, 9/1966, pp. 111–17; S. Bolski, *Życie gosp.*, 3/7/1966, p. 10; D. Soky and B. Talas, in *Studies in International Economics*, T. Földi (ed.), Akademiai Kiado, Budapest 1966, pp. 91–141.

It is often emphasized in the Bloc that the exports from many Socialist countries to the West do not reflect their vast industrialization achievements under Socialism. Imports from the West are largely paid for by the products of agriculture, which is under-capitalized and sadly inefficient. Thus Poland chiefly exports farming products to Western Europe, yet the productivity in her poultry and dairying industries is only about half of that in Belgium, Denmark or Holland.[1] Farming exports are subject to wide fluctuations in Western markets and to the vagaries of the weather in Socialist countries. Moreover, owing to the protection of agriculture and strategic considerations in the West, many Socialist exports (meats, eggs, dairy products, certain metals, oil) are faced with different forms of discrimination.

At the same time, it must be pointed out that imports from the West, containing as they do advanced technology, and being carefully planned to fit the Socialist countries' developmental ambitions, have greatly accelerated their industrialization. In the past, the Bloc countries often imported prototypes only and copied various Western achievements without proper compensation [see Ch. 11 E(c)]. Even the substantial imports of grains, again mostly from the West, have proved providential to Socialist countries, not only in extricating the Communist regimes from serious embarrassment and possible internal unrest but also in enabling them to forge ahead with their industrialization. Besides, Socialist countries have in many cases obtained these grains at lower than domestic prices in the exporting countries [see Chs. 9 A and 11 E(b)]. Whilst the West has been and still is the only source of many imports for the Bloc, Western countries have alternative sources of supply for practically all their needs, either in the West or in the Third World. The Socialist Bloc is hardly in a position to harm the West either by withholding its exports or by retrenching its imports.

If complete information were available on the prices at which transactions actually take place, it would enable a more accurate evaluation of which side secures a higher share of micro-economic gains from East-West trade. There are several reasons, however, to believe that on the whole the Bloc trades with the West at less advantageous prices to itself than the prevailing world market prices. Socialist countries are likely to be securing lower than world prices for their exports when they are

[1] E. Harasim, *Handel zagr.*, 2/1965, pp. 60–61.

anxious to earn badly needed currencies for unexpected urgent imports, to break into the highly competitive market and to secure non-commercial advantages. Inability to adapt their goods to the highly whimsical Western markets, ignorance of prices, and poor marketing techniques also often result in less profitable terms. Besides, Socialist exporters have to overcome various forms of discrimination, such as the inapplicability of tariff preferences to them, exclusion from well-established commercial channels, unofficial boycotts, etc.[1]

At the same time, in some cases Socialist countries may have to pay higher than world prices for their imports from the West, especially when they insist on paying in counter-sales and when endeavouring to secure embargoed goods. When a state trader, being a large and unwieldy buyer, is known to be in the market, it often leads to an inflation of the prices of the articles affected (see Chs. 6 A and 8 B).

The question naturally poses itself as to whether the Socialist countries' terms of trade with the West are better or worse than in intra-Bloc trade. Curiously enough, practically nothing has been published on this subject in the Socialist Bloc. But this problem has received considerable attention in the West, particularly after the publication of two articles by H. Mendershausen in 1959 and 1960,[2] since when A. Kutt, F. D. Holzman, M. Kaser, H. Köhler, Feng-hwa Ma, E. Hoffman (in West Germany), G. L. Amundsen (in France), I. Agaston (in Switzerland) and many others have joined in the discussion.[3] The conclusions, based on average unit prices calculated from official Socialist sources, indicate that the Bloc countries pay lower prices on

[1] It was pointed out in a Czechoslovak source that, according to recent studies in purchasing power, US $1.00 was equal to 20–25 korunas but, on the average, it takes 31 korunas to earn $1.00 from exports to the West, largely because of various forms of Western discrimination. *Reporter*, Prague, 8–15 May, 1968, pp. 20–21.

[2] H. Mendershausen, 'Terms of Trade between the Soviet Union and Smaller Communist Countries' and 'The Terms of Soviet-Satellite Trade: A Broadened Analysis', *Rev. of Econ. and Stat.*, May 1959, pp. 106–18 and May 1960, pp. 152–63.

[3] See especially A. Kutt, 'Exploitation in Soviet-Bloc Trade', *East Europe*, May 1962, pp. 21–24, and his *Prices and Balance Sheet in 10 Years of Soviet-Captive Countries Trade, 1955–1964*, New York 1966; F. D. Holzman, 'Soviet Foreign Trade Pricing and the Question of Discrimination', *Rev. of Econ. and Stat.*, May 1962, pp. 134–47, and 'More on Soviet Bloc Trade Discrimination', *Soviet Studies*, July 1965, pp. 44–65; M. Kaser, *COMECON*, Oxford UP 1965, pp. 140–57; H. Köhler, *Economic Integration in the Soviet Bloc*, Praeger, New York 1965, Feng-hwa Ma, 'The Terms of Sino-Soviet Trade', *China Quarterly*, Jan.–March 1964, pp. 174–91.

their imports from Western Europe than from the USSR, and they receive higher prices for their exports to Western Europe than to the USSR.

According to calculations made by Kutt, over the ten-year period 1955–64, on the average the USSR charged 31·2% higher prices to the European Socialist countries than to Western Europe, and paid 16·3% lower prices to them than to W. Europe.[1] Holzman's argument is that the apparent exploitation by the USSR is a consequence of Western discrimination against the Bloc countries and of the artificial limitation of these countries' trade with the West, particularly in the goods in which they have a comparative advantage, largely under Soviet pressure.

The problems involved in comparing the Socialist countries' terms of trade with the West with those in intra-Bloc trade are complex and probably insuperable, except perhaps to a few top Socialist officials. The interpretation of gains or losses derived from unit values covering limited samples of comparable exports and imports is certainly fraught with dangers. The author has attempted to work out the terms of trade for most CMEA countries with the West and with the USSR in recent years using his own method. But no clear-cut conclusion could be reached, and besides the samples at his disposal were considered to be too small and not enough details were available on multiangular operations and switch deals, investment outlays in joint projects relevant to the partners' trade, and other pertinent facts. A study recently carried out by Heinz Köhler on East German-Soviet terms of trade also showed no conclusive answer.[2] But Soviet attempts to refute the Western allegations of exploitation by the USSR are unconvincing. They are loaded with emotional overtones and superficial assertions.[3]

In fact, several Soviet economists have gone further recently, endeavouring to demonstrate that it is the other CMEA members (especially Czechoslovakia, East Germany and Hungary) that exploit the

---

[1] By Kutt's calculations, the total amount of exploitation of the seven Eastern European countries by the USSR in trade over the 10-year period reached $12,773 m., of which $7,274 m. was overcharged on Soviet exports to, and $5,499 m. was underpaid on Soviet imports from, these countries. A. Kutt, *Prices and Balance Sheet, op. cit.*, p. 5.
[2] *Op. cit.*, esp. pp. 357–59.
[3] For example see F. Abramov, *Vnesh. torg.*, 10/1963, pp. 13–17; S. Zavolzhky and L. Lukin, *International Affairs*, Moscow, 1/1967, pp. 8–13.

USSR.[1] Similarly, many leaders in the smaller Socialist countries also refute the possibility of exploitation by the USSR. It is maintained that if there is any exploitation in intra-CMEA trade, it is rather of the more developed by the less developed countries, in accordance with the Charter of the Socialist International Division of Labour (adopted in 1962) postulating 'evening out of economic levels' amongst member countries.[2]

To the question: Are Socialist countries' terms of trade in East-West trade better or worse than those in intra-Bloc trade?, this writer has no definite answer that can be substantiated quantitatively. But the study of the problem prompts him to make the following observations and conclusions. There are strong reasons to believe that several Eastern European countries have been exploited commercially, mainly due to the fact that they obtain most of their imports, especially raw materials, from the USSR, instead of from the cheapest sources outside the Bloc. Already two decades ago it was known that the production costs in Soviet extractive industries were rising steeply, but the increasing raw material requirements consequent upon fast industrialization in the CMEA area has markedly pushed these costs drastically up. Being in a stronger (politically and economically) bargaining position, the USSR has prevailed upon member countries to agree to the so-called 'corrections' to the average world market prices in intra-CMEA trade, partly

[1] The essence of the argumentation is that the Soviet Union mainly exports fuels and other raw materials to the CMEA countries (56% of all fuels and raw materials in intra-CMEA trade is supplied by the USSR), whilst she chiefly imports light manufactures and machinery from them. It is argued that to earn 1 foreign exchange rouble from the CMEA countries, she has to invest 5–9 times more in the extraction of coal, iron ore, oil and raw materials for fertilizers than in the export of machinery; this burden is further increased by long periods of construction of the investment projects and, further, heavy transport costs. It is stated that the receipts from exports of raw materials to the CMEA area in some cases do not even cover prime costs. Moreover, it is pointed out that the USSR pays average world prices for the imported manufactures and yet they are not up to world market standards. Several Soviet economists have advocated larger investment participation by other CMEA countries in Soviet extractive industries, and that the prices payable to the USSR should be raised. This question was apparently discussed at the July 1966 meeting of the CMEA Council in Bucharest. See I. Dudinskii, *Vop. ekon.*, 4/1966, pp. 84–94, esp. pp. 88–90; O. Bogomolov, *Mirovaya ekonomika i mezhdunarodnye otnosheniya* (World Economy and International Relations), Moscow, 5/1966, pp. 15–27, esp. p. 18, and by the same author: *Kommunist*, 18/1966, pp. 13–24.

[2] See, e.g., A. Apro (Vice-Premier of Hungary), *Tarsaldami szemle* (Social Review), Budapest, 11/1967, p. 32.

in her favour. In some cases these countries have also shared the cost of investment in Soviet raw material producing industries, e.g. Bulgaria in timber exploitation, Czechoslovakia in oil extraction and iron ore mining and Bulgaria, East Germany, Hungary and Poland in potassium mining.

In effect, the USSR has been able to shift some of the cost burden of her inefficient extractive industries to other 'fraternal' countries. Thus, as a consequence of the artificially induced diversion of trade into intra-CMEA channels, the terms of trade of the member countries (including those of the USSR) are almost certainly not as favourable as those in their trade with the West. If CMEA adopts a price structure completely divorced from the world market, as advocated by the Soviet Union (partly supported by Bulgaria and Rumania), the prices of raw materials will rise further in relation to manufactures. In such a case, the terms of trade of Czechoslovakia, East Germany, Hungary and Poland would further become worse in trade with the USSR than with the West.[1]

However, the extent of the overall exploitation by the USSR has probably been exaggerated by most Western writers on the subject. It is likely that, by market economy standards, most CMEA countries' terms of trade with the USSR have been worse than those with the West (although less so in recent years as compared with the 1950s). But endeavouring to teach these countries what is best for them savours of naïveté. Socialist countries take a broader view of foreign trade – they are guided more by macro-social long-run cost-benefit considerations than by immediate commercial terms of trade. Apart from ideological and political hostility, such realities as instability and discrimination in Western markets are significant factors to be taken into account.

Where losses to the smaller Socialist countries have occurred, they have probably been partly compensated for by the benefits deriving from the reliability of raw material supplies and the assured market for their finished products, which a politically allied country like the USSR has been in a position to provide. Long-run stability of prices has been another advantage, and it is possible that 'losses' over some years may

[1] For example, Soviet economists recently argued that cost ratios in the CMEA area are such that a CMEA exporter for 1 railway passenger car should be paid by a country like the USSR only 1,300 tons of oil instead of 3,400 tons according to the world market structure, for 1 milling machine only 140 tons of iron ore instead of 520 tons, for 1 man's suit 3·5 kilogrammes of wool instead of 7·5 kgs. V. Zhukov and Y. Olsevich, *Vop. ekon.*, 3/1967, p. 78.

have been offset by 'surpluses' over some other period. In addition, the possibility of substantial intra-Bloc trade strengthens the bargaining position of Socialist countries in the West. Otherwise, their terms of trade with the West, were they at the mercy of the Western countries for trade to the extent that they were between the two world wars, would almost certainly be worse than now, and perhaps worse than in their trade with the USSR.

Besides, these countries have received much more in the way of designs, licences and patents from the Soviet Union than they have given in exchange.[1] This know-how received free of charge has, in fact, enabled them to export certain items to the West in competition with the USSR. If the exchange of technological data is placed on a commercial basis at world market prices, as has been recently advocated by several Soviet economists, these countries will miss an undoubted advantage. But even then, they would be no worse off in this respect than in East-West trade (assuming no poaching), because they would still be able to buy certain types of Soviet know-how which Western countries might refuse to sell on strategic grounds.

The enthusiasm and zeal with which some economists in the leading Western countries have taken up the cause of the smaller Socialist countries is commendable, whatever their reasons. It is high time that stronger countries stopped exploiting their superior bargaining power over economically and politically weaker trading partners. But this advice equally, if no more, applies to the leading Western nations in their trade with underdeveloped Capitalist countries, where the 'Prebisch effect' has, after all, been most conclusively demonstrated.

No doubt, in their foreign-trade-efficiency studies, Socialist countries must be making comparative evaluations of their gains from trading with Western and with other Socialist countries. It is perhaps not without significance that no such studies, covering long periods and showing details of the methods used, have been published.[2] The fact that Socialist

[1] According to a Soviet source, by 1965 the USSR had supplied to other Socialist countries more than 12,000 m. foreign-exchange roubles' (at world market prices) worth of designing and technical documentation, but received only 2,000 m. roubles' worth from them. S. Yovczuk, *International Affairs*, Moscow, 11/1966, p. 111.

[2] It is known that studies of the terms of trade have been carried on in several CMEA countries for years. The Hungarian Central Statistical Office and the Chamber of Commerce began to make calculations of the terms of trade in 1959, and Hungary is the

countries have planned and achieved a slower growth in intra-Bloc trade in the last decade than in extra-Bloc trade (see Ch. 3 C, esp. Table XIII, p. 55) appears to suggest that (even by their criteria) their trade with Capitalist countries has proved more gainful.

A brief discussion of benefits from East-West trade beyond the immediate commercial gains will not be out of place. On the Western side, trade with the Bloc has to some extent relieved the balance-of-payments problems of such countries in particular as Australia, Canada and the USA at critical times. Moreover, the substantial Soviet gold sales in recent years have improved Western liquidity. Some countries, notably the United Kingdom, have profited from invisible earnings arising from the Bloc's trade with the West. The growing volume of exports to the Bloc has also contributed to a higher level of employment in the West. In view of the limited contacts with the Bloc by other means, trade has become an important avenue for demonstrating the Western way of life, its affluence and the fact that free enterprise and political freedom can produce very good results.

Apart from the contribution of imports from the West to the Socialist industrialization and technological advancement already discussed, other advantages of a broader nature accruing to the Bloc may be identified. Socialist countries have easier access to Western markets and they have a greater variety of goods to choose from than the West has in the Bloc (see Ch. 8 B). Western markets are still treated, although less now than in the past, as a convenient reservoir to absorb unexpected surpluses or to ease bottlenecks which may arise out of planning errors or unforeseeable fatalities.

Trade with the West also provides opportunities for gauging world market prices which are used as a basis for guiding intra-Bloc trade and to some extent the allocation of resources. Confrontation with Western markets, through both exports and imports, provides a stimulus to the

---

first Socialist country to publish such results. Over the period covering 5 years, 1957–1961, the Hungarian terms of trade with Capitalist countries, although fluctuating from year to year, on the whole improved more than with Socialist countries. The Polish Chamber of Foreign Trade publishes quarterly figures of the Polish terms of trade with Capitalist countries only, although these countries claim only one-third of Poland's trade. See Imre Vajda, *The Role of Foreign Trade in a Socialist Economy*, Corvina Press, Budapest 1965, p. 279; P. Bożyk, *Handel zagr.*, 8/1964, pp. 370–73 and 4/1965, pp. 175–79.

efficiency of many Socialist industries and a yardstick to its evaluation. Finally, trade also helps cultivate a better Socialist image in the West. This, not infrequently, produces practical benefits too, when the commercial and industrial pressure groups interested in trade with the Bloc defend and perhaps champion the Socialist cause.

In attempting to draw an overall assessment of the gains from East-West trade to each side, it would appear that the following conclusion is warranted. In some respects, chiefly in the prices of actual deals, the West probably strikes a better bargain, but in others, particularly where non-measurable benefits are involved, the Bloc almost certainly gains more. On balance, in the writer's estimate, the total gains derived from East-West trade by the Bloc are greater than those by the West.

E. FORMS OF WASTE

Waste in East-West trade is even more difficult to estimate than gains, and certainly no quantitative measurement is possible. What follows is an attempt to highlight the main forms of losses consisting of the direct extra costs of government intervention and, what is thought to be of greater magnitude, of missed gains.

For a variety of reasons, East-West trade in relation to its size is more complex and costly for partner countries to regulate than trade which involves other Capitalist or Socialist nations. There are the extra direct costs of the administration of various controls, such as strategic embargo, quantitative import restrictions, anti-dumping measures, discriminatory tariff applications, foreign-trade efficiency calculations and market research. To this, we must add the high cost of negotiating bilateral trade agreements, annual protocols and even individual contracts. The high degree of uncertainty prevailing in East-West trade, affecting trading undertakings on both sides, associated with such matters as the issue of export and import licences, credits, trade disputes, also add extra cost in the form of risk.

The missed gains in East-West trade derive chiefly from discrimination, bilateralism and fluctuations. It may be observed that the leading countries on each side (more so in the West) have often been concerned more with potential gains to the Socialist countries than with their own missed benefits. Some controls have been considered beneficial if their own losses were thought to be smaller than the missed potential advantages to the partner, with retaliations often following (see Chs. 11 B and 12 B).

On the Western side, the forms of discrimination practised against Socialist countries are those of tariff discrimination (including denials of MFN, see Chs. 6 C and 8 A), licensing and quantitative restrictions on imports [Chs. 7 B(b) and 8 B], anti-dumping measures (Ch. 9 D), strategic embargo (Ch. 12), boycotts and currency transferability (Ch. 8 B), credits (Ch. 10 E) and the export of subsidized articles [Chs. 7 B(b) and 9 A]. These measures are either specifically directed against Socialist countries (quotas, strategic embargo, credits) or in practice affect these countries more than others.

On the Bloc's side, the policies and practices of a discriminatory nature include the diversion of trade into intra-CMEA channels through direct controls (see Ch. 3 B), evasion of the full MFN reciprocity (Ch. 7 A, B), administrative measures – such as the directive coefficients of the relative value of foreign currencies [see this chapter Section B(e)] – the low priority assigned to imports of consumer goods from hard currency areas and market disruption through price undercutting (Ch. 9 B, C).

The economic waste consequent upon bilateralism is well known. Trade is reduced to the capacity of the weaker partner country, or otherwise unwanted goods have to be accepted by the stronger partner as part-payment. There are price distortions and inflexibility, and such trade is more likely to be marred by non-commercial considerations (see Ch. 10 C). Even if remedied by occasional multiangular operations, it provides no better than a 'second best' approach. Not infrequently, goods acquired in bilateral or multiangular deals have to be resold or even re-exported – an obvious waste when goods have to be moved instead of monetary claims.

Although bilateral trade is obviously profitable to both partners (as it would not take place otherwise), gains are not maximized. The missed gains on the part of the Socialist countries are to some extent compensated for by several advantages that bilateralism entails for them (such as simplifying the planning process, minimizing currency transactions, securing export markets, making discrimination possible and aiding political manœuvring; see Ch. 10 C).

A study of trade figures from year to year shows that East-West trade has been, on the whole, less stable than trade either among Western or among Socialist countries. This is corroborated by independent studies carried out in the last decade. Mikesell and Behrman concluded that, 'Not only has bilaterally planned trade with the Soviet bloc been wide of the agreement targets, but it has also been less stable and more subject to erratic fluctuations than unplanned trade among free world countries.'[1] A study carried out by the Political and Economic Planning, based on the experience of British businessmen, indicated that firms trading with Socialist countries were confronted with the 'sudden emergence of gluts or shortages of particular products.'[2]

It was also shown in several investigations carried out in the USA that neither the USSR nor the Soviet Bloc as a whole was more stable than the seven leading Western countries as a market for the principal primary commodities entering world trade.[3] Similar conclusions were reached in a study of Australia's trade experience with the Socialist Bloc.[4] There were suggestions made in the West that a scheme be established under the United Nations (e.g. within the IMF and IBRD framework) 'to provide special assistance to countries whose exports to the bloc were suddenly terminated.'[5]

The Socialist view of trading with Capitalist countries is synonymous with unpredictability, a natural consequence of the anarchical market forces – one of the important reasons for the State foreign trade monopoly and the insulation of the domestic from the world market.[6] In

[1] R. F. Mikesell and J. N. Behrman, *Financing Free World Trade with the Sino-Soviet Bloc*, Princeton University 1958, p. 80.
[2] Political and Economic Planning, 'East-West Trade', *Planning*, May 1965, p. 122; also see *The Economist*, 10/9/1966, p. 1,054.
[3] See E. Neuberger, 'Is the USSR Superior to the West as a Market for Primary Products?', *Rev. of Econ. and Stat.*, August 1964, pp. 287–93; US Senate, *A Background Study on East-West Trade*, Prepared for the Committee on Foreign Relations, GPO, Washington 1965, pp. 26, 59; also see US Senate, *East-West Trade*, Hearings before the Committee on Foreign Relations, Part I, GPO, Washington 1964, p. 239.
[4] J. Wilczynski, 'Trade between Market and Centrally Planned Economies: Australia's Experience with the Communist Bloc', *Economic Record*, Dec. 1965, pp. 588–89.
[5] R. F. Mikesell and D. A. Wells, 'State Trading in the Sino-Soviet Bloc', *Law and Contemporary Problems*, Summer 1959, p. 453.
[6] The elements of risk and uncertainty confronting a Socialist country in trade with the West were succinctly brought out in Z. Kamecki, H. Sołdaczuk and W. Sierpiński, *Międzynarodowe stosunki ekonomiczne* (International Economic Relations), PWE, Warsaw 1964, pp. 86–91, 269–97. Also see F. G. Piskoppel, *Zasady badania koniunk-*

contrast to the systematically planned trade with other Socialist countries (especially within CMEA), trade with Capitalist countries is largely treated as residual. Even where amounts are bilaterally agreed upon, no great importance is attached to the fulfilment of commitments to Capitalist countries.

Erratic fluctuations produce uncertainty and lead to losses on both sides. The adverse effects are probably more painful on the Western side where there is no comparable in-built protective system and where the risk is borne mostly by private traders. However, it must be pointed out that these fluctuations have not been as wide as one would expect from the whimsical course of East-West political relations.

A very obvious source of waste in the case of Socialist countries is that their economic system has no automatic mechanism to indicate which trade is not gainful. So far no simple and reliable system has been evolved. This, together with the peculiarities of the pricing policies pursued, must lead to substantial economic waste.

Gains from trade may also be adversely affected by mistakes. There is no doubt that errors are made in both a market and a centrally planned economy. But the magnitude and persistence of errors under a highly bureaucratic and centralized system is likely to be greater, and this is recognized in the Bloc:

> there is inherent danger of errors on a large scale whose effects, owing to the complex and unwieldy machinery, may not be signalized in time. As a result, corrective measures may not be applied swiftly enough to stem a flood-tide of losses consequent upon an erroneous decision – erroneous in the first instance, or otherwise made erroneous by a changed situation in world markets.[1]

A free enterprise economy has an in-built error-correction system. Errors lead to losses which affect profits. If errors are not corrected the firm has to leave business. But in a centrally planned economy pricing

---

tury w gospodarce kapitalistycznej (Principles Governing the Study of Trade Cycles in Capitalist Countries), in Polish translation from the Russian original, PWE, Warsaw 1962, esp. pp. 247–304.

[1] M. Orłowski, *Teoria kursów walutowych* (Theory of Exchange Rates), PWG, Warsaw 1961, p. 199. Also see, T. Morgan, 'The Theory of Error in Centrally Directed Economic Systems', *Quart. Jour. of Econ.*, August 1964, esp. p. 400. For a broader study of this subject see, H. Köhler, *Welfare and Planning*, An Analysis of Capitalism versus Socialism, John Wiley, New York 1966.

confusion and the chain of bureaucratic procedures are likely to lead to the multiplication of errors. They can be large because they are committed on a national scale, and they can remain undetected and unrectified for long periods.

As a result of the peculiar conditions considered above, the pattern of East-West trade has been too far removed from its optimal size, structure and direction. The degree of East-West 'under-trading' is roughly indicated by the fact that although each camp contributes two-fifths, or more, of the world industrial output, their participation in each other's trade is unjustifiably low. The Western share in the Bloc's trade has never exceeded 26%, and the Bloc claims less than 5% of the Western trade, whilst before the war the respective proportions were 75% and 10% (see Ch. 3 C, esp. Table XII, p. 54).

The composition and direction of the partner countries' trade is not in accordance with the equi-marginal principle to ensure the maximization of gains, i.e. East-West trade is not carried to the equilibrium pattern where the ratios of the marginal costs of products are equated with their marginal revenues.[1] These man-made market imperfections on a large scale lead to a misallocation of resources on both sides. It may also be generalized that, for a variety of reasons, the controls administered on each side in effect militate against the domestic consumers' welfare (limitation of imports, higher domestic prices) but favour the interests of the domestic industries.

Looking in retrospect, one wonders whether the direct costs involved in administering the controls in East-West trade and the potential gains sacrificed *by both sides* have been compensated for by non-commercial advantages *to both sides*. One can hardly refrain from noting an element of analogy between the interference in East-West trade and a vision of a nuclear World War III – each side striving to win at the expense of the other but both in fact losing. However, recent trends suggest that the extent of waste in East-West trade is on the decline, conditioned by the improving political climate and the growing liberalization of trade on both sides.

Of all countries, the USA and the USSR have shouldered the costs and sacrificed gains with the least apparent concern. This is largely due

[1] This is also true of intra-Western trade (mainly due to tariffs and subsidies) but the extent to which it exists in East-West trade is far greater.

to the fact that their dependence on trade is relatively small and that they have taken upon themselves the leadership of the respective camps. On the other hand, the remaining countries, being substantially dependent on foreign trade and being sadly conscious of the costs and missed opportunities, have been relaxing their controls and assigning an increasing role to economics at the expense of politics. We shall examine the extent of these changes in the next chapter.

15 East-West Trade as an Avenue of Convergence

A. BROAD PATTERNS OF CONVERGENCE

EXAMPLES of pure free enterprise and of pure centrally planned economies can be found only in text books. In reality the economic systems existing in the West and in the Bloc are mixtures, which they have always been ever since they began to confront each other. But borrowings and adaptations from each other, even though unconscious in most cases, have become quite pronounced more recently. This tendency of the Capitalist and Socialist economies towards evolving similar attitudes, institutions and practices proved obvious enough for Tinbergen to formulate his well-known convergence thesis.[1] Many Westerners have eagerly seized upon this theory in their belief in the ultimate coalescence of Capitalism and Communism as being historically inevitable.

Departures from the ideal of *laissez-faire* free enterprise in the Capitalist world have a long history, and the Keynesian revolution and the acceptance of the postulate of rapid economic development have vested them with theoretical and pragmatic respectability. The more pronounced changes in the Socialist Bloc are relatively recent. The wisdom of extreme centralization, authoritarianism and isolationism had already begun to be seriously questioned soon after Stalin's death, but some far-reaching reforms have been initiated only since 1962 and are still being implemented in all European CMEA countries. The evolutionary processes towards an increasing resemblance and *rapprochement* of the two systems can be observed not only in the sphere of economics but also in the social and political arena. We shall now bring these tendencies out.

---

[1] See J. Tinbergen, 'Do Communist and Free Economies Show a Converging Pattern?', *Soviet Studies*, April 1961, pp. 333–41 (it also appeared in translation in, *Hamburger Jahrbuch für Wirtschafts– und Gesellschaftspolitik*, 1963, pp. 11–20). Also see his 'Concrete Concepts of Co-existence', *Co-existence*, no. 1, 1964, pp. 15–20.

CH. 15 §A   EAST-WEST TRADE 349

(*i*) *Ownership of the means of production.* In the West there is a tendency for increasing State ownership and for some diffusion of property in favour of the working classes. This is exemplified by the nationalization of key industries (such as coal mines, the iron and steel industry, banks, railways), heavy death duties and a tendency for workers to own shares especially in the firms in which they are employed.[1] In the Socialist Bloc, there has been considerable de-collectivization of farming land in the last decade, and a large proportion of livestock is now privately owned. Private enterprise also plays an important role in handicrafts, retail trade, catering and fishing.[2]

(*ii*) *Economic planning.* Since World War II practically all Western countries have adopted some form of economic planning ('indicative' or 'frame' planning, planning 'by objectives', supplemented by 'regional' and 'structural' planning) to promote a high level of employment, stability and social welfare. Long-term plans have been adopted by Belgium, France, Italy, Japan, the Netherlands, Norway, Turkey and others.[3] Even in the United States a good deal of planning is done through the Treasury, the Federal Reserve System and various government instrumentalities, with many influential groups favouring even

[1] To quote Soviet sources, nearly 100% of the coal and gas, 80% of the power, 50% of the automobile and 33% of the chemical fertilizer industry in France is State-owned. 20–25% of the workforce in Britain and in Italy is employed in State enterprises or service. Over 25% of the national income in Austria and in Sweden is contributed by the State sector. A. A. Arzumanian, *Pravda*, 2/8/1965, pp. 3–4; B. Denisov, *Voprosy ekonomiki*, 5/1967, 80.

[2] Of the 12 Socialist countries, only in the USSR and Mongolia is land nationalized, but even there private plots allowed to collective farmers play an important part (about 17% of agricultural output in the USSR is contributed by private plots). In Poland 86% (nearly as much as in Yugoslavia), in Hungary 25%, and even in China 5–7% of agricultural land is privately farmed. 33% of livestock and 88% of poultry in Hungary (and similar proportions in other Socialist countries) are privately raised. The number of privately owned enterprises (not including farms) in Poland exceeds 200,000, and the number of registered private tradesmen in Bulgaria increased from 10,000 in 1965 to 26,000 in 1966. The proportion of total production contributed by the private sector in 1964–65 in Poland, Albania, East Germany, Rumania and Czechoslovakia were: 23%, 9%, 7%, 5% and 4% respectively. Based on: *Vop. ekon.*, 10/1966, p. 61; *Far Eastern Economic Review*, 21/4/1966, p. 154; statistical yearbooks of the countries concerned.

[3] For a broad and thought-provoking treatment of the subject see N. W. Chamberlain, 'Western Economic Planning and Convergence Thesis', a paper presented at the 79th Annual Meeting of the American Economic Association, 29/12/1966. A Socialist view of planning under Capitalism is examined by J. Tudrej, *Współczesny kapitalizm i planowanie* (Contemporary Capitalism and Planning), ŁTN, Łódź 1964.

more.[1] At the same time in Eastern Europe, there is a trend away from centralized command planning to what Professor Ota Šik of Czechoslovakia calls 'planning by orientation', whereby industrial-branch associations and enterprises participate in working out the details of plans. Quantitative planning is gradually giving way to the defining of production plans in value terms. The former contempt for mathematical methods and computers has been replaced by enthusiasm in applying them to economic planning.[2]

(iii) Economic management. A naïve faith in the beneficial working of the free market mechanism and unrestricted competition is now well outdated in the West. The traditional monetary policy is now increasingly supplemented with budgetary and even direct controls. Apart from the direct operation of certain key industries, the State intervenes in the marketing of certain products and regulates big business through anti-monopoly legislation. Many large concerns invite trade unions to participate in some details of management. In Socialist countries the idea that workers can manage enterprises was dropped long ago and the position of local management is being further strengthened. In many ways economic management is being decentralized and greater scope is given to the initiative of individual directors of enterprises who in several respects now resemble Western managers. In the more developed Socialist countries, especially in Czechoslovakia, East Germany, Hungary, Poland and the USSR, and even in Bulgaria and Rumania, monetary and credit policy is being increasingly used as a tool of economic policy.[3]

(iv) Profits. Profit is no longer such a dominant factor in determining economic activity in Western countries. To many enterprises the goodwill of the public is more important than the maximization of profits at all costs, and State participation in economic activity is usually not

---

[1] See G. Colm, 'Economic Planning in the United States', *Weltwirtschaftliches Archiv*, Kiel, vol. 93, no. II, 1964, pp. 31–54; Yu. Vassiliev, *Plan. khoz.*, 6/1966, pp. 73–82.

[2] A. Bömisch, *Aussenhandel*, East Berlin, 12/1965, pp. 27–30.

[3] On the latter question, see an interesting treatment by G. Garvey, 'Banking and Credit in the Framework of New Economic Policies in Eastern Europe', *Banca Nazionale del Lavoro*, Sept. 1966, pp. 223–49.

CH. 15 §A EAST-WEST TRADE   351

prompted by the profit motive. There are also profit-sharing schemes and in some cases the State regulates the size of profits. On the other hand, in all European CMEA countries profit is being adopted as the chief indicator of efficiency and part of the enterprise profit is shared by the workers and management. Even in China, profit is an important feature of enterprise accounting.

(*v*) *The role of the consumer.* The consumer in the West is no longer as sovereign as the classical assertion 'the consumer is king' would imply. Collusion among producers, advertising, consumer loyalty and State intervention operate in favour of 'producer sovereignty', whilst the consumer, like all kings nowadays, has little real power. At the same time, in many Socialist countries on the threshold of mass-consumption, increasing attention is being given to consumers' preferences. One of the important reasons for this is to avoid accumulation of stocks of unsaleable goods not in demand, an embarrassment which has plagued many Socialist countries in recent years.

(*vi*) *Prices.* Owing to the distortions by subsidies and indirect taxes, few prices in the West now accurately reflect factor cost. Besides, especially in the marketing of certain primary products, there are governmental or semi-governmental price stabilization schemes whereby price ceilings or price floors are artificially imposed. In manufacturing industries, many large firms pursue stable price policies over long periods, irrespective of short-run changes in the conditions of supply and demand. On the other hand, most Socialist countries are adopting a more flexible approach to prices. Interest and even rent are gradually being considered as genuine costs and are being reflected in pricing. In all Socialist countries free market prices exist for agricultural produce privately grown, and steps are taken in some countries (especially in Bulgaria, Czechoslovakia and Hungary) to extend the system to many industrial consumer goods.

(*vii*) *Distribution of national income.* Inequalities of income in Western countries are being reduced by heavy, progressive taxation and the expansion of social services. In many of them there are also legal or *de facto* minimum-wage schemes protecting the lower-grade worker. On the other hand, equalization of income has been forsaken in most Socialist countries long ago. The disparities in income between successful authors, actors and scientists on the one hand, and unskilled labourers and collective farmers on the other would surprise many a communist dreamer in the West. The growing role of material incentives (China excepted)[1] is further militating against the Marxian Communist ideal 'from each according to his ability, to each according to his needs'.

(*viii*) *Social structure.* Class distinctions in the West are being obliterated by rising affluence, broadening educational opportunities and a gradual rise of the working class to middle-class status. The employers' power has been moderated by a continuous high level of employment, powerful trade unions, the labour vote and State intervention. At the same time, there is little evidence of a classless society in Socialist countries. Even in the Soviet Union, the oldest Socialist country, three social classes are officially acknowledged (workers, peasants, intelligentsia) and the increasing influence of technocracy and managers is accentuating the distinctions. Judging by the tightening up of the legislation and penalties against 'parasites', juvenile delinquents and crimes against property since the mid-1950s, the failure of Lysenkoism officially conceded, and the popularity of material incentives, the Socialist society is not moving closer to the ideal of a new Communist man devoid of acquisitive appetites.

(*ix*) *Peaceful co-existence.* The idea of peaceful co-existence was put forward by the Soviet Union to the West in 1956,[2] and the proposition was further reaffirmed and elaborated at the 22nd Party Congress in

---

[1] But some 300,000 capitalists in China are reported to be still receiving interest and dividends on their nationalized enterprises – one of them as much as the equivalent of US $400,000 a year. However, according to a recent Peking poster, fixed interest compensation payments to capitalists are to be ended. See B. M. Richman, 'Capitalists and Managers in Communist China', *Harv. Bus. Rev.*, Jan.–Feb. 1967, pp. 58–59; *Far Eastern Economic Rev.*, 9/2/1967, p. 188.

[2] The idea can be traced back to the early 1920s when Lenin advanced it in his speeches and writings as a necessary temporary stage until the final victory of Communism over Capitalism. However, the phrase was first used with its present popularized connotation in the Sino-Indian declaration of 1954 ('Five Principles of Peaceful Co-existence').

1961.¹ A well-known American diplomat and scholar aptly described the Western reaction: 'the West has no choice but to accept the quest for peaceful co-existence as the basis for policy towards the countries of the Communist world.'² The year 1963 saw the virtual end of the Cold War when in August the Nuclear Test Ban Treaty was signed by most Capitalist and Socialist countries, and this was followed by the Tripartite Agreement (USA, UK, USSR) banning nuclear weapons in space (January 1967) and the Non-Proliferation Treaty (June 1968). The *rapprochement* has been aided by (generally) greater Western moderation and a decline of imperialism and colonialism. On the other hand, the CMEA countries have rejected Stalinism (after 1956), have dropped the postulate of class war in their internal relations (after 1961) and their former revolutionary fervour.

(*x*) *Disintegration of Western and of Socialist unity.* The developments bringing the West and the East closer together have been paralleled, and indeed enhanced, by the waning solidarity of each camp. The former clearly recognizable bipolarity radiating from Washington and Moscow has been overshadowed by polycentric tendencies, so that the extremist inclinations of the leading powers on each side are now being partly frustrated by a lack of cohesive unity. With their economies booming and the fear of war in Europe receding, many Western countries have come to resent the leadership of the United States and her proclivity for questionable entanglements and escalation of wars in other parts of the world. France has practically withdrawn from NATO and she is more interested in integrating Europe eastwards to the Urals than westwards to the Rockies. The formation of economic groupings has further put the West in disarray. In the Socialist Bloc, the denunciation of Stalinism by Khrushchev, who also officially conceded the feasibility of 'different

¹ Peaceful co-existence was declared to embody the following principles: 'renunciation of war as a means of settling international disputes, and their solution by negotiation; equality, mutual understanding and trust between countries; consideration for each other's interests; non-interference in internal affairs; recognition of the right of every people to solve all the problems of their country by themselves; strict respect for the sovereignty and territorial integrity of all countries; promotion of economic and cultural co-operation on the basis of equality of mutual benefit.' *The Road to Communism*, Documents of the 22nd Congress of the Communist Party of the Soviet Union, FLPH, Moscow 1961, p. 506.

² G. F. Kennan, *On Dealing with the Communist World*, Harper & Row, New York 1964, p. 21.

paths to Socialism', at the 20th Party Congress in 1956 produced a ferment with far-reaching consequences. More recent developments such as the Sino-Soviet dispute, Rumania's bold moves in CMEA and in the Warsaw Pact, the military intervention in the reformist Czechoslovakia, the dissent between the less and the more developed countries and differing views on the 'German question' have played havoc with the former monolithic Bloc unity.

East-West trade, of course, occupies a special position in the relations between the two world divisions because it represents a tangible and continuous line of contact. In the remaining sections of this chapter we shall test the convergence hypothesis against the tendencies in East-West trade and the conditions underlying such tendencies in certain specific fields on each side. In this section we shall only bring out the evidence of a general nature, such as the attitude to the principle of comparative costs, the role of politics in trade and the significance of trade in the *rapprochement* of the two world divisions.

Ever since the abandonment of free trade, the theory of comparative costs has been, to some extent, irrelevant in explaining the foreign trade of the market economies, and its limited applicability as a guide to the foreign trade of the less developed economies is now generally recognized.[1] At the same time, especially since the early 1960s, many Socialist thinkers have expressed second thoughts on the theory. The principle of comparative advantage has, of course, been implicitly accepted in export efficiency studies, and it is now being extended to cover some imports as well (see Ch. 14 B, C). The idea of national self-sufficiency or even autarky on a CMEA scale has been abandoned many years ago. This new attitude is commonly entertained even in the country which one would think is least interested in foreign trade.[2]

[1] See, for example, H. Myint, 'The Classical Theory of International Trade and the Underdeveloped Countries', *Econ. Journal*, June 1958, pp. 317–37; J. Bhagwati, 'The Theory of Comparative Advantage in the Context of Under-development and Growth', *Pakistan Development Review*, 2(3), 1962, pp. 339–53; G. Haberler, 'An Assessment of the Current Relevance of the Theory of Comparative Advantage to Agricultural Production and Trade', *International Journal of Agrarian Affairs*, May 1964, pp. 130–150; B. R. Schiller, 'The Compatibility of the Theory of Comparative Cost with the Development Needs of Today's Economically Less-Developed Countries', *Indian Econ. Journal*, July–Sept. 1965, pp. 1–12. Also see Ch. 4 C, pp. 73–74.

[2] For example, a Soviet scholar recently pointed out: 'But it is obvious that all countries are economically interconnected and interdependent, that the broad development

At one stage several prominent Western economists, such as L. v. Mises, L. Robbins and J. Viner, contended that the existence of central planning and state foreign trade monopoly must inevitably lead to autarky. Their argument ran along the following lines: foreign trade depends largely on external factors which are beyond the control of central planners and other Socialist authorities; to remove the elements of uncertainty threatening to disrupt planned development, the State finds itself under constant pressure to reduce foreign trade to a minimum.

These assertions are emphatically refuted in modern Socialist literature.[1] It is pointed out that disruptive elements and uncertainty in trade with Capitalist countries can now be reduced to insignificance by

(a) entering into long-term trade agreements;

(b) participating in international commodity agreements and in the work of various international institutions promoting stability of trade;

(c) concentrating on trade with the most reliable partner countries;

(d) adjusting the structure of trade in such a way as to minimize the role of articles subject to unexpected fluctuations;

(e) accumulating larger foreign-exchange reserves to be able to cushion changes in world markets;

(f) making the Socialist foreign trade system more flexible by reforms such as those currently implemented in Eastern Europe.[2]

In fact, central planning and the State monopoly of foreign trade can apply these remedies to better effect than would be possible under private enterprise. Besides, it may be observed that the unstable element in the Bloc countries' foreign trade, i.e. trade with the Capitalist World, represents only one-third (one-quarter with the West) of their total trade.

---

of world trade is an objective necessity, and that it enables the partners to enjoy all the advantages of the world-wide division of labour and helps to strengthen world peace.' N. Lyubimov, 'Soviet Foreign Trade Problems', *International Affairs*, Moscow, 8/1965, p. 5. Similar statements were made on several occasions by Khrushchev; see, e.g., *Izvestiya*, 31/12/1963, p. 1 and *Pravda*, 23/3/1964, p. 1.

[1] See, e.g., Z. Kamecki, J. Sołdaczuk and W. Sierpiński, *Miedzynarodowe stosunki ekonomiczne* (International Economic Relations), PWE, Warsaw 1964, pp. 502–506; Imre Vajda, *The Role of Foreign Trade in a Socialist Economy*, Corvina Press, Budapest 1965, esp. pp. 291–98.

[2] *Ibid.*, pp. 503–504.

A converging trend can also be discerned in parallel attempts to integrate the theory of international trade with the theory of growth.[1] There is at least one Western scholar who believes that the West and the Bloc (and the Third World) will overcome their differences and will 'converge through growth'.[2] It is obvious that the possibility of convergence through trade and development is greater between Western and Eastern Europe than between other parts of the West and East.[3]

East-West trade is increasingly regarded as the soundest practical way of promoting *rapprochement* between the two world divisions. In an interview with an American publisher in 1958 Mr Khrushchev stated: 'Trade constitutes that sound and stable basis upon which co-existence between countries with different social and economic systems can successfully develop and be consolidated.'[4] It has been asserted on numerous occasions in both the East and the West that trade promotes broader contacts and understanding not only between traders but also other members of the public in general. Mr du Cann, the (then) Minister of State, Board of Trade, voiced the British view by stressing: 'We believe that an expansion of trade plays an important part in encouraging the spirit of *détente* between East and West which all of us want so much.'[5]

Largely as a result of the marked improvement in the political climate, East-West trade is becoming 'de-politicized', and as such it is commanding greater confidence and esteem. It has become apparent to each side that the advantages that can be derived from manipulating trade for non-commercial ends were greatly exaggerated in the past. Judging by the experience of the 1950s, the economic cost was usually substantial whilst expected concessions proved almost invariably disappointing to each side (see Chs. 11 F and 12 D, E).

[1] Of the notable Socialist contributions, we must mention I. Sachs, *Handel zagraniczny a rozwój gospodarczy*, PWE, Warsaw 1963, which has been translated into English (*Foreign Trade and Economic Development of Underdeveloped Countries*, Asia Publishing House, London 1966).
[2] C. A. Zebot, *The Economics of Competitive Co-existence: Convergence Through Growth*, Praeger, New York 1964, esp. chs. 1 and 11.
[3] See J. Siotis, 'ECE in the Emerging European System', *International Conciliation*, 1/1967.
[4] Quoted in *International Affairs*, Moscow, 5/1958, p. 3.
[5] *Board of Trade Journal*, 26/6/1964, p. 1,373.

B. 'PECUNIA NON OLET'

We shall not argue at this stage whether the evolutionary changes outlined in the preceding section merely represent a superficial resemblance or if they foreshadow a substantive coalescence of the two systems. Most of these changes are rather self-generated developments to overcome the weaknesses which are becoming too obvious in each system under the impact of technological revolution. Neither side would easily concede the superiority of the other system to be worth imitating. The differences in basic ideologies are still fundamental and intact, and the possibility of ideological reconciliation is most emphatically denied, particularly by Socialist leaders (this question will be pursued in the concluding section of this chapter). We shall now consider how, in spite of this inherent cleavage, East-West trade has been evolving into a strange marriage of convenience.

If the course of East-West trade, as reflected in the figures of trade turnover over the last decade or so, is accepted as indicative of the convergence or divergence of the West and the Bloc, then our answer must unequivocally be: yes, the two systems are converging. Recusant ideologues on each side may recall Alfred Marshall's age-tested observation that material gains 'harness man's strongest, though not necessarily the highest, motives', but – perhaps paradoxically – it is materialism that appears to be bringing the two divisions together. The changing patterns of direction of trade were considered in Ch. 3, but some figures highlighting the trends relevant to our present discussion may be restated here.

Ever since the Korean War, the role of East-West trade has been increasing – in absolute as well as in relative terms. Its share in world trade has in fact more than doubled – from 1·3% (£766 m.) in 1953 to 2·8% (£4,400 m.) in 1967 (see Table XI, p. 52). The relatively fast expansion of East-West trade can be brought out by the following figures showing the average annual rates of increase over the 1953–67 period (derived from Table XI):

Western trade
intra-Western	8·4%
with the Socialist Bloc	13·3%
with the Third World	5·1%

Socialist trade
 intra-Bloc 5·6%
 with the West 13·3%
 with the Third World 16·1%
WORLD TRADE 7·0%

Thus East-West trade has been expanding about twice as fast as either intra-Western or intra-Socialist foreign trade, or in fact world trade as a whole. The rate of increase in Western trade with the Bloc has been about three times as fast as with the Third World.[1] As a result of this remarkable growth, whilst in 1953 trade with the Socialist Bloc represented only 2% of total Western trade, the proportion rose to 4% in 1967. Similarly, the share of the West in the Bloc's total trade climbed from 14% to 25% in the same period (see Table XII, p. 54). In the traditional conflict between ideology and economics in East-West relations, obviously the latter has proved triumphant.

The former Western reluctance to trade with Socialist countries because trading means giving tacit approval of the social system in force, is not much heeded now by the business community. Competition for markets in the West and in the Developing World is becoming more acute. The Socialist Bloc with its high rates of growth has been pictured as an insatiable market, a picture that has been embellished in a masterly manner by Socialist officials and political leaders. Technological innovations have tended to produce a surplus capacity, and the large orders typical of Socialist deals have been difficult to resist.

It is rather strange that in this feverish race for the Bloc market, most Western monopolies – which could hardly be accused of much sympathy for communism – have been in the forefront. And they have moreover had a welcome reception from the bewildered Socialist officials oblivious of Marx's polemics on 'surplus value' and Lenin's dicta on the 'parasitism and decay of capitalism'.[2] More recently, even many smaller firms have

[1] It will be noted that Socialist trade with the Third World has been rising faster than with the West. However, the high percentage rise is largely due to the low absolute value of that trade at the beginning of the period (1953), and even in 1967 the absolute value of that trade was rather small. The respective absolute values of the Socialist Bloc's trade with the Third World and with the West in 1967 were £2,000 m. and £4,400 m. (see Table XI, p. 52 and Table XXVIII, p. 257).

[2] K. Marx, *Capital*, Parts III, IV and VIII, V. I. Lenin, *Selected Works*, Lawrence & Wishart, vol. v, esp. pp. 61–68, 91–99.

been looking for salvation in the Bloc. As a Socialist economist observed, 'integration in Western Europe prompts the weaker enterprises to look for new outlets in the Socialist countries.'[1] In the face of the economic integration in Western Europe, the imminent (as it appeared at the time) British entry into the Common Market and the development of woollen synthetics, the managing director of the International Wool Secretariat, when questioned on wool exports, is reported to have said that he 'would deal with the Devil if he could make a sale'.[2] The following year, Senator Fulbright urged the Americans to 'overcome the myth that trade with Communist countries is a compact with the Devil'.[3]

That money obtained from Socialist countries does not smell, is further illustrated by the evasions and erosion of the strategic embargo. Illicit trans-shipment and smuggling of the most critical embargoed items were particularly brisk at the height of the strategic export controls during the Korean War. Since that time, mainly due to pressure from interested business circles, and in spite of the stubborn opposition of the American Government, the scope of the embargo has been whittled down to a bare minimum (see Ch. 12 A, D). Most Western governments have become adept at availing themselves of the 'hardship escape clause', and the embargo in recent years has been more conspicuous in its breaches than its observance.

Judging by the unusual growth of Australia's, Canada's, Japan's and West Germany's trade with many Socialist countries, it appears that the absence of diplomatic recognition does not stand in the way of lucrative commercial exchanges (see Ch. 11 C, F). Nor does the war in Vietnam in which Western and Socialist countries, if not all *de facto* at least ideologically, confront each other.

The Socialist ideological contempt for the West is much greater than the West's for Socialism, so that the eagerness with which the Bloc countries have been hurrying into trade with the bourgeois nations is the more remarkable. The Bloc's trade with the West has been rising more than twice as fast as intra-Bloc trade, and the latter now represents 62% of the total as compared with 80% in 1953 (see Table X, p. 46). Many a

---

[1] Karl-Heinze Domdey, 'Economic Contacts between Socialist and Capitalist Countries of Europe', *Peace, Freedom and Socialism*, 9/1965, p. 10.
[2] *The Bulletin*, Sydney, 15/6/1963, p. 47.
[3] J. W. Fulbright, *Old Myths and New Realities*, Jonathan Cape, London 1965, p. 14.

Stalinist diehard must view these developments as evidence of degenerate revisionism or even infamous collusion with the decadent West. These epithets were in fact drawn from the Chinese repertoire of invectives describing the behaviour of the Soviet Union and other CMEA members. Yet of all Socialist countries, China's trade has been diverted most away from intra-Bloc channels – from a share of 75% in 1953 to about 25% in 1967.

The temptation to trade with the West has been too great ever since the Korean War. It is now well appreciated that trade with the industrially advanced Capitalist countries represents one of the few remaining growth factors. On the one hand, as is well known, imports of highly advanced machinery and equipment – apart from saving domestic resources – enable Socialist countries to participate in the technological and scientific revolution in the West. On the other, exports to the highly demanding Western buyers' markets 'play an extremely important role in modernizing the economy'.[1] As such, however distasteful on other grounds, trade with the West strengthens the position of Socialism in its contest with Capitalism in the economic arena. 'Combined with the full use of technological achievements', concluded a Socialist writer, 'it increases socialist accumulation, promotes the development of the socialist mode of production and the socialist world economy, thereby strengthening the positions of the socialist countries in the economic competition.'[2] In May 1968, the (then) Czechoslovak Premier, Mr Černik, suggested a new role for Western capital in his country.

The pangs of ideological conscience have not been strong enough to prevent Socialist countries from exporting to the West articles desperately needed by consumers at home or by other 'fraternal' Socialist nations, to earn hard currencies – and often at lower prices than those charged to domestic buyers (see Chs 9 C, E, and 10 B). The fact that most Socialist countries have been endeavouring to attract Western tourists, does not mean that the authorities are particularly interested in a greater freedom of travel for the sake of cultural *rapprochement*, but rather in earning badly needed foreign exchange. The authorities in Eastern Europe and in China have also devised all sorts of subtle tricks to secure remittances of hard currencies from nationals resident outside the Bloc, even though

[1] S. Leszkowicz, *Handel zagraniczny* (Foreign Trade), Warsaw, 4/1966, p. 132.
[2] Domdey, *op. cit.*, p. 14.

realizing that these people do not, generally speaking, approve of Communist regimes.

In the traditional Marxist view technical knowledge, just as material means of production, should belong to the society and not to private owners, and consequently trading in patents is unethical. For nearly half a century the USSR conveniently subscribed to this philosophy, poaching Western know-how while herself having little of interest to the West. But with technical progress, the Soviet Union has found in recent years that she herself has technology to sell. Many observers were mystified when in 1965 she decided to accede to the International Union for the Protection of Industrial Property. Which shows that ideological tenets are a matter of relativity.

Similarly, China has not hesitated to engage in extensive illicit opium traffic, and Vietcong guerillas to make prostitutes earn American dollars for the North-Vietnamese cause (see Ch. 10 B, p. 201). It has been recently reported in a British source that in 1966 Chinese steel was sold through intermediaries in Singapore to the American forces in South Vietnam for the construction of new military bases to escalate the war against the Vietcong.[1] The fact that the Peking regime has so far not taken over Hong Kong and Macao has puzzled many a Western (and Asian) observer for the past decade, but the explanation is quite simple. These colonies in their present state are most valuable trade links with Capitalist countries and very important sources of Western currencies. Unquestionable historical right, national pride and the impatient local Communist Parties are sacrificed, at least for the time being, to commercial expediency.

C. INSTITUTIONAL CONVERGENCE

A converging trend between the two systems in respect of institutional forms and relations can be discerned in the growing resemblance of the

---

[1] The report was written in Singapore by Dennis Bloodworth and it appeared in the *Observer* (18/12/1966, p. 1). According to this account, the transaction took place at the beginning of 1966, it was worth £357,000 and the payment was effected through banks in Hong Kong. Only China could meet the required specifications, quantities and the six-week delivery date. The denials that were made by China and the USA immediately, before proper investigations could be made, were unconvincing.

organization of foreign trade, widening membership of the same international organizations, increasing participation in the work of such an important United Nations body as the European Commission for Europe, and growing participation in international trade fairs and other forms of pursuits bearing on East-West trade. What follows is an attempt to substantiate these propositions.

(a) Organization Forms and Relations

If we closely examine the organizational forms prevalent in Western foreign trade today, we find that the picture of independent private producers or merchants engaging in external trade in keen competition amongst themselves, belongs more to the past than to the present. First, the degree of centralization in foreign trade is now quite substantial. This is exemplified by commodity-trade associations (such as the Timber Trade Federation in the United Kingdom), producers' and exporters' associations (e.g. the Associated Chamber of Manufacturers of Australia) and specific bodies for the promotion of trade with Socialist countries such as the Japan Association for Soviet and East European Trade. Although such bodies have (generally speaking) been privately organized, their membership is usually encouraged by the government, and not infrequently is made compulsory.

Second, there has been a tendency for the size of firms engaging in foreign trade to increase through amalgamations and takeovers on a national and even an international scale, as well as a formation of international cartels. Third, State trading is now a not unimportant feature even of Western countries' trade.[1] In general, it has made greater inroads into foreign trade than domestic trade, export (and to a smaller extent import) of primary products being the most favoured field of State trading. In most of these countries (especially in Australia, Canada, France, Italy, Japan, New Zealand, South Africa, USA) government or semi-government marketing boards have been established to handle exports, and even imports in some cases, of such commodities as wheat, barley, rice, dairy products, oil seeds, salt, alcohol, narcotics, tobacco,

---

[1] State trading has, of course, made great headway in the Developing Capitalist countries. See especially UNCTAD, *State Trading in Countries of the ECAFE Region*, Doc. E/CONF. 46/32, 22/1/1964.

matches, etc. Such boards or agencies are a necessary part and parcel of the price or income stabilization plans in agriculture, or otherwise an effective means of enforcing State monopolization of production or distribution for fiscal, health or security reasons.[1]

Even in the United States, commonly regarded as the main bastion of Capitalism and usually most critical of 'creeping Socialism' in other countries, has succumbed to State trading. In fact the scale of State trading in the USA is in a sense greater than in any other Western country, and it is increasing. The value of exports handled by the Commodity Credit Corporation (an offshoot of the Department of Agriculture) alone runs into thousands of millions of dollars annually,[2] which is much more than the average value of *exports and imports* handled by a Soviet foreign trade corporation.[3] It may also be observed that the CCC is a big factor in the world market for cotton and wheat, it engages in barter and it operates at a huge loss.[4] According to Spulber, at one stage the possibility of establishing a State trade monopoly to deal with Socialist countries was seriously considered in France and in the United States at government level.[5] The evidence of American tolerance of Socialism is further borne out by her continued aid to India and other Developing nations in spite of the adoption by these countries of several elements of State trading and central planning.

Japan is sometimes contrasted with Mainland China as an example of a successful free enterprise economy. Yet its Ministry of International Trade and Industry is not that much different from a ministry of foreign trade in a Socialist country. MITI has been described as a 'monolith' and 'a very overstaffed and hard-headedly bureaucratic agency... pushing its authority into every facet of foreign trade'. It has the right to

---

[1] For further details see M. Quin, 'State Trading in Western Europe', *Law and Contemporary Problems*, Summer 1959, pp. 388–419; *State Trading in Countries of the ECAFE Region, op. cit.*, pp. 8–9, 21–22.

[2] The value of the export of price-support commodities alone amounted to: $211 m. in 1953, $3,040 m. in 1958, and $1,290 m. in 1961; the figures published since 1961 are not comparable to those published before but the sales and donations of price-support commodities reached $3,260 m. in 1960 and $2,340 m. in 1966. See, *Statistical Abstract of the United States 1962*, p. 632, and *1967*, p. 619.

[3] For 1967 the figure worked out at 510 m. roubles, or less than $570 m.

[4] $1,140 m. on exports for dollars alone in 1966. *Statistical Abstract of the United States 1967*, p. 394.

[5] N. Spulber, 'The Soviet-Bloc Foreign Trade System', *Law and Contemporary Problems*, Summer 1959, p. 432.

approve all licences, royalty and joint-venture agreements negotiated with foreign countries, and to govern production volume.[1] As if this were not enough, the Japan External Trade Organization has urged for years that the Japanese Government should set up a single export channel for dealings with Socialist countries.[2]

The economic reforms initiated in most European Socialist countries several years ago (see Ch. 14 C) have tended to produce organizational forms and relations closer to those prevailing in the West. Although in essence the foreign-trade monopoly still prevails in all Socialist countries, its very principle is being increasingly questioned, and there have been some significant departures in practice.[3] This has been the case particularly in East Germany, Czechoslovakia, Hungary and Poland since the early 1960s, and more recently in Bulgaria and Rumania.[4] The monopoly has also been weakened by the growing number of joint East-West undertakings whereby direct dealings are established between Socialist and Western enterprises, usually by-passing the ministry of foreign trade and even foreign-trade corporations (see Section D of this chapter below).

The reforms have also produced several decentralizing effects. Much of the responsibility of the ministries of foreign trade has been transferred to the economic councils, industrial branch associations, the enterprises producing for export and (in some cases) to those relying on imports, thus allowing them greater participation in working out foreign-trade plans and greater freedom of initiative.[5] Many such enterprises

[1] *Far Eastern Economic Review*, 3/3/1966, pp. 395, 397–98.
[2] *FEER*, 24/2/1966, p. 379.
[3] For a representative selection of articles on the subject see V. Černiansky and J. Pleva, 'On Theoretical Questions of Foreign Trade Management', *Hospodářské noviny* (Economic News), Prague, 9/1965 (translation in *The American Review of Soviet and East European Foreign Trade*, Jan.–Feb. 1966, pp. 37–55, esp. p. 42); F. Enderlein, *Aussenhandel*, 2/1966, pp. 9–20; J. Szanyi, *Aussenhandel*, 2/1967, pp. 37–40; G. St. Georgiev, 'The Essence and Forms of the Foreign Trade Monopoly under the New System of Managing the National Economy', *Vunshna turgoviya* (Foreign Trade), Sofia, 4/1967, pp. 6–9 (translation in: US Dept. of Commerce, Joint Publications Research Service, *Translations on East European Foreign Trade*, 21/6/1967, pp. 12–19).
[4] In Yugoslavia the foreign-trade monopoly has been gradually abandoned by the reforms of 1952, 1961 and 1965. Exports and imports are handled by several hundred semi-independent enterprises.
[5] On the role of the industrial branch associations or economic councils in the Eastern European countries see R. Evstignyev, *Vop. ekon.*, 9/1965, pp. 98–104; B. Muszycki, *Handel zagr.*, 2/1968, pp. 67–70.

have been granted the right of conducting their own foreign-trade operations in *Capitalist countries* (but not so much in other Socialist countries). Besides, special licences are occasionally issued to other undertakings (such as co-operatives and internal trading corporations) to carry out particular export or import transactions.

A decentralizing effect is also being produced by the gradual increase in the number of foreign-trade corporations (from 150 in the mid-1950s to 250 in the late 1960s in the whole Bloc). It must be pointed out that the corporations have been given a far wider latitude of freedom in dealing with Capitalist firms than with corporations in other Socialist countries.

For a long time the Marxist-Leninist postulate of divorcing production from distribution was basically unquestioned, because the two were considered antagonistic[1] and because their separation fitted so neatly into 'command planning'. But this practice is being abandoned in favour of a closer relation between industry and foreign trade. Closer links are being established between industrial enterprises and foreign-trade corporations by making them co-responsible for the production and marketing of exportables through a newly devised system of material incentives (see Ch. 14 C).[2]

The link between production and foreign trade is even more obvious in the case of the industrial enterprises which have been granted authority to operate in Western markets directly. It may be observed that in this respect there is a parallel tendency in the more dynamic European Socialist and Western countries. Larger enterprises, particularly those producing complicated machinery and equipment, tend to handle the marketing of their articles abroad themselves, including the installation of plant, the training of local personnel, servicing, etc.

One can also detect a changing attitude in the European Socialist countries towards the role of banking institutions in foreign trade. All these countries (with the exception of Albania) now have specialized

[1] On the need for closer co-operation between industry and foreign trade see especially G. Hamman, *Aussenhandel*, 10/1965, pp. 7-12; F. Enderlein, *Aussenhandel*, Parts I and II, 3/1966, pp. 1-6 and 4/1966, pp. 5-6; L. Dzikiewicz, *Handel zagr.*, 8/1967, pp. 299-301.

[2] The economic reforms in the USSR have not gone as far as in Bulgaria, Czechoslovakia, East Germany, Hungary, Poland and Rumania. But the change in the economic administration from a territorial to a branch-of-industry basis is closer to the Western practice, and it makes for easier adaptation in producing for export. See G. Rubinshtein, *Vop. ekon.*, 9/1966, pp. 111-17.

foreign-trade banks responsible for carrying out foreign exchange and credit operations, and all their central banks (except the East German and Soviet State Banks) are members of the Bank for International Settlements (situated in Basle). The Soviet Union has a highly successful bank in London (and its branch in Beirut),[1] one in Paris and a newly established one (in 1966) in Zürich; it is also reported that steps have been taken towards establishing similar banks in West Germany, Italy and Turkey.[2] Czechoslovakia also has a bank in London, while Hungary has one in Paris and another in Zürich. It may be noted in passing that the Charter of the International Bank for Economic Co-operation, established by CMEA countries in 1963, provides for a possibility of membership by Capitalist countries (see Ch. 10 D, p. 221). Some sort of association between EFTA and CMEA, and even between EEC and CMEA, has been advocated on occasions in both Eastern and Western Europe.

(b) Membership of International Organizations

Since World War II, the world has witnessed an unprecedented internationalization of human activities.[3] For a variety of reasons, Western countries have traditionally participated in international organizations to a far greater degree than have Socialist countries.

In general, Socialist countries have been more inclined to seek participation in technical fields, as for example in the sphere of transport and communications. Socialist leaders are fully aware of the fact that many practical problems can best be overcome by international co-operation, but they have often been critically disposed to international organizations in the economic, social and political fields. This is only natural, as attempts to solve common problems in these fields unavoidably lead to clashes conditioned by the opposing ideologies and

---

[1] The harmonious relations prevailing between the Narodny Bank and the banking institutions in the leading financial centre of the Western World, London, was stressed by the Lord Mayor when welcoming Mr Kosygin at Guildhall in February 1967.

[2] The Economist, *Foreign Report*, 17/2/1966; also see the interview with Mr. Dubonosov, chairman of the Narodny Bank in London, reported in *The Banker*, 3/1967, pp. 190–98.

[3] According to the Union of International Associations (of Brussels), the numbers of international organizations were: 210 in 1913, 480 in 1947, 1,150 in 1954, and over 2,130 in 1966. *International Associations*, 11/1966, p. 664; *Yearbook of International Organizations* for the years 1948, 1954–55, 1966–67.

practices peculiar to each system. Besides, most international organizations, by virtue of the circumstances in which they were established and their membership, have been dominated by Western ideas and interests.[1]

The membership of Western and Socialist countries in the international organizations which have a bearing on East-West trade is set out in Table XXXII. The Western predominance in the membership of the 35 organizations listed is conspicuous. In 1954 the 25 Western countries represented 48%, and the 12 Socialist countries only 7%, of the membership of these organizations (the total number of countries in the world was about 90).

Even in 1966, when the *percentage* of Western membership declined to 36% and that of the Socialist countries increased to 8%, Western prominence was still obvious. For the sake of a rough comparison, in 1966 the 25 Western countries represented 20% and the 12 Socialist countries 10% of the 125 countries in the world capable of becoming members of international organizations.

If we examine the trend in the membership of the 35 organizations since 1954, it becomes evident that both Western and Socialist countries have displayed an increasing inclination to join these international bodies relevant to East-West trade. Between 1954 and 1966, the Western countries' membership increased by 15% and the Socialist countries' by 66%. But the remarkable feature of these tendencies is that, as compared with the West, the Socialist predisposition to join these organizations has been much greater. Thus the Socialist reluctance to participate in a common solution of problems pertinent to East-West trade is no longer as patent as it was in the first decade after the war. Socialist countries would probably join more of these organizations were there no opposition from Western nations (e.g. in the case of GATT).

Other observations that can be made from Table XXXII may be briefly noted. So far as the 35 organizations are concerned, the most membership-minded countries on the Western side are (in descending order): France, Belgium, Italy, the Netherlands, the United Kingdom and Austria, but even the remaining Western countries belong to most

[1] By number, 95% of all international organizations have their headquarters in Western countries. Of the total number of 2,114 international meetings held in 1964, 1,610 (or 76% of the total) took place in the 25 Western countries, and only 90 (4%) in the 12 Socialist countries; the respective figures for 1954 were: 1,094, 900 (82%) and 14 (1%). Based on: *International Associations*, 4/1966, pp. 207-209; 11/1966, p. 664.

TABLE XXXII WESTERN AND SOCIALIST MEMBERSHIP OF INTERNATIONAL ORGANIZATIONS RELEVANT TO EAST-WEST TRADE, 1954 AND 1966

ORGANIZATION[1]	WESTERN COUNTRIES[2] Total number: 25 (1954)	1966	SOCIALIST COUNTRIES[3] Total number: 12 (1954)	1966
I. United Nations Organization				
1. United Nations New York, 1945; (60), 115	(16) a, b, c, d, e, f, g, i, j, k, l, m, n, o, p, q, r, s, t, v, w, x, y	23	(3) A, B, C, E, G, J, K, L	8
2. Economic Commission for Asia and the Far East Bangkok, 1947; (24), 28	(7) a, g, h, m, n, o, u, w, x	9	(1) G, L	2
3. Economic Commission for Europe[4] Geneva, 1947; (18), 29	(18) b, c, e, f, g, h, i, j, k, l, n, p, q, s, t, u, v, w, x, y	20	(7) A, B, C, E, J, K, L	7
4. Food and Agriculture Organization Rome, 1945; (71), 113	(25) a, b, c, d, e, f, g, h, i, j, k, l, m, n, o, p, q, r, s, t, u, v, w, x, y	25	(–) J, K	2
5. International Bank for Reconstruction and Development New York, 1945; (57), 103	(20) a, b, c, d, e, f, g, h, i, j, k, l, m, n, o, p, q, r, s, t, v, w, x, y	24	(1)	–
6. International Labour Organization Geneva, 1919; (67), 113	(25) a, b, c, d, e, f, g, h, i, j, k, l, m, n, o, p, q, r, s, t, u, v, w, x, y	25	(6) A, B, C, E, J, K, L	7
7. International Monetary Fund Washington, 1945; (57), 103	(20) a, b, c, d, e, f, g, h, i, j, k, l, m, n, o, p, q, r, s, t, v, w, x, y	24	(1)	–

TABLE XXXII—*Continued*

ORGANIZATION[1]	WESTERN COUNTRIES[2] Total number: 25 (1954) 1966	SOCIALIST COUNTRIES[3] Total number: 12 (1954) 1966
8. Universal Postal Union Berne, 1874; (91), 126	(25) 25 a, b, c, d, e, f, g, h, i, j, k, l, m, n, o, p, q, r, s, t, u, v, w, x, y	(7) 8 A, B, C, E, G, J, K, L
II. Other inter-governmental organizations		
9. Bank for International Settlements Basle, 1930; (25), 26	(19) 20 b, c, e, f, g, h, i, j, k, l, n, p, q, s, t, u, v, w, x, y	(6) 6 A, B, C, E, J, K
10. General Agreement on Tariffs and Trade[5] Geneva, 1948; (34), 81	(19) 24 a, b, c, d, e, f, g, h, i, j, l, m, n, o, p, q, r, s, t, u, v, w, x, y	(1) 2 C, J
11. International Bureau for Weights and Measures Paris, 1875; (34), 40	(21) 22 a, b, c, d, e, f, g, h, k, l, m, n, p, q, r, s, t, u, v, x, y	(6) 6 B, C, E, J, K, L
12. International Commission for Agricultural Industries Paris, 1934; (47), 41	(15) 13 b, c, e, g, i, l, m, n, p, s, v, x, y	(5) 3 B, C, E
13. International Cotton Advisory Committee Washington, 1939; (30), 40	(19) 20 a, b, c, d, e, f, g, h, l, m, n, p, q, s, t, u, v, w, x, y	(–) 1 L
14. International Exhibition Bureau Paris, 1928; (19), 32	(14) 17 b, c, d, e, f, g, h, i, l, m, n, o, p, q, t, u, w	(1) 6 B, C, E, J, K, L
15. International Lead and Zinc Study Group New York, 1959; (–), 25	(–) 17 a, b, c, d, e, f, g, h, l, m, n, p, r, s, t, w, y	(–) 3 C, J, L

TABLE XXXII—*Continued*

ORGANIZATION[1]	WESTERN COUNTRIES[2] Total number: 25		SOCIALIST COUNTRIES[3] Total number: 12	
	(1954)	1966	(1954)	1966
16. International Rubber Study Group London, 1944; (19), 28	(11) a, b, c, d, e, g, h, l, m, n, t, w, x	13	(1) C, E	2
17. International Sugar Council London, 1953; (24), 45	(12) a, c, d, e, g, h, k, l, m, n, o, q, r, w, x	15	(4) C, E, J, L	4
18. International Union for the Protection of Industrial Property Geneva, 1883; (34), 74	(24) a, b, c, d, e, f, g, h, i, j, k, l, m, n, o, p, q, r, s, t, u, v, w, x, y	25	(5) B, C, D, E, J, K, L	7
19. International Union for the Protection of Literary and Artistic Works Geneva, 1886; (43), 54	(24) a, b, c, d, e, f, g, h, i, j, k, l, m, n, o, p, q, r, s, t, u, v, w, y	24	(5) B, C, E, J, K	5
20. International Union for the Publication of Customs Tariffs Brussels, 1890; (59), 73	(22) a, b, c, d, e, f, g, h, i, j, l, m, n, p, q, r, s, t, u, v, w, x, y	23	(6) A, B, C, E, J, K, L	7
21. International Wheat Council London, 1949; (43), 48	(17) a, b, c, d, f, g, h, i, j, k, l, m, n, o, p, q, r, s, t, u, w, x	22	(–) L	1
22. International Wool Study Group London, 1947; (31), 39	(22) a, b, c, d, e, f, g, h, i, k, l, m, n, o, p, q, r, s, t, u, v, w, x	23	(1) C	1
III. *Non-governmental organizations*				
23. Baltic and International Maritime Conference Copenhagen, 1905; (43), 62	(22) b, c, d, e, f, g, h, i, j, k, l, m, n, p, q, r, s, t, u, v, w, x, y	23	(1) C, E, J, K, L	5

CH. 15 §C EAST WEST TRADE 371

TABLE XXXII—*Continued*

ORGANIZATION[1]	WESTERN COUNTRIES[2] Total number: 25		SOCIALIST COUNTRIES[2] Total number: 12	
	(1954)	1966	(1954)	1966
24. International Cargo Handling Co-ordination Association London, 1952; (35), 70	(23) a, c, d, e, f, g, h, i, j, l, m, n, o, p, q, r, s, t, u, v, w, x, y	23	(–)	2 C, J
25. International Credit Insurance Association Zürich, 1946; (14), 21	(12) b, c, e, f, g, h, i, k, l, n, p, r, s, t, u, w, x	17	(1)	2 C, J
26. International Fur Trade Federation London, 1949; (15), 19	(14) a, b, c, d, e, f, g, h, l, n, p, r, s, t, u, w, x	17	(–)	2 C, L
27. International Organization for Standardization Geneva, 1946; (34), 53	(22) a, b, c, d, e, f, g, h, i, k, l, m, n, o, p, q, r, s, t, u, v, w, x, y	24	(5)	8 A, B, C, E, H, J, K, L
28. International Union of Aviation Insurers London, 1934; (17), 29	(14) a, b, c, e, f, g, h, k, l, m, n, p, q, s, t, u, v, w, x, y	20	(1)	3 C, E, J
29. International Union of Marine Insurance Zürich, 1874; (35), 37	(23) a, b, c, d, e, f, g, h, i, k, l, m, n, o, p, q, r, s, t, u, v, w, x, y	24	(2)	6 B, C, E, J, K, L
30. International Union of Official Travel Organizations Geneva, 1925; (48), 93	(22) a, b, c, d, e, f, g, h, i, k, l, m, n, o, p, q, r, s, t, u, v, w, x, y	24	(–)	7 B, C, E, G, J, K, L
31. International Union of Railways Paris, 1922; (36), 38	(18) b, c, d, e, f, g, h, i, k, l, m, n, p, q, s, t, u, v, w, y	20	(5)	5 B, C, E, J, K

TABLE XXXII—*Continued*

ORGANIZATION[1]	WESTERN COUNTRIES[2] Total number: 25		SOCIALIST COUNTRIES[3] Total number: 12	
	(1954)	1966	(1954)	1966
32. Permanent International Assn of Navigation Congresses Brussels, 1900; (46), 69	(20) a, b, c, d, e, f, g, h, i, j, k, l, m, n, o, p, q, r, s, t, u, v, w, x, y	25	(2) B, C, D, E, J, K, L	7
33. Permanent International Assn of Road Congresses Paris, 1909; (37), 63	(20) a, b, c, d, e, f, g, h, i, k, l, m, n, o, p, q, r, s, t, u, v, w, y	23	(2) B, C, D, E, J, K, L	7
34. Union of International Fairs Paris, 1925; (16), 30	(10) a, b, c, f, g, h, i, l, m, n, q, s, t, v, w, x, y	17	(3) B, C, D, E, J	5
35. World Power Conference London, 1924; (37), 61	(22) a, b, c, d, e, f, g, h, i, j, k, l, m, n, o, p, q, r, s, t, u, v, w, x, y	25	(3) B, C, E, J, K, L	6
TOTAL COUNTRY MEMBERSHIP IN THE 35 ORGANIZATIONS LISTED:				
(1,300), 2,021	(637)	733	(92)	153
Percentage share in each year (100%), 100%	(49%)	36%	(7%)	8%
Percentage comparison between 1954 and 1966[6] (100%), 15%	(100%)	115%	(100%)	166%

[1] The name of each organization is followed by: the place of its headquarters, year of foundation; (total world membership in 1954), total world membership in 1966. Membership figures in all cases include full, associate, provisional and participating members.

[2] The names of the Western member countries are given *for 1966*; they are indicated by *small* letters:

a = Australia,	f = Finland,	k = Ireland,
b = Austria,	g = France,	l = Italy,
c = Belgium,	h = W. Germany,	m = Japan,
d = Canada,	i = Greece,	n = Netherlands,
e = Denmark,	j = Iceland,	o = New Zealand,
	p = Norway,	u = Switzerland,
	q = Portugal,	v = Turkey,
	r = S. Africa,	w = UK,
	s = Spain,	x = USA,
	t = Sweden,	y = Yugoslavia.

Smaller European countries (Cyprus, Luxemburg, Malta, Monaco, etc.) are omitted in Column 2 for the sake of simplification, but if they are members of the organization listed they are included in total figures in Column 1.

[3] The names of the Socialist countries are given *for 1966*; they are indicated by *capital* letters:

A = Albania,	D = E. Germany,	G = Mongolia,	J = Poland,
B = Bulgaria,	E = Hungary,	H = N. Korea,	K = Rumania,
C = Czechoslovakia,	F = M. China,	I = N. Vietnam,	L = USSR.

Byelorussian SSR and Ukrainian SSR are not regarded as separate countries; where these Republics are members (in addition to the USSR) the total figure in Columns 1 and 3 does not include them.

[4] Including Cyprus, Luxemburg, Malta, Switzerland (an associate member), and the USA. Byelorussian SSR and Ukrainian SSR are also members but are not included in the total of 29.

[5] Including Iceland (a 'provisional' member).

[6] The total figure of membership in the 35 organizations in 1954 in each case is taken as 100%; the membership in 1966 is taken as a percentage of the total membership figure in 1954.

− = nil;   n.a. = not available.

Sources. Based on: *Yearbook of International Organizations 1954–55* and *1966–67* (Brussels), *Europa Year Book 1968*, London; *International Associations* (published monthly in Brussels) and Western and Socialist daily press.

---

of them. On the Socialist side, the membership of these organizations is virtually limited to 7 European countries, whilst East Germany and the 4 Asian countries belong to hardly any of them. The most favourably disposed to the 35 organizations are (in descending order): Czechoslovakia, Poland, Hungary, USSR, Bulgaria, Rumania and Albania. Mainland China and North Vietnam do not belong to any of the 35 organizations listed.

(c) *Participation in the Work of the European Commission for Europe*

All Western European countries (plus the USA) and all Eastern European countries (except East Germany) are members of ECE. Of all international organizations, ECE has proved the most fruitful meeting ground for tackling East-West problems. In fact, one of the main reasons for establishing the Commission was to normalize trade between Eastern and Western European countries. In the mind of its first Secretary, Gunnar Myrdal, its ultimate if not immediate task was to go even further – to promote integration on an all-European scale, and efforts towards this objective have been resumed in the last decade.[1]

Up to the mid-1950s, the Commission was more a forum for mutual recriminations than a channel for *rapprochement*, for which both sides must be equally blamed. However, since that time attitudes have been changing in favour of mutual understanding and co-operation, although this has not been without occasional setbacks.

The member countries have co-operated in many fields, but those most relevant to the promotion of East-West trade include: the general conditions of sale of certain products, the standardization of commercial documents, trade agreements, market disruption and discriminatory surcharges, the application of MFN, quotas, insurance and re-insurance contracts, payments and multilateralism, inland transport and commercial arbitration. This work has been carried on mostly under the dynamic leadership of the Committee on the Development of Trade. It was established in 1949 (replacing the 'Ad Hoc Committee on Industrial Development and Trade' formed in 1948); it was dormant during the 'frigid stage' of the Cold War, but it has resumed regular meetings since 1953.

Amongst the most successful forms of co-operation under the auspices of the Commission have been the meetings of economic advisers to member governments, begun in 1961. In 1967 practical measures were worked out for the removal of several economic and administrative obstacles to the growth of trade, and in the following year problems of long-run development were examined. It may also be added that up to the mid-1950s, there were few nationals from Eastern Europe on the staff of ECE, but the number has been increasing since. At the end of 1966, of the total number of 77 on the professional staff of the ECE Secretariat, 24 were from Socialist countries.[2]

[1] See J. Siotis, *op. cit.*, *passim.*, esp. pp. 5–6.
[2] Ibid., p. 35.

(d) *International Trade Fairs, Exhibitions and Similar Forms of Co-operation*

Trade fairs and exhibitions held in the leading industrial and commercial centres in the West and in the Bloc are being patronized by larger and larger numbers of exhibitors and representatives from the other side. Such occasions provide inestimable opportunities for broader contacts between officials and industrial and commercial personnel from each side interested in East-West trade. It is also noticeable that in recent years, with some exceptions, governments have offered support and even active encouragement and extra facilities to make these events successful.[1]

The places in the West which have proved particularly valuable in the last decade for periodical reunions of Western and Socialist industry and commerce include Belgrade, Brussels, Frankfurt, London, Lyons, Marseilles, Milan, Montreal, Munich, Osaka, Paris, Stockholm, Sydney, Tokyo, Utrecht, Vienna and Zagreb. Brno, Bucharest, Budapest, Canton, Leipzig, Leningrad, Moscow, Peking, Plovdiv, Poznan, Prague, Tientsin and Warsaw are the well-known converging points in the Bloc. The immense service rendered to the cause of East-West trade by the Leipzig Spring and Autumn Fairs over the past fifteen years deserves special acknowledgment.

In the early 1950s, where Socialist countries participated at all (as a Western observer noted) 'Eastern exhibits tended to be long on impressive displays and short on goods for sale.'[2] This is no longer true. Socialist countries are most anxious to promote exports to the West in this way, and indeed the amount of business transacted at the fairs is usually considerable.

It appears that most Socialist countries are now much more inclined to exhibit in the West than in the Bloc. Thus in 1964 Hungary participated in 6 international trade fairs held in the Bloc but in as many as 19

[1] Although in the past West German and American firms were usually discouraged by their governments from exhibiting at the Leipzig International Trade Fairs and elsewhere in East Germany, the enterprising businessmen attended these fairs all the same, quietly negotiating lucrative deals from their hotel rooms. However, American firms started exhibiting at the Leipzig Fair in 1965, and in 1968 at least 100 US firms exhibited there. The Bonn Government now favours participation in the Fair, too. See *The Economist*, 14/3/1964, p. 1209; *Amer. Rev. of East-West Trade*, 4/1968, p. 6.

[2] M. L. Hoffman, 'Problems of East-West Trade', *International Conciliation*, 1/1957, p. 299.

in the West;[1] in 1966 the respective figures for Czechoslovakia were 5 and 21,[2] for Poland 11 and 29,[3] and for East Germany 7 and 10.[4] Since 1954 Czechoslovakia and Hungary have joined the Union of International Fairs (Bulgaria, East Germany and Poland had joined before), and Bulgaria, Czechoslovakia, Hungary, Poland and the USSR (in addition to Rumania) have acceded to the inter-governmental organization, the International Exhibition Bureau (see Table XXXII, p. 369).

Another form of improving East-West understanding is represented by the increasing number of inter-governmental agreements on industrial, technical, scientific and even cultural co-operation between Western and Socialist countries. For example, as reported in the Western and Socialist press in the last few years, such bilateral East-West agreements have been concluded by at least thirty pairs of countries.[5]

An interesting case of multilateral efforts towards a new approach to co-operation is the 'Group of Nine', the remarkable feature of which is that it includes 2 NATO countries (Belgium and Denmark), 3 Warsaw Treaty countries (Bulgaria, Hungary and Rumania) and 4 non-aligned nations (Austria, Finland, Sweden and Yugoslavia). The Group, sponsored and formed at the United Nations Assembly in September 1965 (although the idea had already been mooted by Rumania at the 1963 Assembly), has called on the European governments to improve economic, political and diplomatic relations with each other, to reduce tension and to strengthen peace and security. Its work is being carried on through diplomatic channels, and international conferences on the question are also planned.

[1] *Handel zagr.*, 12/1964, p. 601.
[2] *Handel zagr.*, 4/1966, p. 164.
[3] *Czechoslovak Foreign Trade*, 2/1966, p. 23.
[4] These figures include collective participation by the foreign-trade corporations only. If individual participation by firms is included the respective figures were 90 and 161. *Statistisches Jahrbuch der DDR 1967*, East Berlin, p. 408.
[5] E.g., Belgium with Bulgaria, Czechoslovakia, Poland and the USSR; Canada with the USSR; Denmark with Bulgaria, Czechoslovakia and Poland; France with Czechoslovakia, Hungary, Poland, Rumania and the USSR; Greece with Rumania; Italy with Bulgaria, Czechoslovakia, Poland, Rumania and the USSR; Japan with the USSR; the Netherlands with Rumania; Sweden with East Germany and Poland; the United Kingdom with Bulgaria, Czechoslovakia, Poland and the USSR; the United States with Poland, Rumania and the USSR. It appears that there are at least 35 British institutes which maintain fruitful relations with 39 Soviet institutes in the field of science, and the USA has about 105 agreements in force with the USSR. *Amer. Rev. of East-West Trade*, 3/1968, p. 44; *U.S. News & World Report*, 27/3/1967, p. 50.

CH. 15 §C EAST-WEST TRADE 377

Other examples of improving East-West relations that may be cited include: the liberalization of regulations for passports and visas; a constant procession of official and unofficial trade missions both ways on a scale inconceivable ten years ago; the mutual extension of air-service links;[1] the construction of the Rhine-Danube Canal (undertaken by West Germany, to be completed by 1970), and plans have also been made under the auspices of ECE to link the Danube-Oder-Rhine with the Dnieper-Oder; and the laying down of gas pipelines from the Soviet Union to Finland and to Austria and Italy (which are likely to be extended to France).

D. JOINT EAST-WEST VENTURES

Joint Socialist-Capitalist undertakings already existed in the early 1920s, when up to 5% of Soviet imports and up to 10% of exports was handled by joint Soviet-Western trading companies.[2] However, this partnership did not last long. In the case of other Socialist countries, some joint trading companies established before the war have continued their operations after the Communist take-over.[3] There is 'no legal

[1] For example, the Soviet *Aeroflot* now operates regular flights to 25 Capitalist cities (including Amsterdam, Brussels, Copenhagen, Helsinki, London, Montreal, New York, Paris, Rome, Stockholm and Vienna). The first steps to initiate flights between Moscow and New York go back to 1935; after many breakdowns in negotiations, an agreement between the two countries was finally signed in November 1966. In exchange for the right of fly-over for her planes over Denmark, Norway and Sweden, the USSR granted similar rights to Scandinavian airlines operating flights to Japan, India and Iran.

[2] Such as *Russoangloles* (Soviet-English Timber Trading Company), *Russogollandoles* (Soviet-Dutch Timber Trading Company), *Russogertorg* (Soviet-German Trading Company). 51% or more of the shares was Soviet-owned. A. Baykov, *Soviet Foreign Trade*, Princeton UP 1946, p. 13; S. Szczypiorski, *Handel zagr.*, 6/1961, p. 270.

[3] The most dynamic of these companies appears to be the Polish *Dal*, established in 1937, which under Socialism has been transformed into a foreign-trade corporation. Its subsidiary *Anglo-Dal* renewed its operations in 1946 and it acts now as an agent for several Polish foreign-trade corporations in the United Kingdom, especially in the field of consumer goods; 99% of its shares is Polish-owned. In 1959, another subsidiary, *Daltrade* was established in London to develop Polish exports of consumer durables to Britain; shares are owned on a 50:50 basis by Poland and by British investors. In 1962, *Daltrade* established a new company in Nigeria, with 30% of the capital owned by Nigeria (since that time the British share of capital has been bought out by *Dal*). Other *Dal*'s subsidiaries or associate companies include *Dalimpex* – in Canada, *Armida* – in

prohibition preventing Socialist enterprises entering into joint ventures with Capitalist firms'.[1] However, up to 1964 such partnerships were rare, they were in fact limited to distribution and their effects on East-West trade were insignificant.

Since 1964 a new era in East-West economic relations seems to have been foreshadowed. Examples of joint ventures entered into by Socialist governments (however indirectly) and private Western firms are given in Table XXXIII. The most interested Western countries in these schemes so far appear to be West Germany, Austria, Italy, France, Belgium, Sweden and the United Kingdom, whilst on the Socialist side Hungary,[2] Bulgaria, Czechoslovakia and Poland are the most active proponents.[3]

The Western firms participating in these schemes include *Krupp*, *Siemens-Reiniger*, *IBAG* (Internationale Baumaschinenfabrik), *Rheinische Stahlwerke* and *Daimler-Benz* of West Germany; *Alpine Montangesellschaft* and *Simmering-Graz-Pauker* of Austria; *Krebs and Hamon* of France; *Alfa-Laval* and *Electrolux* of Sweden; *English Electric, Jones Cranes, Gallaghan & Sons* and *Rolls-Royce* of Britain; *Simmons Machine Tool Corporation, Inter-Continental Hotels* and *Coca-Cola* of the United States.

Panama, *Falconda Venezolana* – in Venezuela, *Dal International Trading Co.* – in Lebanon and *Indopol* – in India. The annual foreign trade turnover of *Dal* exceeded $100 m. in 1967. For further details, see *Handel zagr.*, 9/1964, pp. 457–58 and 12/1967, Supplement.

[1] Szczypiorski, *op. cit.*, p. 269.

[2] The degree of significance attached by the Hungarian Government to this form of co-operation is indicated by the formation of the Office for Foreign Trade Technical Co-operation in 1964 under the joint sponsorship of the Ministry of Foreign Trade and the Ministry of Heavy Industry. Its responsibility is to act as a clearing house for Hungarian and Capitalist enterprises interested in commercial and technical partnership.

[3] Yugoslavia is very active in co-operating with both the East and the West, and this is mostly done through the Progres Invest Business Association situated in Belgrade. Important joint enterprises have been established with East Germany (ceramics, electronics, metallurgy), Poland (chemicals), Hungary (harbour equipment) and also with Bulgaria, Czechoslovakia and the USSR. There are numerous examples of co-operation in production and marketing with American, British, French, West German, Italian and other enterprises. In 1963 special 'free tariff zones' were established to facilitate joint production, and in 1967 legislation was passed to admit foreign risk capital whereby foreign investors are permitted to own up to 50% of an enterprise's capital.

Table XXXIII Recent examples of joint
East-West undertakings

COUNTRIES WITH
CO-OPERATING ENTERPRISES — FORMS OF PARTNERSHIP

1. Bulgaria–Australia — Trade in certain consumer goods and raw materials.
2. Bulgaria–West Germany — Repair and service stations for Mercedes cars in Bulgaria.
3. Bulgaria–Italy — Co-production and joint marketing of grinding equipment.
4. Bulgaria–Netherlands — Co-operation in the marketing and servicing of certain Bulgarian machines.
5. Bulgaria–Switzerland — Export of certain industrial machinery to third countries.
6. Bulgaria–Turkey — Joint canning and marketing of fruits and vegetables.
7. Bulgaria–USA — Co-operation in bottling and sale of soft drinks in Bulgaria.
8. Czechoslovakia–Austria — Co-operation in the production of ski-bindings.
9. Czechoslovakia–France — Co-production and joint marketing of horizontal drills.
10. Czechoslovakia–West Germany — Co-operation in road construction in third countries; co-operation in the production and marketing of gramophone records.
11. Czechoslovakia–Italy — Joint construction and ownership of a holiday resort in Sardinia; joint production and marketing of motorcycles, sportcycles and pumps.
12. Czechoslovakia–Japan — Co-operation in the production of spinning machines for third markets.
13. Czechoslovakia–Sweden — Co-production and joint marketing of lathes.
14. Czechoslovakia–United Kingdom — Joint sales and servicing of Skoda cars, trucks and tractors in Britain; a British distributor marketing Czecho-

TABLE XXXIII—*Continued*

COUNTRIES WITH CO-OPERATING ENTERPRISES	FORMS OF PARTNERSHIP
	slovak machines in the British Commonwealth in conjunction with complementary British-produced fibre-amalgamating machinery.
15. Czechoslovakia–USA	A Czechoslovak machine tool factory acting as a sub-contractor for an American firm, the latter being responsible for marketing of the combined production; co-operation in the production of records.
16. East Germany–Belgium	Co-operation in the production of East German machine tools in Belgium to be marketed in EEC.
17. East Germany–West Germany	Limited co-operation in the manufacture of specialized components on a short-term basis.
18. East Germany–Sweden	Co-operation in the production of furnaces, cranes and tool machines.
19. Hungary–Austria	Mutual exchange of rolled metals between two co-operating firms; co-production of artificial fertilizers, pharmaceuticals and synthetic materials; co-production and marketing of welding equipment; co-operation in the construction of power stations in third countries.
20. Hungary–West Germany	Co-production of steel pit props; joint manufacture and marketing of a new programme-controlled lathe developed in Hungary; joint production of component instruments for X-ray equipment for third countries; co-operation in the production of certain types of steam engines.

TABLE XXXIII—*Continued*

COUNTRIES WITH CO-OPERATING ENTERPRISES	FORMS OF PARTNERSHIP
21. Hungary–United Kingdom	Co-production of tractors and hydro-electric apparatus; co-operation in the production of British-developed thread-grinding machinery in Hungary.
22. Hungary–USA	Co-operation in the construction and operation of a luxury hotel in Budapest (similar hotels also planned for Bucharest, Prague and Warsaw).
23. Poland–Austria	Co-operation in the production of aircraft parts.
24. Poland–Belgium	Co-operation in the production of machine tools, marine engines, railway equipment and textile machinery.
25. Poland–France	Joint marketing of certain Polish consumer and capital goods in France.
26. Poland–West Germany	Joint production and marketing of equipment for chemical and food processing industries; co-operation in the production of West German diesel engines in Poland; co-operation in the production and export of clothing made in Poland from West German cloth.
27. Poland–Italy	Co-operation in the production of measurement instruments.
28. Poland–Switzerland	Co-operation in the production of marine diesel engines.
29. Poland–United Kingdom	Co-operation in the production of British buses and sacking paper in Poland; joint marketing of certain Polish consumer goods in Britain.
30. Poland–Austria, Denmark, France, West Germany, Italy, Sweden	Co-operation in the export and installation of complete plants in third countries.

TABLE XXXIII—*Continued*

COUNTRIES WITH CO-OPERATING ENTERPRISES	FORMS OF PARTNERSHIP
31. Rumania–USA	Co-operation in the construction of a meat-canning factory in Rumania and marketing of the output in the USA.
32. USSR–Belgium	Marketing of Soviet oil, cars and certain other consumer goods in Belgium.
33. USSR–Finland	Co-operation in the construction of a gas pipeline to, and distribution of Soviet gas in, Finland. Operation of a joint navigation company.
34. USSR–Italy	Co-operation in the construction of a gas pipeline to, and distribution of Soviet gas in, Italy.
35. USSR–Japan	Joint Moscow–Tokyo air service with Soviet planes and pilots and Japanese cabin crews; joint development of natural gas resources in Sakhalin.

Sources. Compiled from Western and Socialist daily press and periodicals.

An example of a joint East-West enterprise is *Depolma* (Deutsch-Polnische Maschinenhandels, G.m.b.H.). According to the agreement signed in September 1965, the Polish *Polimex* foreign trade corporation owns 55% and the West German IBAG 45% of the initial capital. Its operations consist in the joint buying of components, in production and in the marketing of equipment for the chemical, food processing and other industries.

Joint East-West ventures assume different forms:
  (i) The mildest form is the exchange of licences, designs and industrial trainees.
  (ii) Co-operation in exporting parts of complete plants to third countries.
  (iii) Co-production ventures where a Socialist enterprise is usually supplied by a Western firm with initial key equipment and then

certain key components, technical designs and perhaps technical advisers. The Western firm is entitled to an agreed portion of the production of the complete article.

(iv) Dual production and marketing undertakings where a Socialist enterprise is supplied with similar assistance as under (iii), but the final stages of production are usually completed in the West ('vertical co-production'). Subsequently the Socialist enterprise undertakes the marketing of the complete article in the Socialist Bloc whilst the Western partner does it elsewhere.

(v) A Western enterprise, using its own key equipment, technical know-how, management methods and technical staff, carries on production in a Socialist country. The latter supplies buildings, raw materials and labour. The Western enterprise is guaranteed an agreed share of production.

(vi) A different type of joint venture is that operated by Mainland China, known as 'Overseas Chinese Investment Corporations', established by the authorities with the capital contributed by Overseas Chinese. Under 1957 regulations, the corporations are allowed to pay dividends of up to 8%, half of which under certain conditions may be transmitted to shareholders abroad. The share capital remains the property of the investors entitled to recall it in Chinese currency or reinvest it after twelve years.[1]

The initiative in the new drive for joint production and trading schemes has originated primarily from the Socialist side, particularly from the more dynamic Eastern European countries. It must be observed that they are not seeking ordinary economic aid. Each scheme is a venture based on a commercial *quid pro quo*.

This newly re-discovered fascination with what one would think a rather incongruous association, can be explained by several factors. For Western firms an obvious attraction of partnership with Socialist firms is lower labour costs, the advantage further accentuated by shortages of labour which have plagued many industries in France, West Germany and Sweden.

Furthermore, in the face of economic integration in Western Europe, many Western firms, within and without the groupings, have found it

[1] Pauline Lewin, *The Foreign Trade of Communist China*, Praeger, New York and London 1964, p. 39.

difficult to compete with more efficient firms; even many strong multi-product firms are encountering difficulties in pushing certain lines. A partnership with a Socialist enterprise may offer a possibility of reducing overheads and provide a sheltered market in that country and even in other Bloc countries. Besides, Socialist countries have built up a sound reputation for strict adherence to the terms of agreement and established an excellent payment record (see Ch. 10 F). At its February 1967 meeting in Paris, the International Chamber of Commerce – for years silent on the question of East-West economic relations – declared its wholehearted support for these ventures.

But the driving force has come mainly from Socialist countries which have been prompted by the following considerations. First, to secure Western technological know-how and to keep abreast of the latest achievements in the West. Second, to master and apply the latest Western organizational and management methods as well as the marketing techniques which produce results in the highly competitive Western markets. Third, to secure capital. These countries realize that for continued growth, capital of the sort that the West alone can provide is essential. Some of them, such as Poland, are faced with unemployment. Fourth, to ease their desperate foreign-exchange situation through direct inter-enterprise arrangements as to the provision of capital, and by availing themselves of Western marketing channels.

E. SOLVING EAST-WEST TRADE PROBLEMS

East-West trade is a more fertile plane for bringing the West and the Bloc together on a sound basis than any other sphere of their relations. Trade is so obviously of tangible benefit to both sides and, as the last decade has demonstrated, given sufficient goodwill on each side most problems arising on this plane are not insoluble. In this section we shall briefly consider how the East and the West have been brought closer together by a gradual process of removing obstacles to trade which separated the two divisions for a long time, and which indeed some ten years ago appeared to defy solution.

There is still a large number of outstanding problems in East-West trade, but the concessions made on each side so far have eliminated many glaring cases of discrimination, provided an easier access to markets and have created a vested interest in further accommodation and reconciliation.

(*i*) *Quantitative restrictions.* Many discriminatory restrictions in the past were in fact defensive and retaliatory measures, but with improving goodwill on both sides they are becoming pointless. A very large proportion of Western imports from most European Socialist countries have been gradually freed from the previous highly specific and detailed annual quotas rigidly enforced. Experience has shown that the latter countries have not recklessly flooded Western markets following this liberalization. Quantitative restrictions and prohibitions on exports of strategic value to the Bloc are no longer a significant factor in impeding further growth of East-West trade. In the Bloc, especially in the European CMEA countries, foreign-trade plans are now more flexible, and the actual quantities of many categories of goods to be exported or imported are left to the initiative of the foreign-trade corporations and industrial enterprises. Trade agreements with Western countries are not as specific as with other Socialist or with Developing countries; they are rather terms of reference ('umbrella agreements') than rigid quantitative plans. In contrast to their previous practice, the more developed Socialist countries are now prepared to import more consumer goods from the West.

(*ii*) *Pricing of exported and imported goods.* Foreign-trade efficiency calculations, a new approach to costs and the planning of foreign trade in value terms in most Socialist countries are reducing the risk of erratic pricing of their exports, otherwise typical of these countries in the past. On many occasions in recent years, all Bloc countries have exhibited a remarkable degree of restraint in pushing low-priced exports which might cause market disruption in the West. At the same time, the authorities in Western countries have also shown more restraint than in the past in declaring any Socialist export drive as 'dumping'. As a result of the work jointly carried out under the auspices of the European Commission for Europe, Western countries also appear to be less inclined to impose arbitrary surcharges (internal taxes, differentiated transport rates, etc.) on imports from Eastern Europe. Some Socialist countries, notably Czechoslovakia and Hungary, have taken steps to price some imports at their foreign-exchange equivalents to expose their domestic enterprises to healthy competition, so as to achieve greater efficiency.

(*iii*) *Tariffs*. Today, Western countries extend the MFN tariff treatment to more Socialist countries than they did ten years ago, and the latter have usually undertaken to increase their imports in return. The reluctance to put retaliatory measures into effect against the Common Market and EFTA indicates the conciliatory disposition of the Bloc countries. In 1963–64 the ECE Ad Hoc Group, consisting of Western and Eastern European experts, examined the question of MFN in application to market and centrally planned economies, and worked out some practical solutions to ensure effective reciprocity (see Ch. 8 C).

(*iv*) *Multilateralization of trade and payments*. The appeal of bilateralism to Socialist countries is no longer as strong as it used to be (see Ch. 10 B). The degree of multilateral balancing in East-West trade has been increasing in the last decade (see Table XXVI, p. 209), aided by the extension of multiangular operations, the voluntary clearing scheme operated by ECE and the gradual extension of the transferability of balances accorded by Western to most Socialist countries. The multilateral system of settlements under CMEA (the International Bank for Economic Co-operation) provides a promising step towards creating favourable conditions for the multilateralization of East-West trade [see Ch. 10 D(*c*), (*d*)]. The increasing liberalization of imports from Socialist countries has helped in easing the main brake on the growth of East-West trade – the Bloc's shortage of convertible foreign exchange.

(*v*) *Credits*. In the last decade, particularly since 1963, Western countries have gradually overcome their previous reluctance to extend credits to the Bloc. Today, practically all Western nations grant credits for periods of up to fifteen years on exports of both manufactures and of primary products, and most Western governments now provide guarantees on such credits (see Ch. 10 E). Socialist countries have proved reputable borrowers. So far they have repaid all commercial credits in full, and often ahead of the due dates (see Ch. 10 F).

(*vi*) *Uncertainty*. With the Cold War having receded and the primacy of commercial considerations gaining ground, much of the uncertainty that surrounded East-West trade in the past has been removed. A stabilizing effect is also produced by the recent tendency for East-West trade agreements to cover longer periods – 3–6 years instead of the annual periods common in the past. When Mr Kosygin paid his well-publicized visit to Britain in February 1967, he made an offer to enter into an 8-year trade and development agreement between the two countries. In 1966 the United Nations published a detailed bibliography of the economic plans and intentions of the 12 Socialist and 19 Western countries.[1] Hopes have been expressed in both the East and the West that similar publications will be continued in the future.

(*vii*) *Commercial practices*. The challenge of working out norms to regulate commercial practices in trade between different economic, social and legal systems has been taken up by ECE since its inception. In the past, conditions of trade were generally determined by the older and stronger Western countries, in fact mostly prescribed by British trade associations. As a result of the work of the ECE Trade and Development Committee, several sets of rules have been reformulated so that neither private trading nor State trading enjoys special advantages, nor is either penalized because of the system in force. The rules which have particularly contributed to a healthy normalization of East-West practices include General Conditions of Sale (applicable to durable goods and other engineering articles), insurance and re-insurance contracts, and the standardization of commercial documents.

(*viii*) *Trade promotion*. In contrast to the frosty phases of the Cold War, there is now a growing propensity and scope for trade promotion in the Bloc as well as in the West. Since 1963 there has been a marked relaxation of travel restrictions by the more trade-oriented European Socialist countries, favouring both incoming and outgoing commercial, technical and management personnel. Contrary to what is generally believed in the West, market research is no longer the royal preserve of a developed market economy. A Socialist trade expert recently stated, 'The

[1] United Nations, *Economic and Social Development Plans*, New York 1966.

planning of foreign trade is, in fact, becoming more and more perspective market research.'[1] Moreover, methods of market analysis are becoming nearly identical under Capitalism and Socialism – public opinion research, the law of diminishing utility, the equalization of marginal utilities, income elasticity of demand, substitution effect, cyclical changes, etc.[2] Prompted by foreign-trade efficiency studies (see Ch. 14 B, C) and the need for more foreign exchange, Socialist countries have taken to intensive studies of Western markets and are even hiring Western agencies for the purpose. Apart from trade fairs and exhibitions, advertising is now an important medium in East-West trade promotion. Socialist advertisements in the West are becoming a common feature. Advertising by Western firms is now permitted in practically all European Socialist countries, and it is done quite regularly in trade journals, special directories, on radio and even television,[3] and, as well, Western newspapers and magazines are now more easily available. In their search for market opportunities in East Europe, Western firms can avail themselves of the services not only of the Socialist Chambers of Commerce but also of market research institutes, publicity companies and agencies which have been mushrooming in these countries recently. In 1968 there were at least a dozen agency companies in existence in Bulgaria (2), Czechoslovakia (3) and Hungary (8) established to represent foreign firms seeking business in these countries.[4] Plans are not as rigid as they were in the past and there is scope for demand creation, particularly in respect of items relevant to developmental programmes. The scope for developing market opportunities in Albania and the Asian Socialist countries is still severely limited.

[1] H. Ehrlich, *Handel zagr.*, 11/1965, p. 544.

[2] Especially see the following articles: S. Varga, 'The Importance of Market Research in Socialism', *Øst Økonomie*, Oslo, Dec. 1962, pp. 233–43; H. Rymarcewicz *Aussenhandel*, Parts I, II and III 1/1966, pp. 17–20, 3/1966, pp. 24–26 and 5/1966, pp. 21–24; A. H. Krzymiński, *Handel zagr.*, 7/1966, pp. 313–16.

[3] Foreign firms can now advertise on Soviet radio at $600 and on television at $2,000 per minute, provided that the content is 'informative and intelligent'. (Reported in the *Amer. Rev. of East-West Trade*, 6/1968, p. 91.) For details of the theory and practice of advertising under Socialism see I. Ivanov, *Vnesh. torg.*, 10/1964, pp. 36–37; T. Sztucki, *Plan i rynek w obrocie towarowym* (The Role of Planning and the Market Mechanism in Trade), PWE, Warsaw 1966, esp. pp. 192–202; W. Kielanowski, *Handel zagr.*, 2/1967, pp. 72–75; W. Kupferschmidt, *Aussenhandel*, 2/1967, pp. 44–46.

[4] *Amer. Rev. of East-West Trade*, 6/1968, p. 80.

CH. 15 §E EAST-WEST TRADE 389

(*ix*) *Settlement of trade disputes.* Many Western and Socialist countries worked together for a number of years to prepare mutually acceptable rules for the arbitration of trade disputes. By now most of them have ratified the UN Convention on the Recognition and Enforcement of Foreign Arbitral Awards of 1958, and the European Convention on International Commercial Arbitration of 1961 (see Ch. 13 C). These are great achievements, which for a long time seemed hardly possible. The existence of a satisfactory system for the settlement of disputes tends to regularize trade, and thus to lower its cost and to reduce tension.

The cases outlined above do not represent complete solutions to East-West problems, but at least they provide promising openings to further concordant developments. The fact that these countries, in spite of basic differences in their political, legal, social and economic systems, have managed to work out common solutions to their mutual satisfaction and have agreed to abide by them, makes one wonder if there is any gulf in the area of East-West trade too wide to be bridged.

The degree of commercial convergence has been substantial, and indeed conspicuous, if we compare the situation in the late 1960s with that in the early 1950s, and if we narrow down East-West trade to that between Eastern and Western European countries. For a long time it was virtually impossible to find a kind word in Socialist literature on the Western approach to East-West trade, but referring to recent trends a Socialist economist concluded: 'The new emerging relations between the two systems are basically founded on the principles of equality and mutual advantage as well as respect for the interests of all countries.'[1]

F. BARRIERS TO CONVERGENCE

A study of convergence between the two world divisions via East-West trade would be incomplete without examining the forces operating against the coalescence of the two systems. We shall now bring out the confines circumscribing the scope of commercial co-operation as well as the conditions of a broader nature that may continue to impose limits to

[1] Karl-Heinz Domdey, 'Economic Contacts between Socialist and Capitalist Countries of Europe', *Peace, Freedom and Socialism*, Prague, 9/1965, p. 11.

the further development of organic reconciliation in the sphere of East-West trade.

The evolutionary changes taking place in the form of 'creeping Socialism' in the West and the adoption of elements of Capitalism in Eastern Europe are, upon reflection, not incompatible with the existing system in each case. Endeavouring to minimize the fundamental differences still prevailing is bound to be misleading.

The emerging similarities in the institutional forms and relationships in foreign trade under each system do not necessarily lead to identity in substance. For example, the apparent resemblance of State trading, industry-trade relations, profits and price management, upon closer examination, still embody essential differences. In fact, selective adaptations may remove main weaknesses, thus strengthening each system and preventing further convergence. On each side, there is too much vested ideological and economic interest in preserving the existing order and even hostility to the other system. As long as the US Government does not adopt a policy of disarmament, the large American concerns, which could easily increase sales of manufactures to the Bloc, will be reluctant to do so for fear of antagonizing the Department of Defense, their largest and most regular customer.

East-West trade, even though steadily growing, has proved in several respects a rather precarious bond linking the two world divisions. Accusations of discrimination in East-West trade have a long history and it is difficult to see if the grounds can be removed completely in the future. Some cases of discrimination have been engineered as calculated schemes to weaken the other side. Others, although a logical consequence of the system in force, have been interpreted by the other party as deliberate acts of economic warfare. Co-operation in the selected fields has been prompted not by lofty yearnings for international harmony but simply by the pressing need for devising remedies to common problems, each side thinking only of its own advantage.

The co-operative effort has been, in fact, concentrated on 'working agreements', i.e. on removing the most obvious practical obstacles, scratching the surface rather than going to the very roots of the issues. The need for a complete and mutually acceptable set of rules, practices and discipline has been felt by the trading community in both the West and in the Bloc for a long time. But so far, no such general agreement has

CH. 15 §F EAST-WEST TRADE   391

proved possible, not even in the Economic Commission for Europe. The conclusion on the efforts in this direction reached by a member country's delegation is worth quoting: 'it seems not practical in the Austrian view, to establish general rules for east-west trade . . . it has rather to be left to each member country to judge for itself in which way an optimal development of east-west trade based on the principle of mutual advantages can be reached.'[1]

There are still many undercurrents in the West, some of them not easily identifiable, running counter to mutual understanding and the synthesis of the two systems. The relaxation of Western restrictions and other discriminatory measures has not, in general, applied to half the number of the Bloc countries (Albania, East Germany, Mainland China, Mongolia, North Korea and North Vietnam). Taking the West as a whole, its trade with the Bloc is of no critical importance (see Table XII, p. 54) and, owing to the acute shortage of foreign exchange in Socialist countries, the West does not see any spectacular trade opportunities there.

Although the United States has partly abandoned her previous anti-Communist crusading fervour, she has not given up the idea of goading Eastern European countries into further reforms and greater independence from the Soviet Union. Professor Brzezinski (who was appointed in 1966 a leading adviser to President Johnson on East-West relations), as well as many other experts, advocates a more active manipulation of trade for American political ends by a system of 'rewards' and 'penalties'.[2] This not only tends to alienate the USSR but is also considered crude and distasteful by many Eastern Europeans, and is viewed as an attempt to interfere in their internal affairs.[3] Brzezinski's ideas on the reunification of Western and Eastern Europe under the leadership of the United States is not acceptable to Socialist countries because it means continued American support of West German re-

---

[1] ECE, *Further Work of the Ad Hoc Group to Study Problems of East-West Trade in Implementation of Commission Resolution 9 (XVI)*, Doc. E/ECE/553, 3/3/1965, Annex, p. 1 (this fact and quotation were first pointed out by R. Nötel, 'The Role of the United Nations in the Sphere of East-West Trade', *Economia internazionale*, Nov. 1965, p. 656).

[2] See especially Z. Brzezinski, *Alternative to Partition*, McGraw-Hill, New York 1965, p. 154. Also see Ch. 11 B, C, pp. 241-52 above.

[3] For example see R. Werfel, *Nowe drogi* (New Paths), Warsaw, 2/1967, pp. 99–111.

militarization and demands at the expense of Eastern neighbours.[1] This brings us to the forces militating against convergence which operate on the East side.

These forces are, in fact, more numerous and powerful in the Bloc than in the West. Even Liberman, who has become to the Westerners a symbol of economic revisionism, is most emphatic in denying evolutionary trends in the USSR towards capitalism.[2] The reforms in the Soviet Union have been most cautious, and the liberalization has not in fact been extended to foreign trade. In other European CMEA countries, whilst the approach to exports is being liberalized the conduct of imports is still subject to extreme centralization. In Mainland China as well as in Albania, North Korea and North Vietnam, the present regimes are strongly against economic revisionism and against peaceful co-existence with the West.

Even those Socialist leaders who have preached peaceful co-existence limit it in fact to the pragmatic plane, i.e. they really mean peaceful competition in the economic field, trade included. But they categorically refuse to admit the possibility of ideological reconciliation.[3] 'Peaceful co-existence', it was pointed out recently in the editorial of the official organ of the Presidium of the Supreme Soviet, 'does not extend to the sphere of ideology ... ideological struggle between the two social systems cannot cease because it is part and parcel of the class struggle'.[4] Khrushchev, the most vocal propagator of peaceful co-existence of them all, stated frankly in an article written for a leading Western journal on international affairs: 'It can be said without fear of exaggeration that there is no good basis for improvement of relations between our countries other than development of international trade.'[5] Peaceful

---

[1] *Ibid.*, esp. pp. 105–10.

[2] See especially his letters to *The Economist*, 31/10/1964, p. 459 and 26/2/1966, pp. 782–86.

[3] Socialist literature on this subject is quite extensive. Amongst the most interesting articles published in English are: Y. M. Melnikov, 'Critique of the Imperialist Theory of "Ideological Reconciliation",' *International Affairs*, Moscow, 8/1963, pp. 28–30; V. P. Karpov, 'The Soviet Concept of Peaceful Co-existence and Its Implications for International Law', *Law and Contemporary Problems*, Autumn 1964, pp. 858–64; M. Senin, 'The Socialist Countries' Economic Reforms and Foreign Policy', *Intern. Affairs*, Moscow, 2/1966, pp. 5–11.

[4] *Izvestiya*, 28/5/1968, p. 1.

[5] N. Khrushchev, 'On Peaceful Co-existence', *Foreign Affairs*, Oct. 1959, p. 16.

co-existence as viewed by Socialist leaders does not include an outright condemnation of war; revolutionary civil wars, wars against counter-revolution and wars of national liberation are still accepted by all Socialist regimes as justified.[1]

In fact Socialist thinkers, in the USSR in particular, go even further: they bluntly refute Western speculation on recent converging trends or the possibility of convergence in the future.[2] Whilst the economic revisionism in Eastern Europe has been quickly hailed by Westerners as an evolutionary move towards Capitalism, Socialist leaders view the departures from *laissez-faire* Capitalism in the West not as evidence of a welcome converging trend towards Socialism, but as a process further aggravating 'inherent contradictions' bound to lead to the breakdown of Capitalism.[3] To Socialist leaders, the increasing size of East-West trade does not indicate convergence. Even Lenin and Stalin advocated the use of trade whereby Capitalist countries would merely 'finance their own destruction'. The avid Western response to East-West trade is seen as a proof of contradictions in the Capitalist world.

The value of intra-Bloc ideological conflicts to the West, although of inestimable benefit so far, may be exaggerated in the long run. Whilst there are sharp differences amongst Socialist countries and leaders on the means ('paths'), they still subscribe to the same basic philosophy of Marxism-Leninism. The ultimate goal is crystal-clear to all of them: the inevitable victory of Communism and the collapse of the Capitalist order. The increased diversity in the Bloc, as compared with the Stalinist period, does not necessarily mean that its members will rush

---

[1] The fact that in the Socialist view liberation wars are legal and consistent with peaceful co-existence and with the Charter of the United Nations was reflected in the discussion at the UN Special Committee in New York in March and April 1966. Most Developing countries supported the Socialist stand, against the opposition of the leading Western countries (Australia, Canada, the United Kingdom and the USA). See A. N. Talalayev, *Review of Contemporary Law*, Brussels, 1/1966, pp. 9–17; A. Olszowka, *Sprawy międzynarodowe* (International Affairs), Warsaw, 2/1967, pp. 86–96, esp. p. 88.

[2] For example see, A. P. Butenko, *Voprosy filozofii* (Problems of Philosophy) Moscow, 2/1964, pp. 3–13; V. Smolianskii, *Planovoe khoziaistvo* (Planned Economy), Moscow, 7/1965, pp. 18–24; E. Bregel, *Mirovaya ekonomika i mezhdunarodnye otnosheniya* (World Economy and International Relations), Moscow, 1/1968, pp. 3–14.

[3] See M. B. Mitin and V. S. Semenov, *Voprosy filozofii*, 5/1965, pp. 35–46; A. Pokrovskii, *Mirovaya ekonomika...*, 3/1966, pp. 70–80; I. Dvorkin, *Mirovaya ekonomika...*, 2/1967, pp. 51–63.

into the arms of the West; in fact it may prove a new source of strength. In spite of many acrimonious quarrels, Rumania after all has not deserted CMEA, neither China nor the USSR has defected to the West, nor has Czechoslovakia, whilst Yugoslavia is slowly returning to the Socialist fold.

The national interests of the Eastern European countries postulate close co-operation with the Soviet Union, their most important trading partner and an indispensable ally against West German militarism and revanchism. The more Western-inclined of these countries will continue to be restrained by the USSR from too much involvement with the West, and by East Germany from reconciliation with West Germany. Some sort of working accommodation in Sino-Soviet relations cannot be ruled out after Mao Tse-tung and the Cultural Revolution fade away from the scene, and this may be followed by a redirection of China's trade back into intra-Bloc channels.

Although Western and Socialist countries have joined many international organizations bearing on East-West trade, membership in itself does not necessarily mean active and harmonious participation in the work of such bodies.[1] Besides, hardly any Asian Socialist countries are represented in them. For a variety of political and economic considerations, the Socialist Bloc has been looking for trade to Developing nations, and in fact since the Korean War the Bloc's trade with them has been rising at a much faster rate than with the West (see Table XXVIII, p. 257). There are many good reasons for this trend to continue in the future. Socialist countries are likely to keep on pressing for an International Trade Organization under the wings of the United Nations to replace GATT. In such an organization they are almost certain to side with the Developing World against the West, as they did at the 1964 United Nations Conference on Trade and Development.

The growth of joint East-West ventures has been, and will continue to be, hampered by several factors. In most cases the co-operation has been rather limited in scope and often short-lived. Western firms find little freedom of manoeuvre in the centrally planned economies, whilst their

[1] For example, on the clashes between Western countries and the USSR in the United Nations see R. N. Gardner, 'The Soviet Union and the United Nations', *Law and Contemporary Problems*, Autumn 1964, pp. 845–57. Also see A. Z. Rubinstein, *The Soviets in International Organizations. Changing Policy Towards Developing Countries 1953–63*, Princeton UP 1964.

Socialist partners are virtually unrestricted in their operations in the West. The Bonn Government is against West German firms' partnership with Socialist enterprises in East Germany or those in the ex-German territories now forming part of Poland. On the other hand, Socialist countries are critical of the Western concerns' designs for 'islands of Capitalist property'. A Polish economist expressed this discomfort in the following words: 'In some cases, capitalist concerns, especially West Germany, are anxious to acquire property in the Socialist countries. These transparent designs, aimed at weakening the resistance of socialist countries to imperialist infiltration and undermining their unity, are all pathetic attempts to return to a past that has gone never to return.'[1]

Other factors which have tended to destabilize East-West relations and trade, and which are likely to continue to do so in the future, include the regional economic groupings, the great-power chauvinism, and the question of the two Germanies, Chinas, Koreas and Vietnams. The work of the European Commission for Europe will continue to be, as it has been, handicapped by the exclusion of East Germany from membership. Besides, new divergencies, no doubt, will crop up sooner or later.

There are many indications suggesting that East-West trade will continue to grow, in the near future at least. But there will have to be a lot more converging along the East-West trading front in the brave new world to come to restore the relative importance of East-West trade to its pre-World War II level. This can be gauged from the figures for 1938 and 1967 given below:

East-West trade as a percentage

	1938	1967
(a) of world trade	6·4%	2·8%
(b) of total Western trade	9·5%	4·1%
(c) of the Bloc's total trade	73·8%	25·2%

If the trend since the Korean War (1953–1967) continues in the future, East-West trade will regain its relative pre-World War II importance in world trade not earlier than in the year 2,000. The growth of trade in itself is, of course, no guarantee of the coalescence of the two systems or even of peaceful co-existence.

[1] S. Kozinski, 'Economic Relations Between the Socialist and Capitalist Countries', *Peace, Freedom and Socialism,* 7/1965, p. 13.

A Selected Bibliography

I. UNITED NATIONS SOURCES

A. Periodical Publications

Commodity Trade Statistics, New York; annual.

Direction of International Trade and *Direction of Trade*, International Monetary Fund and International Bank for Reconstruction and Development, New York; annual and monthly issues.

Economic Bulletin for Europe, Economic Commission for Europe, Geneva; about three issues a year.

Economic Survey of Europe, Economic Commission for Europe, Geneva; annual.

Economic Survey of Asia and the Far East, Economic Commission for Asia and the Far East, New York; annual.

Monthly Bulletin of Statistics, Statistical Office of the United Nations, New York.

Staff Papers, International Monetary Fund, Washington; three issues a year.

Statement of Treaties and International Agreements, New York; monthly.

Yearbook of International Trade Statistics, Statistical Office of the United Nations, New York.

Yearbook of National Accounts Statistics, Statistical Office of the United Nations, New York.

B. Books, Monographs, Reports

European Commission for Europe, *Further Work of the Ad Hoc Group to Study Problems of East-West Trade in Implementation of Commission Resolution 9 (XVII)*, Doc. E/ECE/553, Geneva, 3/3/1965.

United Nations Conference on Trade and Development, *Proceedings of the United Nations Conference on Trade and Development, Geneva 23 March–16 June 1964*, New York 1964; 8 volumes.

UNCTAD, *State Trading in the ECAFE Region*, Doc. E/CONF. 46/32, Geneva 1964.

II. WESTERN SOURCES

A. Periodical Publications

American Economic Review, American Economic Association, Stanford; quarterly.

American Journal of International Law, American Society of International Law, Washington; quarterly.

American Review of East-West Trade, Symposium Press, New York; monthly.

Asian Survey, University of California, Berkeley; monthly.

The Battle Act Report, Mutual Defense Assistance Control Act, Washington; annual (formerly semi-annual).

Board of Trade Journal, HMSO, London; weekly.

China Quarterly, Congress for Cultural Freedom, London.

Co-existence, Oxford; semi-annual.

Columbia Law Review, Columbia University, New York; 8 issues a year.

East-West Commerce, London; monthly.

Economia Internazionale, University of Genoa; quarterly.

Economica, London School of Economics; quarterly.

Economic Journal, Royal Economic Society, Cambridge; quarterly.

Economic Record, Economic Society of Australia and New Zealand, Melbourne; quarterly.

Economics of Planning, Norwegian Institute of International Affairs, Oslo; three issues a year.

Economie Appliquée, Institute of Applied Economics, Paris; quarterly.

The Economist, London; weekly.

Exports by Commodities, Dominion Bureau of Statistics, Ottawa; monthly.

Foreign Affairs, Council on Foreign Relations, New York; quarterly.

Intereconomics, Hamburg Institute for International Economics; monthly.

International Affairs, Royal Institute of International Affairs, London; quarterly.

International and Comparative Law Quarterly, British Institute of International and Comparative Law, London.

International Associations, Union of International Associations, Brussels monthly.

Kyklos, Basle; quarterly.

Law and Contemporary Problems, Duke University, Durham (USA); quarterly.

Minerals Yearbook, US Dept. of Mines, Washington.

Mining, London; monthly.

Oriental Economist, Tokyo; monthly.

Oversea Trade Bulletin, Commonwealth Bureau of Census and Statistics, Canberra; annual.

Parliamentary Debates (House of Representatives, Senate), Commonwealth of Australia, Canberra; irregular.

Petroleum Press Service, London; monthly.

Proposed Economic Assistance Programs, Agency for International Development, Washington; annual.

Reports, Tariff Board, Canberra; irregular.

Review of Contemporary Law, International Association of Democratic Lawyers, Brussels; semi-annual.

Review of Economics and Statistics, Harvard University; quarterly.

Soviet Studies, University of Glasgow; quarterly.

Statistical Abstract of the United States, US Dept. of Commerce, Washington; annual.

United Kingdom Balance of Payments, Central Statistical Office, London; annual.

The Wheat Situation, Bureau of Agricultural Economics, Canberra; semi-annual.

Wirtschaftsdienst, Hamburg; monthly.

World Wheat Statistics, International Wheat Council, London; semi-annual.

Yearbook of International Organizations, Union of International Associations, Brussels; bi-annual.

B. Books, Monographs, Reports

G. Adler-Karlsson, *Western Economic Warfare 1947–67*, Almqvist & Wicksell, Stockholm 1968.

Z. Brzezinski, *Alternative to Partition*, McGraw-Hill, New York 1965.

S. F. Clabaugh and R. V. Allen, *East-West Trade – Its Strategic Implications. Analysis and Inventory of Congressional Documents 1959–63*, Center for Strategic Studies, Washington 1964.

Committee for Economic Development, *East-West Trade – A Common Policy for the West*, New York 1965.

W. M. Corden, *Recent Developments in the Theory of International Trade*, Princeton University 1965.

A. Eckstein, *Communist China's Economic Growth and Foreign Trade*, McGraw-Hill, New York 1966.

European League for Economic Co-operation, *East-West Commercial Relations*, Study Conference Held in May 1965, Brussels 1965.

M. I. Goldman, *Soviet Foreign Aid*, Praeger, New York 1967.

Pauline Lewin, *The Foreign Trade of Communist China*, Praeger, New York 1964.

J. D. Montgomery, *Foreign Aid in International Politics*, Prentice-Hall, New York 1967.

F. O'Brien, *Crisis in World Communism*, Committee for Economic Development, New York 1965.

J. W. Fulbright, *Old Myths and New Realities*, Jonathan Cape, London 1965.

GATT, *Anti-Dumping and Countervailing Duties*, Geneva, July 1958.

GATT, Report of Group of Experts, *Anti-Dumping and Countervailing Duties*, Geneva 1961.

K. Grzybowski, *The Socialist Commonwealth of Nations*, Yale UP, New Haven and London 1964.

G. Haberler, *A Survey of International Trade Theory*, Princeton University 1961.

M. L. Harvey, *East-West Trade and United States Policy*, National Association of Manufacturers, New York 1966.

G. F. Kennan, *On Dealing with the Communist World*, Harper & Row, New York 1964.

H. Köhler, *Economic Integration in the Soviet Bloc, with an East German Case Study*, Praeger, New York and London 1965.

A. Kutt, *Prices and Balance Sheet in 10 years of Soviet – Captive Countries' Trade 1955–1964*, Assembly of Captive European Nations, New York, March 1966.

F. L. Pryor, *The Communist Foreign Trade System*, George Allen & Unwin, London 1963.

H. Rosovsky (ed.), *Industrialization and Foreign Trade*, John Wiley & Sons, New York 1966.

C. M. Schmitthoff, *The Sources of the Law of International Trade with Special Reference to East-West Trade*, Stevens & Sons, London 1964.

P. E. Uren (ed.), *East-West Trade*. A Symposium. Canadian Institute of International Affairs, Toronto 1966.

US Congress, House, Select Committee on Export Control, *Investigation and Study of the Administration, Operation and Enforcement of the Export Control Act of 1949 and Related Acts*, GPO, Washington 1964.

US Senate, *A Background Study on East-West Trade*, Prepared for the Committee on Foreign Relations, GPO, Washington 1965.

US Senate, *East-West Trade*, Hearings before the Committee on Foreign Relations; Part I, March 13, 16, 23, April 8, 9, 1964, GPO, Washington 1964; Part II, February 24, 25, 26, 1965, GPO, Washington 1965.

US Senate, *US Policy with Respect to Mainland China*, Hearings before the Committee on Foreign Relations, March 8, 10, 16, 18, 21, 28, 30, 1966, GPO, Washington 1966.

III. SOCIALIST SOURCES

A. Periodical Publications

Annuarul statistic al Republicii Socialiste România (Statistical Yearbook of the Rumanian Socialist Republic), Central Statistical Board, Bucharest.

Aussenhandel, East Berlin; monthly.

Czechoslovak Economic Papers, Czechoslovak Academy of Sciences, Prague; irregular.

Czechoslovak Foreign Trade, Chamber of Commerce, Prague; monthly.

BIBLIOGRAPHY

Ekonomicheskaya gazeta (Economic Gazette), Central Committee of the Communist Party of the Soviet Union, Moscow; weekly.

Ekonomista (The Economist), Polish Economic Society, Polish Academy of Sciences, Warsaw; bi-monthly.

Finanse (Finance), State Economic Publications Centre, Warsaw; monthly.

Gospodarka planowa (Planned Economy), State Economic Publications Centre, Warsaw; monthly.

Handel zagraniczny (Foreign Trade), Polish Chamber of Foreign Trade, Warsaw; monthly.

Hung-ch'i (Red Flag), organ of the Chinese Communist Party, Peking; daily.

Ikonomicheski zhivot (Economic Life), Central Committee of the Bulgarian Communist Party, Sofia; weekly.

International Affairs, All-Union Society 'Znaniye', Moscow; monthly.

Izvestiya (The News), Presidium of the Supreme Soviet of the USSR, Moscow; daily.

Jin-chi Yen-chiu (Economic Research), Peking; monthly.

Kommunist (The Communist), Central Committee of the Communist Party of the Soviet Union, Moscow; 18 issues a year.

Közgazdasági szemle (Economic Review), Institute of Economics, Budapest; monthly.

Külkereskedelem (Foreign Trade), Budapest; monthly.

Mirovaya ekonomika i mezhdunarodnye otnosheniya (World Economy and International Relations), Institute of World Economics and International Relations, Academy of Sciences of the USSR, Moscow; monthly.

Nowe drogi (New Paths), Central Political Committee of the Polish United Workers' Party, Warsaw; monthly.

Peace, Freedom and Socialism, Prague; monthly.

Peking Review; weekly.

Plánované Hospodářstvi (Planned Economy), State Planning Committee, Prague; 10 issues a year.

Planovoe khoziaistvo (Planned Economy), State Planning Commission of the USSR, Moscow; bi-monthly.

Pravda (The Truth), organ of the Communist Party of the Soviet Union, Moscow; daily.

Rocznik statystyczny (Statistical Yearbook), Central Statistical Office of Poland, Warsaw.

Rocznik statystyki handlu zagranicznego (Yearbook of Foreign Trade Statistics), Central Statistical Office of Poland, Warsaw.

Ruch prawniczy, ekonomiczny i socjologiczny (Developments in Law, Economics and Sociology), University of Poznan; quarterly.

Sprawy miedzynarodowe (International Affairs, Polish Institute of International Affairs), Warsaw; monthly.

Statisticka Ročenka CSSR (Statistical Yearbook of the Czechoslovak Socialist Republic), Central Commission for Control and Statistics, Prague.

Statistisches Jahrbuch der Deutschen Demokratischen Republik, State Central Statistical Office, East Berlin.

Vjetari Statistikor i Republikës Popullore te Shqipërise (Statistical Yearbook of the Albanian People's Republic), Statistical Board, Tirana.

Vneshnaya torgovlya (Foreign Trade), Ministry of Foreign Trade of the USSR, Moscow; monthly.

Vneshnaya torgovlya SSSR. Statisticheskii obzor (Foreign Trade of the USSR, Statistical Survey), Ministry of Foreign Trade of the USSR, Moscow; annual.

Voprosy ekonomiki (Problems of Economics), Institute of Economics, Academy of Sciences of the USSR, Moscow; monthly.

Vunshna turgoviya (Foreign Trade), Ministry of Foreign Trade of Bulgaria, Sofia; monthly.

Die Wirtschaft, East Berlin; fortnightly.

Wirtschafts Wissenschaft, East Berlin; monthly.

Życie gospodarcze (Economic Life), Warsaw; weekly.

B. Books, Monographs, Reports

A. Bodnar, *Gospodarka europejskich krajów socjalistycznych. Zarys rozwoju w latach 1950–1975* (The Economies of the European Socialist Countries. An Outline of the Development in the Years 1950–1975), KiW, Warsaw 1962.

R. Chwieduk et al., *Ekonomia polityczna* (Political Economy), PWN, Warsaw 1966; volume II.

L. Ciamaga, *Od wapólpracy do integracji. Zarys organizacji i działalności RWPG w latach 1949–1964* (From Co-operation to Integration. An

BIBLIOGRAPHY

Outline of the Organization and Activity of CMEA over the Period 1949–1964), KiW, Warsaw 1965.

P. Glikman, *Efektywność inwestycji związanych z handlem zagranicznym* (Effectiveness of Investment Relevant to Foreign Trade), PWE, Warsaw 1965.

S. Góra and Z. Knyziak, *Współpraca krajów RWPG a rachunek ekonomiczny* (Co-operation amongst CMEA Countries and the Calculation of Economic Efficiency), PWE, Warsaw 1966.

M. Guzek, *Zasada kosztów komparatywnych a problemy RWPG* (The Principle of Comparative Costs in Relation to the Problems Facing CMEA), PWE, Warsaw 1967.

Z. Kamecki, J. Sołdaczuk and W. Sierpiński, *Międzynarodowe stosunki ekonomiczne* (International Economic Relations), PWE, Warsaw 1964.

J. Krynicki, *Problemy handlu zagranicznego Polski* (Poland's Foreign Trade Problems), PWN, Warsaw 1958.

L. V. Kantorovich, *The Best Use of Economic Resources* (translated from Russian), Harvard UP 1965.

T. Földi (ed.), *Studies in International Economics*, Institute of Economics, Hungarian Academy of Sciences, Budapest 1966.

A. B. Frumkin, *Kritika sovremennykh burzhuaznykh teorii mezhdunarodnykh otnoshenii* (Critique of the Contemporary Bourgeois Theories of International Relations), Vneshnotorgizdat, Moscow 1964.

O. Lange, *Ekonomia polityczna* (Political Economy), vol. I, PWE, Warsaw 1959; vol. II, PWE, Warsaw 1966.

O. Lange, *Essays on Economic Planning*, Asia Publishing House, London 1961.

O. Lange (ed.), *Zagadnienia ekonomii politycznej socjalizmu* (Problems of Socialist Economics), PWN, Warsaw 1958.

J. Masztalerz, *Wymiana towarowa organizacji handlu wewnętrznego* (Foreign Trade and Internal Trading Corporations), IHW, Warsaw 1964.

J. Mujżel, *Stosunki towarowe w gospodarce socjalistycznej* (Commodity Relations in a Socialist Economy), PWE, Warsaw 1963.

Ewa Raszeja-Tobjasz, *Protekcjonizm w rolnictwie Europy Zachodniej* (Protectionism in Western European Agriculture), KiW, Warsaw 1965.

A. Rolow, *Rachunek ekonomiczny w handlu zagranicznym* (Economic Calculations in Foreign Trade), PWG, Warsaw 1960.

J. Rutkowski, *Światowy rynek kredytowy* (The World Credit Market), PWE, Warsaw 1964.

I. Sachs, *Handel zagraniczny a rozwój gospodarczy* (Foreign Trade in the Context of Economic Development), PWE, Warsaw 1963.

G. L. Shagalov, *Ekonomicheskaya effektivnost tovarnogo obmena mezhdu sotsialisticheskimi stranami* (Economic Effectiveness of Commodity Exchanges between Socialist Countries), Mysl, Moscow 1966.

J. V. Stalin, *Economic Problems of Socialism in the USSR*, Foreign Languages Publishing House, Moscow 1952.

T. Sztucki, *Plan i rynek w obrocie towarowym* (Planning and the Market Mechanism in Commodity Circulation), PWE, Warsaw 1966.

The Road to Communism, Documents of the 22nd Congress of the Communist Party of the Soviet Union, Foreign Languages Publishing House, Moscow 1961.

W. Trzeciakowski, *Metody wyznaczania kursu granicznego i uproszczone metody analizy efektywności handlu zagranicznego* (Methods of Determining the Marginal Exchange Rate and Simplified Methods of Analysis of Foreign Trade Effectiveness), Institute for the Study of Economic Fluctuations and Prices in Foreign Trade, Warsaw 1964.

J. Tudrej, *Współczesny kapitalizm a planowanie* (Contemporary Capitalism and Planning), LTN, Łódź 1964.

B. S. Vaganov, *Vneshnaya torgovlya sotsialisticheskikh stran. Voprosy teorii* (Foreign Trade of Socialist Countries. Problems of Theory), Mezhdunarodnye Otnosheniya, Moscow 1966.

Imre Vajda, *The Role of Foreign Trade in a Socialist Economy*, Corvina Press, Budapest 1965.

W. Wilczyński, *Rachunek ekonomiczny a mechanizm rynkowy* (Economic Calculation and the Market Mechanism), PWE, Warsaw 1965.

J. Zieleniewski and S. Szczypiorski, *Zasady organizacji i techniki handlu zagranicznego* (Principles of the Organization and Conduct of Foreign Trade), PWE, Warsaw 1963.

IV. OTHER SOURCES

A. *Periodical Publications*

China Mainland Review, University of Hong Kong; quarterly.

China Trade Report, Far Eastern Economic Review, Hong Kong; monthly.
Current Scene, Hong Kong; monthly.
Far Eastern Economic Review, Hong Kong; weekly.
Yearbook, Far Eastern Economic Review, Hong Kong.

B. *Books, Monographs, Reports*

Kao Hsian-kao, *Chinese Communist Foreign Trade and Diplomacy*, Asian People's Anti-Communist League, Taipei 1964.

Index of Names

Abramov, F., 337n.
Adenauer, K., 275
Adler-Karlsson, G., 128n., 261n., 288n.
Agaston, I., 336
Akihiro Amano, 69n.
Allen, R. V., 399
Altman, O., 126n., 196n., 214
Amundsen, G. L., 336
Apro, A., 338n.
Arzumanian, A. A., 349n.
Aubrey, H. G., 146n.

Babashkin, L., 330n.
Balassa, B., 69n.
Balazsy, S., 322n., 329n.
Balogh, T., 73n., 179
Bareau, P., 196n.
Baruch, B. M., 275
Baykov, A., 377n.
Belous, T., 128n.
Behrman, H. J., 307n.
Behrman, N., 107n., 109n., 203n., 206, 344
Berg, M. von, 196n.
Bhagwati, J., 354n.
Bielecki, J., 217n.
Bird, Jean, 239n.
Biro, J., 78n.
Bloodworth, D., 361n.
Böckenstiegel, K. H., 295n.
Bodnar, A., 50n.
Bodnar, J., 226
Bogomolov, O., 266n.
Böhmisch, A., 350n.
Bolski, S., 128n., 334n.
Bornstein, M., 215n.
Bożyk, 341n.
Brauer, R., 66n.
Bregel, E., 393n.
Bresciani-Turroni, C., 63
Brus, W., 99n.
Brzezinski, Z., 195n., 225n., 238, 249n., 391
Budinov, I., 89n.
Bukowski, W., 128n.

Bush, K., 196n.
Butenko, A. P., 393n.
Byé, M., 63

Campbell, R. W., 215n.
Castro, F., 276
Černiansky, V., 66, 312, 364n.
Černik, O., 360
Chamberlain, N. W., 349n.
Chamberlin, E., 63
Chenery, H. B., 73n.
Ch'in Liu-fang, 180n.
Chou, S. H., 179n.
Chou En-lai, 236
Churchill, W. C., 236
Chwieduk, R., 135n., 316n.
Ciamaga, L., 50n.
Clabaugh, S. F., 399
Colm, G., 350n.
Conner, A., 89n.
Corden, W. M., 64n.
Cornelisse, P. A., 26n.
Coudert, A. C., 159n., 174n.
Czepurko, A., 114n.

Dalrymple, Dana, 185
Denisov, B., 349n.
Diatchenko, V., 162n., 187n.
Dillon, D., 273n.
Domdey, K.-H., 229n., 265n., 359n., 360n., 389n.
Domke, M., 132n., 133n., 301n.
Donnelly, D., 307n.
Drummond, I. M., 89n.
Dubonosov, A. J., 366n.
Dudinskii, I., 338n.
Dvorak, L., 67n.
Dvorkin, I., 393n.
Dzikiewicz, L., 365n.

Eckstein, A., 196n., 201n., 203n., 399
Edgeworth, F. Y., 63
Ehrlich, H., 112n., 388n.
Ellsworth, P. T., 63
Enderlein, F., 364n., 365n.

INDEX OF NAMES 407

Engels, F., 64
Eorsi, G., 299n.
Erroll, F., 107n., 160
Evstignyev, R., 364n.

Falkowski, M., 67n.
Fawcett, J. E. S., 132n.
Feng-hwa Ma, 336
Fensterwald, B., 243n.
Fiszel, H., 327n.
Földi, T., 41n.
Frumkin, A., 71n., 171n.
Fulbright, J. W., 256, 359

Gardner, R. N., 394n.
Garvey, G., 350n.
Georgiev, G. S., 77n., 364n.
Glikman, P., 312n.
Głowacki, J., 61n., 324n., 329n.
Goldman, M. I., 89n., 253n.
Gondos, P., 114n.
Góra, S., 66n., 74n.
Gräbig, G., 61n.
Griffith, W. E., 249
Grote, G., 114n., 326n.
Grzybowski, K., 295n., 296n., 307n.
Guzek, M., 74n.

Haberler, G., 63, 64n., 69n., 73, 135n., 354
Hamman, G., 365n.
Hamouz, F., 333n.
Harasim, E., 127n., 335n.
Harrod, R. F., 64
Harvey, M. L., 29n., 62n., 239n., 241n.
Hazard, J. N., 132n., 133n., 241n.
Heckscher, E., 63
Herman, K., 314n.
Hirschman, A. O., 64
Hodges, L., 228
Hoffman, E., 336
Hoffman, M. L., 88n., 107n., 134n., 375n.
Holzman, F. D., 125, 126n., 169n., 336, 337
Hsueh Mu-ch'ao, 182n.
Hume, D., 63
Humin, S., 318n., 322n.
Humphrey, H., 274
Hungdah Chiu, 299n.
Hunsicker, J., 330n.

Ivanov, I., 388n.

Jakubowski, J., 302n.
Johnson, H. G., 11–14, 63
Johnson, L. B. J., 248ff., 391

Kaganov, E. D., 61n.
Kaldor, N., 64
Kamecki, Z., 50n., 51n., 71n., 73n., 111n., 136n., 176n., 180n., 344n., 355n.
Kantorovich, L. V., 215
Kao Hsiang-kao, 237n., 287n.
Kaser, M., 336
Karpov, V. P., 392n.
Kennan, G. F., 268, 353n.
Kennedy, J. F., 250
Khrushchev, N., 29, 135n., 161, 236ff., 284, 292, 353, 355n., 356, 392
Kielanowski, W., 388n.
Knyziak, Z., 66n., 74n.
Köhler, H., 336, 345n.
Kolacz, J., 179n.
Konnik, I., 333n.
Konopka, J., 234
Kornai, J., 66, 326
Korovushkin, A., 97n.
Kos Rabcewicz-Zubkowski, L., 307n.
Kosygin, A., 74n., 366n., 387
Kosk, H., 92n.
Kotyński, J., 73n.
Kovacs, L., 86n.
Koziński, S., 395n.
Królak, Z., 212n., 213n.
Krynicki, J., 311n.
Krzymiński, A. H., 388n.
Kück, G., 128n.
Kupferschmidt, W., 388n.
Kutt, A., 169n., 336, 337
Kyosuke Hirotsu, 252n.

Labedz, L., 215n.
Lange, O., 215, 222, 327n.
Lenin, V. I., 20, 64n., 171, 239, 358n., 393
Leontyev, L., 61n.
Leszkowicz, S., 360n.
Lewin, Pauline, 263n., 383n.
Liberman, E., 114, 392
Lim, E. R., 115n.
Lipson, L., 307n.
Liska, T., 312, 326
Litvinov, M., 263
Liu Jih-hsin, 198n.
Lukin, L., 337n.
Luxemburg, Rosa, 64
Lysenko, T. D., 352
Lyubimov, N., 293n., 355n.

McEwen, J., 141n.
Machlup, F., 63
Maier, Erica, 74n.
Maneli, M., 310n.
Mao Tse-tung, 299n., 394

INDEX OF NAMES

Marias, A., 66, 312n.
Marshall, A., 63, 357
Martos, B., 326
Marx, K., 64, 72, 171n., 204n., 224n., 310, 358n.
Masztalerz, J., 86n.
Mazal, J., 303n., 306n.
Meade, J. E., 63
Meissner, K., 86n.
Melnikov, Y. M., 392n.
Mendershausen, H., 169n., 336
Metzler, L. A., 63
Michaely, M., 207n.
Mikesell, R. F., 107n., 109n., 203n., 206, 344
Mill, J. S., 63
Mises, L. von, 355
Mitin, M. B., 393n.
Molotov, V., 91n.
Montgomery, J. D., 253n.
Morgan, T., 345n.
Muszycki, B., 86n., 364n.
Myint, H., 73n., 354
Myrdal, G., 374

Nai-Ruenn, 92n.
Najniger, B., 258n.
Nazarkin, K., 219n., 220, 296n.
Nesterov, M. V., 239
Neuberger, E., 344n.
Niesiołowski, M., 262n.
Nikolov, I., 86n.
Nitz, H. J., 66
Nove, A., 307n.
Nurkse, R., 64
Nykryn, J., 66, 314n.

O'Brien, F., 399
Ohlin, B., 63
Olsevich, Y., 339n.
Orłowski, M., 96n., 97n., 345n.
Otto, G., 330n.
Ovchinnikov, V., 201n.

Pareto, V., 63
Patolichev, N. S., 254
Perroux, J., 63
Pavlat, V., 128n.
Pien Ching-chung, 182n.
Pisar, S., 111n., 302n., 307n.
Piskoppel, F. G., 344n.
Pleva, J., 364n.
Pokrovskii, A., 393n.
Polaczek, S., 323n.
Porowski, J., 180n.
Pryor, F. L., 26n., 207n.
Przelaskowski, W., 217n.

Rachkov, B., 128n., 259n., 260n., 261n., 262n.
Ramzaitsev, D. F., 306n.
Raszeja-Tobjasz, Ewa, 403
Reubens, E. P., 181n.
Ricardo, D., 63, 69
Richman, B. M., 352n.
Robbins, L., 355
Robinson, Joan, 63, 73n.
Roginskii, G., 71n.
Rolow, A., 66, 312n., 322n., 327n.
Rosovsky, H., 400
Rouscik, L., 66
Rubinshtein, G., 334n., 365n.
Rubinstein, A. Z., 394n.
Rusk, D., 236, 276
Rutkowski, J., 226n., 255n.
Rymarcewicz, H., 388

Sachs, I., 67n., 71n., 356n.
Samuelson, P., 64
Sanders, P., 21n., 307n.
Sawyer, Carole A., 253n.
Schermer, G., 62n.
Schiller, B. R., 73n., 354n.
Schmidt, J. L., 67n.
Schmitthoff, C. M., 296n.
Schroeder, G., 249n.
Semenov, V. S., 393n.
Senin, M., 392n.
Senkowski, H., 296n., 297n.
Shabad, T., 199n.
Shaffer, H. W., 225
Shagalov, G. L., 310n., 312n., 314n., 327n.
Sheynov, K., 78n.
Shiina, E., 229n.
Sierpiński, W., 50n., 51n., 71n., 73n., 111n., 136n., 176n., 344n., 355n.
Šik, O., 350
Siotis, J., 212n., 356n., 374n.
Silyanov, E., 114n.
Smolianskii, V., 393n.
Soky, D., 334n.
Sołdaczuk, J., 50n., 51n., 71n., 73n., 111n., 136n., 176n., 344n., 355n.
Sölle, H., 83n.
Spulber, N., 363
Stalin, J. V., 48, 49n., 53n., 171n., 393
Stefański, M., 114n.
Stolte, S. C., 146n., 260n.
Struminski, J., 92n.
Szabados, J., 324n.
Szanyi, J., 364n.
Szczypiorski, S., 81n., 86n., 87n., 103n., 111n., 112n., 113n., 200n., 297n., 303n., 377n., 378n.

INDEX OF NAMES 409

Sztucki, T., 388 n.
Sztyber, W., 182
Szwarc, K., 330 n.

Talalayev, A. N., 393 n.
Talas, B., 334 n.
Tarnovskii, O., 92 n.
Thornton, H., 63
Tinbergen, J., 348
Toczek, S., 41 n., 110 n., 175 n.
Torrens, R., 69
Toynbee, A. J., 268 n.
Trammer, H., 296 n., 297 n.
Trąmpczyński, W., 328 n.
Truman, H., 237
Trzeciakowski, W., 61 n., 66, 323, 324
Tudrej, J., 349 n.

Uren, P. E., 89 n.

Vaganov, B. S., 66 n.
Vajda, I., 62 n., 66 n., 71 n., 72 n., 226, 254 n., 341 n., 355 n.
Vassiliev, Y., 350 n.
Viner, J., 63, 64, 138, 355
Vvedensky, G. A., 260 n.

Weiler, J., 63

Wells, D. A., 254 n., 344 n.
Werfel, R., 391
Werner, J., 243 n.
Wesołowski, J., 99 n., 100 n., 323 n.
Więckowski, H., 127 n., 243 n.
Wierzbołowski, J., 310 n., 327 n., 328 n., 329 n., 333 n.
Wilczynski, J., 89 n., 141 n., 163 n., 264 n., 344 n.
Wilczyński, W., 61 n., 62 n., 88 n.–89 n., 163 n., 264 n.
Wojciechowski, B., 329 n.
Wowczyk, W., 233 n.
Wyczalkowski, M. R., 216 n.

Yntema, T. O., 138 n.
Yoshida, S., 229
Yovczuk, S., 179 n., 340 n.

Zahalka, V., 214 n.
Zauberman, A., 169 n., 215 n., 326 n.
Zavolzhky, S., 337 n.
Zebot, C. A., 356 n.
Zhukov, V., 339 n.
Zieleniewski, J., 81 n., 86 n., 87 n., 103 n., 111 n., 112 n., 113 n., 200 n., 297 n., 303 n.
Zwass, A., 96 n., 217 n., 219 n.

Subject Index

Absolute sovereign immunity, doctrine of, 301 n.
'Active Eastern policy', 238
Advertising, 216, 388
Albania, 32, 49n., 76n., 79, 99, 101, 108, 143, 197, 202n., 204, 259n., 263, 274, 278, 295, 349n., 373, 391
Aluminium, 95, 149, 160ff., 175
Anti-dumping arrangements, 126, 143, 155, 172, 173n., 174n., 188
Anti-economism, 114
Australia, 25, 30, 34, 43, 75, 77, 90n., 94, 108, 113, 128, 140ff., 154ff., 180, 191, 193, 210, 223, 227, 244, 262ff., 270ff., 277, 341, 362, 393n.
Austria, 29, 43n., 108, 125, 210, 296ff., 349n., 365, 376ff.
Autarky, 26, 55, 62, 65, 244, 250, 354

Balance-of-payments equilibrium, 68, 98, 324
'Balanced' economic development, 71, 309
Banks in East-West trade, 226, 365–6, 368–9
Barley, 96, 113, 144, 167, 176, 181n., 201
Battle Act, The, 271, 292
Belgium, 25, 31, 75n., 87, 108, 174n., 210, 262n., 271, 292, 349, 365, 376ff.
Berne Union rules, 230
Bilateralism, 51, 94, 105–10, 170, 185, 191, 203–7, 211–12, 218, 220–3, 241, 251, 271, 276, 309, 343
  advantages to Socialist countries, 204–6
  bilateral agreements on industrial, scientific, technical and cultural co-operation, 376
  bilateral balancing of trade, 191, 203–4, 212, 220
  bilateral clearing account, 94, 221
  'bilateral justice', 223
  bilateral trade agreements, 105–10, 190, 203n., 206–7, 211–12, 218, 241, 251, 271
  degree of bilateralism, 204

  different meanings of, 203
Boycotts, 126, 126n., 127n., 243, 253
'Building bridges', 238, 248–9
Bulgaria, 25, 32, 37, 39, 71ff., 78, 83ff., 92, 99ff., 108, 113, 135, 148ff., 200, 204, 216, 233n., 263ff., 278, 295ff., 311, 339, 350, 364, 376, 378ff., 388
Buyer's markets, 104–5

Canada, 25, 30, 34, 43, 74n., 77, 108, 113, 144, 174, 192, 210, 227, 262, 268, 270, 283, 292, 341, 362ff., 393n.
Capital charges, 179, 328, 330
Cellulose, 95, 167
Cement, 95, 149, 167, 180
Ceylon, 95, 146
Chambers of Commerce, 87–8
Chemicals, 95, 152, 156
China, Mainland, 19n., 25, 28, 32, 36ff., 49n., 65, 71ff., 79, 87, 92, 95, 99, 108, 114, 122, 134, 141ff., 173ff., 178ff., 185, 194ff., 208, 229ff., 245, 250ff., 263ff., 272ff., 277, 282ff., 292, 295, 349n., 361, 373, 391, 394ff.
Chin-Com, 272, 285
Clearing of bilateral balances, 183, 212, 219, 221, 223–4
CMEA, 40, 49–51, 61, 65, 68, 73, 85, 102, 122, 179, 191, 218, 305, 337–9, 385
Coal, 166–7, 182, 287
Co-Com, 25, 271–4, 290
Coefficient of investment discount, 322
Coefficients of the relative value of foreign currencies, 98, 322–4
Cold War, 41, 53, 117, 236–41, 246, 267–8, 353
COMECON, see CMEA
Commercial considerations clause, 131–2
Commercial practices, 117, 296, 300, 387
Commercial reputation of Socialist countries, 117, 232–3, 306–7
'Commodity inconvertibility', 126, 214
Comparative advantage, see Theory of comparative costs

Computers, 280–1, 326, 329–30
Consultative Group, 271, 291
Consumer goods, 36, 125, 244, 385
Containment of communism, 237, 242
Convergence of Capitalism and Socialism, 73, 225, 348–54, 361–77, 389, 395
Convertibility of currencies, 137, 183, 213, 218–19, 221, 225, 323
Copper, 252, 278
Co-responsibility of production and foreign trade, 84
Counter-purchases, 94, 200, 206, 260
Countervailing duty, 174
Credits, 62, 141, 144, 219–21, 226–32, 283, 386–7
  as a form of economic aid, 231
  discrimination, 228
  extended by Socialist countries, 226, 386–7
  government guarantees, 228–9
  insurance, 227–9
  interest rates, 227
  liberalization of Western policy, 229–31
  on wheat exported to Socialist countries, 141, 226–7
  short-, medium- and long-term, 226 n.
Creeping socialism, 363, 390
Cuba, 20, 49 n., 76 n., 87 n., 102 n., 130 n., 182, 251, 263, 270, 273, 274, 276 ff., 286
Currency transferability, 53, 133–4
Czechoslovakia, 21, 25, 32, 35 ff., 71, 73, 78 ff., 83 ff., 88 n., 92, 95, 99 ff., 108, 113, 125, 130, 135, 148 ff., 174, 178, 199 ff., 233 n., 254, 259 n., 265 n., 270, 277, 281 ff., 287, 295 ff., 305 ff., 311, 316 n., 318, 332 ff., 377 ff., 350, 364, 373, 376 ff., 386 ff.

Debts and compensation agreements, 233–5
Decentralization, 75, 77, 79, 84, 216, 331–2, 364–5
Denmark, 30, 43 n., 108, 210, 376, 378 ff.
Developing countries, 19, 37, 51, 55, 65, 67, 101, 107, 129, 182, 190, 212, 252, 256–8, 269, 357–8, 394
Development strategy, *see* Industrialization
Diplomatic relations, 269–70
Directive means, 105–6, 112, 116
Discrimination, 41, 104–5, 121–2, 126–32, 138–9, 170, 185, 205, 223, 225, 228, 336, 339, 343 n., 374, 391. *See also* Price discrimination
Dual production, 383
Dumping, 23, 138–90
  accusations by Capitalist countries, 148–54
  and benefits to buyers, 186
  and domestic shortages, 185–6
  and Gresham's law, 154
  by Socialist countries, 146–61
    by China, 147–8
    by Eastern European countries, 147–148
    by the U.S.S.R., 146–8
  by Western countries in the Bloc, 140–6
    of chemicals in China, 145
    of wheat, 141–4
  definitions, 138–9
  disguised, 153–4
  d. duty, 174
  indirect, 182
  'injurious', 139, 145–6, 154–61, 175, 187
  intermittent, 188, 190
  overall appraisal of Socialist, 161–2
  protection against, in a market economy, 172–3
    in a planned economy, 171–2
  reciprocal, 182
  reverse, 138
  specific d. complaints against Socialist countries, 155–7. *See also* Antidumping arrangements

East-West Payments Union, proposed, 226
East-West Trade, 20–33, 41–2, 52–4, 298–9, 246, 251–2, 269–70, 334–42, 354–8, 360, 395
  and 'bourgeois contradictions', 251
  and 'class struggle', 238–9
  and employment, 246
  and Western Communist Parties, 252
  as a growth factor, 360
  changing structure, 41–2
  dependence on, 28–33, 43
  'depoliticizing' of, 269–70, 356
  distinguishing features, 21–4
  in the world scene, 27
  increasing importance of, 44
  proper meaning, 20–1
  role to the Socialist Bloc, 54, 334–6, 341–2
  role to the West, 54, 246, 341–2
  small size of, 27–8, 52
  tendencies in, 52–4, 357–8, 395
ECE, 136, 212, 225, 368, 373–4, 386, 387, 391, 395
Economic integration, 50 n., 60, 122, 220, 359, 374. *See also* CMEA; EEC; EFTA

SUBJECT INDEX

Economic reforms, 68, 77–8, 83–4, 88, 92, 101, 112, 114, 214–18, 265, 330–4
Economic stagnation, 66, 216
EEC, 102, 125, 128, 133, 191, 193, 223, 261, 305, 359
Effective reciprocity, 122–3
Efficiency of foreign trade, *see* Foreign-trade efficiency
EFTA, 47, 386
Egypt, 141, 261, 269
Equimarginal principle, 182, 346
'Equivalent' exchange, 72 n., 125–6. *See also* Gains from trade; Prices; Terms of trade
Errors of judgement, 183–4, 345–6
Exchange rates, 60, 66, 70–1, 96–100, 113, 163–4, 201, 215
and gold, 97
commercial, 97, 99
in a market economy, 96
in a Socialist economy, 97–100, 113
limiting (or marginal), 322–4
multiple, 97
non-commercial, 98–9
relative value of foreign currencies, 322–4
Exploitation in intra-Bloc foreign trade, 169, 336–41
Export prices, 93–4, 164, 181–3, 335–6, 385–6. *See also* Prices
Extensive growth factors, 62, 217

Finland, 28 ff., 43 n., 88, 94 n., 108, 205, 210, 260, 298, 376 ff.
Fluctuations, 68, 198, 206, 256, 344–5
Foreign aid, 115, 251–6, 269, 271
Foreign exchange, *see* International liquidity reserves
Foreign trade corporations, 60, 78–83, 95, 97, 112–13, 125–6, 137, 169–70, 241, 312, 363, 385
criteria for the field of operation, 80–1
monopolistic-monopsonistic power, 78–9, 95, 125
performance and efficiency, 79
Foreign-trade disputes, *see* Settlement of trade disputes
Foreign-trade efficiency studies, 65–7, 98, 311–30
generalized model of the optimization of foreign trade, 325–6
historical development, 312–14
index of the capital-intensity of foreign-trade production, 321
index of the foreign-exchange effectiveness of import, 319

index of the foreign-exchange effectiveness of import for the retail market, 319–20
index of the foreign-exchange effectiveness of import-replacement production, 320
index of the foreign-exchange equivalent of labour, 317
index of the gross foreign-exchange effectiveness of export, 315–16
index of the market effectiveness of export, 315
index of the net foreign-exchange effectiveness of export, 316
index of the pure net foreign-exchange effectiveness of export, 317
limitations of the calculations, 326–9
of exports, 314–18
of imports, 313, 318–20
of investment, 66, 217, 320–2
partial and global indexes, 318
relative and absolute effectiveness of foreign trade, 324–5
synthetic index of the foreign-exchange effectiveness of foreign trade, 322
value of the analysis, 329–30
Foreign-trade theory, 59, 63–8, 354–6
Socialist, 64–8
Western, 63–4, 67
See also Theory of comparative costs
France, 25, 30, 34, 36, 43, 88, 90 n., 93, 110 n., 113, 144 ff., 234, 262, 264 n., 268 ff., 278, 288, 292, 298, 349, 362, 367, 378 ff., 383
'Friendly firms' in Japan, 245, 252

Gains from trade, 176–85, 225, 308–10, 326–9, 332, 334–42
balance of, in East-West trade, 334–42
criteria, 308–10
gains from dumping, 176–85
indexes of foreign-trade efficiency, 314–22
missed gains from East-West trade, 342–7
GATT, 59–60, 102, 129–33, 138, 189, 252, 369, 394
Germany, East, 19 n., 21, 32, 37 ff., 43, 73, 76 n., 78, 92, 99, 101, 108, 113, 148 ff., 164, 174, 199 ff., 203 ff., 216, 254, 265 n., 282, 295 ff., 311, 316 n., 318, 326, 337 ff., 349 ff., 364, 375 ff., 391, 394 ff.
Germany, West, 19 n., 25, 30, 34 ff., 43, 108, 110 n., 113, 196, 204, 210, 246, 262 ff., 270, 292, 298, 378 ff., 383, 391, 394 ff.

SUBJECT INDEX

Gold, 129, 196, 198–9, 202–3, 206, 213 ff., 228
Greece, 29, 79, 107 ff., 210, 260, 298
Group of '48', 77

Hallstein doctrine, 270
Hong Kong, 134, 191, 283, 287, 302, 361
Horizontal co-production, 383
Horizontal trade, 49
Hungary, 21, 25, 32, 35, 37 ff., 71, 73, 78, 83, 92, 99 ff., 108, 113, 135, 164, 169, 174, 178, 199, 216, 233, 254, 259 n., 263 ff., 281, 295 ff., 311 ff., 316, 318, 322, 329, 332, 337 ff., 349 ff., 364, 373 ff., 378 ff., 386 ff.

IBEC (International Bank for Economic Co-operation), 218–22
Iceland, 28, 30, 107, 260
Ideology and trade, 327–8, 357–61, 392–3
IMF, 60, 96, 100, 197, 368
'Implicit import surplus', 126
India, 128, 141, 146, 269
Indices of foreign-trade efficiency, see Foreign-trade efficiency studies
Industrialization, 60, 65, 68, 104, 184, 187, 269
Insulation of the domestic market, 70, 100, 116, 333
Intensive growth factors, 62, 217
Interest, 179, 196, 205–6, 255
'Internal convertibility' of currency, 214
International Bank for Economic Co-operation, 218–22
International Chamber of Commerce, 87, 274, 384
International liquidity reserves, 36, 129, 194–203, 215, 223
 of China, 196–7
 of Eastern European countries, 197
 of the Socialist Bloc, 196–8
 of the U.S.S.R., 196
 of the West, 196, 199–200
 of Yugoslavia, 197
International Trade Organization, 128 n., 133, 135, 190, 394
International Union for the Protection of Industrial Property, 266, 370
Intra-Bloc foreign trade, 46, 48–51, 55–6, 209, 337–40, 358
Intra-Western foreign trade, 44–7, 55–6, 209, 357
Ireland, 31, 75, 108
Iron and Steel, 151, 176, 178, 280, 288, 339, 361
Italy, 25, 30, 36, 43, 88, 91 n., 108, 210, 113, 261, 263, 268, 271, 278, 349, 362, 365, 378 ff.

Japan, 21, 25, 30, 36, 43 n., 75, 88, 108, 134, 145, 192, 210, 229, 252, 268 ff., 278, 288, 293, 298, 349, 362 ff.
Joint East-West ventures, 377–83, 394–5
 benefits to each side, 383–4
 examples, 379–82
 forms, 382–3
 limitations, 394–5

'Kennedy Round', 102, 122
Korea, North, 19 n., 28, 32, 49 n., 87 n., 99, 108, 143, 148 ff., 169, 197, 199, 263, 272 ff., 277, 282, 292, 295, 391, 395

Leipzig trade fairs, 243
Liberalization of controls, 110–11, 224, 229–31, 248–50, 330, 377
Licences, see Technology
Licensing, 110–11, 130
Limiting exchange rate, 323–4

Malaysia, 133, 191, 193
Manufactures in East-West trade, 35–43, 127, 334–5, 341
Marginal exchange rate, 323–4
Market disruption, 95, 132, 138, 160, 175, 374
Market mechanism, 59–60, 90–1, 222–3, 331–3, 348–52
Material incentives, 113–14, 180 n., 215, 331, 327
MFN (Most Favoured Nation), 23, 101, 121–3, 125–6, 130–6, 243, 246, 250, 374
Middle East, 259, 282
Military-supporting base, 277, 280, 286
Mongolia, 33, 49 n., 99, 108, 391
Multilateralism, 122, 206–26, 374, 386
 and convertibility, 214, 222
 degree of multilateral balancing of trade, 207–11
 elements of, in East-West Trade, 211–214
 IBEC and multilateral settlements, 218–22
 multiangular operations, 206, 212, 214

NATO, 134, 175, 232, 240, 251, 305, 353
'Nesterov figures', 239
Netherlands, 25, 28, 31, 36, 43, 108, 210, 271, 298, 349, 365
New Zealand, 28, 31, 34, 43, 108, 174, 191, 193, 223, 271, 273 n., 277, 362

SUBJECT INDEX

Non-commercial considerations, 51, 53, 71, 95, 122, 183, 205, 228, 237–52, 267, 329, 346
Normal value, 139, 142, 172–4, 189
Norway, 30, 108, 210, 298, 349

OECD, 134, 175, 232, 240, 305
Oil, 149, 161, 166–7, 178, 259–62, 339
Optimization of foreign trade, 61, 325–30
'Own path to socialism', 353–4

Pakistan, 141, 269
Payment performance by Socialist countries, 232–5
Peaceful co-existence, 62, 161, 250, 265, 307 n., 352, 389, 395
'Peaceful engagement', 238
Planning of foreign trade, 60–1, 112, 189–90, 216–17, 331–3, 350, 355
Poland, 21, 25, 28, 32, 35, 38 ff., 71, 73, 78 ff., 83, 87 n., 92, 94 n., 99 ff., 108, 113, 127, 130, 133, 135, 144, 148 ff., 163 ff., 174 n., 178, 182, 199 ff., 216, 232 ff., 259 n., 263 ff., 277, 287, 295 ff., 302, 305 ff., 311 ff., 316 n., 318, 328, 339, 350, 355, 364, 373, 376 ff., 395
Politics in East-West trade, *see* Cold War; Credits; Discrimination; MFN, Non-commercial considerations; Strategic embargo
Polycentrism, 249–51, 268, 353
Portugal, 31, 79
Prices, 33, 51, 66–8, 90–6, 181, 215, 218, 330–1, 336–42, 351, 385–6
  allocative function of, 308–9
  computational, 330
  fixing of, 218
  formation of, in Western countries, 90–1
  goal, 33
  in East-West trade, 22, 93–6, 335–6, 340–2, 385–6
  in intra-CMEA trade, 93 n., 336–41
  procurement, 181
  'objectively determined valuations', 215
  reforms of, in Socialist countries, 92, 330–2
  'shadow', 330
  structure of, 218
  'trial and error', 215
  See also Dumping; Price discrimination
Price discrimination, 128, 162–70, 183, 336–41
Profits, 61, 114, 179, 216, 331, 345, 350
Property claims, 233–5
Protection, 76–7, 100, 103, 105, 126, 187, 224

Quantitative restrictions, 60, 110, 126, 132–3, 160, 174, 242–4, 385, 391

Rapprochement in East-West relations, 248–9, 254–6, 360. *See also* Convergence
Re-exports, 182–3, 206
Reorientation of trade, 46, 48, 52, 360
Rice, 253, 283, 287
Rubber, 95, 252, 277, 288
Rumania, 28, 32, 36 ff., 43, 71 ff., 78, 84, 99, 101 ff., 108, 113, 146 ff., 178, 199, 216, 233 n., 259, 263, 277, 295 ff., 298, 311, 339, 354, 373

Scientific and technological co-operation, 62, 266, 269–72, 276, 378–83
Seller's markets, 104, 217
Settlement of trade disputes, 111 n., 294–307, 374, 389
  advantages of arbitration, 307
  college of arbitrators, 296
  Convention on the Recognition and Enforcement of Foreign Arbitral Awards, 298
  domestication of foreign trade litigations, 297, 302–3
  European Convention on International Commercial Arbitration, 298
  force majeure, 302
  foreign trade arbitration courts in Socialist countries, 294–8
  impartiality of arbitrators and judges, 299, 301, 304
  'juridically incestuous' relation, 300–2
  proceedings *in camera*, 304
  set-up in Western countries, 294
  sources of conflict in East-West trade, 294, 299–304
Silver, 199, 203, 213–14
Sino-Soviet dispute, 51, 285, 394
Social benefit, 178, 181, 309, 339
Social cost, 181, 309, 339
Socialist Bloc, 19–20
Solutions of East-West problems, 367, 373–4, 384–9
South Africa, 28, 31, 108, 362
Spain, 30, 108, 210, 270
Special China embargo list, 264, 272, 277, 287
State foreign-trade monopoly, 61, 76–7, 85, 116, 125, 170, 241, 355, 363–4
State trading, 77, 253. *See also* State foreign-trade monopoly
Sterling Area, 133, 191, 193, 211, 223
Strategic embargo, 53, 60, 75, 110, 240, 271–93, 359

SUBJECT INDEX 415

beginnings, 271
'bottleneck theory' of denials, 286–7
Cuba, 273, 276–7
definition of 'strategic', 275, 287
direct administrative cost to the West, 289
effects on China, 283, 285, 288
effects on East-West trade, 284, 290
effects on smaller socialist countries, 286
effects on the U.S.S.R., 284–5, 288
effects on the West, 289
illicit trans-shipment, 287
large-diameter pipes, 286, 293
limited effectiveness, 281, 285–8
objectives, 276
on technology, 280, 284
relaxations of, 272–4, 277–8
'special national interest or hardship', 288, 359
U.S. controls, 271–4, 290–3
Strategic lists, 272, 276, 278–80
Strategic pre-emption, 278
Strategic vulnerability of the Bloc, 278–83
Subsidies, 112–14, 142–4, 157, 164, 170, 188, 216, 330
Subversive activities, 252, 392–3
Sugar, 96, 167, 181–2
Sweden, 30, 34, 43, 87, 91 n., 108, 113, 210, 262 ff., 293, 376 ff., 383
Swing credits, 203 n., 205
Switch deals, 183 n.
Switzerland, 25, 30, 87, 109, 169, 174 ff., 210, 234, 296, 298

Tariffs, 68, 100–2, 122–6, 129, 148, 386. *See also* MFN
Technology, 62, 104, 264–6, 340, 358, 360–1, 364, 382–3
growing trade in patents, 265–6
joint utilization, 382–3
Socialist ideological attitude to patents, 264–5
Socialist need of Western technology, 264, 360
Western complaints of poaching, 126, 265
Terms of trade, 68, 336–41
Textiles, 95, 150, 156–7, 161, 181, 185–6, 244
Theory of comparative costs, 69–74, 188, 205, 269, 308
acceptance in continental Western Europe, 69
and higher stages of economic development, 73–4

and underdeveloped countries, 71–2, 354
and Western economic domination, 71
critical Socialist view of, 70–3
dynamic view, 72, 354
static view, 72, 354
Third World, *see* Developing countries
Tin, 93, 95, 146, 182, 252, 277, 287
Trade agreements, 76, 88, 105–9, 253–4
Trade deficits and surpluses, 191–3, 207, 211–12, 219, 224, 230
Trade delegations, 87
Trade divorced from politics, 269–70, 357–61
Trade fairs, 372, 375
Trade missions, 86, 246–8, 270, 377
Trade promotion, 387–8
Trade protocols, 76, 93, 106, 189–90, 218
Trade representation, 86–7
Transferable rouble, 218, 221
Trans-Siberian Railway, 283
Trilateral deals, 206, 211
Turkey, 21, 25, 29, 107, 109, 210, 349

Uncertainty in East-West trade, 355, 387
UNCTAD, 255, 394
Under-trading, 26 n.
'Unfair' competition, 154, 159, 175
United Kingdom, 30, 34 ff., 43, 87 ff., 109 ff., 133, 145, 174, 191, 193 ff., 204, 210, 223, 234, 269 ff., 277 ff., 288, 290, 292, 341, 349 n., 353, 365, 376 n., 378 ff., 393 n.
U.S.A., 25, 28, 31, 34, 36, 75, 87, 102 n., 109, 113, 126 ff., 144, 159, 192, 208, 210, 231, 234, 240 ff., 254, 262 ff., 267 ff., 274 ff., 289 ff., 341, 343–4, 346, 349, 353, 362 ff., 376 n., 393 n., 390 ff.
U.S.S.R., 25, 32 ff., 43, 48, 65, 74 n., 83 ff., 88, 92 ff., 99, 101, 108, 110 n., 111 n., 127, 133 n., 135, 146 ff., 163, 165, 167, 178, 182, 185, 194, 196 ff., 202 ff., 211, 227, 244 ff., 251, 254, 259, 261, 263 ff., 267, 269, 274, 276, 278, 282 ff., 293, 295 ff., 302, 305 ff., 311, 329, 337 ff., 346, 350, 353, 361, 365 n., 373, 376, 391 ff.

Vertical co-production, 383
Vertical trade, 41
Vietnam, North, 19 n., 28, 32, 39 n., 49 n., 99, 108, 113 n., 146 ff., 197, 200, 263, 272 ff., 277, 295 n., 361, 373, 391, 395

War debts, 234–5
Wars, those ideologically justified, 392–3

Waste in East-West trade, 342–7. *See also* Discrimination

Wheat, 74n., 90n., 91n., 96, 113, 140, 142–4, 176ff., 181n., 185, 188, 201, 262–4, 270, 283, 370

Wool, 96, 244

World trade, participation in, 24–6

Yugoslavia, 20, 25, 28ff., 43, 49, 72n., 76n., 80, 87n., 102n., 109, 113n., 130, 197n., 210, 251, 277, 295n.ff., **298**, 311n., 349n., 364n., 376, 378